Guide to Personal Financial Planning for the Armed Forces

7th Edition

Colonel S. Jamie Gayton
Major Scott P. Handler

Contributing Associates, Department of Social Sciences,
The U.S. Military Academy, West Point, New York:

Major Hartleigh Caine
Professor Dean Dudley
Major Matthew P. Fix
Major Daniel Gade
Ms. Nicole Gilmore
Major Jessica D. Grassetti
Captain Liesl Himmelberger
Major Jacob M. Johnston
Major Hugh W. A. Jones

Lieutenant Colonel Paul Kucik
Major Conway Lin
Major Brian Miller
Major Fran Murphy
Major Jeffrey S. Palazzini
Major Riley Post
Major Sukhdev S. Purewal
Major Lee Robinson
Major Todd Schultz

STACKPOLE BOOKS

0   11557 00371   0

To the members of the armed forces and their families
who serve in support of overseas contingency operations

Former editions published under the title *Armed Forces Guide to Personal Financial Planning*

Published by
STACKPOLE BOOKS
5067 Ritter Road
Mechanicsburg, PA 17055
www.stackpolebooks.com

Printed in the United States of America

10 9 8 7 6 5 4 3 2 1

Cover design by Tessa J. Sweigert

Library of Congress Cataloging-in-Publication Data

Gayton, S. Jamie.
  Guide to personal financial planning for the Armed Forces / S. Jamie Gayton,
Scott P. Handler. — 7th ed.
      p. cm.
  Rev. ed. of: Armed forces guide to personal financial planning : strategies for
securing your finances at home while serving our nation abroad / Margaret H.
Belknap ... [et al.]. 6th ed. 2007.
  Includes bibliographical references and index.
  ISBN 978-0-8117-0371-0
  1. Finance, Personal. 2. Soldiers—United States—Finance, Personal. I. Handler,
Scott P. II. Belknap, Margaret H. Armed forces guide to personal financial planning.
III. Title.
  HG179.P55 2011
  332.0240088'35500973—dc23
                    2012005524

Contents

PART I

FINANCIAL BASIC TRAINING

1

Realizing Your Financial Goals

Many individuals daydream about a better life, but very few exert the effort to learn how to achieve a higher standard of living through financial planning. Many of these same individuals believe that achieving a higher standard of living requires either saving so much that they must forego opportunities while young, or being lucky enough to "beat" the stock market or win the lottery. Neither of these beliefs is true for the vast majority of individuals; in most cases, one achieves a higher standard of living by making small changes whose impacts compound over time. Some financial experts believe that as much as 90 percent of achieving a higher standard of living is attained through behavior change while as little as 10 percent is a function of individual investment choices. The important take-away is that positive behavior change is the key to achieving a higher standard of living. This book outlines the steps necessary for families and individuals to make behavioral changes in personal finance so that they can accomplish their financial goals and live the lives they have always dreamed of having.

Personal finance is about evaluating future earnings (all sources of revenue) and future expenses (the costs of typical life "events") to understand the impacts of one's decisions on one's future standard of living and to enable informed choices. This book provides servicemembers with the tools to develop a sound financial plan. It helps them better assess future earnings by addressing additional sources of revenue and future costs by reviewing typical lifetime expenditures.

This chapter provides a process for examining the decisions individuals and families make, and the tradeoffs between current and future consumption (exposing the significant rewards of delaying consumption). Specifically, this chapter outlines a process for establishing personal financial planning goals, weighing costs of the goals, and developing a strategy to accomplish the goals. By establishing and implementing a financial plan and budget, individuals and families gain a degree of control over their destiny. However, they must maintain self-discipline in adhering to their plans. A sound financial plan allows individuals and families to protect themselves against accumulating

Introduction

This edition of *Guide to Personal Financial Planning for the Armed Forces* continues a tradition that began in 1987 with the first edition of the *Armed Forces Guide to Personal Financial Planning*. For 25 years, servicemembers and civilian faculty members of the Department of Social Services at West Point have donated their personal time to writing and revising this book in order to help fellow servicemembers achieve their personal financial goals. All royalties earned by the authers are donated to the Military Education Endowment in the Association of Graduates at West Point to support cadet enrichment and development activities. This edition could not be any more timely, given the financial crisis facing this nation since 2008—the worst since the Great Depression. Economic conditions—including uncertainty concerning the duration of the recession and major cuts projected for defense spending—point to less generous pay and benefits, decreased job stability, and increased responsibility for managing one's own retirement account. These factors make it imperative for servicemembers to evaluate their current personal financial situations and, plan—not just for their long-term futures, but also for possible short- and mid-term economic challenges.

This book provides servicemembers with the basic knowledge and tools that will allow them to put themselves and their families on the road to financial security. In too many circumstances, the authors have heard "seasoned" servicemembers say, "I wish I had known the power of managing my personal finances and the impact of compounding returns 20 years ago!" Readers of this book have no more reason for excuses. This book serves as an introduction to these topics and encourages servicemembers and their families to take a greater responsibility for their personal finances. People (servicemembers and civilians alike) spend an inordinate amount of time trying to earn extra money (working second jobs or looking for slightly higher-paying jobs) but relatively little time managing their finances. This book highlights the benefits and demystifies the process of actively managing one's finances, in order to provide confidence to servicemembers and their families that they can achieve financial security, independence, and success. This book should also serve as a reference when major financial decisions arrive in the lives of servicemembers and their families.

On behalf of all of this book's contributors, we hope that you find this book useful and an impetus to take control of your future financial security. We have written this as a gesture of thanks to all of those who serve, and to their families who support our nation's servicemembers. We are indebted to all of you.

S. Jamie Gayton, Ph.D.   Scott P. Handler, Ph.D.
Colonel, U.S. Army   Major, U.S. Army

unmanageable debt, take full responsibility for their financial future, and reach their financial goals.

BIG RETURNS TO SOUND FINANCIAL PLANNING

Becoming educated about sound financial planning has several positive results. First and foremost, the only way to consume more in a given year than you earn by working, without going into debt, is to have saved some money in a previous year. The power of compounding interest enables savings to multiply exponentially, giving you more financial freedom and the ability to improve your standard of living and achieve your goals. This is called "letting your money work harder for you, rather than you always working harder for your money." Patience, aside from being a personal virtue, also carries a financial reward. A useful rule of thumb is that if you divide 72 by the annual interest rate you expect, you get the number of years required for the investment to double.

For example, if a first lieutenant put $10,000 into an investment account expected to earn 7% annually, the account would hold about $20,000 in ten years, $40,000 in twenty years, and $160,000 in forty years. Figure 1-1 shows the growth of a $10,000 investment over a 45-year period for several different annual interest rates. Figure 1-1 is based on a one-time $10,000 investment. In most circumstances, people will continue to add to their savings, especially as their current income grows. If, for example, the lieutenant continued to add $5,000 to her savings each year, she would have $1,738,000 after 45 years, assuming a 7% return. See Fig 1-2, page 4, for a graph of this option.

The lieutenant's ultimate reward depends on the rate of return she expects to earn—which varies by the type of investment—and on the length of time she expects to hold the investment. The longer an investor holds an investment,

Figure 1-1
Growth of $10,000 for Multiple Interest Rates

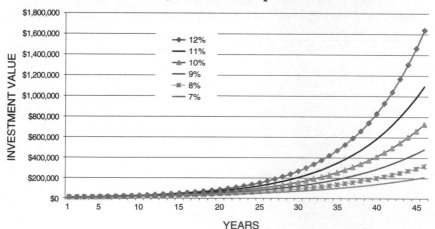

Figure 1-2
One-Time Investment of $10,000 vs. Adding $5,000 to Initial $10,000 Investment Each Year

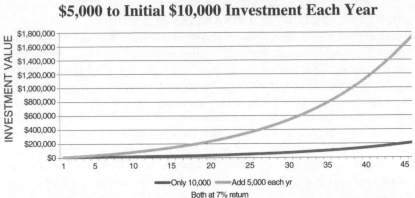

the more powerful the effect of compounded interest. Figure 1-1 shows that there is very little difference between the accumulated returns at the different interest rates initially; however, as time progresses, the accumulated wealth associated with the higher interest rate grows exponentially faster. Therefore, the sooner a family starts saving, the greater the financial returns in the future. Consider that starting an investment ten years later than desired equates to not earning one last "doubling," still assuming a 7% return. If a family's final investment value is $1.5 million dollars, they have foregone an additional $1.5 million by delaying their investment start date by 10 years. This should highlight the importance of starting *now*—even if the monthly investments are small, compounding will provide significant rewards in the long-term.

Of course, prices are likely to rise during the time the lieutenant is waiting for her money to grow. The pace at which prices of goods and services rise in a particular period is called the inflation rate. Recently, the U.S. inflation rate has averaged a little less than 3% each year. If prices rise at 3% each year, then an item that costs $1,000 today would cost $1,030 next year and $1,344 in ten years.

Since inflation erodes a family's true purchasing power, it is even more important to save money in an investment with a positive return greater than the rate of inflation; otherwise, the value of cash will decrease in real terms over time. A family's true purchasing power is the difference between the future value of savings and the future cost of living. This is called the real rate of return on the original investment, and it yields the total real dollars (adjusted for expected inflation) available at the end of the period. The real rate of return is the difference between the stated (or nominal) rate of return on savings and the rate of inflation:

$$\begin{array}{ccc} 7\% \text{ (nominal rate} & 3\% \text{ (rate} & 4\% \text{ (real rate} \\ \text{of return)} & - \quad \text{of inflation)} & = \quad \text{of return)} \end{array}$$

Using the real rate of return yields a better measure of an individual's future financial well-being. If the lieutenant in our example chose to leave her $10,000 as cash each year rather than invest it, she would lose purchasing power of her money due to inflation. With an inflation rate of 3%, after 40 years her $10,000 would have a purchasing power of less than $3,000. Figure 1-3 compares the real value of her $10,000 at a 4% real rate of return to the real value if the $10,000 is left as cash at an inflation rate of 3%. Therefore, the best protection against the effects of inflation is to wisely invest your family's savings.

Figure 1-3
Comparison of $10,000 at 4% Real Rate of Return to $10,000 Left as Cash

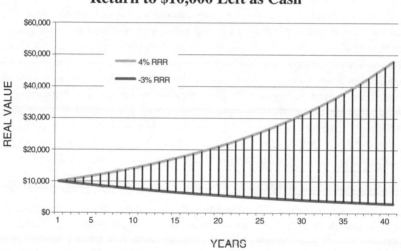

Figure 1-4
Comparison of Different Real Rates of Return on $10,000

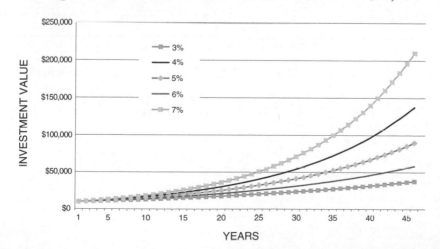

Historically, investors in the United States have earned real rates of return between 1% and 5% annually. The specific rate depends upon the amount of risk the investor is willing to accept, as well as the prevailing interest rate established by the U.S. Federal Reserve. Riskier assets should offer higher expected returns as compensation for that risk. Figure 1-4 shows different returns for our lieutenant, given the returns for different risk levels. The most conservative expected rate of return shown in the graph is 3%; this rate of return will grow to more than $30,000, inflation-adjusted, in forty years. The most aggressive investment shown, 7% real rate, will return over $150,000 in forty years from the initial $10,000 investment. Achieving such returns requires financial planning, budgeting, and starting early to allow investments to compound over time.

STEPS IN FINANCIAL PLANNING

Only servicemembers and their families can determine the ultimate financial priorities for their household. Everyone knows that middle-class life in America is expensive, but the good news is that military personnel, especially those serving longer careers, do earn sufficient income to achieve many of their financial or lifestyle goals. However, achieving one's goals requires careful financial planning and budgeting. The steps below outline a general process for setting financial goals. Setting aggressive yet achievable goals takes time and should involve everyone in the household. Families should review goals following every major life change, such as a marriage, divorce, birth of a child, relocation, promotion, change in spouse's career status, and retirement.

Step 1: Brainstorm

As a first step, investors should develop a list of their family's "life" objectives. Consider the necessity of each item, as well as the family's willingness to wait for it. It may be helpful to place each item in a matrix like the one shown in Table 1-1. For example, a one-week vacation in Florida might be in the "Nice to Have" column in the table, or in a column for things to do next year. An emergency fund to cover unexpected expenses might be in the "Must

TABLE 1-1
PERSONAL FINANCIAL GOALS

Goals	Next Year	3 Years	5 Years	20 Years	Retirement
Must Have	3–6 months emergency fund; essential furniture	Engagement ring	Spouse's tuition	Home repairs	Manageable house payment
Should Have	New car	Small wedding	New furniture	Tuition for child	
Nice to Have	Nice vacation in Florida		Home down payment	Lakefront home	

Have" column. (Most financial planners recommend that individuals save two to six months of after-tax income for such a fund.) Another example of something that might go under "Must Have" is having a manageable home mortgage payment by the time an individual retires. The longer one postpones planning for future goals, the more difficult achieving those goals can become due to the compounding factor described earlier.

This phase of the planning process could take some time, depending on the complexity of the family's household and how long it takes to achieve reasonable consensus. In addition, the matrix might be quite large, with each block containing multiple entries. In the end, the matrix should accurately reflect the family's current needs and future dreams; it should serve as a useful roadmap for the family's financial planning.

Step 2: Determine Cost of Goals (in Today's Dollars)
Today's society has raised consumption to an art form. The median price of a new home in the United States was $234,500 in May 2012, and the average price of a new vehicle in April 2012 was $30,748. In 2011, the average American wedding cost over $27,000. After the wedding, the U.S. Department of Agriculture has estimated that it costs between $163,440 and $377,400 to raise a child through the age of seventeen. The College Board rubs salt in the wound by reporting that a "moderate" college budget for all expenses at an in-state public college was $21,477 (over $85,000 for four years) for 2011–2012, and a private college was $24,224 (nearly $170,000 for four years).[1]

In America, every conceivable product and service is available—for a price. The cost of a particular item can vary markedly depending on its size and quality. The cost can also vary widely by region of the country; this geographical variation is particularly important for goods that cannot easily be traded across state borders, such as housing, personal services, and educational services. Fortunately, the Internet provides a powerful tool for researching the prices of different items in your financial plan. A useful starting point is Consumer Reports (http://www.consumerreports.org), which evaluates the quality of various products relative to their prices.

Once you have assigned prices for each item, you can expand the matrix. Table 1-2 includes prices for a few items and also estimates the total funds needed at each stage of the financial plan. Although this chapter has mentioned the importance of inflation, it is possible to use today's prices for planning future expenses, as long as investors use the real rates of return to estimate their needed savings. Using the real rate of return ensures that investors understand true purchasing power and that they compare apples with apples—today's dollars with inflation-adjusted dollar investment return.

---

[1] Sources: http://www.census.gov/construction/nrs/pdf/newressales.pdf, http://content .usatoday.com/communities/driveon/post/2012/04/car-prices-hit-record/1, http://www .nada.org/NR/rdonlyres/0798BE2A-9291-44BF-A126-0D372FC89B8A/0/NADA_ DATA_08222011.pdf, http://www.cnpp.usda.gov/publications/crc/crc2010.pdf, and http://www.collegedata.com/cs/content/content_payarticle_tmpl.jhtml?articleId=10064.

TABLE 1-2
PERSONAL FINANCIAL GOALS WITH "PRICE TAGS"

Goals	Next Year	3 Years	5 Years	20 Years	Retirement
Must Have	3–6 months emergency fund; essential furniture	Engagement ring (down payment)	Spouse's tuition (pay off debt)	Home Repairs (fix roof)	Manageable house payment ($325,000 paid off)
Prices	$9,000	$8,000	$36,000	$20,000	$325,000
Should Have	New car	Small wedding	New furniture	Tuition for child	
Prices	$20,000	$24,000	$10,000	$40,000	
Nice to Have	Nice vacation in Florida		Home down payment	Lakefront home down payment	
Prices	$3,000		$35,000	$20,000	
Grand totals	$32,000	$32,000	$81,000	$80,000	$325,000

To estimate a monetary goal for each period (i.e., a price tag for the financial plan), the family must add all of the subtotals in the bottom row. The grand totals in the very modest example in Table 1-2 vary by sub-period, from $32,000 this year to $325,000 by retirement age. In principle, the grand totals could be much higher, since our table includes *very* few items. The "magic number" may seem daunting, even unachievable. Before losing hope, remember that time is the investor's best ally and allows achievement of many seemingly unattainable goals. The establishment of a goal worksheet is a dynamic process that encourages frequent updates to capture changes in goals, the economy, and investment progress. Investors may decide to get a car loan instead of paying with cash or to reduce the size of a house down payment to allow savings to continue to grow. Families may achieve more than they expect. They may also develop some priorities to guide them if it becomes necessary to scale back their goals.

Step 3: Estimate the Total Savings Needed
Now that you have set monetary goals for each period, you must work backwards to estimate the savings needed to reach each goal in the time allotted. Most people have a variety of investments that earn different rates of return, depending on the risk they are willing to accept in saving for each goal and the time available before reaching that milestone. Refer to part III of this book for an in-depth discussion of how best to match a particular savings goal with the most appropriate type of investment.

For now, this chapter keeps matters fairly simple, by using a 3% annual real return rate to illustrate the basic procedure for estimating the savings nec-

TABLE 1-3
WHAT YOU NEED TO SAVE TODAY TO REACH A FUTURE GOAL

Real rate of return	If you need $1,000 in 10 years, then today you must save	If you need $1,000 in 20 years, then today you must save	If you need $1,000 in 40 years, then today you must save
1%	$905.29	$819.54	$671.65
2%	$820.35	$672.97	$452.89
3%	$744.09	$553.68	$306.56
4%	$675.56	$456.39	$208.29
5%	$613.91	$376.89	$142.05

essary to achieve one's goals. The math required to estimate the needed savings is simple. For example, a $1,000 investment today will be worth $1,344 in ten years. One finds that number by multiplying the initial savings, or present value (PV), of $1,000 by $(1.03)^{10}$, where .03 is the annual expected return and it is raised to the power of 10 for the ten years. This following formula demonstrates how to calculate future value:

$$\text{Future value} = \text{present value} \times (1 + \text{expected annual return})^{\text{number years}}$$

One can rearrange this expression to determine how much to save today to achieve a particular goal in the future.

$$\text{Present value} = \frac{\text{future value}}{(1 + \text{expected annual return})^{\text{number years}}}$$

The higher the expected real rate of return and, more importantly, the longer the investor's time horizon, the more powerful one's savings today becomes. As Table 1-3 shows, if the family needs $1,000 in forty years, and expects to earn 3%, then it must make a $306.56 investment today. However, if the family needs the money in ten years, it must make a much larger investment today, about $744.09 at that same rate.

Step 4: Account for Your Taxes
Since investors pay taxes on investment income, they should account for tax implications when planning for the future. This book covers several scenarios where families can find tax-efficient means of saving, meaning that families will pay less in taxes over time to achieve financial goals. The good news, however, is that the government exempts many components of military pay from taxation. Moreover, the government provides numerous investment options that can reduce or eliminate the tax on savings. Chapter 4 explains tax rates, while chapter 12 discusses tax-friendly investment plans.

Step 5: Calculate the Monthly Allotment

Unless they have just earned a bonus, received an inheritance, or returned from deployment, most investors do not have large lump sums to invest today. Instead, they will have to meet future goals in incremental steps. A monthly contribution, usually called a "system of automatic investment" plan, is a series of regular deposits into a savings instrument. Because the savings earn an expected rate of return every year, the cumulative effect of these monthly payments is highly significant. For military personnel, an allotment from your monthly paycheck to a mutual fund is an example of such an automatic investment plan.

The two tables below provide a guide to the monthly payments needed to save $10,000 by a given future date. Table 1-4 uses lower rates of return because short-term investments tend to be more conservative. Table 1-5 uses higher rates of return because investors often seek more aggressive returns in the long term. Again, time is a powerful ally. At a 4% annual return, an investor must save $261.91 each month to reach $10,000 in three years, but only $67.91 each month to reach $10,000 in ten years.

TABLE 1-4
MONTHLY PAYMENTS NEEDED TO SAVE $10,000
OVER A SHORT PERIOD

Real rate of return	Number of Years				
	1	2	3	4	5
1%	$829.52	$412.69	$273.75	$204.28	$162.60
2%	$825.72	$408.74	$269.76	$200.28	$158.61
3%	$821.94	$404.81	$265.81	$196.34	$154.69
4%	$818.17	$400.92	$261.91	$192.46	$150.83
5%	$814.41	$397.05	$258.04	$188.63	$147.05

TABLE 1-5
MONTHLY PAYMENTS NEEDED TO SAVE $10,000
OVER A LONGER PERIOD

Real rate of return	Number of Years				
	10	15	20	30	40
4%	$67.91	$40.64	$27.26	$14.41	$8.46
6%	$61.02	$34.39	$21.64	$9.96	$5.02
8%	$54.66	$28.90	$16.98	$6.71	$2.86
10%	$48.82	$24.13	$13.17	$4.42	$1.58
12%	$43.47	$20.02	$10.11	$2.86	$0.85

Saving $67.91 each and every month is challenging, but it is considerably easier than finding $6,756 to invest all at once, which is the lump sum an investor would need to invest today to reach $10,000 in ten years. Further, because a servicemember's income is likely to rise over his or her lifetime, the savings plan should become easier to fund over time.

Step 6: Determine the Appropriate Investment Vehicle(s)

Finally, with the help of this book, you should determine the investment vehicle you will use for each goal. As noted earlier, a person with a long time horizon and some tolerance for risk may be comfortable with aggressively invested funds. A person with a shorter time horizon or lower tolerance for risk may be more comfortable with safer bonds and savings instruments. A diversified portfolio provides investors with greater stability and ensures somewhat higher expected returns than just a savings account.

DEVELOPING A MONTHLY BUDGET AS A PLANNING TOOL

The monthly budget is the key tool in establishing a financial routine and reaching a family's financial goals. A monthly budget brings financial self-awareness by providing answers to central questions: (1) What are my sources of revenue? (2) What are my expenditures or costs now and in the future? (3) How much could I save to achieve my financial goals? Once investors identify revenues and expenditures, they can create priorities for planning their monthly spending.

The Internet has a number of sources available for helping an investor establish a monthly budget and track current expenditures. For example, most major banks have web tools that allow investors to categorize their monthly purchases and show them how they allocated their monthly income. Investors can establish goals for each category to monitor progress towards their desired plan. There are also free resources, such as https://mint.com, where investors can use a web-based system to track all of their accounts, create and manage their budgets, and monitor their bills. There is also an application available for mobile devices that sends monthly summaries and alerts. And, for a fee, one can download traditional software, such as Quicken, that allows families to monitor all aspects of their financial plans, including their budgets, bank accounts, investments, and credit card expenditures. These tools all help families monitor progress towards their goals.

Three Common Excuses for Not Budgeting

1. Negative attitude: "Budgets are depressing and constricting."
2. Unrealistic expectations: "Budgets are easy—just save half your income!"
3. Low motivation: "This budget is not really my problem."

Budgeting, despite its usual connotation as an exercise in self-depriva-
tion, is better viewed as a necessary step toward financial well-being. Instead
of thinking of a budget as a financial diet, consider it more as a set of well-balanced meals. Attitude is the key to successful budgeting. If you approach your
monthly budget as unachievable and as an external constraint, you are likely
to fail. If you consider it a personal choice and a path toward meeting a personal goal, you are more likely to succeed. Remember, personal financial success comes largely from making positive behavioral changes, such as sticking
to a budget.

Establishing the structure of a monthly budget is simple: 1) develop a
measure of available disposable income—what is left after paying taxes and
other mandatory expenses, and 2) develop a measure of monthly expenses—
where all disposable income goes. In a financially healthy household, monthly
disposable income exceeds monthly expenses, allowing the household to save
and reach its financial and personal goals. In an unhealthy situation, the
household spends more than its income, and accumulates stressful credit card
debt, or falls behind on paying bills.

Five Good Reasons to Establish a Monthly Budget

1. Take control of the family's financial destiny.
2. Get out (and stay out) of consumer (high–interest rate) debt.
3. Build confidence in managing unexpected changes.
4. Provide the family with a working financial plan while the servicemember is deployed.
5. Realize the family's dreams.

The following section will show how a budget can accurately account for
a servicemember's income, both taxable and nontaxable. Because of its complexity, the section focuses on special issues involving military pay. The subsequent section shows how a budget can guide monthly spending for a
household, yielding many positive results: financial security, reduced friction
among household members, confidence during a financial emergency, and a
sense of financial well-being for the servicemember and the family throughout
a deployment.

Understanding A Servicemember's Military Income

While serving in the armed forces, a servicemember's total "pay" is the sum
of numerous forms of monetary and nonmonetary compensation. Several elements of pay apply to everyone in the military; other elements only apply to a
servicemember's specific individual circumstances. In addition, some components of income are taxable, while others are not. It is crucial that service-

TABLE 1-6
ESTIMATED NOMINAL MONTHLY PAY FOR AN OFFICER
OVER THE FIRST FIVE YEARS OF SERVICE

	Years				
	1	**2**	**3**	**4**	**5**
Basic Pay	$2,784.00	$3,402.31	$3,990.64	$5,112.06	$5,739.57

We assumed a promotion schedule of O-2 before the two-year mark and O-3 at the three-year mark, starting with the 2011 pay charts; cost-of-living increases are estimated at 3%.

members have a complete grasp of their total after-tax income when they develop their financial plans and household budgets.

A servicemember's basic monthly pay varies with rank and length of service, and is taxable. Consequently, a financial plan—complete with current pay and expected future pay—must account for expected changes in base pay. Fortunately, over time, basic monthly pay follows a fairly predictable path, which is valuable in financial planning. Table 1-6 displays the trend in pay that a second lieutenant (O-1) commissioned in 2011 can anticipate over the first five years of service.

The Department of Defense has approved incentive pay for critical-need occupations and duties that augments monthly basic pay. Personnel in highly skilled branches—such as medical and aviation officers—receive incentive pay, as do personnel performing particularly hazardous or onerous duties. This form of compensation is taxable.

A servicemember's basic allowance for housing (BAH) varies—based on the location of his or her current duty station, and on whether the servicemember has any dependents. For example, the housing allowance is more generous if the servicemember is assigned to a high-cost area of the country and has dependents. The basic allowance for subsistence (BAS), intended for food, does not vary by location or household status.

Additionally, military personnel may be eligible for many additional forms of pay—usually temporary in nature, depending on the nature of the assignment. Foremost, a servicemember receives additional pay while at sea or deployed to a hostile theater of operations, with most military income becoming nontaxable during a combat deployment. Go to the Defense Finance and Accounting Service (DFAS) websites mentioned below to review military pay and entitlements.

Table 1-7 summarizes the many forms of military compensation. Because of the large number of permutations, it is unproductive to print all of the pay and allowance tables here. They are easily available on the DFAS website governing military pay. The Defense Travel website of the Department of Defense offers a convenient calculator for helping to determine BAH at any location.

TABLE 1-7
MAJOR COMPONENTS OF MILITARY COMPENSATION

Component	Description	Factors	Tax Implications	Keep in Mind	More Information
Basic monthly pay	Monthly pay for services	Rank; years of service	Taxable unless deployed to a hostile theater (limits may apply)	Periodically adjusted to keep up with inflation	DFAS; myPay
Basic Allowance for Subsistence	Compensation for basic food expenses	Rank; availability of rations and mess permissions	Not taxable	Periodically adjusted to keep up with inflation	DFAS; myPay
Basic Allowance for Housing	Compensation for basic housing expenses	Location of duty station; rank; dependent status	Not taxable	Periodically adjusted to keep up with inflation	DFAS; myPay
Uniform and Clothing Allowances	Compensation for expenses related to duty uniforms	Rank; officers get one-time allowance	Not taxable	Limits apply	DFAS; myPay
Duty-related Travel and Relocation (TDY)	Compensation for travel related to official duties and for expenses related to permanent change of station	Reason for travel; type of expense	Taxable; some TDY not taxable	Limits apply	DFAS; Joint Forces Travel Regulations and Defense Travel System (DTS)
Occupational Incentive Pay	Incentive to encourage personnel to choose assignments in critical areas		Taxable unless deployed to a hostile theater (limits may apply)	Types of incentive pay include: aviation pay, hazardous duty pay, medical officer special pay, and career sea pay	DFAS
Hostile Fire Pay	Additional compensation for deployment to a hostile theater of operations	Length of deployment	Not taxable	Hostile theater is determined by your orders (issuing authority)	DFAS

TABLE 1-7 (continued)
MAJOR COMPONENTS OF MILITARY COMPENSATION

Component	Description	Factors	Tax Implications	Keep in Mind	More Information
Family Separation Allowance	Additional compensation for your dependents during an assignment that takes you away from your permanent duty station	Length of assignment; number of dependents	Not taxable		DFAS
Enlistment Bonuses	Additional compensation available at time of enlistment and/or reenlistment	Prior service; length of active-duty service obligation	Taxable, unless awarded in a combat zone	Periodically changed to encourage entry into specific branches and occupations	DFAS
Disability Severance Pay	Entitlement for duty-related injury or illness, received upon separation	Source of disability	Taxable, unless injury or illness related to combat	Requires official action by VA	DFAS

Defense Finance and Accounting Service

Home page: http://www.dfas.mil
Military Pay: http://www.dfas.mil/militarymembers/payentitlements/
    militarypaytables.html
BAH charts: http://www.defensetravel.dod.mil/site/bahCalc.cfm
My Pay: https://mypay.dfas.mil

Understanding the Tax Implications of Military Pay

Many components of military compensation are exempt from federal or state taxation. In addition, some taxable components of pay become exempt from taxes when servicemembers deploy to a combat zone. This tends to complicate the ability of families to develop estimates of income that are comparable to regular civilian pay. Chapter 4 explains the calculation of taxes and procedures for managing a servicemember's taxes in greater depth. At this point, investors simply need to become familiar with a few key points.

Taxable income and nontaxable income cannot be compared directly because tax-exempt income is worth more than regular, taxable pay. To convert a nontaxable payment into the equivalent amount of taxable income, you need to use your marginal tax rate, which is the amount of tax you must pay on your last dollar of income earned.

For most civilians, wages and salaries are fully taxable and constitute the bulk of their total taxable income. Such income is frequently called gross (pretax) income. Total after-tax income refers to the income remaining after all taxes have been paid. It is also called disposable income, which means the money available to a family to meet expenses and to save to meet their financial goals. For military personnel, disposable income is the sum of after-tax regular income and any nontaxable income:

Disposable income = all taxable income − taxes + all nontaxable income

For sound financial planning and budgeting, servicemembers must develop accurate estimates of their monthly disposable income. This number becomes the natural limit on monthly expenses within the framework of the budget. To derive that figure, servicemembers should review their information by using the myPay electronic system. On myPay, servicemembers can view their leave and earnings statements for the past year, and their recent W-2 statements documenting the taxes they have paid. (The website for myPay is at https://mypay.dfas.mil.)

Servicemembers who have income from other sources, such as investment and savings accounts, rental income, or spousal income, should also collect statements reflecting these income sources for the past year. If other income is not earned on a monthly basis, estimate an average for each month by taking the total for the year and dividing by twelve. Place the family's best estimate of monthly disposable income in the budget table.

Table 1-8 compares a single lieutenant's monthly sources of revenue when deployed and when not deployed. The lieutenant receives additional pay for being in a hostile fire zone and is no longer taxed on her basic pay. The table also includes other sources of income, such as basic allowance for subsistence (BAS) and basic allowance for housing (BAH), assuming that Fort Hood is the duty station. If the lieutenant were married, BAH would accrue at the "with dependents" rate, and the soldier would receive Family Separation Pay.

Income, especially military income, is relatively predictable. There can be surprises, however, and it is useful to track expected income and actual income—at least for a few months—until you become fully aware of everything going into your bank account each month.

Developing realistic spending goals

The next step in creating a viable household budget is developing realistic spending goals. To get started, collect bank statements, credit card bills, and

TABLE 1-8
DISPOSABLE INCOME FOR A SINGLE SECOND LIEUTENANT
DURING A TYPICAL MONTH

Income Type	Non-Deployed (after-tax income)	Deployed (after-tax income)
Basic and special pay (before taxes)	$2,784	$2,784
Federal taxes on basic and special pay	($310)	$0
BAH at Ft. Hood with no dependents (tax-exempt)	$1,026	$1,026
Hostile fire pay	$0	$225
Interest and investment income	$75	$75
BAS (tax-exempt)	$223	$223
TOTAL	$3,799	$4,333

other receipts of expenditures for the past twelve months. Begin to review your spending patterns, sorting the spending items into categories as you go. Table 1-9 (page 19) provides a set of spending categories to help with this step. After reviewing your bills and records, add up all expenditures within each category. Divide the total by twelve to calculate a monthly average for each item.

The list in Table 1-9 is not exhaustive; servicemembers should add lines to account for spending on items not found in the table. The point of this exercise is to create an accurate picture of how the family is spending household income. This process should generate a frank dialogue about household finances. These conversations require honesty and patience as families assess, without hurtful recrimination, what everyone is currently spending.

In some cases, current spending exceeds current income, meaning that the family is accumulating debt, often on credit cards. In many other cases, current spending (excluding contributions to savings and investments) is barely covered by current income, meaning that the family is living paycheck to paycheck. When these patterns exist, the household cannot achieve its future financial goals.

If the family finds itself in this situation, it must carefully consider ways to reduce current spending. The family should develop concrete and realistic solutions to solve this problem, such as reducing services like cell phones, cable TV, and internet service, or reducing purchases of coffee, soda, snacks, cigarettes, alcohol, or meals at high-cost restaurants. Military OneSource (http://www.militaryonesource.mil) is a great resource available to military families that offers counseling (in person and by phone) and guides servicemembers in addressing financial, personal, legal, or marriage issues. They have exceptional resources for helping families overcome debt and the mismanagement of funds. Additionally, service-specific organizations like Army

Community Service (ACS) and its service equivalents offer similar counseling through installation assets.

The ultimate goal of this step is to derive a spending limit for each category that will allow the family to increase its capacity to save each month. This process requires kind, honest, and patient negotiation among all family members in order to change ingrained spending patterns. It is common for people to feel anxious about spending limits because today's culture often confuses moral worth with material wealth. One way to alleviate these frictions is to keep your financial goals handy (Table 1-2) and remind everyone in the family that today's savings will bring a sense of achievement, security, and reward in the future.

As a family works through its spending goals, the family must also consider its monthly savings goal and ask, "What is possible? What is desirable?" Again, it is common to feel concerned about your family's capacity to reach its goals. How can $50 each month really make any difference? The simple answer is that *any* monthly savings moves a family closer to its financial goals. As Table 1-5 showed, regular monthly savings of $61, invested at a 6% (real) rate of return, would generate $10,000 in ten years (in today's dollars). If you could double that amount to $122, you could double your future savings to $20,000.

When a family abides by a budget, they take full responsibility for their future. They save for the household and create a sustainable pattern of spending, one that they can maintain even in the servicemember's absence. Imagine the lieutenant's peace of mind, *knowing* that when she is deployed, her husband and children will have the tools they need to manage the household finances and maintain the family's financial security. Imagine the sense of financial independence and satisfaction your family will feel after reaching your financial goals. Families and individuals must take control of their futures through careful financial planning and budgeting.

USEFUL RESOURCES AND SUGGESTED READING
Financial Planning: http://www.financialplan.about.com
AARP: http://www.aarp.org/work/retirement-planning/retirement_calculator
National Endowment for Financial Education: http://www.nefe.org
Military OneSource: http://www.militaryonesource.mil
Mint: http://www.mint.com

Additional Investing Guides
Gardner, David, and Tom Gardner. *The Motley Fool Personal Finance Workbook: A Foolproof Guide to Organizing Your Cash and Building Wealth.* New York: Fireside Books, 2003.
Tyson, Eric. *Personal Finance for Dummies* (7th Edition). New Jersey: Wiley, 2012.

TABLE 1-9
HOUSEHOLD SPENDING

Expenses	Planned Spending	Actual Spending	Notes
Housing			
Mortgage or rent on primary residence	_____	_____	_____
Homeowners/renters insurance	_____	_____	_____
Property taxes	_____	_____	_____
Home repairs/maintenance/lawn	_____	_____	_____
Household supplies	_____	_____	_____
Home improvements	_____	_____	_____
Utilities (phone, electricity, water, gas/oil)	_____	_____	_____
Expenses on any secondary properties	_____	_____	_____
Food			
Groceries	_____	_____	_____
Eating out	_____	_____	_____
Family obligations			
Child support	_____	_____	_____
Alimony	_____	_____	_____
Day care, babysitting	_____	_____	_____
Health and wellness			
Insurance (medical, dental, vision)	_____	_____	_____
Unreimbursed medical expenses (co-pay)	_____	_____	_____
Fitness (club memberships, classes, equipment)	_____	_____	_____
Personal grooming	_____	_____	_____
Toiletries	_____	_____	_____
Habits (smoking, coffee, alcohol)	_____	_____	_____
Transportation			
Car payments	_____	_____	_____
Gas	_____	_____	_____
Auto repairs/maintenance	_____	_____	_____
Auto insurance	_____	_____	_____
Other costs (tools, public transportation)	_____	_____	_____
Travel-deployment related	_____	_____	_____

table continued on next page

table continued from previous page

TABLE 1-9
HOUSEHOLD SPENDING

Expenses	Planned Spending	Actual Spending	Notes
Entertainment/Social			
Cable TV/videos/movies	_____	_____	_____
Internet expenses/online accounts	_____	_____	_____
Computer equipment	_____	_____	_____
Hobbies	_____	_____	_____
Subscriptions/dues (clubs, church, other)	_____	_____	_____
Vacations	_____	_____	_____
Cell phone	_____	_____	_____
Celebrations/parties	_____	_____	_____
Pets			
Food	_____	_____	_____
Grooming, vet	_____	_____	_____
Moving/relocation			
Packing supplies	_____	_____	_____
Moving expense	_____	_____	_____
Clothing			
Casual/personal	_____	_____	_____
Professional	_____	_____	_____
Charity and gifts	_____	_____	_____
Debt payments			
Credit cards	_____	_____	_____
Loans (home equity, student)	_____	_____	_____
Other loans	_____	_____	_____
Direct Allotments from Military Pay			
Allotment A	_____	_____	_____
Allotment B	_____	_____	_____
Allotment C	_____	_____	_____
Contributions to savings and investments			
401(k) or IRA	_____	_____	_____
Stocks/bonds/mutual funds	_____	_____	_____
College savings	_____	_____	_____
Emergency fund	_____	_____	_____
Other savings	_____	_____	_____

2

Smart Banking

A convenient and cost-effective relationship with a bank is essential for military families. Understanding what banks offer and how to choose the best one is an important first step toward responsible financial management. Banks are an essential part of the economy for many reasons, but most importantly for individuals, banks: 1) hold deposits of paychecks and savings, 2) enable commerce by allowing account holders to write checks or make debit payments to purchase goods, and 3) make loans to homeowners, automobile purchasers, and businesses.

Banks themselves are businesses that make money by paying account holders a nominal rate of interest to keep deposits at the bank and then loaning that money to others to earn a higher rate of interest. Banks can vary in type, size, and capabilities (see Table 2-1, page 25).

SELECTING A BANK
There are several factors to consider when selecting a bank. Convenience and cost of services are the most important considerations.

Convenience
People use banks because they want to make purchases conveniently and because they want to ensure that their money is quickly accessible. Since convenience is a major reason for using a bank, it is a major factor to consider when choosing a bank.

> *Choose a bank that is convenient, cost-effective, and offers online banking services and ATMs worldwide.*

Today, cash is instantly available at twenty-four-hour automatic teller machines (ATM). The better ATM networks share sites and allow clients to obtain cash from machines far removed from the particular bank where they hold an account; many include international access. Look for a bank that has

ATM services with convenient home or workplace access. Keep in mind that banks normally charge a fee for using an ATM associated with another bank. However, some banks refund all or part of other banks' ATM usage fees. For example, USAA (http://usaa.com) does not charge a fee for the first ten ATM withdrawals; it also refunds up to $15 in other banks' ATM usage fees during each statement cycle.

Another way to access cash is to write a check. A check is simply a note between a client and his/her bank telling the bank to transfer a specified amount of money from the client's account to someone else. While checks are convenient for transferring money to another person or business, they are at times inconvenient to receive. Due to bank branch locations and operating hours, some people find it difficult to deposit checks into their own accounts or to cash them. However, new applications offered by a growing number of banks on mobile devices are making check depositing more convenient.

Another challenge with checks is that some merchants do not accept them, so a more convenient method to make purchases is to use a debit card. A debit card looks and is used like a traditional credit card. The fundamental difference is that the use of a credit card is a loan—a loan that eventually must be repaid. A debit card acts much like a check in that it draws against the current balance of either a savings or checking account. There are some differences between a debit card and a check. Checks typically take one to three days to clear an account, while debit card transactions usually clear on the same day. If lost or stolen, debit cards require knowledge of a personal identification number (PIN) to make a fraudulent transaction, whereas checks often involve only a forged signature. Finally, debit card use can be monitored electronically for unusual transactions (potentially fraudulent activity)—unlike check transactions, which are just processed through a check clearing center. The end result is that while money may come out of an account sooner if you use a debit card, there may be a slightly lower risk of fraudulent activity if the card is lost or stolen.

A drawback to using debit cards is that they may provide less control over charges against their linked account. Particularly with car rentals and hotel stays, merchants may place holds on debit cards for the estimated cost of the transaction. If the cardholder uses the debit card to purchase something from another merchant while the hold is in place, an account overdraft can occur. An overdraft is when someone withdraws more money from an account than is currently available in that account. Most banks offer overdraft protection against this occurrence (for a fee). Banks charge higher fees or penalties to their clients who draw in excess of their account funds without overdraft protection.

There are two types of debit card transactions. Purchasers may complete transactions by using either a PIN or a signature. "Signature" debit card transactions function like a credit card transaction; purchasers select the "credit" rather than "debit" option on the payment machine. "Signature" transactions help customers avoid the transaction fees that some banks charge for PIN transactions. A signature debit will be withdrawn from the associated savings or checking account, but it may take a day or two longer to clear than a PIN transaction. Additionally, Visa and MasterCard protect signature debit card transactions with "zero liability" protection against fraudulent charges. Finally, banks usually make signature debit card transactions eligible for their rewards programs, whereas check transactions and PIN debit card transactions are not usually eligible. For these reasons, consumers generally should use the signature transaction for debit card purchases.

One of the most important convenience features that banks offer service-members is direct deposit. A direct deposit arrangement establishes a direct link between the military pay system and a servicemember's checking or savings account. On payday, the Defense Finance Accounting Service (DFAS) automatically sends pay to the servicemember's bank account. Servicemembers can find out details about the pay deposit by accessing their Leave and Earnings Statement (LES) through DFAS's myPay website (https://www.mypay.gov). The most important convenience of direct deposit for service-members is that their paychecks are deposited and their money is available even when they are away from their duty stations—on leave, TDY, or deployment.

Many military families maintain bank accounts in the locality where they are assigned. This necessitates closing old accounts and opening new ones at each duty station. Because closing and opening bank accounts and shopping for the best banking services are time-consuming tasks, it is worth considering whether a local bank is really necessary. An alternative to transferring banks with each change of duty station is to maintain a permanent or hometown bank so that the family can continue to write checks and maintain savings balances while in transit from one assignment to the next. The disadvantage to this option is that the family's permanent bank may not have a branch near the new duty station, making in-person transactions (check cashing and depositing) much more onerous. It may be prudent to investigate the number and location of branches before committing to a permanent bank. Some banks such as Bank of America, Wells Fargo, Citibank, and Chase have nationwide branches that may make it easier for servicemembers to maintain a more permanent relationship.

Similarly, with technological advances in online banking, it may be most convenient to use a virtual bank, such as USAA (https://www.usaa.com) or E*TRADE (https://www.etrade.com), which servicemembers can use regardless of duty location. Many banks have expanded their virtual services, including those that can be accessed through mobile devices, to include depositing checks, transferring funds, paying bills, and obtaining balances. Virtual banks generally offer the same services as brick-and-mortar banks, but with lower fees and greater convenience. The decision about the type of bank that would best serve a military family's needs should be a function of the family's comfort with accessing the bank's resources through virtual technologies (Internet, phone, chat, and mail). Military families should ask the following questions to determine if a virtual bank can meet a family's banking needs:

- Does the bank provide a means for electronically depositing checks?
- Is it possible to access cash conveniently if the family is unable to go to a local branch to cash a check?
- Does the bank have a national or international ATM network?
- Does the bank offer online banking, and does the military family have access to a computer with an Internet connection or a mobile device that can access the online banking system?
- Does the bank offer convenient loan service by Internet, mail, or phone?
- Does the bank allow for transfers between savings, checking, or other accounts by Internet or phone?

If the answer to most of these questions is "yes," a virtual bank may offer the best value (cost-effectiveness and convenience). At most banks, online banking is free; however, some still charge a monthly fee for paying bills using the bank's online service. You should be able to find a bank that does not charge an online bill-paying fee. For example, USAA federal savings bank does not charge fees for this service; it also offers to pay penalties if the funds do not transfer to the recipient on time. Online bill paying offers further value in that it saves time and postage, and online bankers can use the service from anywhere with Internet access (even during some deployments). Servicemembers should judge online banking services in the same manner as they judge a brick-and-mortar bank; the fundamental analysis remains the same. Remember, the goal is to find the bank that provides you with the maximum value (balancing convenience and cost).

Cost of Services

Comparison shopping is an important step in selecting a bank. Offers of $100 or free items to new customers should give you an idea of how important customers' business is to banks. Banks competing for your business is good for you as long as you review and assess the competition to get the best possible combination of desired services at the best possible cost.

The military family should shop around to compare the fees different banks charge and the interest that they pay on deposits before committing to a financial institution. Banks compete with other banks in both price and service in order to earn customers. In developing a price strategy, most banks try to attract the most profitable customers; therefore, their pricing schemes encourage or discourage specific types of customers. It is important to understand the banks' pricing schemes, and for servicemembers to find a bank whose fee structure best matches their customer type. Additionally, by minimizing the number of accounts the family opens with a bank, the family can simplify the banking process and hold down the cost of financial services as well.

TABLE 2-1
BANKING CHOICES

Type of Bank	Advantages	Disadvantages
Commercial bank	Complete range of services, including online banking, multiple ATMs and branches	Higher Fees
Credit union (not-for-profit)	Low fees	Fewer ATMs; limited hours
Savings & loan	Lower fees; personal service	Fewer branches
Virtual bank (online only—no branches)	Higher interest rates on deposits; time-saving	Must mail in deposits or deposit via smartphone, ATM, or computer and scanner; limited check-cashing service
Brokerage firm or investment company	One-stop shopping	May require higher minimum balances; limited loan services

Table 2-1 summarizes the advantages and disadvantages of different types of banks, taking into account convenience and costs.

TYPES OF BANK ACCOUNTS

There are a number of necessary services that banks offer to meet their customers' basic needs, such as checking and share draft accounts for transactions; savings accounts or money market deposit accounts for emergency funds; and certificates of deposit for short- and medium-term savings. Investment options for meeting servicemembers' short-, medium-, and long-term financial goals are discussed further in part III of this book.

Checking Accounts

A checking account or share draft account (which is the equivalent of a checking account at a credit union) is the best banking service for conducting multiple monthly transactions. Checking accounts come in two basic varieties: noninterest-bearing and interest-bearing. As their name implies, noninterest-bearing accounts offer no interest on the deposited funds. Since banks pay no interest on these accounts, they are cheaper for the bank to provide. Banks generally encourage depositors who plan to keep very small balances (less than $500 or $1,000) to use noninterest checking accounts.

Some banks charge a per-check fee along with a service fee for a checking account. Banks levy per-check fees on each check written against the account; the fees cover expenses related to processing and clearing checks. Banks may also levy monthly service fees, designed to compensate the bank for the costs of maintaining small accounts, on some checking accounts. Many banks will waive these fees for direct-deposit customers, and most credit unions associated with the military do not have them at all. These fees can really add up, so it is worth shopping around to avoid them. There is *no* reason to pay a per-check fee or a monthly checking account fee—many military-friendly banks do not charge them.

Banks often advertise "free" checking accounts, with no per-check or service fees. The catch on some of these free checking accounts is that the bank waives the fees only if the customer maintains a minimum average balance each month; the minimum may be $1,000 or more. In other cases, banks or credit unions offer free checking if the customer maintains a savings account or time deposit above a required minimum (either for deposits in one of those accounts, or for total deposits in all accounts).

Overdraft Protection

It is essential that all military personnel have overdraft protection on their checking accounts. If the family writes a check for more than the balance of the account, the family has "bounced" a check. A bounced check, or a check presented for insufficient funds, can be detrimental to a military career. Good money management and fiscal responsibility are attributes of good officers and noncommissioned officers. The military chain of command will generally view a bounced check as an irresponsible or careless act. Bouncing a check is also expensive. Banks will generally charge $25 to $50 for the administrative cost of handling the check, and the retailer will likely charge a fee as well.

> *Finding a bank that offers overdraft protection along with free checking is a basic financial goal: The best bank may also pay interest on larger balances.*

Families can avoid concerns and fees associated with bounced checks by subscribing to overdraft protection. Overdraft protection is simply a money transfer from a linked account, or a short-term loan from a credit card, that prevents a check from bouncing. For example, if you write a check for $100 but have a balance of only $50 in your checking account, with overdraft protection, the bank would immediately transfer $50 from a linked savings account to your checking account and then process the check. Some banks require the link to be to a bank-issued credit card rather than a savings account in order to qualify for overdraft protection. When the account is linked to a credit card, a customer overdraft will usually be billed as a cash advance, resulting in a fee for the loan and interest accruing immediately on the credit card balance. Although these fees can be costly, they will likely cost the customer less than the fees and penalties associated with bouncing a check. Simply put, do not bank without overdraft protection, and strive to have the protection linked to a savings account to minimize potential fees.

Savings Accounts

An essential part of any financial plan is savings. Unlike checking account deposits, families generally do not need constant access to savings deposits. Therefore, banks can rely more on using funds from savings deposits to make the loans to other customers that will generate additional bank revenue. Banks provide three basic choices for these funds: savings accounts, money market savings accounts, and certificates of deposit (CDs). These accounts are relatively low-risk instruments for achieving short- and medium-term financial goals.

Savings Accounts. These accounts normally have tiered annual percentage yields, or rates of return; larger deposits earn greater rates of return. Generally, savings accounts are not an appropriate means for attaining long-term financial goals because the interest rates on these accounts do not provide the returns necessary for many investors to achieve their goals. Typically, traditional savings accounts provide the lowest yield, money market accounts provide a slightly higher yield, and CDs provide the highest yield of the three. All three of these savings vehicles are FDIC (Federal Deposit Insurance Corporation) insured. (The FDIC guarantees certain bank accounts for up to $250,000 in the event of a bank failure.)

Money Market Accounts. Money market deposit accounts (MMDAs) available from banks offer higher yields than traditional savings accounts, along with additional restrictions (usually higher minimum balances and limited check writing or per-check fees). Money market funds (MMFs), also known as money market mutual funds, are available from brokerage firms and mutual fund companies. They offer yields and restrictions comparable to those of MMDAs, however they are not FDIC insured. The easiest way to access the most up-to-date information about the best money market accounts and trends in banking is Bankrate.com (http://www.bankrate.com).

> *Open a savings account that earns interest and immediately start saving. Aim to accumulate two to six months' worth of income as an emergency fund.*

Certificates of Deposit. For short- to medium-term investments, you might want to consider certificates of deposit (CDs). Certificates of deposit pay higher interest rates than regular savings accounts but require that the amount deposited remain in the account for a set time period; banks levy early withdrawal penalties on funds removed before the maturity date. CDs are usually available in one-, three-, and six-month, and one-to-seven-year increments, with higher interest rates for the longer maturity periods. Generally, you should use CDs when you have funds beyond what you need for the short term and in case of emergencies. For example, if a servicemember already has an emergency fund with two months' pay and no other short-term needs for the excess funds, a CD that pays a higher interest rate than a savings account is a good way to save for a short-term goal.

A great advantage of CDs is that the interest is guaranteed for the entire life of the certificate, so a CD enables customers to "lock in" an attractive rate of interest for a known amount of time. Savings accounts do not offer this advantage, typically paying very low interest rates or money-market rates that fluctuate weekly or monthly. However, guaranteeing an interest rate for several years is a double-edged sword, because inflation rates ultimately determine one's real rate of return (how much one's purchasing power increases or decreases). For example, a CD with a 4% guaranteed rate of return for five years may seem attractive today if savings deposits are paying 3%, but the 4% rate is much less attractive if money market rates rise to 6% next year (as a function of prevailing inflation and interest rates).

Do not let the fear of an early withdrawal penalty eliminate CDs as an investment option. If you really need your money, or if interest rates shoot way up, you can always get your deposit out of the CD by paying the withdrawal penalty. The penalty usually involves forfeiting interest earned to date, but the principal remains intact. As with all bank deposits, it is important to fully understand the terms of a CD before investing in one. Chapter 11 discusses how a CD may fit into a portfolio of financial assets.

EMERGENCY FUNDS
High-yield savings accounts, CDs, MMDAs, and MMFs with check-writing privileges are all candidates for emergency funds. With respect to emergency funds, families should be much more concerned with the ability to access money quickly than with maximizing the interest earned on such funds. Families must be willing to balance the need for liquidity against the desire to get higher rates of interest. Families should fund their emergency fund first; however if this is not possible, the family should maintain a no-fee credit card with a sufficient line of credit—to provide peace of mind that they will be able to pay for immediate emergency requirements.

The emergency fund provides immediate cash if a disaster or adverse event occurs. Families must first determine the size of their needs. Most financial advisors suggest between two and six months' worth of living expenses. Two months' base pay may be sufficient if the family has a good credit history and quick and easy access to credit. Families should anticipate what emergencies might arise that would require immediate payments. Certainly the fund should be large enough to buy plane tickets home for the entire family. In other cases, the family would want to be able to cover the deductible on automobile insurance in case of an accident, or to pay for a significant automobile repair. Families should use common sense to assess their needs, and then adapt the magnitude of their emergency fund to meet their expectations. The family may need a larger fund if they anticipate the death of an immediate family member that would require traveling a great distance, or if the service-member is contemplating changing careers or starting school (in which case income will become less guaranteed). Even though the family may pay for such emergencies with a credit card, the balance will be due within the month. Emergency funds help prevent families from falling deep into debt and having to pay high consumer-credit interest payments.

LOANS

Most people find it necessary to borrow money from time to time. You may not have the cash available to pay for expensive items like major appliances or cars, and you certainly will need to borrow money to buy a house. It often makes sense to spread the cost over the period of time you anticipate using the purchase, and to do so you must borrow money and pay interest for that con-venience. A credit card is a type of loan, and banks are just one type of insti-tution that issue credit cards. You should compare different credit card companies before selecting one. Chapter 3 explains how to evaluate the credit services offered by banks and other credit card companies, and part II of this book addresses borrowing money to finance major purchases like a home or automobile.

Rates are negotiable! Rates on loans are negotiable before and during the term of the loan. This is particularly true for those with strong credit ratings. In order to negotiate a lower rate, scour the Internet for lower rates from rival financial institutions. Armed with this information, call your bank and request

---

TABLE 2-2
SELECTING A BANK

Service	Available?	Cost?/Fees?	Rate?
Checking Account			
Checking account pays interest	Require	Avoid	Compare
Nationwide ATM use reimbursement	Require	Avoid	N/A
Check deposit via scanner & computer or smartphone	Advised	Avoid	N/A
Deposit via affiliated organizations	As Required	Compare	N/A
Web bill-paying service	As Required	Avoid	N/A
Online banking and mobile banking	Require	Avoid	N/A
Cash back or rewards on debit card purchases	Preferred	Avoid	Compare
Monthly service fees	Avoid	Avoid	N/A
Overdraft protection	Require	Avoid	N/A

table continued on next page

table continued from previous page

TABLE 2-2
SELECTING A BANK

Service	Available?	Cost?/Fees?	Rate?
Checking Account (continued)			
Checks	N/A	Free	N/A
FDIC insured	Require	N/A	N/A
Credit Card			
Rate (APR)	N/A	N/A	Compare
Annual Fees	Avoid	Avoid	Avoid
Fees for exceeding credit limit	Avoid	Avoid	Avoid
Cash back or rewards on credit card purchases with no annual fee	Preferred	Avoid	Compare
Savings Account			
National/international ATM use	As Required	Avoid	N/A
Rate	N/A	Avoid	Compare
Fund transfers	Require	Avoid	N/A
Monthly service fees	N/A	Avoid	N/A
FDIC insured	Require	N/A	N/A
Certificates of Deposit (CDs)			
Terms (time to maturity) Available	Compare	Compare	Compare
Fixed rate	Compare	Compare	Compare
Adjustable rate	Compare	Compare	Compare
Variable rate	Compare	Compare	Compare
FDIC insured	Require	N/A	N/A
MMDA/MMSA	Require	Avoid	Compare

that the bank match the rival institution's rate. See chapter 3 for a more detailed discussion of interest rates.

Table 2-2 provides a summary of the topics discussed in this chapter, highlighting the factors a family financial planner should evaluate when selecting a financial institution for routine banking.

3

Using Credit Wisely

Borrowing to finance the purchase of durable goods such as cars, furniture, and appliances has long been a traditional feature of American life. More recently, gasoline, candy bars, and fast food have been added to the American borrowing culture. This chapter discusses the wise use of consumer credit, costs of consumer credit and debit cards, the operation of traditional bank-loan services, and some of the different types of loans available to consumers. It concludes with a review of the uses, abuses, and costs of consumer credit.

THE BASICS OF CREDIT

Before discussing the wise use of credit and borrowing, it is important to understand where borrowed money comes from. You also need to be familiar with some terms that are necessary for understanding the credit process: interest rate, interest payment, principal payment, opportunity cost, risk premium, and outstanding balance.

Most people view borrowed money as coming from some large institution, such as a bank or a credit card company, and do not consider where these institutions acquire the money to loan out. Every dollar these institutions loan out comes from some person who has chosen not to spend all of his or her current income—someone who has chosen to defer consumption. In short, every dollar loaned comes from someone's savings.

Individuals and households save money so that they can make purchases in the future. They may set current income aside as savings so that they can have an extravagant night out next month, take a vacation next year, go to college in four years, purchase a house in fifteen years, or retire comfortably in thirty years. Some people may set these savings aside in the sock drawer for easy access, but most savers store their money in a financial institution such as a bank, where the savers expect the savings to grow over time. This growth rate is called the interest rate.

To explain what interest rate, interest payment, principal payment, inflation, opportunity cost, risk premium, and outstanding balance are and how they come to be, consider the following story of Jack and Jill. Jill has $100 she could use to buy a bicycle that is priced at $100. Jack has failed to appear at his court date for a speeding ticket and has been arrested on a bench warrant. Jack needs $100 to post bail or he must stay in jail until his next court date, exactly one year from today. Jack asks to borrow the $100 bail from Jill. If Jill loans Jack the $100, she must put off buying the bicycle for one year (opportunity cost), so she is saving $100. Having borrowed the $100, Jack now has $100 (outstanding balance) he owes to Jill. So far, Jill has saved $100 by putting off current consumption opportunities and Jack has borrowed and spent $100 he did not originally have.

Jumping forward a year to Jack's court date, things in Jack and Jill's world have changed. For Jill, the price of the bicycle has risen to $105 (inflation). Since Jill had originally wanted to use her money to buy that bicycle, it is reasonable for her to expect Jack to cover the extra inflation cost so that she comes out even. So Jack needs to pay Jill $100 plus $5 for a total of $105 to cover inflation. Jill has also given up a year's worth of bicycle riding and she wants compensation for that loss. It turns out that Acme-Rent-All, the local bicycle renting agency, rents bicycles for $10 per year. Jill wants Jack to pay an extra $10 to cover the rent for that year of bicycle riding (opportunity cost). Lastly, Jack is not the most reliable person. There was a 10% chance that Jack would forget his court date and Jill's bail money would have been forfeited. If Jack and Jill were in the habit of making this arrangement, Jill would need an extra $10 for each loan to cover the $100 lost each time Jack forgot to appear in court (risk premium).

To make it a beneficial opportunity for Jill to give up purchasing the bicycle (saving $100) and make the money available to Jack for bail (borrowing $100), Jack must agree to pay Jill the $100 principal plus a $25 fee one year later. That $25 fee is called interest and it consists of three parts:

1. $5 or 5% for inflation,
2. $10 or 10% for opportunity cost of capital, and
3. $10 or 10% for risk premium.

In this situation, if Jack wants to borrow $100 from Jill, he must agree to a 25% annual interest rate. All posted interest rates are a sum of the expected inflation rate, the opportunity cost of capital, and an expected risk premium. If Jack pays all of the $125 he owes Jill, he will make a $100 principal payment and a $25 interest payment. If, on the other hand, he pays Jill the $100 he gets from the court clerk when his bail is refunded, he will make a $25 interest payment and a $75 principal payment, leaving an outstanding balance of $25. If he waits until the end of the next year to pay off the rest, Jack will owe the $25 principal plus $6.25 in accrued interest ($25 x 25% = $6.25) for a total balance of $31.25.

CREDIT HISTORIES AND CREDIT SCORES
Of the three components of the interest rate a borrower faces—the inflation rate, the opportunity cost of capital and the risk premium—there is only one

that is directly influenced by the borrower's behavior—the risk premium. Jack, from the example above, is in control of how reliable he is. As with Jack, individual borrowers build a history of financial reliability through their bill paying and borrowing habits. This reliability is called credit worthiness. Companies that collect and organize this history in the United States are called credit bureaus. The three major credit bureaus are: Experian, Equifax, and Trans-Union. These are private companies that face strict government regulation through the Fair Credit Reporting Act (FCRA) and the Fair Credit Billing Act (FCBA) and are overseen by Federal Trade Commission (FTC) and the Office of the Comptroller of the Currency (OCC).

Since lenders use the credit histories collected by the credit bureaus to determine a potential borrower's credit worthiness, individuals are entitled to a free annual credit report. Individuals can go to AnnualCreditReport.com (https://www.annualcreditreport.com) to get their free credit report. Individuals should obtain and review their credit report from each agency annually, ideally spacing out the requests among the three credit agencies at four-month intervals. This quarterly spacing ensures that individuals do not pay for the "free annual service," while ensuring their credit history is up-to-date and accurate. Mistakes on a credit report can severely impact an individual's terms of, and ability to obtain, consumer credit. Under the FCRA, a potential borrower is entitled to an additional free credit report within 60 days of being denied credit or being granted unfavorable credit terms.

The information on a person's credit report is consolidated into a single number called a Credit Score. There are many algorithms used to generate credit scores, but the most common is the credit score calculated by the Fair Isaac Corporation (FICO). The FICO credit score is a value ranging from 300 to 850. The credit score is a measure of a potential borrower's credit worthiness and impacts the risk premium a lending institution will add into the borrower's interest rate. The higher the credit score, the more credit worthy the borrower is assumed to be, and the lower the additional risk premium the borrower faces in the interest rate. A credit score is determined by five types of information:

1. Payment History
2. Outstanding Balances and Available Credit
3. Length of Credit History
4. Amount of New Credit
5. Types of Credit

Credit scores can have a big impact on your financial opportunities. A borrower is unlikely to qualify for a car loan with a FICO score under 650, unlikely to qualify for a mortgage with a FICO score under 620, and unlikely to qualify for a credit card with a FICO score under 600 (see Table 3-1, page 34).

TABLE 3-1
FAIR ISAAC'S REPORT OF AMERICAN CREDIT SCORES IN 2011

Credit score	Percentage of Population
499 and below	2 percent
500-549	5 percent
550-599	8 percent
600-649	12 percent
650-699	15 percent
700-749	18 percent
750-799	27 percent
800 and above	13 percent

Source: http://yourcreditscorerange.com/2011/understanding-the-fico-credit-score-range

THE ROLE OF CONSUMER CREDIT IN A PERSONAL BUDGET

Today, consumer credit is easy to get—so easy that many families find themselves in financial distress. The danger of too much debt is that there may not be enough income both to pay off the debt and to provide for the basic needs of food and shelter, much less save for future needs. As emphasized in chapter 1, success in personal financial management requires planning and perseverance. An absolute requirement for any family is a regular savings plan. If large monthly debt payments make regular saving impossible, take immediate steps to reduce the amount you owe. Although this situation is easier to prevent than to cure, it is never impossible to get out of debt.

This is not to say that military families should never borrow. Virtually everyone needs to borrow money to finance major purchases, such as automobiles and furniture, or to pay educational expenses. Additionally, very few people can afford to buy a house with cash alone. Without credit, a family could not buy some of these costly items unless they had saved enough money to pay for these purchases outright. If a family has the money available to cover such purchases from their own resources, even if that money was intended for some other long-range goal, they should evaluate the interest rate the lending institution would charge, as it may be more advantageous to use their own funds, or "borrow from themselves," rather than borrow from a lending institution. If the rate of return foregone on savings is lower than the interest rate a lender would charge for a loan, then "borrowing from oneself" is a wise financial decision. A family can then replenish their savings by "repaying" themselves each month with the amount they would have paid the lender. If, on the other hand, they can secure a very low interest loan and their savings are in a high-interest savings vehicle, it is better to borrow from the lender.

If a family find themselves using consumer credit to finance routine day-to-day needs, they need to reassess their budget and financial goals and return to living within their available income. A good practice is to only use consumer credit for items that will have useful lives of at least the time it takes to repay the debt—for example, durable goods such as cars and furniture, and long-lasting assets such as education. Families should not routinely carry unpaid credit card balances for purchases of clothes, entertainment, groceries, and other such nondurable items. They should cover this spending with current income. Using credit to finance routine purchases or to splurge on extras is a sure sign of personal financial mismanagement.

While one appropriate use of consumer credit is to defray the costs of the occasional emergency, such as airfare for a funeral or a major automotive repair, families should try to handle these situations by using their savings or by seeking assistance from aid agencies that make low-cost loans and grants to servicemembers and their families in times of crisis. One such agency is Army Emergency Relief (http://www.aerhq.org).

Since not everyone reading this book will likely adhere to this strict view of consumer credit, the following paragraphs and Table 3-2 offer some guidance on how much consumer debt is too much. Consumer debt refers to all debts incurred to finance purchases—including car loans and credit card debt, but excluding real estate mortgages or rent. One useful rule of thumb is that monthly payments on consumer debt should be no more than 20% of monthly disposable income, which is income after subtracting mortgage or rent, food, utilities, and taxes. Another guideline is that a family's total outstanding consumer debt should be less than one-third of their annual disposable income. The important point is that careful planning for consumer debt is one component of a monthly budget, which must also include adequate provisions for regular savings to establish an emergency reserve. To see how to apply these guidelines, consider the following examples.

Debt-Payment Guideline Example. An E-6 at Ft. Drum, New York, with over 8 years of service is living off-post with a spouse and two children and has an after-federal-tax monthly income of about $4,200. This military family has $1,400 in monthly rent, $100 in monthly utilities, and food costs of about $500 per month. Let's say this leaves the family with about $2,358 a month in disposable income. According to the first guideline, installment debt payments should not exceed $452 per month (20% of $2,358). However, just because it meets the Debt-Payment guideline does not guarantee it is a good choice for a family. How long would it take this family, with $15,000 in consumer debt at an interest rate of 15%, to retire their debt—making the maximum $452 per month payment? Approximately forty-four months, and the family will have paid $4,500 in interest. You can make similar calculations based on your own debt situation by using a calculator at www.bankrate.com or by typing "credit card calculator" into an Internet search engine.

TABLE 3-2
CONSUMER DEBT GUIDELINES

Situation	Annual Basic Pay[1]	Annual BAH[1]	After-tax income[1]	Monthly Fixed Spending[2]	Monthly Disposable Income	Max Monthly Payment	Max Consumer Debt
E-4; 2 years of service; 0 dependents	$24,168	$14,976	$36,420	$1,800	$1,235	$247	$4,940
E-6; 8 years of service; 3 dependents	$37,128	$17,568	$51,092	$2,000	$2,358	$452	$9,031
O-2; 2 years of service; 0 dependents	$43,836	$17,532	$54,612	$2,000	$2,551	$510	$10,204
O-3; 6 years of service; 1 dependent	$62,268	$21,564	$73,477	$2,200	$3,923	$785	$15,692

[1] Basic Pay, BAH and Federal Taxes from 2011. Tax liability assumes the servicemember claims standard deduction and exemptions. The residual income is taxed according to the 2011 tax brackets.
[2] Monthly disposable income was calculated by subtracting median rent (adjusted for household size and income), food ($500 per month), and utilities ($100 per month) from monthly after-tax income.

Total-Debt Guideline Example. This rule is a bit more constraining than the debt-payment guideline. Modifying the preceding example, the same family stationed at Ft. Drum with an annual disposable income of $28,296 should not owe more than one-third of their disposable income, or $9,432, in consumer debt. Either calculation method will provide a ballpark figure for the maximum debt anyone should carry.

Table 3-2 provides examples of the maximum monthly payments and maximum total consumer debt amounts that junior and mid-level enlisted servicemenbers and officers should undertake.

WHAT ARE CREDIT, ATM/DEBIT, AND CHARGE CARDS?

One of the most popular forms of consumer credit is the credit card. Banks, credit unions, and thrift institutions usually offer either MasterCard or VISA, and sometimes both. Additionally, Discover Bank issues the Discover Card through the Discover Network, and American Express offers the AMEX card through their network (American Express offers a credit card in addition to their traditional charge card). Most military credit unions and financial services companies, such as USAA, offer credit cards with no annual fee and very low interest rates; in fact, shopping around will reveal this to be the case with most credit cards today.

A credit card contract is an arrangement between the lender and the holder of the credit card; it opens a line of credit that the cardholder can borrow against. When the cardholder makes a purchase with a credit card, the lender makes an instant loan to the cardholder for the amount of the purchase. The lender pays the merchant for the goods and bills the cardholder for loan repayment.

From the cardholder's perspective, the credit card is a very effective substitute for cash or checks in making routine purchases. Credit cards eliminate the insecurity and inconvenience of carrying currency, and the uncertainty about the acceptance of personal checks, since so many retail establishments (including post or base exchanges) accept the nationally known credit cards. Use of a credit card allows the cardholder to make a single payment for all the small purchases made during the month. A cardholder could buy nearly everything needed during the month with credit cards and then repay the entire balance right after payday. In essence, the cardholder receives an interest-free loan on all purchases made throughout the month as long as the balance is paid in full by the due date. However, the constant danger is in spending beyond one's means, carrying a balance, and paying interest on routine purchases.

One of the best features of credit cards is that they represent a reserve of purchasing power that can be tapped immediately in an emergency. When applying for a credit card, ask for a credit limit that is high enough to finance emergency expenditures. Remember that only the unused portion of a credit line serves as an effective source of reserves. This is a good reason to repay the entire balance each month.

Credit cards can also prove particularly useful during international travel. They reduce the need for converting currency because they are so widely accepted. Furthermore, the exchange rate used by the card companies to convert foreign currency charges into dollars is generally competitive and often better than the exchange rate you would receive at a bank or exchange office.

In addition to credit cards, most bank-like financial institutions offer automatic teller machine (ATM) cards that provide access to savings and checking accounts from machines throughout the world. An ATM card's use is restricted to banking functions one would perform at a teller window at a bank. The cardholder can make remote and off-hour deposits and cash withdrawals from checking and savings accounts, as well as limited account management actions such as balance transfers and electronic bill paying. Often these ATM cards are also debit cards that can be used anywhere a credit card is accepted. Debit cards have many of the same advantages as a credit card except they do not extend any credit at all. When a transaction is completed with a debit card, the account associated with the card is reduced by the amount of the transaction, plus any fees associated with the transaction. A debit card transaction is exactly like writing a check and must be recorded and tracked as such. While the cardholder is not in danger of carrying an outstanding balance across years as with a credit card, he or she is in danger of overdrawing from the account and being charged punitive fees by the bank. For this reason, many debit cardholders associate a bank line of credit with the debit card account for overdraft protection.

The final category of cards available to consumers is charge cards. The most familiar charge cards are American Express, Diner's Club, and Carte Blanche. They extend credit but under quite different terms than credit cards. These cards exist only for purchasing convenience and do not allow the cardholder to carry a balance. These cards offer the cardholder many of the same advantages as credit cards, except the ability to extend the payment of purchases across long periods of time. The cardholder is expected to pay all monthly purchases in full at the time of the statement.

HOW CREDIT CARD COMPANIES MAKE MONEY

Credit card companies have three basic sources of income from two different groups—the participating merchants and the cardholders. The merchants, in exchange for a payment option often more secure than checks, commit to pay the credit card company a host of fees (Table 3-3).

Cardholders may pay both fees and interest. These fees include both card membership fees and financial transaction fees (Table 3-4).

In addition to fees, cardholders pay interest on unpaid balances. To truly understand the interest income that credit card companies make, one must understand the effect of the credit card interest rate applied to the monthly balance.

TABLE 3-3
FEES CREDIT CARD COMPANIES CHARGE MERCHANTS

Fee Type	Charge
Annual Fee: A yearly fee for maintaining a credit card account.	Usually from $80 to $400 per year.
Transaction Fee: A fee charged for each transaction.	Usually $0.25 per transaction.
Authorization Fee: A fee charge for card authorization.	This is in addition to the transaction fee and applies whether the transaction completes or not.
Interchange Fee: A fee charged on the total amount transferred.	Usually 1-6% of the balance per transfer. It averages 2% and depends on the merchant's volume.

TABLE 3-4
FEES CREDIT CARD COMPANIES CHARGE CARDHOLDERS

Fee Type	Charge	How to Avoid It
Application Fee: A fee charged when you apply for a credit card.	Many have no application fee; others charge from $10 - $50 per application.	Ask your creditor to waive the fee.
Annual Fee: A yearly fee for the having the credit card.	Many have no annual fee; others charge from $25 to $300/year.	Ask your creditor to waive the fee. Some credit cards waive the fee if you make purchases during the year.
Cash Advance Fee: A fee charged when making a cash advance.	Usually 1-3% of the advance per transaction or a fixed minimum amount.	
Balance Transfer Fee: A fee charged when transferring balances between credit sources.	Usually 1-3% of the balance per transfer or a fixed minimum amount.	
Late Fee: A charge for a less-than minimum payment or a payment after the due date.	Usually $15 - $39 for each infraction.	Pay your bills on time or call your creditor to make payment arrangements. If you have otherwise good credit, ask them to waive it.
Finance Charge:A monthly charge for the convenience of carrying a balance.	A minimum fee or the interest due for the right to carry a balance.	Pay your balance before the grace period expires.

How Balances Are Computed
Credit card issuers use different methods to determine the balance on which they charge interest. As with bank deposits and loans, the method used to calculate the outstanding balance can have an important effect on the total interest expense.

The most common method used by card issuers is the average daily balance (ADB) method. This method applies the daily interest rate to the average of a cardholder's daily balances during the billing cycle. If the consumer pays the entire statement balance by the due date, the card company charges no interest. If the consumer carries a balance from the previous month, then the balance and all new charges incur interest charges daily until the new balance is paid in full.

There are two other frequently used methods—the previous balance method and the adjusted balance method. In the previous balance method, finance charges are levied on the previous balance due as of the beginning of the billing period. The adjusted balance method levies the charge on the amount of the previous balance minus any payments made during the billing period. Thus, the adjusted balance method results in the lowest finance charge, the previous balance method has the highest charge, and the ADB method falls somewhere in between.

A less-often used balance calculation method is the two-cycle billing method. This is a more costly method than the others. This method takes the average of a cardholder's balance over the previous two billing cycles and applies the finance charge to that. Using this method, it is possible to carry no unpaid balance for a month and still be charged interest based on the balance of the previous month.

The Effective Annual Interest Rate
When considering using any form of consumer credit, including credit cards, the borrower must understand that the advertised interest rate is not usually the effective interest rate paid. Most advertised credit card interest rates are the nominal Annual Percentage Rate (APR). The nominal APR's effect on a loan contract is straightforward: A higher nominal APR will yield a higher annual interest payment for a stable outstanding balance across a year. A second consideration is how often the card company calculates interest and adds it to the outstanding balance. A credit card with an 18% nominal APR, a stable ADB of $1000 across a year—with its interest payment calculated, or compounded, monthly—has an Effective Annual interest Rate (EAR) of 19.56%. If the APR is compounded daily, then the EAR is 19.72%. Most credit cards compound the nominal APR daily. The EAR is calculated based on the following formula, where n is the number of times the interest is compounded in a year:

$$EAR = (1 + (APR/n))^n - 1$$

Typical credit cards offer nominal APRs that range from 7% to 35%, yielding EARs of 7.44% to 41.88%. Often a credit card will offer low introductory nominal APRs of 0% to 2% for the first six to eighteen months. These teaser rates usually only apply if the balance is paid off by the end of the introductory time period. The higher standard interest rate will apply retroactively if the balance is not paid on time.

HOW CONSUMERS CAN BENEFIT FROM CREDIT CARD USE
The main benefit consumers derive from credit cards is convenience. The consumer does not have to carry large quantities of cash for large purchases. The consumer does not have to worry about whether the merchant will accept a personal check. The consumer can smooth out large consumption events such

as Christmas shopping or back-to-school spending across several months by taking advantage of the short-term loan aspect of the credit card's line of credit. The consumer also builds a credit history by making on-time payments, which can favorably influence his or her credit score.

Credit cards offer a "grace period"—a window of time across which new purchases are not assessed interest charges. This period can be as little as 20 days and as long as 50 days, depending on the particular card. Some cards offer introductory 0% interest rates for extended periods of time. This no-interest window gives the consumer the opportunity to pay off a purchase without accruing a finance charge. Most cards do not apply the grace period on new purchases if the account has a previous outstanding balance. So, if the cardholder does not pay off the outstanding balance each billing period, there is no grace period.

There is a kind of credit card called a reward, or affinity, credit card. Reward credit cards allow the card user to accumulate points on a subset of their purchases. Reward card users can redeem these points for discounts on certain classes of future purchases. These points might be spent on hotels and travel, home improvements, brand name merchandise, and much more. Some of the reward credit cards offer cash back refunds. These refunds vary between 1% and 5% of specified purchases; on rare occasions card companies offer 10% cash back rewards for purchases from very select merchants. For those who pay off their monthly balances, reward credit cards are a source of found money. A cardholder who charges most of the family's monthly expenses might charge $3,000 per month, or $36,000 per year. This charge pattern would earn $360 in rewards at 1%, $720 at 2%, and up to $1800 at 5%.

Two good sources for credit card offers and information are Credit CardGuide.com (http://www.creditcardguide.com) and BankRate.com (http://www.bankrate.com/credit-cards.aspx).

Credit cards offer the cardholder quick, easy access to a line of credit that is very useful in cases of emergency. Unexpected costly events, such as emergency leave or large car repairs, often require large, instantaneous expenditures. In many cases, the only source of payment for unexpected large expenditures is a credit card. Once the purchases are charged on the credit card, it is more cost-effective for the cardholder to use savings to pay off as much of the credit card debt as possible—if the APR of the credit card exceeds the return on the savings. If the card has a low introductory APR that expires at some time in the future, treat that particular credit card balance as a closed-end loan by establishing a time period for repayment and faithfully making regular monthly payments.

CAUTIONS TO CREDIT CARD USE

Although credit cards offer great utility to consumers, their misuse costs cardholders many millions of dollars in unnecessary interest expenses. Accumulating credit card debt is an easy trap for an undisciplined consumer and a sure sign that he or she has become dangerously overextended on credit. It is best to repay the entire balance during each billing cycle.

While the convenience and temporary free credit feature of credit cards make them potentially useful to everyone, many consumers accumulate large unpaid balances on their card accounts and continually make sizable interest payments. The card issuers make this easy by asking that the cardholder repay only a minimum monthly amount, which is usually far less than the unpaid balance. This minimum payment can be little more than enough to cover the finance charge of the previous month and 1% or 2% of the principal. Cardholders making only the minimum payment will take a long time to repay their debt and guarantee the card companies a hefty return on the loan. Occasionally, often right after Christmas, credit card companies encourage consumers to take a payment holiday and skip a month's payment. The interest charges, of course, accrue on the unpaid balance, making it a very expensive holiday for the consumer when he or she eventually has to pay the bill with additional interest.

A quick way to establish a reasonable payment plan is to divide the balance on the statement by the number of months needed to repay the balance, then add estimated finance charges. This becomes a monthly payment plan. For example, to repay an entire $2,000 balance in ten months requires a payment of $200 on the principal each month. To calculate the total monthly payment, add the $200 principal payment to the finance charge from the previous month's statement. It is generally wise to use any leftover funds from other parts of the budget to reduce credit card debt as quickly as possible.

Cardholders who accrue large card balances that they cannot easily repay within a short period of time should consider getting a signature loan from a bank or another financial institution to consolidate their debts at the lower signature loan rate. Such a loan adds the discipline of fixed monthly installment payments. Banks will consider the credit limits of all active credit cards when they decide whether to approve a loan. After all, there is nothing that stops a consumer from immediately going out and incurring new charges on a credit card once the signature loan is used to repay the credit card balance.

In summary, avoid carrying a balance on credit cards. If carrying a balance is necessary, make it a priority to reduce or eliminate it quickly. In general, repay credit card debt before trying to save, since credit card APRs tend to be higher than returns on savings. If you are carrying balances on more than one credit card, pay the minimum on the cards with the lowest APR and concentrate on eliminating the credit cards one at a time, starting with the card with the highest APR.

CREDIT CARD INSURANCE
Occasionally, credit card issuers will encourage cardholders to buy credit card insurance. There really is little reason to pay for such insurance, because cardholder liability for unauthorized use of their cards is generally limited to $50,

and few issuers actually attempt to get their cardholders to pay even that. Cardholders must make sure that they report any lost credit card within twenty-four hours. One technique for keeping track of credit cards—in case a purse or a wallet is lost or stolen—is to empty the contents of the purse or wallet onto a copy machine and make a copy of the credit cards. Do this now and on each birthday. Put the copy in a safe place at home. This provides a quick and convenient record in case of a loss or theft.

CHOOSING A CREDIT CARD

There are three primary factors that potential cardholders should assess as they determine the card that is best for them: annual fees, rewards programs, and costs associated with interest rates, late fees, and balance computation methods. Cardholders will generally have to prioritize the benefits of the three factors, oftentimes accepting less than optimal circumstances in one factor to achieve desired outcomes in the other two. For example, having a no-annual-fee card with great rewards might require accepting a higher effective interest rate on purchases; having a no-annual-fee card with a low interest rate might require sacrificing the rewards program.

Today, virtually anyone in the military who wants a credit card can get one, and many servicemembers have more than one. This has changed the strategy of card issuers—from simply reaching new credit users to trying to lure credit card customers away from one another. The competition has expanded further by offering incentives for making card expenditures over cash expenditures, making expenditures on one card over another card, and carrying a balance. Credit card companies promote these behaviors by an array of ever-expanding/increasing rewards payments to card users. Another common technique for lenders to increase credit card use, especially among those users who expect to carry a balance, is to offer a low introductory APR (such as 0.9%) for a six-month to one-year period. At the end of the introductory period, the APR often jumps up significantly. It is common for lenders to exclude cash advances from these introductory rates and to switch to the higher, "regular" APR if cardholders exceed the credit limit or have a late payment. Credit cards are a lucrative business for card companies. As such, potential cardholders should carefully review card amenities and their spending and payment patterns in order to select the card that will allow them to best maximize their value in this mutually beneficial arrangement.

Annual Fees. Servicemembers should not pay an annual fee to use a credit card. Better-educated consumers have caused many financial institutions to offer credit cards with no annual fees and to compete for credit card-holders' business in other ways. There are so many no-fee cards available that servicemembers should not pay an annual fee unless there is some financial reason to do so. Some rewards cards charge annual fees, but many do not. Unless a card holder can justify the annual fee with a cost-benefit analysis that shows the benefits from the card with an annual fee (subtracting out the fee) exceed the benefits from a no-annual-fee rewards card, paying an annual fee does not make sense.

Rewards Programs. There are rewards cards that focus on gas rebates, expenditures with certain merchants (such as Amazon.com), and even car companies. Servicemembers should review rewards cards and select the card that offers the maximum rewards on the expenditures for which they make a majority of their purchases.

Interest Rates and Balance Compounding Periods. If a cardholder expects to maintain an outstanding balance on a card, then interest rates and compounding periods are important factors. If the cardholder expects to pay off balances each month, then the rates are a less important consideration. Servicemembers who expect to maintain an outstanding balance want a card with a consistently low effective annual interest rate and one that uses a compounding method that minimizes costs.

In selecting the credit card that offers the maximum value, cardholders should prioritize the factors that best match the card features with their individual spending patterns. In almost all cases, a servicemember should select a card with no annual fee. Servicemembers who repay their balances nearly every month should select a card with no annual fee and the best rewards program available. Servicemembers who maintain a balance most months should select a card with no annual fee and a low effective annual interest rate.

Additional Considerations When Maintaining a Card Balance

If you have some compelling reason to carry a credit card balance for a while, because of an emergency or other high-cost event, consider taking advantage of low introductory rate offers. If necessary, transfer any remaining balance to another low-rate introductory offer when the original introductory period expires. However, keep in mind that there may be a balance transfer fee associated with such an offer; if not, check to see if interest will accrue immediately. With the intense competition among lenders, such offers are generally available. In addition, maintain a card whose regular APR is lower than the rate that takes effect after the introductory periods of the other cards expire. *Money* magazine (http://money.cnn.com) and the other financial websites and periodicals referenced in this book are the best sources of credit card interest rate information.

Also, keep in mind that the number of credit cards held, their limits, and current balances all affect a borrower's credit score and will appear on the borrower's credit report. This information is readily available to anyone making a decision on whether to offer a potential borrower more credit. Because nothing stops a cardholder from "maxing out" all open credit cards after receiving a new bank or car loan, thus increasing their risk of default, creditors take a customer's available credit on revolving accounts into consideration before extending additional credit.

Sources for free, objective information about credit cards:

CreditCardGuide.com:
  http://www.creditcardguide.com/credit-card-deals.html
BankRate.com: http://www.bankrate.com/credit-cards.aspx

HOW ATM/DEBIT CARD COMPANIES MAKE MONEY

Like credit card companies, debit card companies have two basic sources of income—the participating merchants and the cardholders. In exchange for a payment option often more secure than checks, merchants pay the debit card issuer a host of fees (Table 3-5). Debit cards are processed in one of two ways. They are processed as a prepaid credit card if the cardholder presses the credit option when making a purchase. Under this option, or the Offline Debit System, merchants pay fees as if the transaction were a credit transaction. Transactions are processed like a check when the cardholder presses the debit option. Under this option, or the Online Debit System, merchants pay fees as if the transaction were a check transaction.

  Debit cardholders may pay fees, which may include card membership fees, overdraft fees, and financial transaction fees. (See Table 3-6, page 46.)

TABLE 3-5
FEES DEBIT CARD COMPANIES CHARGE MERCHANTS

Fee Type	Offline Debit System Charge	Online Debit System Charge
Annual Fee: A yearly fee for maintaining a debit card account.	Usually from $80 to $400 per year.	N/A
Transaction Fee: A fee charged for each transaction.	Usually $0.10 per transaction.	Usually $0.10 per transaction.
Authorization Fee: A fee charge for card authorization.	This is in addition to the transaction fee and applies whether the transaction completes or not.	This is in addition to the transaction fee and applies whether the transaction completes or not.
Interchange Fee: A fee charged on the total amount transferred.	Usually 1-6% of the balance per transfer. It averages 2% and depends on the merchant's volume.	N/A

TABLE 3-6
FEES DEBIT CARD COMPANIES CHARGE CARDHOLDERS

Fee Type	Charge	How to Avoid It
Application Fee: Fee charged when a customer applies for a debit card.	Many have no application fee; others charge from $10 - $50 per application.	Ask your creditor to waive the fee.
Annual Fee: A yearly fee for the having the credit/debit card.	Many have no annual fee; others charge from $0 to $50/year.	Ask your creditor to waive the fee. Some credit cards waive the fee if you make purchases during the year.
Cash Advance Fee: A fee charge when making a cash advance.	Usually 1-3% of the advance per transaction.	Usually waived at the card issuer's ATMs
Overdraft Charge: A monthly charge for the convenience of carrying a balance.	A minimum fee for exceeding your bank account balance.	Record your transactions. Request overdraft protection by linking account to another account (deposit or credit).

HOW CONSUMERS CAN BENEFIT FROM ATM/DEBIT CARD USE

Debit cards offer consumers convenience over cash and checks, but no line of credit. A cardholder's own deposits back these cards, so they are not a form of consumer credit unless the bank account has an associated overdraft protection line of credit. In a very real sense, debit cards are just a more generally accepted form of checks.

Debit card issuers make more revenues from offline debit system transactions than online debit system transactions. To encourage offline transactions, some debit card issuers offer reward debit cards. These cards are very similar to the reward credit cards discussed earlier. The consumer has the opportunity for "found money."

Prepaid debit cards or gift cards are an attractive option that allows the convenience of card-based payment opportunities to individuals unable to secure a credit card, or to individuals too young to open a checking account.

CHARGE CARDS

Charge cards, those issued by American Express, Diner's Club, and Carte Blanche are used just like credit cards but differ in a very important way from credit cards such as Visa, MasterCard, or Discover. Issuers of the charge cards expect their cardholders to use the cards only for the convenience of eliminating cash and check purchases—not for revolving credit. That means the cardholder must pay the full balance when it is due. Failure to use the cards as prescribed may result in very stiff penalties, including interest rates of up to 2% per month and probable cancellation of the agreement. Additionally, these companies market the cards as prestigious and elite, generally charging large annual fees for the privilege of carrying the card with their logo. Servicemembers should carefully consider the costs and benefits of these cards and use them only if the prestige factor is important to them, if they value the extra benefits provided by the cost (such as airport lounge access), and if they will pay off the entire balance each month.

GOVERNMENT TRAVEL CARDS

The General Services Administration (GSA) provides a worldwide payment system for government employees to acquire travel and travel-related products and services. There are two different types of travel card accounts—Centrally Billed Accounts (CBAs) and Individually Billed Accounts (IBAs)—in the Government Travel Card program.

CBA cards pay for official travel charges (air and rail) and for other official travel-related expenses (hotel, rental car, conferences, etc.) and are most often used by travel service providers; they are also used by a limited number of individual government travelers. Purchases on these accounts are billed directly to a government central billing account. The government is liable for authorized charges made to the CBA.

IBA cards are used for the same purposes as the CBA cards—and are the travel card the government's designated card provider issues to most servicemembers. The major difference between these two cards is that an IBA cardholder is personally liable for all charges, excluding those not made by the cardholder when a card is reported as lost or stolen or charges under dispute. The cardholder is also responsible for paying any balance by the due date and for complying with the terms and conditions of the Government Travel Card Cardholder Account Agreement. Payment in full is required for all charges incurred by a cardholder. The cardholder will receive a statement of account detailing all transactions made by the cardholder during the billing cycle. The cardholder must remit the payment by the due date on the statement.

There are six methods that a cardholder can use to make payments:
- *Split Disbursement.* Reimbursement for authorized TDY travel expenses made directly by the government to the credit card company.
- *Check Payments.* Cardholders can send payment through regular mail using the payment coupon and window envelope provided with the statement.
- *Wire Payments.* A cardholder can initiate a wire payment by obtaining a cash letter from a financial institution.
- *Automated Clearing House (ACH) Payment.* The cardholder may elect to have payments deducted from his or her demand deposit account.

- *In-Person Payments.* Citibank branch offices will accept cardholder payments during normal business hours.
- *Online Payments.* A cardholder can use a third-party online banking system or a credit card's website.

An IBA card is considered past due if the government's designated card provider has not received payment for the undisputed principal amount within forty-five calendar days of the closing date on the statement of account in which the charge appeared. If payment for the undisputed principal amount has not been received within sixty-one calendar days from the closing date on the statement of account in which the charge appeared, the card issuer will suspend the account—unless otherwise informed by the cardholder's agency or organizational program coordinator of any mission-related extenuating circumstances for which the account should not be suspended.

There are four reasons for which an IBA card will be canceled:

1. The account has been suspended two times during a 12-month period for undisputed amounts and is again past due.
2. The account is 120 days past due for undisputed amounts, and the procedures for suspension of the account have been met.
3. Use of the card for other-than-authorized purchases and cancellation is approved by the agency or organizational program coordinator.
4. The account has had two or more non-sufficient funds checks written against the account within a 12-month period.

Policies and conditions on Government Travel Card use can be found at Citi Transaction Services (http://www.transactionservices.citigroup.com/card_solutions/commercial_cards) under Public Sector Solutions or at the Department of Defense Travel Card homepage (http://www.defensetravel.dod.mil/site/govtravelcard.cfm).

TYPES OF CONSUMER LOANS AND THEIR COMPONENTS

The most common type of consumer loan arrangement is the installment loan. With this kind of loan, consumers repay the amount borrowed plus interest over a predetermined period in equal monthly payments. Automobile loans and home mortgages are common examples of installment loans.

Some lenders also use single-payment loans, but this is less common. In a single-payment loan, borrowers must repay the full amount plus interest at the loan's maturity date. This form of loan is often used by lenders who offer "payday loans." A loan with a combination of periodic payments and a large repayment at the end is called a balloon loan. It is important to be aware of a common variety of this type of loan, the "same as cash" terms offered by retailers for large-ticket items such as electronics, appliances, and furniture. In this case, the borrower applies for a retailer's credit card and commits to making nominal payments during the course of the "same as cash" period, which ranges typically from six months to two years. If the borrower repays the entire balance of the loan in this period, the interest is waived. However, if the borrower has not paid the loan in full when the term expires, the merchant will charge the borrower interest for the entire period of the loan, usually at an interest rate approaching the maximum allowed by law.

The following section will focus on variants of installment loans because they are more common.

THE "TRUE INTEREST RATE"

As discussed in the credit card section, which explained that nominal APR did not reflect the effective annual interest rate (EAR) faced by cardholders, the nominal APR is not the whole interest rate story with installment loans either. Servicemembers shopping for installment loans should compare three features: the annual percentage rate (APR), the term (length) of the contract, and any prepayment penalties or other fees. The APR's effect on a loan contract is straightforward: A higher APR will yield a higher monthly payment for the term of the loan and will increase the total interest the borrower will pay over the loan's life. The impact of the loan's term is subtler. A longer loan term will lower the loan's required monthly payments. However, the total interest paid by the borrower will be higher because the lender's money is being used longer. In loan contracts, the total amount of interest over the life of the loan is called the total finance charge; it is one of the items, along with the APR, that lenders must disclose in every loan agreement, as required by the Truth in Lending Act.

Lenders use several different methods to compute the monthly payment on an installment loan. Two loans that appear to be the same (the same amount, duration, and interest rate) can have different monthly payments, finance charges, and APRs, based on how the lender calculates the interest. Consumers typically must choose among loans with different durations, different lengths until the first payment is due, and any number of other variables. The APR is a standardized calculation that allows consumers to compare the true interest rate for different loans in order to determine which loan offers the lowest cost of borrowing.

Tables 3-7 and 3-8 illustrate the differences between the monthly balance and the add-on interest methods of charging interest on a loan for $2,000 at a 12% nominal APR, repaid in twelve equal monthly payments. These two loans appear identical, but they are not. The monthly balance method is the usual way that loans are repaid. When interest is computed using the monthly balance method, the monthly payments are $177.70 and the APR is 12% per year. The add-on interest method charges interest on the entire amount borrowed over the whole year, even though some of the principal is being repaid each month. When interest is computed using the add-on interest method, the monthly payments are $186.67 and the APR is 22% per year.

Tables 3-7 and 3-8 show two different formulas for calculating the APR, and there are many others (one for every type of consumer loan). The bottom line is that all APR formulas are very good approximations of the true interest cost of the loan. Consumers do not have to calculate the APR; they need only compare the APRs that the law requires lenders to reveal.

It is clear that the monthly balance interest method is less costly than the add-on interest method. The point of the examples in Tables 3-7 and 3-8 is to show how much of a difference the method of computing interest can make. Do not rely on the nominal APR in a loan contract. Find the APR in the Truth in Lending Act section. Compare the APR the lender is offering to typical loan rates reported at websites in the "Money Rates" section of either the *Wall Street Journal* (http://www.WSJ.com) or *Barron's* (http://www.barrons.com), or in frequent surveys published in *Money* (http://money.cnn.com) or *Consumer Reports* (http://www.consumerreports.org). It pays to shop around for loan terms.

TABLE 3-7
MONTHLY BALANCE INTEREST METHOD
$2,000 AT 12% FOR 1 YEAR, 12 MONTHLY PAYMENTS

Month	Payment	Interest	Principal	Outstanding
				$2,000.00
1	$177.70	$20.00	$157.70	$1,842.30
2	$177.70	$18.42	$159.28	$1,683.02
3	$177.70	$16.83	$160.87	$1,522.15
4	$177.70	$15.22	$162.48	$1,359.67
5	$177.70	$13.60	$164.10	$1,195.57
6	$177.70	$11.96	$165.74	$1,029.83
7	$177.70	$10.30	$167.40	$862.43
8	$177.70	$8.62	$169.08	$693.35
9	$177.70	$6.93	$170.77	$522.58
10	$177.70	$5.23	$172.47	$350.11
11	$177.70	$3.50	$174.20	$175.91
12	$177.70	$1.79	$175.91	$0.00
	$2,132.40	$132.40	$2,000.00	$1,103.08*

*Average outstanding balance (sum of last column divided by 12).

$$\text{APR} \;=\; \frac{\text{Finance Charge}}{\text{Average Balance}} \;=\; \frac{\$132.40}{\$1,103.08} \;=\; 0.12 \ (12\%)$$

TABLE 3-8
RESULTS WITH ADD-ON INTEREST METHOD
$2,000 AT 12% FOR 1 YEAR, 12 MONTHLY PAYMENTS

Month	Payment	Interest	Principal	Outstanding
				$2,000.00
1	$186.67	$20.00	$166.67	$1,833.33
2	$186.67	$20.00	$166.67	$1,666.66
3	$186.67	$20.00	$166.67	$1,499.99
4	$186.67	$20.00	$166.67	$1,333.32
5	$186.67	$20.00	$166.67	$1,166.65
6	$186.67	$20.00	$166.67	$999.98
7	$186.67	$20.00	$166.67	$833.31
8	$186.67	$20.00	$166.67	$666.64
9	$186.67	$20.00	$166.67	$499.97
10	$186.67	$20.00	$166.67	$333.30
11	$186.67	$20.00	$166.67	$166.63
12	$186.63	$20.00	$166.63	$0.00
	$2,240.00	$240.00	$2,000.00	$1,083.32*

*Average outstanding balance (sum of last column divided by 12).

$$\text{APR} = \frac{\text{Finance Charge}}{\text{Average Balance}} = \frac{\$240.00}{\$1,083.32} = 0.22 \ (22\%)$$

Not knowing the market for consumer loans can cost a borrower a lot of money. It is common today for auto loans to offer low APRs, but as discussed in chapter 6, the low-rate loans are often available only if other purchasing conditions are met. To determine whether the offered interest rate is attractive, identify the costs of purchasing conditions placed on the loan. One example might be that the borrower must qualify for the advertised APR by having a high enough credit score.

The loan conditions of particular banks may also be important criteria in the selection of the financial institution where you choose to deposit your paycheck. Loan approval and repayment options will often be easier in conjunction with a bank that receives the borrower's direct deposit; this includes the ability to establish monthly automatic deductions from a demand deposit account. However, this is often possible with many financial institutions simply by providing a voided check and signing an agreement to allow such automatic deductions. Such methods save both the borrower and the lender from monthly hassles and add credibility to the borrower's repayment commitment.

PREPAYMENT PENALTIES

A borrower should also investigate potential loan contracts for any prepayment penalties. Strangely enough, if a borrower decides to repay a loan in a shorter period than the contract specifies, the borrower may have to pay more interest on the loan than originally stated in the terms. The lender must tell the borrower, in writing, how much it will cost to pay off a particular loan early. Seek loans without prepayment penalties.

THE ROLE OF COLLATERAL IN CONSUMER LENDING

For many loans that consumers use to finance major purchases, the item purchased becomes the collateral for the loan. That is, the bank takes a lien (or has some ownership rights) against the item, so that if repayment is not made as agreed, the bank may repossess the property and sell it for cash. The two best examples of this practice are auto and home loans. Remember that banks are lending their depositors' money and want to have some protection if a borrower fails to repay. Collateral for loans can also include other property, such as stocks and bonds, equity in a home, and sometimes jewelry. In some cases, the bank will insist on taking physical possession of the collateral.

Collateralized, or secured, loans are less risky for banks because they offer some protection in the event the borrower defaults. As a result, the interest rate on a secured loan tends to be lower than for an unsecured or "signature" loan. This is worth remembering when borrowing for a purpose such as a child's education, where the asset being financed cannot be used as collateral. It may be worthwhile to use some other assets, such as equity in a home, to secure a loan in such cases. Also consider selling the assets for cash, since this may be cheaper than borrowing; however, bear in mind that some assets may have a great deal more use and value to the seller than the amount they sell for on the open market.

PAYDAY LOANS

In a payday loan, the lender provides a short-term unsecured loan to the borrower. The borrower is expected to pay the principal, interest, and fees on the borrower's next payday. The most common practice is for the lender to give the loan in exchange for a post-dated check that covers the loan agreement. When the post-dated check matures, the lender claims payment. Online variants of this process, where the lender directly deposits the loan to the borrower's account, then electronically withdraws the principal and fee on an agreed upon date, are becoming popular. Since these loans are unsecured and traditionally risky to the lender, the APRs on these loans are very high.

Since borrowers are usually seeking this type of loan when under severe financial circumstances, default rates are high. In addition to penalties from the lender, the defaulting borrower is likely to face insufficient funds fees from the bank when the post-dated check is deposited or the automatic withdrawal is engaged.

In addition to payday loans, there is the tax refund anticipation loan. This loan is very similar in structure to the payday loan but is backed by the borrower's anticipated tax refund. Professional tax preparers provide these loans. As with the payday loan, the APR on this type of loan is typically very high.

Servicemembers have an alternative to payday loans through the PenFed Foundation's Asset Recovery Kit (ARK); in which the Foundation helps military families by providing short-term loans for a small processing fee (at a fraction of the payday loan costs). These loans come with a requirement to receive credit counseling from a local consumer credit counselor (identified by the Foundation and at no cost). For more information, visit the Foundation's website at http://www.pentagonfoundation.org and select ARK from the menu.

HOME EQUITY LOANS

A popular form of collateralized borrowing involves second mortgages and lines of credit secured by the borrower's equity in a home. Equity in a home is the difference between the value of a home, as determined by an appraiser, and what the homeowner still owes the mortgage holder.

Second mortgages and home equity lines of credit allow homeowners to borrow money at interest rates lower than those of normal consumer loans because the loans are secured by the property. The interest on home equity loans is usually tax-deductible. One should consult with a tax advisor to learn more about the tax implications. Another advantage of home equity loans is that homeowners can borrow relatively large amounts of money for long periods of time, often up to fifteen years.

Home equity loans have several disadvantages. They can be fairly expensive to set up because of the closing costs—the transaction fees involved in real estate lending. These closing costs can run into several hundreds or thousands of dollars. In addition, lenders can charge points, where a point is a fee of one percent of the amount borrowed on a loan. Points are an up-front fee charged by the lender to initiate a loan. Finally, the interest rate on a second mortgage will be a few percentage points higher than the going rate on first mortgages.

If a borrower needs a large amount of money with a reasonably long period to repay, such as financing a child's college education, a second mortgage on a home may be a good alternative. For smaller amounts and shorter repayment periods, shop carefully for more conventional loans before committing to a second mortgage. Weigh the tax and interest rate advantages against the sizable up-front closing fees.

Home equity lines of credit are similar to second mortgages: The equity in a home secures the loan, and one pays closing costs to establish the credit line. However, once established, the credit line has a great deal of flexibility and can be used in many ways. In most cases, the borrower can draw cash against the credit line by simply writing a check, and can repay on any schedule that is convenient to the borrower. In this sense, the line of credit is almost like a low interest rate credit card. Borrowers pay interest only on the outstanding balance. The closing costs and other fees on a home-equity line of credit are lower than on a second mortgage for most lending institutions. Some consumers use home-equity credit lines to finance cars, appliances, educational expenses, and many other needs that they have traditionally financed by conventional bank loans. An obvious potential danger in using a home's equity as a source of funds is the risk of losing the home if the borrower defaults on the payments and the lender forecloses.

COMMON SOURCES FOR CONSUMER LOANS

Banks are often the first source of credit that comes to mind. However, banks are not the only source of consumer credit. The financial sector of the economy is becoming increasingly competitive as different kinds of institutions enter the market for consumer financial services. Therefore, a potential borrower should also consider credit unions, savings and loan associations, or mutual savings banks. Many of these institutions are consumer-oriented and may offer better loan rates than banks in a borrower's home area. In addition, some stockbrokers will lend money using stocks, bonds, or other qualifying assets as collateral. These "margin loans" are usually used by aggressive investors to leverage their stock portfolios when they believe stock prices are about to rise, but in some cases margin loans may be used for other purposes, as well. The rate of interest on broker loans is generally very close to the short-term Treasury bill rate—the theoretical "risk-free" interest rate used as a reference by financial institutions. A loan from a broker may be cheaper than a loan from any other institution. In addition, the repayment terms on loans from brokers are typically flexible: Repay a margin loan as desired, but remember that interest accrues on the principal as long as it is unpaid.

A potential borrower may be able to borrow against retirement portfolios or pensions. If the borrower has a 401K retirement savings vehicle or a TSP account for government employees, he or she may be able to borrow against the retirement account. The positive side to borrowing from a retirement account is that the borrower is borrowing from his or her self. The principal and interest paid back goes back to the borrower. Since the borrower's employer controls these accounts, there are certain potential pitfalls. If the borrower changes employers, the borrower must pay the loan in full within sixty days or face tax penalties and a 10% surcharge for the early withdrawal of tax deferred savings. This can be quite expensive. A second pitfall is that the loan must be repaid before retirement or the borrower will face the previously mentioned early withdrawal penalties.

Borrowing from a pension is different from borrowing from retirement savings plans. Pensions are technically owned by the employer, and loans can only be secured if the employer allows them. There is a technical work-around if the borrower is vested in a portion of the pension. This means that the employer has incurred an obligation to pay pension funds in the future. A third party may be willing to write a contract, giving a potential borrower funds today for a right to that stream of future income. In exchange for the funds today, the borrower gives up a portion of the pension.

The military provides servicemembers with an interest-free loan in the form of an advance on future pay. This is available only in conjunction with a permanent-change-of-station (PCS) move. With appropriate justification and command approval, servicemembers can obtain one month's advance pay from the departing station and two months' advance pay at the new assignment location. Repayment by payroll deduction will take place over a twelve- to twenty-four-month period. Servicemembers are not charged interest for advance-pay transactions.

Finally, if a potential borrower owns permanent life insurance (whole life), they can borrow against the cash value of the policy at very attractive rates. If a potential borrower already owns a whole life policy with a substantial cash value, this may be his best alternative for borrowing small amounts cheaply. See chapter 13 for details on borrowing against a whole life policy.

HOW TO ADDRESS CREDIT PROBLEMS
Credit and some people just do not mix. Through bad luck, bad management, or just lack of willpower, some people either cannot get credit or cannot handle it well once they do get it.

If someone cannot get either a Visa or MasterCard, it is probably because they are a bad credit risk. Bad credit is a function of several factors: having a history of bankruptcy or unpaid bills; being too young or inexperienced to be offered a credit card; or having no or a limited credit history. People in these situations must take some measures to clean up or build their credit history. Start with a gasoline company credit card—as these cards often have the least strict criteria for approval. Use it and pay the entire balance immediately. Then work up to a department store card and eventually to a bank card. Try a local bank or credit union—most military credit unions will give servicemembers cards with low credit limits, even if they have little or no credit history, because of their government paycheck.

If this fails, get a secured credit card; however, these cards are usually very expensive and operate more like a debit card. There are some banks that will issue cards secured by sizable deposits for people who have destroyed their credit ratings and exhausted their other options. If the cardholders prove that they can use this card reasonably for a while, the card issuer can "graduate" them to a normal credit card.

A servicemember should be wary of online or direct mail offers to check or improve their credit rating or "score." You should not pay for something like this. By law, the leading credit agencies must disclose a person's full credit report annually for free (the free credit report is available at Annual-CreditReport.com) and his or her actual FICO score for a fee. This fee includes a report of the three-digit credit score, how it was derived, and advice on how to improve it. This service also includes a full credit report. Explore MyFICO.com (http://www.myfico.com) for further information.

Potential borrowers who are refused credit can get their credit rating information for free. (See point 9 under Borrowers' Rights, page 57.)

If you find yourself in debt you can no longer service, with high, unpaid, credit card balances, you have a serious problem and you should get help in responding to it. Each of the services has trained financial counselors to help servicemembers develop budgets and structure payments to get out of debt. There are also other agencies in the civilian community, such as the National Foundation for Credit Counseling (800-388-2227 or http://www.nfcc.org), which can assist with personal budgeting and debt management.

The sooner you seek help to work out a solution to a financial problem, the easier it is to get out of debt.

THE SERVICEMEMBERS CIVIL RELIEF ACT

The Servicemembers Civil Relief Act (SCRA) is an expanded and updated version of the former Soldiers' and Sailors' Civil Relief Act (SSCRA). The SCRA provides a wide range of protections for active duty or deployed servicemembers. It is intended to postpone or suspend certain civil obligations entered into prior to entry to active duty, to enable servicemembers to devote full attention to duty, and to relieve stress on the family members of those deployed servicemembers. Examples of financial obligations that servicemembers may be protected against are: outstanding credit card debt, mortgage payments, and taxes. If the servicemember's ability to make payments is "materially affected" by military service, then the lender on an installment contract may be prohibited from repossessing the personal property for nonpayment or breach of contract unless authorized by the court.

BORROWERS' RIGHTS

When considering whether to take advantage of any of the various forms of consumer credit outlined in this chapter, you should know your legal rights as a borrower. Over the years, Congress has passed two major pieces of legislation that protect the borrower's rights: the Consumer Credit Protection Act of 1968 (better known as the Truth in Lending Act) and the Fair Credit Billing Act of 1975. Under these two acts, you, as a borrower, have the following rights:

1. You have the right to know the true interest rate (in APR terms) and total finance charges before signing any loan agreement.
2. Credit card issuers must advertise the true interest rate (in APR terms) charged on their cards.

3. You must be given at least fourteen days from the postmark on your credit card statement to pay off your balance and avoid paying any interest.
4. When considering your application for a loan or a credit card, a financial institution cannot ignore income from child support, alimony, or a pension.
5. In the event that you purchased goods or services in excess of $50 with your credit card and are dissatisfied with the purchase, you have the right to cancel the charges if you make a genuine effort to settle matters with the seller and the purchase was made in your home state or within one hundred miles of your home.
6. In the event that your credit card is used against your will or without your permission (i.e., it is stolen or lost), your liability for the unauthorized purchases is limited to $50. If you are able to notify the credit card issuer of the loss or theft of the card before anyone tries to purchase something with it, you will not be liable for any unauthorized purchases.
7. In the event that your debit card is stolen or lost, you must notify the bank within two business days in order to limit your liability to $50. If you fail to do so, you can be liable for the first $500 taken from your account. If sixty-one days pass after the mailing date of your first bank statement showing unauthorized withdrawals, you may be liable for all the money taken from your account.
8. In the event you are applying for a credit card or loan on your own for the first time (in other words, you have no credit record of your own), you have the right to have your spouse's unblemished credit record considered as your own.
9. Should you ever be denied a loan or a credit card, you have the right to be told the specific reasons why you were turned down. You cannot be denied access to what has been reported about you to a credit bureau. If the credit bureau's report was instrumental in your being rejected for a loan or a credit card, you must be provided access to your file at no charge. If you wish to find out what is in your credit record without having been rejected for a credit application, you can contact the three major credit bureaus: Experian (formerly TRW), Equifax, and TransUnion. Any or all may have a file on you and your report may be accurate at one and inaccurate at another credit bureau. Therefore, you should check your credit report at all three bureaus. To find out how to get your credit report, contact credit bureaus directly by checking Experian (http://www.experian.com), Equifax (http://www.equifax.com), or TransUnion (http://www.transunion.com), or get a free credit report from each of the agencies by visiting AnnualCreditReport.com.

4

Paying Your Taxes

The information in this chapter is by necessity general in nature. Each family's financial situation is different, and tax law is complex. In addition, many of the dollar values for exemptions, credits, exclusions, and deductions change annually. To help, all military installations have legal assistance offices that provide tax forms and offer professional help in tax matters at no charge to servicemembers and their families. The Volunteer Income Tax Assistance (VITA) program at each base provides unit-level volunteers with training to assist with simple tax preparation. In addition, the Internal Revenue Service (IRS) provides a "Free File" site at http://www.irs.gov where it hosts companies offering free tax preparation services. These companies require filers to have an adjusted gross income (AGI) less than $58,000, and certain other stipulations. Through the Military OneSource website (http://www.militaryonescource .mil), servicemembers may complete and file federal and state returns using H&R Block tax software, free of charge.

Additional tax preparation software options are available for purchase; the two most popular are TurboTax and TaxCut, which are very user friendly and formatted in a conversational style. The programs are useful for those filers who have more complicated tax profiles that are beyond the training and support level of the VITA volunteers. Software-based tax preparation makes tax preparation easier over time by storing basic tax information year-to-year. This allows preparers to automatically access previous data, reducing input errors and completion time for the current year's tax preparation. Finally, the Internal Revenue Service (IRS) maintains local offices around the country, a toll-free phone number, and assistance over the Internet at http://www.irs.gov.

With regard to taxes, military compensation has peculiarities that distinguish it from typical civilian pay systems. For example, many military allowances are exempt from income taxation by all three levels of government: federal, state, and local. Considering housing (BAH) and subsistence (BAS) allowances alone, about one-fourth of military compensation is tax exempt. Under specific circumstances, combat zone active duty pay and some bonuses are also tax exempt. In addition, several states either have no state income tax or exempt military income from state income taxes. By exempting military income from taxation, the tax code raises the value of military compensation by providing a "tax advantage" to servicemembers. However, basic military pay, military bonuses, military special and incentive pays, investment income, and spousal income are potentially fully taxable by all levels of government. As a result, a good understanding of tax laws will ensure tax compliance, help incorporate tax considerations into financial planning decisions, and build an understanding of the full value of military compensation.

This chapter discusses the personal tax responsibilities and the peculiarities of federal, state, and local taxation that apply to servicemembers. Servicemembers will learn how to prepare their tax returns and how to tackle the myriad roadblocks that discourage many Americans from preparing their taxes themselves. Information in this chapter provides some general tax planning considerations that should be useful in overall financial planning to help avoid overpaying taxes.

FEDERAL INCOME TAX

This section provides a summary of the general provisions of the federal income tax code. Since tax rules change frequently, it is worthwhile to use tax preparation software, consult the latest IRS tax information, or hire a tax preparer to complete your taxes. As described earlier, servicemembers may use H&R Block's tax software for free through Military OneSource, access the IRS's Free File site, or purchase TurboTax (http://turbotax.intuit.com) or other tax preparation software.

The Internal Revenue Service (IRS) has three basic individual income tax reporting forms. An individual or family only files one of the basic forms: the IRS Form 1040, 1040A, or 1040EZ. The IRS Form 1040 is the full or "long" form. Taxpayers with taxable income below $100,000 who take the standard deduction instead of itemizing deductions can file the IRS Form 1040A—the "short form." Households with no dependents who would also qualify for using the IRS Form 1040A may file the IRS Form 1040EZ—the "easy form." The IRS Form 1040 has eleven possible attachments called schedules. These schedules are:

- Schedule A calculates allowable deductions against income if the taxpayer chooses not to take a standard deduction.
- Schedule B calculates interest and/or dividend income.
- Schedule C calculates profits related to self-employment for sole proprietors.
- Schedule D computes capital gains and losses incurred during the tax year.
- Schedule E reports income and expenses arising from the rental of real property, royalties, or from pass-through entities (like trusts, estates, partnerships, or S corporations).
- Schedule EIC documents a taxpayer's eligibility for the Earned Income Credit.

- Schedule F reports income and expenses related to farming.
- Schedule H reports taxes owed due to the employment of household help.
- Schedule J averages farm income over a period of three years.
- Schedule L calculates an increased standard deduction for certain cases.
- Schedule M claims the Making Work Pay tax credit.
- Schedule R calculates the Credit for the Elderly or the Disabled.
- Schedule SE calculates the self-employment tax owed on income from self-employment (such as on a Schedule C or Schedule F) in a partnership.

The three basic income tax reporting forms have the same purpose and basic structure; the only difference is how complicated the taxpayer's income and tax payments can be. All three forms start out by identifying the household. The second section reports income. The third section determines how much of that income is taxable. The fourth section calculates tax liability. The fifth section calculates taxes paid. The final section calculates taxes owed or tax overpayment due for refund. Fortunately, every IRS form has detailed instructions, and the federal tax computations for the typical servicemember are relatively straightforward. Should you choose to complete your taxes manually, you should be able to calculate your federal income tax liability without professional assistance, although experts say it may take up to twenty hours to gather the appropriate information and complete the forms. However, you can reduce the chance of errors and increase the speed of completion by using tax preparation software. This software carefully walks you through the preparation process by asking straightforward questions that collect the necessary data to complete and file all forms in a timely manner. If you choose, the tax software can save all inputted data for use in subsequent submissions, substantially reducing future preparation time.

TAX BASICS
One of the first things any employee must do is file the Form W-4 with their employer. Any time a servicemember's household composition changes due to a change in marital status or number of dependents, he or she should file a new Form W-4. For all DoD personnel, this is done online at myPay (http://www.mypay.dfas.mil). Form W-4 is used by employers to determine how much federal and state income tax to withhold each pay period. There are two ways to calculate tax withholdings. For single-income households taking the standard tax deductions, the simplest method for calculating tax withholding is through the Personal Allowances Worksheet on Form W-4. The servicemember records marital status, the number of additional dependents, and additional adjustments, which determine the total number of allowances for transfer to form W-4. Servicemembers in multiple-income households, or who itemize deductions, should estimate their household's annual tax liability in

order to determine the appropriate number of allowances to declare. Again, you can calculate this using one of the worksheets on page 2 of Form W-4. The employer will use the declared allowances to calculate the appropriate income tax withholding from each pay period.

Since there are many situations where it is not clear whether or not a person is a servicemember's dependent (for example, when a servicemember cares for elderly parents, has stepchildren, or serves as the primary caregiver for nephews and nieces), servicemembers should visit the IRS website (http://www.irs.gov) and consult the Form 1040 instructions to determine the eligibility requirements for claiming a dependent. Claiming too many allowances may result in inadequate income tax withholding, resulting in a servicemember owing taxes at the time of filing. The IRS may levy fines and penalties on taxpayers who significantly under-withhold. Claiming too few allowances results in excessive income tax withholding, which leads to a tax refund. Some consider this as "found money," but servicemembers should remember that the tax refund is actually the repayment of an interest-free loan provided to the government. The servicemember could have used the money throughout the year, or saved it to earn interest to increase future consumption.

The servicemember's Leave and Earning Statement (LES) has four main columns and reports basic information about the servicemember's pay.

- Entitlements, or the servicemember's income sources from the military, may include basic pay, basic allowance for subsistence, basic allowance for housing, and incentive and specialty pays.
- Deductions, or income withholdings, may include state and federal income taxes, social security and Medicare taxes, government life insurance, thrift savings contributions, and mid-month pay.
- Allotments, or payments that servicemembers authorized the Defense Finance and Accounting Service (DFAS) to make on their behalf, may include payments for on-post quarters, Tricare dental premiums, Army Emergency Relief, and Combined Federal Campaign contributions.
- The summary rolls up the three aforementioned columns to explain the servicemember's end-of-month pay.

The federal and state income tax withholdings reported in the deductions column of the LES are a function of the allowances the servicemember claimed on the Form W-4 filed with DFAS.

IDENTIFYING THE HOUSEHOLD

The first step in filing your taxes is to identify and describe your household. The servicemember, as the income-earning taxpayer, must be a member of the household and report earnings on the IRS Form 1040. If you are married and filing a joint return, then your spouse and his or her income is also reported on the tax form. After identifying your household by providing your name and address, you must decide the household's filing status. There are five categories of filing status: single, married filing joint return, married filing separate return, head of household, and qualifying widower.

Each filing status carries different tax rate schedules and standard deductions and hence has a significant effect on tax liabilities. If single with no qualifying dependents—pets do not qualify—then the you should select filing status "single." If married, under most common circumstances, you will have the lowest household tax liability by choosing the filing status "married filling jointly." Taxpayers in these first two situations with uncomplicated tax situations, such as a single income, may consider filing the IRS Form 1040EZ option. You should reconsider the "married filing jointly" choice if you or your spouse has highly income-sensitive deductions, such as medical bills, theft/property loss, large outstanding IRS tax liabilities, or if one of you has defaulted student loans. There is a small chance that under these circumstances the filing status "married filing separately" will make financial sense. If you are not married, have a dependent, and are not a widow(er), you should choose to file "head of household." Finally, choose "qualifying widow(er) with dependent child," if you meet those criteria. These last three filing statuses require that you use an IRS Form 1040 or 1040A.

To complete the household description, servicemembers must list all dependents. There are two general types of dependents: dependent children and other qualifying dependents. To be claimed as a dependent child, the person must meet four criteria:

Relationship: The person must be the servicemember's child, stepchild, adopted child, foster child, brother or sister, or a descendant of one of these (for example, a grandchild or nephew).

Residence: The person must have the same residence as the servicemember for more than half the year.

Age: The person must be
- under age 19 at the end of the year, *or*
- under age 24 and be a full-time student for at least five months out of the year, *or*
- any age and totally and permanently disabled.

Support: The person did not provide more than half of his or her own support during the year.

In cases of split families, children are sometimes claimed as dependents on multiple separate tax forms. If two or more taxpayers claim a dependent child in the same year, the IRS will use the following test to determine which taxpayer is eligible to claim the dependent. The child will be the dependent of:
- the parent,
- the parent with whom the child lived the longest during the year,
- if the time was equal, the parent with the highest adjusted gross income,
- if no taxpayer is the child's parent, the taxpayer with the highest adjusted gross income.

Taxpayers may claim other relative or non-relative adults and children as dependents. Generally, a taxpayer can claim someone as a dependent if that person did not earn more than a qualifying amount of income all year, the servicemember provided more than half of the dependent's support regardless of where they lived, and the dependent is a citizen or resident alien of the United States, Canada, or Mexico.

Household composition, including the servicemember, spouse, and number of dependents, defines the number of exemptions the servicemember can claim when determining taxable income.

REPORTING INCOME

U.S. households have income from many sources. The more complicated the income sources, the more complicated the tax return one must file. Table 4-1 summarizes the basic income types a household is likely to earn. It also indicates which of the IRS Form 1040s a taxpayer will need to file for the various

TABLE 4-1
TAXABLE INCOME

Tax Form	Taxable Income	Reported
IRS Form 1040EZ	Wages, Salaries, Tips	Form W-2, Online at: mypay.dfas.mil
	Taxable Interest less than $1500	Form 1099INT, End of year statement
	Alaska Permanent Fund	Form 1099MISC
	Unemployment Compensation	Form 1099G
IRS Form 1040A	Dividends less than $1500	Form 1099DIV, End of year statement
	Capital Gain	
	IRA Distributions	
	Pensions and Annuities	
	Social Security Benefits	
IRS Form 1040	Taxable Interest more than $1500	Schedule B
	Dividends more than $1500	Schedule B
	Taxable refunds	Form 1099G
	Alimony Received	
	Business Income/Loss	Schedule C
	Capital Gain/Loss	Schedule D
	Real Estate Rentals, Royalties	Schedule E
	Partnerships, S-Corps, Trusts	Schedule E
	Farm Income/Loss	Schedule F

Sources: http://www.irs.gov/pub/irs-pdf/f1040ez.pdf; http://www.irs.gov/pub/irs-pdf/f1040a.pdf; http://www.irs.gov/pub/irs-pdf/f1040.pdf

types of income. A household will need to file the IRS Form 1040 associated with the income source farthest down the list.

DFAS reports a servicemember's income on a Form W-2. Other employers report additional income or a spouse's income on separate Form W-2s. All W-2s should be available by January 31, after the close of the calendar tax year. Box 1 on the W-2 reports taxable income, including but not limited to wages, tips, salaries, specialty and incentive pays, leave pay, and some scholarships. It does not include nontaxable income such as BAS, BAH, combat zone compensation, and tax-deferred contributions to qualified pension plans like TSP, or a 401(k) from a civilian employer, or qualified medical savings accounts.

In addition to employee income reported on W-2s, it is common for households to have interest income from savings accounts, unemployment income, business income, and so forth. Servicemembers must declare and report all of this income on the appropriate IRS Form 1040 to calculate the household's total income.

ADJUSTED GROSS INCOME

The IRS allows households to make adjustments to their total income for some expenses commonly covered by an employer or for activities the government wants to encourage. An example would be moving expenses. Many employers, including the military, cover job-related moving expenses incurred by their employees. This would be a non-taxed benefit to those employees. To make this benefit available to all employees, the IRS allows employees who incur moving expenses not covered by an employer to adjust their total income by the additional moving expense. According to IRS Publication 3, "Tax Information for Military Personnel," servicemembers can deduct moving expenses that exceed dislocation and travel allowances. Most servicemembers do not qualify because the Army normally reimburses legitimate moving expenses. If you do qualify, you will need to file Form 3903, "Moving Expenses." Remember, you may only deduct expenses that were not reimbursed. Table 4-2 lists the common income adjustments and the IRS Form 1040 that taxpayers must file to claim those adjustments.

TABLE 4-2
INCOME ADJUSTMENTS

Tax Form	Income Adjustments	Reported
IRS Form 1040A	Educator Expenses	
	IRA (Traditional) Deduction	
	Student Loan Interest	
	Tuition And Fees	Form 8917

TABLE 4-2 (continued)
INCOME ADJUSTMENTS

Tax Form	Income Adjustments	Reported
IRS Form 1040	Health Savings Account	Form 8889
	Certain business expenses of reservists, performing artists, and fee-basis government officials.	Form 2106
	Moving Expenses	Form 3903
	Self-Employment Tax	Schedule SE
	Self-Employed Pension	
	Self-Employed Health Insurance	
	Alimony Paid	
	IRA Deduction	
	Domestic Production	Form 8903

Sources: http://www.irs.gov/pub/irs-pdf/f1040ez.pdf; http://www.irs.gov/pub/irs-pdf/f1040a.pdf; http://www.irs.gov/pub/irs-pdf/f1040.pdf

National Guard and Reserve members may make certain business expense adjustments for travel more than a hundred miles from home to perform services as a National Guard or Reserve member. As is required with all adjustments, they must provide receipts, canceled checks, or other records as evidence to support these adjustment claims. Subtracting the income adjustments from the total income leaves what the IRS calls the Adjusted Gross Income (AGI).

TAXABLE INCOME AND TAX LIABILITY

There are two more adjustments that are made to transform AGI into taxable income and then into tax liability: deductions and personal exemptions.

Deductions are qualified expenditures subtracted from a taxpayer's AGI. Taxpayers have two choices as to how to claim their deductions. They can itemize their deductions, or they can claim the standard deduction. Taxpayers who itemize their deductions must do so with an IRS Form 1040 Schedule A. The types of qualified expenditures fall into six broad categories: medical and dental expenses, state and local taxes, mortgage and investment interest paid, charitable donations, casualty and theft losses, and job-related and miscellaneous deductions. Taxpayers choose to itemize when their deductions exceed the standard deduction associated with the taxpayer's filing status.

The standard deduction is the default amount the IRS allows a taxpayer to subtract from their AGI. It is dependent upon the taxpayer's filing status. The standard deduction is higher if the taxpayer or spouse is over sixty-five years of age or blind. Table 4-3 lists the taxpayer's filing status with the associated standard deduction for tax year 2011. A taxpayer filing as "married filing jointly" should take the standard deduction if that taxpayer's itemized deductions are less than $11,600.

TABLE 4-3
FEDERAL INCOME TAX STANDARD DEDUCTION (2011)

Filing Status	Standard Deduction
Single	$5,800
Married Filing Jointly	$11,600
Qualifying Widow(er)	$11,600
Head of Household	$8,500
Married Filing Separately	$5,800

Note: Rates change from year to year; consult www.irs.gov for the most accurate information.
Source: http://www.irs.gov

The personal exemption is a deduction taxpayers may claim for themselves, their spouses, and any dependents in their households. For the tax year 2011, the deduction is $3,700 for every personal exemption. A household that consists of a servicemember, a spouse, and two dependent children has for personal exemptions for a deduction of $14,800 (4 x $3,700) from the household's AGI.

Starting in tax year 2011, the personal exemption deductions phase out as AGI increases beyond a threshold value. The IRS will reduce the exemption by 2% for every $2,500 ($1,250 for married filing separately) earned above the threshold. Table 4-4 lists the AGI phase-out thresholds by filing status.

Taxable income is the taxpayer's AGI less the itemized or standard deduction, and less the deduction for personal exemptions. A taxpayer in a household with four personal exemptions who takes the standard deduction with an AGI of $100,000 and filing status of "married filing jointly" would have a taxable income of:

TABLE 4-4
PERSONAL EXEMPTION OF AGI PHASE-OUT THRESHOLDS

Filing Status	2011	2012
Single	$169,750	$174,450
Head of Household	$212,200	$218,050
Married Filing Jointly	$254,650	$261,650
Married Filing Separately	$127,300	$130,825

Source: http://www.taxpolicycenter.org/taxtopics

$$\frac{\text{Taxable}}{\text{Income}} = \text{AGI} - \frac{\text{Standard}}{\text{Deduction}} - \frac{\text{Personal Exemptions}}{\text{Deduction}}$$

$$\$73,600 = \$100,000 - \$11,600 - \$14,800$$

Since the federal income tax is progressive, higher taxable income is taxed at higher rates. For example, in tax year 2011, the IRS taxes the first $17,000 of taxable income for a taxpayer with filing status of "married filing jointly" at 10%. The IRS will tax all taxable income for that same filer between $17,000 and $69,000 at 15%. These are called tax brackets. Table 4.5 provides a complete listing of tax year 2011 tax brackets.

To calculate the tax liability for the taxpayer discussed above, the $73,600 in taxable income must be put into its tax brackets and taxed at the appropriate rate. The first $17,000 of taxable income is taxed at 10%, the $52,000 of taxable income between $17,000 and $69,000 is taxed at 15% and finally the $4,600 of taxable income between $69,000 and $139,350 is taxed at 25%.

$$\text{Tax Liability} = \$17,000 \times 0.1 + \$52,000 \times 0.15 + \$4,600 \times 0.25$$
$$= \$1,700 + \$7,800 + \$1,150$$
$$= \$10,650$$

Tax software and the tax table provided in the instruction booklets for the various IRS Forms 1040 perform the tax liability calculation for the taxpayer.

For a growing number of taxpayers, a second tax liability is becoming relevant. This is the Alternative Minimum Tax (AMT). The IRS developed the

---

TABLE 4-5
TAX YEAR 2011 IRS TAX BRACKETS ON TAXABLE INCOME BY FILING STATUS

Tax Bracket	Single	Married Filing Jointly	Head of Household
10% Bracket	$0 - $8,500	$0 - $17,000	$0 - $12,150
15% Bracket	$8,500 - $34,500	$17,000 - $69,000	$12,150 - $46,250
25% Bracket	$34,500 - $83,600	$69,000 - $139,350	$46,250 - $119,400
28% Bracket	$83,600 - $174,400	$139,350 - $212,300	$119,400 - $193,350
33% Bracket	$174,400 - $379,150	$212,300 - $379,150	$193,350 - $379,150
35% Bracket	$379,150+	$379,150+	$379,150+

Source: http://www.bargaineering.com/articles/federal-income-irs-tax-brackets.html

TABLE 4-6
TAX YEAR 2011 AMT BRACKETS ON
TAXABLE INCOME BY FILING STATUS

Married Filing Jointly AMT Brackets	Single or Head of Household AMT Brackets	AMT Income Tax Rate	Qualifying Dividend/ Long Term Capital Gains
$0 - $74,450	$0 - $48,450	0%	0% / 15%
$74,451 - $150,000	$48,451 - $112,500	26%	15%
$150,001 - $229,960	$112,501 - $201,460	32.5%	21.5%
$229,961 - $447,800	$201,461 - $306,300	35%	22%
$447,801 or more	$306,301 or more	28%	15%

Source: http://thefinancebuff.com/2010-and-2011-amt-tax-brackets.html

alternative minimum tax to ensure that taxpayers who benefit from deductions and credits still pay a minimum amount of tax. Taxpayers whose taxable income is higher than the AMT exemption amount must complete an AMT worksheet to determine if they should calculate their taxes in the traditional way or if they should calculate the AMT. The AMT calculation starts with the AGI. There is a much higher income threshold on income taxed at a 0% rate. In addition, there are fewer available itemized deductions and the calculations for those allowed are different from the IRS Form 1040 Schedule A. The taxpayer's additional tax liability under the AMT is calculated on an IRS Form 6251. Table 4-6 shows the AMT thresholds.

TAX CREDITS, OTHER TAXES, AND TAXES PAID
A tax credit is money the federal government pretends you have already paid them for engaging in activity they determine to be desirable for social policy reasons or equity considerations. Spending the few minutes to determine whether or not you are eligible for tax credits could save you hundreds of dollars. Table 4-7 shows common tax credits and the IRS Form 1040 that taxpayers must file to claim those credits.

Earned Income Tax Credit (EITC). The most common tax credit and one that many younger servicemembers can take advantage of is the EITC. The government intends the EITC to provide tax equity for those of modest means. Table 4-8 shows the conditions to qualify for the EITC and the maximum credit for tax year 2011. Consult http://www.irs.gov and use the EITC Assistant to determine qualifications and to obtain the most updated information. Computing the EITC is easily done using the IRS worksheet or tax preparation software.

TABLE 4-7
TAX CREDITS

Tax Form	Tax Credit	Reported
IRS Form 1040EZ	Making Work Pay Credit	Schedule M
	Earned Income Tax Credit	Work Sheet
IRS Form 1040A	Dependent Care Credit	Form 2441
	Elderly/Disabled Credit	Schedule R
	Education Credit	Form 8863
	Retirement Savings Credit	Form 8880
	Child Tax Credit	Form 8812
	American Opportunity Credit	Form 8863
IRS Form1040	First Time Home Buyer Credit	Form 5405
	Federal Fuels Tax Credit	Form 4136
	Foreign Tax Credit	Form1116

Sources: http://www.irs.gov/pub/irs-pdf/f1040ez.pdf; http://www.irs.gov/pub/irs-pdf/f1040a.pdf; http://www.irs.gov/pub/irs-pdf/f1040.pdf

TABLE 4-8
EARNED INCOME TAX CREDIT (2011)

Earned Income and AGI Must Each Be Less Than:
• $43,998 ($49,078 married filing jointly) with three or more qualifying children
• $40,964 ($46,044 married filing jointly) with two qualifying children
• $36,052 ($41,132 married filing jointly) with one qualifying child
• $13,660 ($18,740 married filing jointly) with no qualifying children

Maximum Credit:
• $5,751 with three or more qualifying children
• $5,112 with two qualifying children
• $3,094 with one qualifying child
• $464 with no qualifying children

http://www.irs.gov/individuals/article/0,,id=233839,00.html

Credit for Child and Dependent Care Expenses. If a household paid for someone to take care of their children under age thirteen for work purposes, a taxpayer may claim a tax credit for child-care expenses up to a maximum of $3,000 for one child and $6,000 for two or more children. The credit can be as much as 35% of these qualifying expenses—depending on AGI. This credit is not available for households with a non-working spouse. The government intends for this credit to help mitigate only necessary child-care expenses. If a household uses an in-home care provider (e.g., nanny), Form 2441 alerts the IRS of potential social security taxes owed.

Foreign Tax Credit. International mutual funds will likely have paid foreign taxes. These foreign taxes will show up on Forms 1099-Div and 1099-Interest, which mutual fund companies must provide to you at the end of the calendar year. If the foreign taxes come to less than $300 ($600 if filing jointly), simply claim this as a tax credit on line 43 of Form 1040. If you paid more in foreign taxes, you must file Form 1116.

If you or your spouse receive income from a foreign country and pay income taxes to that country, you receive IRS credits for those taxes as paid, alleviating responsibility for taxes to the U.S. government. An example of this is a U.S. servicemember living in Germany whose spouse is a German citizen with a job earning income on the German economy. If the spouse pays taxes in Germany, the servicemember will have to declare that income on the IRS Form 1040. However, filling out Form 1116 will relieve the servicemember from paying taxes to the United States government on that income if the spouse can prove income taxes were paid to Germany.

Child Tax Credit. This allows a credit for each dependent child under age seventeen. For 2011, the amount is $1,000, but it is subject to change in the future. This is perhaps the easiest credit to include on your tax return. If you have dependents under age seventeen, there is no form to fill out. All you have to do is provide the Social Security number for each dependent under age seventeen on the front of your Form 1040.

In addition to tax credits counting towards a taxpayer's tax liability, there are the income taxes already paid through withholdings and reported on the taxpayer's IRS Forms W-2. To calculate the tax refund or tax payment due, the tax form takes the taxpayer's tax liability and subtracts qualified tax credits, as well as taxes already paid.

$$\text{Tax Owed} = \text{Tax Liability} - \text{Tax Credits} - \text{Tax Paid}$$

If the tax owed is positive, the taxpayer will send a payment to the IRS, either electronically or by check. If the tax owed is too great, the taxpayer will have a penalty to pay in addition to the tax owed and should adjust his or her IRS Form W-4 to reduce the underpayment for subsequent years. If the tax owed is negative, the taxpayer will receive a tax refund. If that refund is too big, the taxpayer should adjust his or her IRS Form W-4 to reduce overpayment.

Other Issues

Filing an Extension for Tax Returns. Federal income tax returns and final payments are due on April 15. Military personnel and government employees living outside the United States and Puerto Rico get an automatic extension until June 15. This rule also applies even if only one spouse is out of the country and files a joint return with the one who is not. Attach a statement to the IRS tax return showing that the requirement was met for the extension. Keep in mind that this extension prevents only the assessment of penalties for a late filing and payment of tax; the IRS charges interest on any taxes still unpaid after April 15.

Serving in a Combat Zone. There is special consideration for military pay earned in a combat zone. If you served in an imminent danger area designated by an executive order for any part of a month, then the entire month's pay falls under the exclusion. The amount of the pay that is nontaxable differs for enlisted members and officers. For enlisted members and warrant officers, all basic pay received in a combat zone is nontaxable. Officers may exclude their monthly pay up to the maximum enlisted amount (Sergeant Major of the Army).

Tax Treatment of Servicemembers Who Die in a Combat Zone. The Internal Revenue Code provides tax forgiveness for any member whose death results from a terrorist attack anywhere or while serving in a combat zone. This tax forgiveness applies to income for the taxable year in which the member dies, and for prior years that ended on or after the first day served in a combat zone. Furthermore, any tax liability outstanding against such a member at the time of death will be canceled or reduced.

There is also a military death gratuity, which is a one-time non-taxable $100,000 payment to help surviving family members deal with the financial hardships that accompany the loss of a qualifying active-duty servicemember. There is also a $12,420 gratuity made to eligible beneficiaries when a retired servicemember's death occurs within 120 days after retirement.

Filing When a Spouse is Deployed to a Hazardous-Duty Area. Households still have to file by April 15. In this case, the servicemember should have prepared a power of attorney prior to deployment so that the spouse can sign the joint return. If the servicemember failed to do this, IRS Publication 3 states that the spouse should simply attach a signed statement stating that the servicemember cannot sign the joint return because he or she is serving in a combat zone or qualified hazardous duty area.

Keeping Old Returns. All taxpayers should keep copies of their tax returns for a minimum of seven years. Along with the tax return, keep copies of any supporting documents. These include W-2 forms, 1099 forms, receipts, and mortgage records.

STATE TAXES

State tax codes change constantly, and they can be as complicated as the federal code. Online and commercial tax preparation software is invaluable in preparing state tax returns. Each state treats military compensation differently. A servicemember's military income, and possibly the non-military spousal income (one should contact the tax office of the state where the income was earned to learn how they apply the Military Spouse Residency Relief Act), is taxed according to the servicemember's home of record. A servicemember's non-military income is taxed according to the laws applying to the state in which the income was earned. Seven states (Alaska, Florida, Nevada, South Dakota, Texas, Washington, and Wyoming) have no income tax. If a service-member is a legal resident of one of these states, their military income and possibly their spouse's income from any source will face no state tax liability. Many other states provide special breaks to servicemembers. For example, some do not tax military compensation at all, while other states do not tax military pay if the servicemember is serving outside the state. The remaining states levy some form of tax on military income. One should contact the state tax authorities or a tax preparer for more details.

Changing Your Legal Residence

Military personnel can legally reduce their state income tax by establishing their home of record in a state that does not have an income tax. The service-member must be able to show evidence to meet the criteria to persuade the state tax authorities. Tax authorities are alert for fraudulent domicile changes. Servicemembers should seek advice at their installation legal assistance office to ensure that their actions meet all of the legal requirements.

People establish residence in a state by residing in that state. Residence involves physical presence or the presence of living quarters for a period of time. When the DoD assigns a servicemember to an installation, he or she is usually a temporary resident of that state.

Legal residence, which is synonymous with domicile and home of record for tax purposes, refers to the individual's permanent home for legal purposes. According to the Servicemembers Civil Relief Act, servicemembers are sub-ject to the tax laws in the state of their domicile. Everyone has only one legal residence at any given time. This legal residence may be in the state where a person was born—domicile of origin—or it may be a place he or she has chosen—domicile of choice. Once established, legal residence continues until legally changed. Legal residence changes only by a voluntary and positive action. A mere attempt or desire to make a change is not sufficient. As a rule, to acquire a domicile of choice, a servicemember must meet the following three conditions concurrently:

1. Be physically present in the new state.
2. Have the intention of abandoning the former domicile.
3. Have the intention of remaining in the new state indefinitely.

Once a servicemember has established a legal residence in a particular state, a temporary absence does not cause that legal residence to change. Thus, it is possible for a servicemember to have a home of record in one state and a temporary residence in another.

Servicemembers can use some of the following as evidence of intent when establishing domicile of choice:

1. Place of birth
2. Permanent place of abode
3. Registering to vote and voting by absentee ballot
4. Obtaining a driver's license
5. State from which you entered the military service
6. Filing with state authorities an approved certificate or other statement indicating legal residence

Having legally changed the home of record, the servicemember needs to contact his or her finance office so the finance office can adjust the servicemember's state tax withholding and pay it to the proper state.

Common Rules For State Tax Liabilities

1. The state of home of record may tax military income and other income (such as dividends and interest), regardless of how or where it is earned.
2. The state of temporary residence may not tax military pay. The state of temporary residence (because of military orders) may tax any other servicemember income but cannot not tax spousal income in that state—if the spouse shares the same home of record as the servicemember or maintains a different home of record from the temporary residence.
3. The state of temporary residence cannot tax a servicemember's personal property located in the state. The state of home of record may tax personal property; however, states typically do not tax personal property that is not physically in the state. Real estate is taxed where it is located.
4. The state may tax military pension income if it taxes other pensions in the same manner.
5. If a servicemember obtains state automobile license tags from the state of temporary residence, the servicemember may be exempted from paying certain fees. One should check with the state's Department of Motor Vehicles for more details.

Military Spouses

Under current tax law, a spouse may become a legal resident of the servicemember's stated home of record, or may change his or her residence to the state in which the family is stationed. The spouse's income is taxed according to the laws of the chosen state of residency. The spouse must live in the state— or the servicemember must have a connection to the state—and the spouse must have an intent to return to that state in order to claim residency. Spouses only receive this exemption when they move with the servicemember as a result of military orders. Each state has its own laws and forms for complying with the terms of the Military Spouse Residency Relief Act of 2009 that amended the Servicemembers Civil Relief Act. For more information, contact the tax authorities for the state you live in as well as your state of residency.

SUGGESTED REFERENCES
You may find the following IRS publications (available free from IRS publications centers and on the IRS website) particularly helpful:
- IRS Publication 3, Tax Guide for Military Personnel
- IRS Publication 17, Your Federal Income Tax
- IRS Publication 552, Recordkeeping for Individuals
- IRS Publication 553, Highlight of Tax Changes

An annual income tax supplement to the *Army, Navy,* and *Air Force Times,* published annually (typically in mid-February), contains useful tax tips and information, including detailed information on state taxes.

Software packages for preparing taxes include most forms for printing and transmitting returns directly to the IRS. These include TurboTax and H&R Block's TaxCut.

J. K. Lasser Tax Institute, Prentice-Hall, Commerce Clearing House, and accounting firms such as Arthur Young and PriceWaterhouseCoopers also produce self-help tax guides.

The local tax assistance office on your post and the Staff Judge Advocate (SJA) provide additional resources that you can turn to.

Some useful tax help websites:

Military OneSource: http://militaryonesource.com
IRS: http://irs.gov
myPay: http://mypay.dfas.mil
TaxSlayer: http://www.taxslayer.com
TurboTax: http://turbotax.intuit.com/
TaxCut: http://www.taxcut.com

PART II

FINANCIAL DECISIONS FOR SERVICEMEMBERS

5

Housing

This chapter discusses some of the housing choices military families face and suggests ways to evaluate housing alternatives. Because determining where to live is ultimately a personal decision, each servicemember must adapt these guidelines to fit his or her particular situation. Whether you plan to invest in the purchase of a home, live in military housing, or rent a home or apartment, the decision is financially significant.

When moving to a new area, you should start by reviewing the installation's website and contacting Army Community Service (ACS) and the housing office. The Automated Housing Referral Network (AHRN) is another helpful resource. This DoD-sponsored website, accessible at http://www.ahrn.com, provides information for relocating servicemembers about housing availability. Other sources of information on rental and purchase options include your sponsor, local real estate agents, the local chamber of commerce, the Internet, and newspapers.

The ability to purchase or rent a home depends primarily on your personal financial situation. If you have an excellent credit history, sufficient income, and personal savings for a down payment, you may qualify for a mortgage to buy a home. Most American homeowners budget 30% to 35% of their after-tax household income for their mortgage. Your Basic Allowance for Housing (BAH)[1] may be less than the monthly mortgage payment, but homeownership currently has significant tax advantages that may make it a financially attractive option. BAH is not taxed as income since it is an allowance. Additionally, mortgage interest currently is tax deductible, so servicemembers accrue twice the tax benefit. Refer to chapter 4 for an in-depth discussion of tax deductions.

---

[1] Basic Allowance for Housing (BAH) is the monthly payment the military pays to servicemembers for housing. Because BAH is an allowance, it is not considered part of one's taxable income; thus, servicemembers do not pay income tax on BAH.

THE DECISION TO LIVE ON OR OFF THE INSTALLATION

Living in quarters on the installation is not free. Servicemembers pay their BAH either to the government or to a contractor who manages installation housing, essentially renting quarters from the government. Servicemembers should compare the houses they can afford (based on their BAH) to the quarters they are offered on the installation. For dual military couples electing to live in government or on-post privatized quarters, the senior servicemember forfeits BAH and the junior servicemember retains BAH.

The decision to live on or off the installation is more than just a financial decision and calls for carefully considered cost-benefit analysis. Usually the local real estate market offers greater variety, but often at additional cost. You should prioritize your housing needs in order to decide where to live. In weighing options, it is helpful to identify priorities that may include quality of the school system, proximity to community facilities, taxes, availability of public transportation, commuting costs, and out-of-pocket expenses such as electricity, water, and sewage. Other considerations include the ability to choose neighbors, a sense of security, the flexibility of departure dates due to military necessity, and the responsiveness of maintenance workers. One recommended cost-benefit approach is to put values on these and other relevant factors and crunch the numbers as objectively as possible.

THE RENT VERSUS BUY DECISION

Should you decide to live off the installation, the next decision is whether to rent or buy.

The money you have available for housing is not solely determined by your BAH; it is also a function of other expenses such as transportation, food, entertainment, savings, maintenance, and other budget items. Chapter 1 provides guidance in preparing a personal budget. In addition, many budget templates are available online at sites such as Freddie Mac (http://www.freddiemac.com) or Fannie Mae (http://www.fanniemae.com).[2] It is imperative for any budget to accurately depict spending habits, priorities, and monthly cash flows. A comprehensive needs-based budget will provide a clear picture of what you can afford to spend on housing.

Servicemembers should consider the advantages and disadvantages of each option when deciding to either rent or buy a home. Rent is a payment for the provision of housing services. You should only decide to rent after carefully reviewing total costs and family goals. Renting almost always costs

---

[2] In the United States, Freddie Mac and Fannie Mae (private companies with government charters) purchase the majority of mortgage loans. Thus, they set the mortgage lending criteria. They also provide a wealth of information on buying a home and interest rates on mortgages, as well as analytic tools for evaluating the rent versus purchase decision, preparing budgets, estimating what kind of home one can afford, and calculating mortgage payments.

less than owning an equivalent dwelling. Furthermore, renters are not responsible for large down payments and usually do not incur maintenance and repair expenses. Servicemembers can also break rental agreements with PCS or deployment orders, provided that there is a military clause in the rental agreement or in accordance with the Servicemembers Civil Relief Act (SCRA).

Some servicemembers decide to buy in the expectation that they will make money when they sell the home. However, homeowners do not always make money when they sell because of the risks and costs inherent to real estate investments. The 2007 housing bubble collapse demonstrated such risks when housing prices fell significantly in a short period of time. Despite the collapse, an important consideration is that homeownership currently has many tax advantages. Certain expenses associated with home ownership are tax deductible and thus reduce the amount of income taxes that homeowners pay. Servicemembers with mortgages enjoy an unusual advantage. They receive tax-free quarters allowances (BAH) to pay their mortgages. The primary tax advantage is that the interest paid on a mortgage loan is deductible from the servicemember's income when computing itemized federal income taxes—offsetting part of the loan payment. Other tax advantages include:

- Deduction of points[3] paid to secure an initial mortgage, either in the year of purchase or over the life of the loan. (See Internal Revenue Service Publication 936 "Home Mortgage Interest Deduction" at www.irs.gov.)
- Deduction of property taxes.
- Relief from capital gains tax on profits up to $250,000 for single tax filers and $500,000 for joint filers. Certain criteria apply; for instance, the homeowner must have lived in the home for two of the last five years on the date of sale.

The tax advantages of home ownership are significant, and you should analyze them thoroughly as part of the housing decision. (See IRS Publication 523, "Selling Your Home" at http://www.irs.gov.) At the same time, you need to be careful not to underestimate the risks associated with homeownership. All houses are "money pits" to some extent. Unforeseen costs can include legal fees associated with complications at closing, or repairs needed for undisclosed issues missed during the inspection that arise shortly after the closing. Problems such as water seepage, buried oil tanks, or roof leaks can be expensive to fix. Even if a house has no seasonal or undisclosed issues, it will require renovation and maintenance due to wear and tear. Table 5-1 summarizes the advantages and disadvantages of renting and of buying a home.

---

[3] Discount points are often called points or loan origination fees. A point is equal to 1 percent of the loan amount. Points are considered like interest that one pays in advance; the more points the borrower pays at the closing of the loan, the lower the interest rate.

TABLE 5-1
ADVANTAGES AND DISADVANTAGES OF
RENTING AND BUYING A HOME

RENTING

Advantages

- Pay less in monthly rent (generally) than a mortgage would be for a comparable home.
- Avoid responsibility (most likely) for maintenance and repairs, and maybe utilities.
- Avoid significant down payment or closing costs, although renter will pay a deposit.
- Avoid trouble of selling home upon moving.
- Break contract easily for PCS or deployment through a military clause or the SCRA.

Disadvantages

- Forego the opportunity to earn a capital gain if housing prices rise.
- Choose (maybe) from fewer rental options.
- Fail to capture tax deduction for rent payment.
- Part with interest that would accrue from security deposit if invested.

BUYING

Advantages

- Profit from sale of home if home value increases.
- Avoid capital gains tax payable on gains from home sales (up to $250,000 for single tax payers or $500,000 for a married couple).
- Receive tax deductions for property taxes, mortgage interest, and points.
- Gain ability to borrow against value of home (if needed).

Disadvantages

- Need 10-20% of the home price for a down payment plus closing costs.
- Must have a good credit history.
- Might lose money if house does not appreciate enough to pay off all mortgage, closing costs, and money used for renovations or maintenance when a home is sold.
- Pay for home maintenance and repair costs.
- Part with interest that would accrue from down payment if invested.

TABLE 5-2
INFORMATION NEEDED WHEN DECIDING
BETWEEN RENTING AND BUYING

Personal Information
• Marginal Tax Rate (MTR) based on income tax bracket (see chapter 4).
• The annual return (%) projected for savings that would be applied to a down
  payment on the mortgage

Rental Information
• Estimated monthly rent
• Projected rent increases
• Renters insurance premiums

Purchase Information
• Estimated maintenance costs, homeowners insurance costs, and property taxes
• Potential home price
• Loan terms (down payment, interest rate, maturity, points, and closing costs)
• Estimated housing price appreciation rate

Preparing a net present value analysis is an excellent way to compare renting and purchasing options. Fortunately, you don't need a degree in finance to complete this analysis. Online tools are available to calculate the costs and benefits of each option. The following sites provide tools to facilitate such analysis: FreddieMac.com, Mortgage-Calc.com, and BankRate.com. A simple Internet search for "rent versus buy" will lead to other useful links to financial calculators. It is useful to gather the information listed in Table 5-2 for input into the calculator; much of this information is available from real estate agents, potential mortgage lenders, or online.

You should consider how long you will remain at your duty station when deciding whether to buy or rent, since a decision at the current location may constrain your ability to buy at follow-on duty assignments. If you choose to pay 'points' to reduce your mortgage interest rate, this also increases the length of time you need to own the house (about 5 to 6 years) for the lower interest rate to be cost-effective. Further, the home purchaser assumes the risk that external economic factors will not significantly cause the value of the house to depreciate over the course of a duty assignment or follow-on rental period.

In summary, the decision between renting and buying involves the consideration of many potential advantages and disadvantages. Homeownership offers tax advantages and possible asset appreciation, but with greater financial risk, while renting is generally more convenient and less costly. The upcoming sections of this chapter offer more detail on these costs and other considerations.

RENTAL AGREEMENTS

Upon finding an appropriate rental property, negotiate with the landlord or agent on the price and terms. Then, you should clearly document key rental contract terms, including responsibility for utility payments and repairs, payment terms, duration of rental contract, ability to sublet, restrictions, and deposits. All tenant-landlord agreements should be in writing and should contain a military clause releasing the servicemember from the lease in the event of transfer or deployment. Servicemembers *can* still break their leases under certain conditions granted by the Servicemembers Civil Relief Act, even without the military clause in the lease. But it is still best to have the clause in the lease. Read the contract thoroughly. Before signing any lease, ask the JAG office to review the contract. See RentLaw.com (http://www.rentlaw.com/military/sampleclause.htm) for a sample military clause.

PURCHASING A HOME

Servicemembers who decide to purchase a home should determine how much they can afford to spend. Lenders want to ensure that homebuyers have enough monthly income to make their mortgage payments. They calculate monthly mortgage expenses by adding up the servicemember's mortgage payment, insurance, and taxes. Then, they apply two general tests: the income and debt tests described below.

Income Test
- Mortgage expenses should not exceed 28% of total income.

Debt Test
- Mortgage expenses and other regular debt payments should not be more than 36% of total income.

The lower the interest rate, the lower the mortgage payment will be, which provides savings that can be used to buy a more expensive home. Table 5-3 depicts sample down payments, closing costs, and mortgage payments for a thirty-year fixed-rate loan using two different interest rate scenarios. Anyone can perform these calculations with Excel or an online loan payment calculator, such as the one at FannieMae.com. Ultimately, the interest rate on your loan will depend on your credit history, the type of loan selected, and the amount of down payment at closing. The following section discusses mortgage options in greater detail.

Your mortgage amount will depend on the size of the down payment, which is generally constrained by the balance of your savings. Given the capacity to pay a greater down payment, you should weigh the costs (the interest or dividends you will not earn on the savings that go to the additional down

TABLE 5-3
INTEREST RATE SCENARIOS
FOR A 30-YEAR FIXED-RATE MORTGAGE

Home Price	10% Down payment	Closing Costs	Amount Financed	Monthly Payment at 5% Interest	Monthly Payment at 7% Interest
$150,000	$15,000	$7,500	$135,000	$725	$898
$250,000	$25,000	$12,500	$225,000	$1,208	$1,497
$350,000	$35,000	$17,500	$315,000	$1,610	$2,096
$450,000	$45,000	$22,500	$405,000	$2174	$2694

payment) against the benefits of lower monthly mortgage payments. One generally should not pay more than the minimum down payment, because the after-tax cost of the mortgage will generally be less than the after-tax earnings on other investments.[4] You should discuss the advantages and disadvantages of making a higher down payment with your lender and real estate agent before making a final decision.

The next step is to contact your bank, mortgage company, or credit union to get a commitment letter indicating the maximum loan amount for which you qualify. This letter provides assurance to the seller of your dream home that you will be able to obtain financing. Sellers will more readily accept an offer knowing that the buyers can obtain financing.

THE PURCHASE PROCESS
Deciding which home to buy is an arduous process and largely dependent on your tastes, preferences, and long-term financial expectations. Location is a key consideration in purchasing a home; this includes quality of local schools, availability of mass transportation, recreation facilities, shopping facilities, nearby perceived health hazards (such as electrical grids or power plants), and other factors that could affect potential resale value. Many groups, such as USAA, offer cradle-to-grave relocation services that can help you sell your existing house and buy a new home. USAA offers a website that guides renting versus home purchasing decisions at http://www.homecircle.com. There are several other websites that analyze housing costs in specified neighborhoods for potential homebuyers, such as Trulia (http://www.trulia.com) or Zillow (http://www.zillow.com).

Although it is possible to conduct extensive research via the Internet, most buyers consult real estate agents at this point. Many banks and insurance

---

®4 An after-tax interest rate is the effective interest rate paid on a loan if you deduct interest expense. For example, with an 8% loan in the 25% tax bracket, the after-tax interest rate is 8% × (1− 0.25), or 6.00%.

companies offer relocation assistance, including referrals to real estate agents. If you use these services, you may also receive reimbursement of part of the real estate agent's fee (up to $1,000). Good agents should provide assistance in evaluating potential neighborhoods and homes. However, you should be aware of the different roles, interests, and motivations of brokers and agents.

A broker has a license to operate a real estate company, while an agent works for a broker. The National Association of Realtors is a trade organization that establishes professional standards for its realtor members. Homeowners typically execute agreements with sellers' agents and pay them a commission to sell their homes (generally 5%). Sellers' agents are obligated to disclose certain information about the homes they list, but their incentive is to sell the homes at the highest possible prices. As a homebuyer, you may be better served by choosing your own buyer's agent, whose loyalty is to not to the seller. This agent may require you to sign a buyer's agent agreement, but generally you should not pay additional fees to the buyer's agent, as he or she will receive a sales commission from the seller of the purchased home.

Agents can provide a potential buyer with a market analysis, listings of properties that meet the buyer's criteria in terms of taste and price, as well as advice on neighborhoods and schools. They will show potential homes, answer questions about condition and potential issues, and guide the buyer through the home buying process from offer to closing. It is important to have realistic expectations, stay within a budget, and shop around.

Once you find an ideal home, you should make a purchase offer to the seller. Depending on the local housing market, you may offer less than the seller's asking price and then negotiate to a final bid. Upon acceptance, you must provide a deposit (generally $1,000) to show that the offered price is serious. That deposit will be applied to the purchase price at closing; however, if the bid is withdrawn for reasons other than those authorized in the contract, you may lose this deposit. Following an acceptable inspection and prior to closing, you must provide up to 5% of the principal on the house to take the house off of the market and prevent the seller from accepting other bids. This payment applies to the purchase at closing.

Any purchase offer should be subject to a physical inspection by a qualified, professional inspector. Ideally, it is wise to hire a certified engineer to inspect the home. If at all possible, you should accompany the inspector as you can learn a great deal about any deficiencies in the home this way. The inspector will provide a report of deficiencies that will serve as a basis for negotiating with the seller; the seller may fix the problems prior to the sale or provide a credit against the sale price so that the buyer can perform the repairs after closing. As a supplement to the formal inspection, it may be wise to hire a local carpenter to also look at the house for issues prior to the closing, in order to catch deficiencies that the inspector may have missed. It never hurts to have a second set of eyes on-site. If the deficiencies cannot be resolved, you can withdraw the offer and obtain a refund of any deposit. Potential deficiencies that are overlooked or hidden during the inspection—like seasonal water seepage in a basement—become the buyer's problem after the closing, so it is important to remain alert during the inspection.

It is wise to note the circumstances under which the seller is selling and verify the Certificate of Occupancy (held at the local town hall) prior to closing. If the seller is being transferred or is upsizing or downsizing due to changes in family size, the buyer doesn't need to be as concerned about the house being a "lemon." However, if the seller is moving to a similar home within the same area, he or she may be trying to get rid of a problematic house. An agent should tell you how long the house has been on the market, and the seller is obligated to disclose any issues with the house, but this may not happen in practice. Although not always required, the buyer should confirm that there is a valid Certificate of Occupancy for the house prior to closing. This certificate legally updates changes to the house or property by the seller, which may affect the square-footage or value of the house. Without this certificate upon closing, the new homeowner may be legally mandated to make renovations due to previous unsafe changes to the house or grounds made by the seller. For example, certain states require two points of egress from a basement. If a seller's basement renovations were not approved via this certificate, the buyer would have to add a second exit, an expensive, unexpected project. The certificate can also apply to additions of pools and sheds. To sell the house in the future, you need to be prepared to show potential buyers this Certificate of Occupancy to verify that it meets local building standards.

The final sales contract is executed following a successful negotiation of terms such as final price, expected closing date, expected repairs, and "items that convey" (i.e., appliances, window treatments, and fixtures). Sellers may agree to pay all or part of the buyer's closing costs, and agents may be willing to reduce their commissions, depending on the housing market, in order to facilitate an agreement. It pays to negotiate.

One final consideration is the purchase of additional insurance beyond homeowners insurance. If the house is located in a flood plain, flood insurance, backed by FEMA, is a requirement to receive a mortgage. Additionally, some homebuyers buy a concurrent life insurance policy to cover the cost of the mortgage if they die during the course of the mortgage. This is an all-too-realistic consideration for servicemembers; if you want to fully protect your family, a life insurance policy to match the full value of the mortgage is a prudent option. Any insurance firm, such as USAA, can set up a life insurance policy to pay for the house in this worst-case scenario.

SHOPPING FOR A MORTGAGE

Many different types of mortgages are available through banks, credit unions, and mortgage companies. However, mortgages generally fall into two basic categories: fixed-rate and variable-rate. Fixed-rate loans have constant payments and generally mature in fifteen, twenty, or thirty years. The fixed rate

TABLE 5-4
DETERMINING THE RATE OF AN ADJUSTIBLE RATE MORTGAGE (ARM)

Scenario	Interest Rate
Initial U.S. Treasury (UST) rate	3.1%
Interest rate paid in years 1 through 3 (UST rate plus 3%)	6.1%
Assumed UST rate in three years	5.5%
Interest rate paid in year 4 (UST rate plus 3% is 8.5%, but the interest rate cannot rise by more than 2% per year, so the interest rate is 6.1% plus 2%)	8.1%
Assumed UST rate in four years	6.0%
Interest rate paid in year 5 (UST rate plus 3% is 9.0%, which is not more than a 2% increase this year)	9.0%

allows a "lock-in" of the rate at the time of loan commitment to protect against unexpected rate increases. The interest rate and monthly payments will not increase; they also will not go down if interest rates fall. The fixed interest rate will also be higher than the rate for a comparable variable loan because the lender assumes the risk of interest rate changes.

Another mortgage type is the Adjustable Rate Mortgage (ARM), which generally starts with a lower rate than a fixed-rate loan of the same maturity. This allows homebuyers to qualify for higher loan amounts. The initial rate is fixed for a period of time (e.g., one, three, five, or ten years). Thereafter, the rate can change if interest rates rise or fall. The interest rate is based on an index, such as the London Interbank Borrowing Rate (LIBOR) or the rates on U.S. Treasury Bills, plus a margin. Once the initial period ends, the rate can be adjusted based on the prevailing index, subject to the maximum amounts stated in the loan contract (the caps). A sample specification for an ARM might state: "The initial interest rate will be 3% above the index of U.S. Treasury Securities . . . The rate may be adjusted annually after the initial three-year term. The rate cannot increase by more than 2% per year, and the maximum increase cannot exceed 6 percent." Table 5-4 provides an illustration.

However, while the ARM might allow homebuyers to qualify for higher loan amounts, this type of mortgage can be very dangerous. The homebuyer might purchase a more expensive house than he or she can afford, knowing that the mortgage payments will be lower during the initial time period. Such a homebuyer might be counting on some combination of home value appreciation, decreasing interest rates, or increased personal earnings to kick in before the initial rate changes. If these optimistic events do not occur, the homebuyer might face new, higher mortgage payments at the three-, five-, or ten-year mark that he or she cannot afford. Financial hardship, even foreclosure, could result.

COMPLETING THE LOAN TRANSACTION

It can take thirty to sixty days to close on a mortgage loan. The financial institution that you select will require the following paperwork to process a loan request:

- A loan application
- Income and employment verification
- A financial statement identifying your assets and liabilities
- Verification of cash for down payment

At the time of application, the financial institution will issue a truth-in-lending statement that indicates the annual percentage rate of interest and estimates settlement costs. The Department of Housing and Urban Development (HUD) provides an excellent guide to settlement costs that can be obtained from financial institutions or via the HUD website at http://www.hud.gov. Online sources explain the costs on the HUD-1 Settlement Statement; Home Loan Learning Center (http://www.homeloanlearningcenter.com/files/HUD1.pdf) and About.com (http://homebuying.about.com/cs/titleescrow/a/hud1_settlement.htm) are two good examples. A closing agent from the title company normally disburses required funds between the buyer and seller on the HUD-1. The buyer has to pay settlement charges to the borrower, county and school taxes, and the remainder of the principal (minus the deposit) at the closing. Banks generally charge an application and an origination fee. They will order an appraisal to ensure the value of the home is greater than the loan amount, a survey of the property (paid by the buyer), and a title insurance policy.

Engaging a real estate attorney to review the purchase contract and loan documents is generally a wise investment. Loan closings can be stressful and confusing. At closing, the buyer must provide proof of insurance and bring funds for the down payment and any remaining portion of the closing costs. The closing statement will identify costs associated with obtaining the loan and also payments owed to the seller. These are some of the major expense categories:

- Points (as discussed earlier) are paid to the lender to obtain a lower interest rate, effectively prepaying interest. (Because a dollar today is worth more than a dollar in the future, unless you plan to own the home for a long time, generally more than five to six years, it is not cost-effective to prepay interest.)
- Filing fees to record the mortgage documentation in the county records.
- Lenders' Title Insurance guaranteeing that no one else has an interest in the property. (Obtain a homeowners' title policy for a small additional charge to protect your own interests as well.)
- Mortgage and property taxes.
- Attorney fees.

- Escrow (deposits) for future taxes and insurance payments, generally enough to cover the next six months.

MORTGAGE GUARANTY PROGRAMS

Most homebuyers obtain conventional mortgage loans, which are not guaranteed by any outside agencies. However, the Federal Housing Agency (FHA) and the Veterans Administration (VA) offer loan guaranty programs that may lower mortgage costs or down-payment requirements. It is worth the effort to evaluate the benefits of each program, especially if you do not have savings available to make a large down payment. Each of these options is discussed briefly below.

FHA Loans. Since the Federal Housing Agency insures these mortgages, lenders are more willing to give loans to borrowers with lower qualifying requirements, such as credit problems. FHA loans require only a 3% down payment, thus allowing a buyer to purchase a home with less cash outlay. FHA loans offer competitive interest rates because the loans are insured by the federal government. Specific program terms are identified at the Federal Housing Finance Agency (http://www.fhfa.gov).

VA Loans. The Veterans Administration offers the VA guaranteed home loan program to help veterans finance home purchases with favorable loan terms and at competitive interest rates. Because the VA guarantees a portion of the loan amount (the percent guaranteed varies with the loan balance), eligible participants can obtain loans with little or no down payment, interest rates that may be lower than conventional loan rates, and lower closing costs. Lenders generally currently cap the loan amount at $417,000. However, loan limits may be up to $625,000 for properties in Hawaii, Guam, Alaska, and the U.S. Virgin Islands. Specific requirements and terms are contained in VA Pamphlet 24-6, which can be found at the U.S. Department of Veterans Affairs website (http://www.va.gov).

If you are not able to qualify for an FHA or VA loan and do not have the standard 20% down payment, your bank will require the purchase of Primary Mortgage Insurance. PMI protects the lender against the risk that buyer will not be able make the loan payments. With this type of insurance, it is possible to buy a home with as little as a 3% to 5% down payment. If your loan payment history is favorable, once the loan has been paid down to 80% of the property's value, the PMI requirement will be dropped.

LOWERING THE COST OF YOUR MORTGAGE

Refinancing a home may allow you to lower your cost of borrowing. Refinancing involves obtaining a new loan and paying off the existing mortgage. If interest rates drop after the purchase of the home, you may be able to lower your monthly payments or switch from an adjustable to a fixed-rate loan by refinancing. However, the initial out-of-pocket expenses can be quite substantial. Generally, you will have to pay many of the same closing costs you faced when initially purchasing the home: appraisal, title search, loan application fee, and points.

TABLE 5-5
STRATEGIES TO LOWER THE COST OF HOME OWNERSHIP

Strategy	Benefits
Select a shorter loan term	Switching from a 30-year to a 15-year fixed-rate loan could save $127,000 in interest (55%) on a $200,000 loan at 6% interest.
Make 26 biweekly payments rather than 12 monthly payments	Paying every two weeks, rather than monthly, can save you $50,000 in interest payments on a 6%, 30-year loan for $200,000. The loan would be repaid five years earlier.
Refinance from an ARM to a fixed-rate loan	If interest rates have fallen, you may save money (if interest rates later rise) by refinancing to a lower fixed-rate loan.

Even if you do not have adequate cash to pay the closing costs, you still may be able to refinance. Most lenders allow the addition of these costs to the new loan amount if the value of your home is more than 20% higher than the loan balance. Although the monthly payment will be a little higher, you may still save money in the long run if the difference in interest rates is sufficient.

Before refinancing a mortgage with a new lender, you might ask the holder of your existing mortgage to renegotiate the interest rate. The lender may not go as low as the current market rate but may be willing to split the difference. This kind of deal is beneficial for both parties: The lender retains the borrower as a customer at a higher rate than current market rates, and the borrower saves on closing costs. Your current lender may not be able to renegotiate an interest rate because of financial institution policies, but it never hurts to ask.

A traditional rule of thumb is that if current interest rates are at least two percentage points below your present rate, it may pay to refinance. You should also consider the length of time you plan to own the house, making sure you have sufficient time to recoup the expenses of new closing costs, lawyer fees, and agent fees.

Table 5-5 identifies three other strategies to lower the cost of home ownership.

SELLING YOUR HOME

The average length of time most people own their homes is five to seven years. Uniquely, military members generally move every three years, making the decision to sell or rent their homes critical. If you decide to sell, you need to determine an asking price and whether to use a broker.

You may choose to sell the home independently, or use a real estate agent. The ultimate concern is which choice will give a larger net amount: selling the house independently and avoiding the commission, or using the professional marketing expertise of a real estate agent. For a commission (generally 5 to 6 percent of the sales price), agents provide the following services: determining the fair value of the home, scheduling appointments and screening buyers, and suggesting the most cost-effective ways to improve the home's appearance. They also facilitate contract and closing procedures. Realtors also ensure that one does not miss any important steps in the timeline for preparing for the sale of a house (especially as the closing approaches).

Should you decide to use an agent, you should interview potential candidates and ask them to provide a marketing plan for the home. You can negotiate the type of listing agreement[5] and the size of the commission with the agent you choose. A higher commission may spur the agent to work harder, but it leaves you with less after the sale. You could consider signing a short-term contract at first, perhaps for two or three months, and closely monitoring how aggressively the agent markets the home. An agent's skill and resources can result in quick, efficient, and profitable sales, but agents' abilities and helpfulness vary. Do not renew a contract with an agent who is not working hard to sell a house. Be aware that an agent will not want to bend on many of these points, so you must be an able negotiator to get a listing contract that best serves your interests and not those of the broker.

If market conditions are good and you have the skill and time, you may decide to sell your house without the help of an agent. If you choose this option, make sure to:

1. Screen potential buyers over the telephone to determine how serious they are about buying.
2. Price the house realistically. People often overprice their own homes, so compare your house to others in the area that have sold in the past three to six months.
3. Present the home in the best possible light, as well-presented homes generally sell first and command the best prices.

RENTING ONE'S HOME

This section discusses only single-family homes as rental properties. Although not the optimal real estate investment, this is the type of property the typical servicemember often owns. Other forms of investment property, such as duplexes, condos, apartment buildings, or even commercial buildings, are beyond the scope of this book and beyond the reach of most service-

---

[5] You can discuss the three basic types of listing agreements (Exclusive Right to Sell, Exclusive Agency Listing, and Open Listing) with an agent.

members. If you are interested in these types of investment properties, there are numerous resources devoted to them online and in the financial planning sections of local bookstores and libraries.

As homeowners, military families have the option of turning their homes into income-generating rental properties when they complete a permanent change of station (PCS). Depending on the market (markets are very regional, meaning prices vary by location), this can be a great way to supplement one's income and save; but it is not without risks. Although home prices generally appreciate year-to-year, markets fluctuate broadly, and your home could decrease in value. The supply and demand of homes within a region determine the purchase and rental prices in each market, and these prices tend to move in opposite directions of one another.

Interest rates and taxes are key factors that affect housing demand directly. Historically, low interest rates helped fuel the housing booms through 2008 because mortgage rates were relatively low. Therefore, more people could (or thought they could) afford to become homeowners with lower rates, or could afford more expensive homes. The mortgage payment on a $100,000 loan with a 30-year mortgage and rate of 5% is $536.82 per month. If your rate happens to be 8%, your monthly payment is $733.76, a difference of nearly $2,400 per year. So if rates go up, fewer people are willing to buy, and more people are willing to rent. This is good news for rental property owners, because they can offer rent at a lower cost than a typical mortgage when interest rates are high.

Once you are aware of the risks involved, owning rental property can be a great addition to your investment portfolio. Owning real estate can help offset fluctuations in the stock market. Since real estate typically increases in value (with recessionary periods), and prices are not directly dependent on how well stocks are performing, a house is a good addition to a portfolio of stocks and bonds. However, before you decide to offer a home for rent, you should carefully analyze the situation to determine whether this is the best course of action and whether you can afford the risks involved.

There are several reasons why you may wish to hold onto a home as a rental property. First, you may be unable to sell the home. If the local housing market has cooled, you may want to consider renting the home, since the mortgage has to be paid whether anyone is living in the house or not. While BAH covers housing costs at your new duty station, BAH typically is not enough to cover both housing payments. Renting the vacated home at the previous duty station may be a short-term solution to cover the second mortgage, while waiting for the market for home sales to improve. It is helpful to anticipate the decision to rent after completing a PCS and prior to purchasing a house.

The second reason to rent your home is that you may return to your duty station later in your career, or possibly upon retirement. When a person buys a home, he or she obviously chooses it for some reason, such as location, aesthetics, or feel. Given that you already selected and resided in the home, renting it may be an excellent source of secondary income until you are ready to

TABLE 5-6
EXAMPLE OF MONTHLY RENTAL INCOME
AND COST ANALYSIS

Income	
Rent Received	$1,500.00
Costs	
Property Manager Fees[1]	$150.00
Mortgage[2]	$825.00
Taxes	$250.00
Private Mortgage Insurance (PMI)	$100.00
Repairs[3]	$75.00
Total Monthly Gain or Loss	$100.00

[1] Normally property managers take 10% of current rents. If one manages his or her own property, this expense goes away. However, reputable property managing firms provide one of the most crucial aspects of renting: getting the right person in the home who will pay always and on time.

[2] Mortgage includes principal and interest.

[3] Repairs is a monthly estimate, i.e., replacing air conditioner or furnace, caulking the tub, etc.

reoccupy it. Additionally, having a home you can return to reduces the stress of moving.

The final reason to hold on to a home is solely a financial one. If the rental market is hot, the idea of supplementing an income with monthly rent checks may be appealing. To take full advantage of this situation, the rent you receive must cover not only the mortgage but also taxes, insurance, and repairs (see Table 5-6 for rental income example). If rental income exceeds these costs, then renting will be profitable under normal market conditions. Obviously, having someone else pay all of your mortgage and maintenance costs by living in your house is a winning situation. Depending on the type of mortgage on the home, a renter effectively pays down the principal—a profitable situation that becomes very clear upon the sale of the house, when you can see the appreciation and equity that the house has accrued using someone else's money.

You should carefully weigh the advantages and disadvantages of renting and selling your old house based upon your situation, in order to make the right housing decision upon a PCS. As a landlord, you are operating your own business; therefore, any money received from renting a home is taxable.[6]

[6] There are tools available on the Internet that can calculate the capitalization rate of renting a home. If the calculated rate is less than long-term treasury yields, you should probably sell. One such calculator is available at Forbes.com.

TABLE 5-7
TYPICAL ADVANTAGES AND DISADVANTAGES
OF RENTING YOUR HOME

Advantages
1. Provides additional income every month if rent exceeds the cost of keeping the home.
2. Pays down the mortgage debt on your home at someone else's expense.
3. Allows deduction of expenses and improvements from your income taxes up to the amount of the rent you collect.
4. Gives you the ability to ride out unfavorable selling markets.
5. Hedges against inflation.
6. Diversifies your investor portfolio.

Disadvantages
1. Can consume a great deal of time, including dealing with tenant issues, and the time and money spent to fix up the house between renters.
2. Risk of rental rates dropping below the cost of maintaining and paying for the home.
3. Risk of periods when home is not rented, paying utilities and basic services (i.e., lawn maintenance) in the short-run.
4. Risk of renters damaging the home beyond the value of their security deposit, potentially leading to loss of time and money sunk on costly legal fees.
5. Risk of renters refusing to pay their rent. Varying by city and state, strong tenants' and/or squatters' rights versus those of landlords can make eviction of bad tenants very difficult.
6. Depending on length of rental, may eliminate advantage of the capital gains exemption when you sell (as mentioned earlier in the chapter as one of the advantages of owning a home).

However, there are many ways in which to reduce your tax bill. Serving as a landlord can be an expensive proposition in terms of time and money. Certain (but not all) locations have management firms that monitor property for 8 to 10 percent of the rental proceeds. However, not all management firms are created equal, and virtually none maintain property (and its resale value) with the same care as you would in person. Before buying a house with future intentions to rent, you should solidify your rental plan in advance, whether you intend to use remote management or hire a management firm. Either way, it is smart to check on a rental property at least once a year to examine its condition and take care of maintenance issues.

If you intend to rent, you should consider other factors as well prior to purchasing a home. Every state and city varies in the relative weight that it grants to renters' versus tenants' rights. Certain cities, such as Washington, DC, have strong tenants' rights to protect tenants from abuses by negligent renters. At the same time, these rights can make it difficult to evict a problematic tenant who has stopped paying rent. Prior to purchasing a house with the intent to rent, you can inquire into the local history of tenants' rights issues. Should they arise, such issues could lead to pricey legal battles to evict a tenant or receive payment for damages to the property. If the renter damages the property in an amount greater than the security deposit, this could lead to costly litigation to recover repair costs—often leading the landlord to pay for the repairs out-of-pocket. Even with the best of tenants, once a family leaves the rental property, the landlord needs to invest time and money to prepare the house for new renters or for sale. This could be expensive, depending on how responsibly or irresponsibly the previous tenants lived in the house.

6

Purchasing an Automobile

Most people in the United States consider an automobile a necessity. An individual's automobile is most likely one of the largest purchases he or she will ever make. Transportation expenses are second only to housing in most household budgets; therefore, making a wise decision when buying a car is critical to sound financial planning. The Internet has revolutionized the car buying experience. Consumers never before had access to as much information as they have today. The following sites are a great place to start when researching an automobile purchase: Kelley Blue Book (http://kbb.com), USAA.com, Edmunds.com, and Autobytel.com.

This chapter offers practical advice and identifies helpful references for your quest for an automobile, whether new, used, or leased. It will help you negotiate the maze of automobile decisions and devise a systematic plan to guide you through various automobile purchase choices. If you use the information in this chapter, you will be an informed consumer who is more likely to get a good deal on an automobile that meets your transportation requirements and financial goals.

Every decision you make in buying a new car will affect the amount you ultimately pay. Selecting options, negotiating the purchase price, determining the trade-in value, and financing and insuring your new car are all decisions you must understand to get the best deal for your circumstances. Therefore, take the time to systematically identify which amenities are important—and do some homework before visiting car dealerships.

DETERMINING HOW MUCH YOU CAN AFFORD
It is very important to begin your car-buying process with a solid idea of how much you are willing to spend each month for transportation. Car payments are only a portion of the total monthly cost of driving a car. Insurance and operating expenses, such as fuel and maintenance, add to the total cost of the vehicle. A good rule of thumb is to spend no more than 15% of your pretax income on transportation. To estimate your monthly transportation expenses, you must make estimates for the various expenses associated with automobile ownership. The first step is to determine the amount of your monthly budget to allot for transportation expenses. Your household budget (see chapter 1) is

a useful tool to assess how spending on transportation affects your budget and savings plan.

> *Spend no more than 15% of your pretax income for transportation.*

GATHERING COST INFORMATION
Payments
Automobile payments are usually the largest outlay in most transportation budgets. Table 6-1 shows the monthly payments per $1,000 financed at various interest rates for twenty-four, thirty-six, forty-eight, and sixty months. To use this table: (1) determine the amount you plan to finance after making a down payment; (2) select a payment period shorter than the time you expect to own the automobile; and (3) select the interest rate corresponding to what banks or credit unions offer for car loans. In each column, the amount below the interest rate will be very close to your monthly payments per $1,000 financed. Multiply this number by the amount, in thousands of dollars, you plan to finance. This will give you a close estimate of your monthly automobile payment. For example, financing a $20,000 automobile purchase for four years at a 8% interest rate (assuming no down payment) would result in a monthly payment of approximately $488 (20 × 24.41 = $488.20).

Your monthly payment consists of two components: principal and interest. The principal portion of the payment is really paying for the car; the interest portion is paying for the loan. This process of repaying the loan is known as amortizing the loan. Table 6-2 illustrates the monthly principal and interest payments for a four-year, $25,000 loan at 8%. Online resources such as Bankrate.com will create a loan payment or amortization table that reflects principal and interest payments for each month, to help a prospective buyer

---

TABLE 6-1
MONTHLY AUTO LOAN PAYMENTS (PER $1,000)

Length	Rate of Loan								
	4%	5%	6%	7%	8%	9%	10%	11%	12%
24 months	$43.42	$43.87	$44.32	$44.77	$45.22	$45.68	$46.14	$46.61	$47.07
36 months	$29.52	$29.97	$30.42	$30.88	$31.34	$31.80	$32.27	$32.74	$33.21
48 months	$22.58	$23.03	$23.49	$23.95	$24.41	$24.89	$25.36	$25.85	$26.33
60 months	$18.42	$18.87	$19.33	$19.80	$20.28	$20.76	$21.25	$21.74	$22.24

TABLE 6-2
AMORTIZATION TABLE FOR $25,000 BORROWED AT 8%

Year of Loan	Total Interest Payments	Percentage of Payment to Interest	Total Principal Payment	Principal Remaining on the loan	Total Loan Payments for 12 months
1	$1,800	25%	$5,523	$19,476	$7,324
2	$1,342	18%	$5,982	$13,495	$7,324
3	$845	12%	$6,478	$7,016	$7,324
4	$308	4%	$7,016	$-	$7,324
Total	$4,296		$25,000		$29,295

better understand payments. The important piece to remember is that initially a higher percentage of your monthly payment goes towards interest. For the $25,000 loan, after one year, the buyer will have paid 25% of his payments towards interest and only 75% towards principal. Therefore, if the buyer sells the car any time before the full 48 months, he will have paid a higher interest rate than 8%. Table 6-2 shows the percentage of the loan payment applied to interest for each year of the loan.

If you plan to finance your car purchase, it is crucial to thoroughly compare your options for the best financing terms. The final amount paid over the life of the loan is the amount you want to minimize. There are several online sources that will help a prospective buyer compare interest rates on auto loans. Bankrate.com and Edmunds.com offer auto loan calculators so consumers can compare different financing options. For example, it is in the dealer's best interest to negotiate the whole purchase of the car to include trade-in, financing, and the vehicle, all at one time. However, it is generally in the consumer's best interest to keep each of those as a separate negotiation. Therefore, compare the different options for financing before going to a dealership.

Insurance
Insurance costs vary significantly depending on several factors. You must consider these costs when deciding which car to buy. An insurance company will gladly provide quotes on two or three models you are considering, enabling an accurate estimate of total monthly transportation expenses. The USAA Foundation publishes (at no charge) *The Car Guide* at USAA.com, which compares the safety features of most models; other companies provide similar information. These guides help identify automobiles that have desirable insurance characteristics such as passenger safety in accidents, less damage in accidents, and lower theft rates. *Consumer Reports* (http://www.consumer reports.org) also publishes two annual buying guides, the *New Car Buying*

Guide and the *Used Car Buying Guide,* which review reliability records and safety test reports. A prospective buyer should be aware that most lenders require full coverage (collision and liability) on cars that they finance. Chapter 14 explains in more detail the various types of automobile insurance and coverage guidelines.

> *Your insurance company will gladly give you quotes on the two or three models you are considering so that you can accurately estimate your total monthly transportation expenses.*

Total Transportation Costs

It is important to take into account the total costs of transportation, beyond just monthly car loan and insurance payments. Many car websites such as Edmunds.com offer a "True Costs to Own" calculator that—based upon the selected region—estimates maintenance and repairs, depreciation, loan interest, taxes and fees, and operating (fuel) expenses. This data helps you compare different makes and models of potential vehicle purchases and remain within your transportation budget.

Operation. Operating expenses consist primarily of money spent on fuel. The typical automobile owner in the United States drives 1,000 miles each month. Calculate your estimated operating expenses by dividing the number of miles you expect to drive by the miles per gallon (MPG) rating of the selected automobile. This gives the number of gallons of fuel used each month. Multiply the number of gallons per month by the price per gallon to estimate monthly operating expenses. For example, for 1,000 miles per month, at twenty-five MPG and $4.00 per gallon, the monthly operating expenses would be $160 ([1,000 miles / 25 MPG] × $4.00 = $160).

Other annual costs for most car owners are the annual vehicle registration and inspection fees. Many states require an annual automobile emissions inspection in order to issue a valid vehicle registration for that year. Costs vary widely between states; vehicle registration can range from $50 to over $200.

Maintenance and Repairs. Maintenance expenses include the cost of scheduled maintenance, such as fluid changes, as well as replacing worn out and damaged parts. Maintenance costs vary, depending on the items covered under warranty or through coverage bought under a separate maintenance contract. See the "True Costs to Own" calculator for each model considered to compare the costs per year for maintenance. For the first several years, monthly maintenance costs for a new car should be relatively low. Annual maintenance costs during the fifth year, however, may rise quickly, possibly tripling those in the first year.

TABLE 6-3
DEPRECIATION SCHEDULE

Automobile Age	Value	% Change	Depreciation
New	$25,000		
Moment you leave the lot	$22,250	11%	$2,750
One year old	$18,913	15%	$3,338
Two years old	$16,076	15%	$2,837
Three years old	$13,664	15%	$2,411
Four years old	$11,615	15%	$2,050
Five years old	$9,872	15%	$1,742
Total depreciation (years 0-5)			$15,128
Remaining depreciation (years 6-?)			$9,872

After five years, the car is worth 39% of the original price.

Depreciation. Depreciation is how much resale value a car loses each year. It represents the decrease in the value of an automobile due to time and use. Many automobile owners ignore depreciation because they do not write a monthly check to pay for it, yet it is one of the largest expenses of automobile ownership. "True Costs to Own" calculators provide an expected depreciation schedule for five years for each model under consideration. The reduced amount of depreciation for used vehicles versus new vehicles should be a significant consideration in making a purchase decision. Table 6-3 provides one example of a typical depreciation schedule. It shows that the average $25,000 automobile depreciates more than 60% in five years. For example, the owner could sell the car for $13,664 after three years, but after four years he could sell it for only $11,615. In essence, the owner has paid $2,050 to use the car during that year. Notice that with depreciation the one-year-old car is worth $18,913; however, according to Table 6-2, the buyer would still owe approximately $19,476 principal on the loan. If he were to have an accident or decide to trade in the car for a new one, he would owe more to the bank than the insurance payoff or trade-in value. This is referred to as being "upside down" on a loan.

Depreciation varies considerably across makes and models. New automobiles depreciate much faster than used automobiles; thus, depreciation expenses decrease as automobiles get older. Generally, automobiles lose about 11% when driven off the lot and approximately 15% of the remaining value each year. Models with excellent maintenance and resale records generally hold their value better than average cars. The Kelley Blue Book (http://www. kbb.com) and the NADA Official Used Car Guide at (http://www.nada

guides.com) are good sources for determining depreciation, providing average resale values by model, make, condition of the vehicle, year, and location. The Kelley Blue Book is more liberal in its quotes; therefore, most dealers will utilize the NADA Used Car Guide when determining the value of a trade-in vehicle. A way to gain additional leverage when trading in a vehicle is to get an offer from a used car buying service such as CarMax.com or AutoTrader.com. These and similar companies provide offers to purchase your car, following a short inspection, for a guaranteed price that is generally valid for seven days. Armed with this reservation price, you can negotiate up from this price with the dealership, or—if the dealership does not meet or exceed this amount—sell your car in a separate transaction to the buying service.

An often-overlooked aspect of depreciation concerns the time during the model year when you buy a new car. An automobile bought late in a model year depreciates much more rapidly than the same automobile bought early in that model year. Dealers will typically offer sizable discounts on "old" models to make room for the new models on their lots. You should keep this point in mind, especially if are considering buying last year's model after new car models have been introduced. If you plan to own the car for the entire length of the loan, then buying at the end of the model year may be a wise decision. However, if you plan to sell or trade in the car within a couple of years, then you should keep the effects of depreciation on the value of your car in mind.

TOTAL EXPENSES
After allocating your transportation budget and examining the true cost of owning a car, you can can now calculate (or estimate) the price of a car that you can afford. For example, assume the buyer's monthly transportation budget is $450, based on 15% of a $3,000 pretax income (0.15 × $3,000 = $450); he has about $2,500 for initial costs, and can finance his car at a 8% interest rate for forty-eight months. He has made the following expense estimates for the model he is considering:

Transportation budget	$ 450
Less insurance	– $ 100
Less operation	– $ 160
Less maintenance	– $ 20
Maximum payment	$ 170

This leaves the prospective buyer $170 per month for automobile payments. From Table 6-1, you can see that it costs $24.41 for each $1,000 financed over a forty-eight-month period at 8%. Hence, the buyer can afford to finance about $6,964 ([$170 / $24.41] × $1,000 = $6,964.36).

Initial costs include the down payment and the tax, title, and registration, which average about $1,000. You can estimate these costs more accurately by visiting Edmunds.com and looking up costs in your area for the vehicle that you are about to purchase. Be sure to ask the dealer if military members receive relief from any fees or taxes, as is the case in many locales.

Thus, subtracting $1,000 from the buyer's available $2,500 leaves him $1,500 to make a down payment. The buyer could afford a car that retails for about $8,464 ($6,964 + $1,500). His actual expenses will obviously vary from this example; however, it is clear that a $450-a-month transportation budget will not finance a new $30,000 car. Buyers should be realistic about how far a limited transportation budget will take them.

DETERMINING WHETHER OR NOT TO BUY A USED CAR

In most cases, new cars are much more expensive to own and operate than used cars (when accounting for all costs discussed above). Buying a used car may be more affordable or allow you to set aside more money for your savings plan. Often, a good bet is to buy a used car that is one or two years old. In this case the bulk of the depreciation has already occurred, yet the car's mileage (and subsequent wear and tear on the car) is relatively low. Previously leased cars with low mileage are often good candidates for purchase. These cars may also attract buyers who prefer up-to-date models and styling but cannot afford the latest models.

There are basic expense trade-offs between new and used cars. Depreciation and insurance are more expensive for newer cars; maintenance is more expensive for older, higher-mileage cars. Consider your maintenance aptitude and tolerance for car trouble when making this decision. Since most consumers' individual car needs vary greatly, it is best to look at the "True Costs to Own" on a website such as Edmunds.com to compare the costs of operating a new car and a used car. Table 6-4 illustrates these trade-offs for a 2010 Toyota Camry.

SELECTING THE RIGHT METHOD TO FINANCE YOUR VEHICLE

Once you have decided how much you can afford and whether to purchase a new or used car, the next decision is how to finance the purchase. Most servicemembers have three choices: self-financing (paying cash), borrowing (getting a loan), or leasing. The choice will depend primarily on the buyer's personal financial situation.

You should research financing arrangements before beginning to car shop. Arranging financing in advance serves three purposes. First, you know the price range that fits your transportation budget. Second, it gives you more leverage when negotiating with a dealer. Third, you can recognize a good deal if the dealer offers one.

TABLE 6-4
TRUE COST TO OWN A 2010 TOYOTA CAMRY (4D, 2.5 CYL)

Summary:

True Cost To Own	$35,583
Total Cash Price	$20,636

5 Year Details

	Year 1	Year 2	Year 3	Year 4	Year 5	5-Year Total
Depreciation*	$4,664	$1,831	$1,611	$1,428	$1,281	$10,815
Taxes & Fees*	$1,607	$62	$64	$64	$54	$1,851
Financing**	$1,107	$888	$656	$409	$148	$3,208
Fuel*	$1,696	$1,747	$1,800	$1,854	$1,909	$9,006
Insurance*	$1,335	$1,382	$1,430	$1,480	$1,532	$7,159
Maintenance*	$29	$363	$397	$712	$1,372	$2,873
Repairs*	$0	$0	$97	$234	$340	$671
Tax Credit	$0					$0
True Cost to Own (r)	$10,438	$6,273	$6,055	$6,181	$6,636	$35,583

* Based on the Fort Hood zip code
** Financing is at 6% for a 60 month loan
Source: www.edmunds.com/tco.html

Self-Financing
Even if you plan to pay cash for the car, there is still a financing cost to consider. This financing cost is the opportunity cost of foregone interest. By purchasing the car, you are giving up any interest the money would have earned while deposited in a bank. For example, if the cash (purchase price) was in an investment account earning a 7.5% return and the buyer's marginal tax rate is 15%, his opportunity cost (financing cost) is 6.375% (calculated as 0.075 × [1 - 0.15]). Self-financing is preferable if you have the available cash and if it is difficult to get a consumer loan at a lower rate of interest than the opportunity cost of your investments. Today, many consumers cannot self-finance— or will not because of very attractive interest rates for automobile purchases.

Car Loans
Many Americans borrow money to pay for their cars. As discussed in chapter 3, car loans are a good use of credit since buyers repay the debt as they use the asset. Having estimated the amount you will borrow, you must decide the source and duration of the loan. Your decisions in each of these areas will

affect your credit costs, both the total interest you will pay and the amount of your monthly payments. Financing sources often have loan terms that obscure the actual cost of borrowing money. By law, all lenders must provide borrowers with a rate of interest based on a standardized calculation. This rate of interest is the annual percentage rate (APR). The APR is the most useful method of comparing the cost of different loans.

The two primary sources for borrowing money are dealer financing and third-party loans. Dealer financing is when the car manufacturer lends the buyer money to buy its car. Car dealers often advertise below-market-interest-rate loans or cash-back rebates to attract customers to their products. Timing is often a factor in these promotions. At the end of a model year, dealerships must move the old inventory to make room for the new models. During economic downturns, some automobile manufacturers have offered 0% financing and $0 down payment. Dealer financing can be a good deal, but check online with bankrate.com or another loan broker website to find the lowest available interest rate. BankRate.com also offers a calculator to compare the value of a cash-back rebate from the dealer against varying interest rate options, including those through third party lenders. Be aware that dealers are often less willing to negotiate prices when they offer attractive financing.

A third-party loan is money borrowed from a bank or credit union to buy a vehicle. These institutions are potentially excellent sources to secure automobile financing from. First, banks and credit unions earn customer loyalty by providing competitive services (including loans) and excellent customer service. Car loans are one of their primary businesses, and they want to maintain good relationships with their customers and potential depositors. Second, they are more likely to explain your credit options in detail. Finally, they can provide you with detailed value estimates (wholesale and retail) for both used cars and new cars that you plan to buy. A prospective car buyer should apply to the bank or credit union for a loan at least seven days before begining to shop for the automobile. This allows adequate time to process the loan application and will ensure the approval is ready when needed.

Loans are also available through online institutions. While these institutions often provide attractive options, they can sometimes have hidden costs. For example, an online loan service may distribute credit information to as many lending institutions as possible to solicit the best available rates. This may allow the lending institution to offer very low rates; however, this may also lower the buyer's credit score and put the buyer at greater risk of identity theft. The Internet is a good option, but be sure to use reputable sites. Some suggestions are www.eloan.com and www.USAA.com.

Another alternative for homeowners to finance a vehicle purchase is to use a home equity line of credit. Homeowners who have enough equity in their homes can borrow against their equity rather than taking out third-party loans or using dealer financing. The advantage of this financing option is that the interest on this loan may be tax deductible.

TABLE 6-5
FINANCING UNDER VARIOUS LOAN TERMS

Loan Duration	36 Months 8%	48 Months 10%	60 Months 12%
Monthly payments	$313	$254	$222
Total principal payments	$10,000	$10,000	$10,000
Total interest payments	$1,281	$2,174	$3,347
Total payment to bank	$11,281	$12,174	$13,347

After the decision of how to finance the vehicle purchase, the next major decision is the term, or duration, of the loan. Most lending institutions finance new cars for up to seventy-two months. Most lenders finance used cars for thirty-six months and occasionally for forty-eight or more months. The trade-off is clear: Longer-term loans have lower monthly payments, but the buyer ultimately pays more in interest. Shorter-term loans have higher monthly payments, but the buyer repays the loan faster and pays less in interest. This decision depends on available interest rates and the opportunity costs associated with alternative uses of available money.

Consider the following example. A prospective car buyer wants to borrow $10,000 to purchase a new car. The best available offer is a bank with the following loan schedules: thirty six months at 8%, forty-eight months at 10%, or sixty months at 12%. Table 6-5 shows the buyer's payments under these terms.

As you can see in Table 6-5, the longer-duration loans have smaller monthly payments. But the borrower pays the bank more interest for extending the loan term from thirty-six to sixty months.

You should also consider the value of the car relative to the amount borrowed when choosing your loan duration. The longer the loan period, the slower the loan is amortized (repaid). Because automobiles depreciate very rapidly when they are new, cars may depreciate faster than a long-term loan is amortized. As a result, it is possible for you to receive less on a trade-in (or from insurance if your car is stolen or destroyed) than the outstanding balance on the loan. In the finance business this is called being "upside down" or "financially inverted."

For example, assume our prospective buyer borrows $10,000 for forty-eight months at 10% interest to buy an automobile, but he has a wreck after one year and the car is totaled. On average, the car would have been worth $7,500 after one year, and he could expect the insurance company to pay that amount. However, the principal balance on the loan would be $7,830.18, so the buyer would have to write the bank a check for $330.18 to clear the loan. If the buyer had financed the car for thirty-six months, the remaining principal would have been $6,992.57. In this case the check from the insurance company would fully cover the loan and allow the buyer to apply $507.43 towards a new car. The lesson here is that shorter-term loans not only cost less in interest, but they also reduce the risk of the asset's value falling below the loan principal. You should be as diligent in shopping for financing as you are in your actual automobile shopping. If you ignore financing alternatives, you can easily squander the money you saved through careful research of dealer cost information and skillful negotiations.

LEASING

Leasing is another popular way for buyers to finance automobiles and for dealers to move inventory. Leasing can be an attractive option to some because it allows the lessee to "drive more car for the money." Leasing is similar to renting a car on a long-term basis with an extensive legal contract. The monthly lease price includes the depreciation over the life of the lease (the value the car will lose during the period of the lease [initial value minus value at end of the lease]) and a rental charge that is built into the finance charges. As a a result, a lessee may pay lower monthly payments than a buyer would pay for a loan on the same car. The disadvantage of leasing, despite the lower monthly payment, is that at the end of the contract, the lessee owns nothing.

Car manufacturers have marketed leases aggressively since the 1990s, when cars became prohibitively expensive for many consumers. Leases are lengthy legal contracts that contain many hidden costs (or "fine print"). Some of these costs may include a "capital reduction payment," sales tax, a security deposit equal to the first and last month payments, and an "acquisition fee" that may range from $250 to $700. The lessee must also pay other tax, title, and registration fees, either up front or incorporated into the monthly payments. Prospective lessees must protect themselves by reading the fine print. You should understand all associated expenses, including additional insurance requirements, before signing a leasing agreement.

Leasing an automobile is a sound financial choice for some people. Whether or not you are a good lease candidate depends on your car preferences, personal driving habits, and financial situation. A good lease candidate is someone who fits the following profile:
- Can afford to drive a new car every two to four years.
- Drives less than 12,000 miles per year.
- Wants a smaller monthly payment.
- Takes good care of the car.
- Wants to drive a more expensive car than he or she could afford to buy.

Most lease contracts are closed-ended, meaning that the lessee returns the automobile to the leasing company at the end of the lease period and has no responsibilities other than making the monthly payment, performing scheduled maintenance, and maintaining the required level of insurance. At vehicle turn-in, the leasing company accepts normal wear and tear, but charges the lessee for excess mileage and more substantial wear and tear (e.g., scratched or pitted paint or small dents on the vehicle). One should understand explicitly what "normal wear and tear" is before signing a lease. Dealers often allow lessees to avoid the penalties associated with excess wear if the lessee signs a new lease on another vehicle at the end of the old lease's term. Most leases stipulate the maximum number of miles the lessor allows the lessee to drive during the lease period; this is usually between 10,000 and 15,000 miles. If the lessee exceeds the agreed-upon limit, she must pay a penalty of perhaps 15-30 cents per mile. Additionally, this could also mean that the lessee is in violation of the normal wear and tear clause. When considering a lease, one should ask the lessor what happens if the servicemember deploys, moves to another state, or PCSs overseas. The Servicemembers Civil Relief Act (SCRA) allows servicemembers to terminate a lease early without paying the early termination fee, if any of the following circumstances are met *and* if the lease is in the name of the servicemember or a dependent:

1. Activated reservist or guardsman for more than 180 days.
2. Deployed for 180 days with a military unit.
3. PCS overseas, including Alaska and Hawaii.

The dealer should receive a written termination request with military orders fifteen days prior to the desired termination date.

Leasing Resources

FindLaw: http://library.findlaw.com/1992/Feb/1/130101.html.
Servicemembers Civil Relief Act: www.justicc.gov/usao/az/rights/
    Servicemembers_Civil_Relief_Act.pdf
Federal Reserve Board: www.federalreserve.gov/pubs/leasing/

GETTING THE BEST DEAL
You can purchase a vehicle from several sources: from a dealership, directly from the factory, through a buying service, or from a private party.

Buying from a Dealer
You have to do your homework if you plan to buy from an automobile dealer. You must know exactly what model and options you want. Research the dealer cost for both the base price of the model and the options desired. Have an approved financing plan. You should shop around and get quotes from several dealers in order to negotiate the best possible deal. You can find the dealers' invoice prices online. Do not think that a dealer will not make money if you

buy the car for the invoice price; dealers do not stay in business by making losses. Dealers often receive manufacturer incentives (payments from the manufacturer for cars they sell). These dealer incentive programs can also be found online, and an astute buyer can use this knowledge to his or her benefit during negotiations. You can sometimes find these incentives on the manufacturers' websites or via other consumer sources such as How Stuff Works (http://consumerguideauto.howstuffworks.com).

There are several advantages to buying from a dealer rather than ordering the car directly from the factory. First, you can get a car immediately, or very quickly, from a dealer. If a dealer does not have your desired car on the lot, most will execute a dealer trade within a few days. Second, you can see and thoroughly inspect the actual vehicle before purchasing. Third, dealers are generally more responsive to the maintenance concerns of their sales customers.

There are also some disadvantages to buying from a dealer. First, a dealer's available stock often includes vehicles with undesired, costly options. Second, dealers want to sell from their existing inventory, so you must know your maximum price before starting negotiations.

You can also factory-order a new car through a dealer. Dealers prefer to sell cars off of their lots because they own the vehicles and can use the proceeds to purchase more inventory. By ordering a new car directly from the manufacturer, through a dealer, you get and pay for exactly what you want. However, you have a limited ability to negotiate, must wait generally for four to six weeks for delivery, and cannot inspect the car before purchasing it.

Negotiation with a Dealer
From the moment you enter a dealership, you undergo a battle of wits with the dealer, with several stages of negotiations. Negotiating with a car dealer is an art form. You must realize that successful car dealers are skilled negotiators. Your willingness to engage in negotiation depends upon your personality type. There are numerous books and guides available to help buyers develop a negotiating plan. Additionally, buyers have other available tools to improve their position before beginning the negotiation.

Timing, for example, is a significant indirect negotiating tool. There are times when dealers will accept less profitable offers. Dealers typically have monthly and quarterly sales targets and frequently have bonuses tied to these targets. Dealers are more likely to accept offers more favorable to the buyer towards the end of these target periods, especially if they have not met their goals. Dealers also make deals when business is slow; it is often better to shop in the middle of the week than on weekends. Also, some dealers provide salespeople with a bonus for making the first sale on a weekend, so Saturday morning may be a good time to deal as well. Weather also affects sales; prospective buyers may get better deals during periods of rain or snow. The winter holiday season is also a time when dealers make deals, because people use spending money on other things at this time, and dealerships want to cut year-end inventory for tax purposes. Dealerships often make buyer-friendly deals during the summer as they try to make room for the new models that arrive in the fall.

To maximize your likelihood of garnering the best deal, you should consider using a pricing or buying service (discussed below) to determine the actual dealer cost of the car you want and to get a price quote. If a dealer cannot beat the buying service price, you may not be getting the best deal from the dealer.

Many car dealerships are honest businesses; however, you must beware of the unethical dealers. Understand that you are dealing with experienced professionals who are adept at turning a buyer's money into dealer profit. Some dealerships train their sales representatives to "pass you off" to another representative or the sales manager if they cannot make the sale. A prospective buyer initially negotiates with a salesperson who tries to get the buyer into the closing room. There, the closer, whose specialty is writing sales contracts, finalizes the deal. Sometimes the closer intentionally manipulates the cost, trade-in, down payment, and financing numbers to confuse the customer. Customer confusion can equal dealer profit. Once the purchase order is written, the closer tries to add unnecessary, high-profit options—fabric protection, rust proofing, floor mats, dealer warranties, and even insurance. The closer must then present the purchase order to the sales manager for approval and signature. Passing the buyer off from person to person reduces the buyer's resistance to buying and creates confusion. Each person in the process tries to sell the buyer additional options that he or she does not want, change the terms of the deal, and get more money for the dealership. Remember, these professionals have closed hundreds of sales transactions.

The following are some general guidelines for the purchase of a vehicle with a dealer:

- Know what model and options you want.
- Have financing prearranged/preapproved before going to a dealer's lot with the intention of buying.
- Signal to the dealer that you are a serious buyer and ready to buy a car if the deal is right. You can say to the dealer, "I will buy a car today if you have the car and deal I want."
- Convince the dealer that you have done your homework. Tell the dealer, "I have researched your costs for this car, and I know what your manufacturer's incentives are." Then ask the salesman, "How much are you willing to sell me the car for?" When you confront a dealer with cost information, the dealer will often try to tell you that your information is outdated or incorrect. Do not allow a dealer to convince you that you are wrong. Your cost estimate will be very close. The dealer will also avoid quoting you a price, as an opening price creates an anchor in negotiations. You can negotiate aggressively with the dealer if you have a quote from the buying service to serve as a fallback option.

> *Keep the four major parts of the automobile purchase transaction separate. It is too confusing to discuss a trade-in, down payment, and financing while trying to negotiate the purchase price of a new car. Make each an independent transaction: first negotiate price, then trade-in, and finally the down payment and financing. Tell the salesman, "We can discuss my trade-in and financing when we have agreed on the total sale price."*

- You must be prepared to walk away if not given what you want. Tell the dealer, "I think I can get a better deal by shopping around," and walk out. Dealers hate to hear those words. Record the terms of the deal offered on the back of the dealer's business card.
- After negotiating a satisfactory deal, do not allow the salesperson or another dealer representative to reopen negotiations.
- Make sure that the purchase contract or sales order lists the exact car and options agreed upon, and that it stipulates the dealer will not substitute dealer-installed equipment for factory-installed options.
- Factory orders should stipulate in the contract that the order is contingent on an agreed upon delivery schedule (i.e., within four to six weeks).
- Do not sign a purchase order or sales contract that has blank spaces. Write "n/a" in blank spaces before signing.
- You should not sign a sales contract or purchase agreement without reading every word. Further, you should question any points you don't understand; remember that a buyer's confusion usually means more dealer profit.
- Make sure that the sales manager or an officer of the dealership signs the purchase order or sales contract. Many dealerships will not honor a contract signed only by a sales representative.
- Domestic cars include dealer preparation charges in the basic list price. Dealer preparation charges for imported cars are separate from the list price. Make sure that the purchase order or sales contract is clear on whether there is a separate charge for dealer preparation. Watch out for extra dealer preparation charges and for unwanted dealer-installed options. Dealers sometimes charge customers for dealer preparations that they did not perform, or attempt to add high-profit, dealer-installed options to purchase orders or sales contracts.
- Make sure the purchase order or sales contract records your deposit. The contract should have a stipulation that the deposit is refundable if the dealership does not meet the terms of the contract.
- Make sure the purchase order or sales contract records a trade-in value, if applicable.

- You must ensure that the purchase order or sales contract contains in writing all verbal promises made by the dealership.

Using an Automobile Pricing or Buying Service

If you find the process of buying a new car difficult, expensive, and frustrating, you may consider using a buying service in order to reduce the time and energy you spend searching for a car—and to possibly save money. Buying services allow prospective buyers to order the exact car they want. Depending on the type of buying service, a prospective buyer pays either a predetermined fee or a percentage of the savings for the service. Some buying services are USAA.com, Edmunds.com, Autobytel.com, Sam's Club, or COSTCO. Table 6-6 highlights the potential savings buyers can gain by using the USAA car buying service to purchase a new car. The result in this example is that a prospective buyer saves over $1,880.

TABLE 6-6
COSTS OF USING A CAR BUYING SERVICE

	INVOICE	MSRP	USAA PRICE
Base	$16,945	$17,275	$16,145
Options	$0	$0	$0
Incentives	$0	$0	($750)
TOTAL	$16,945	$17,275	$15,395
Savings off MSRP:	$1,880		

Available from http://usaa.zag.com/configurator.html

Auto pricing services have become increasingly popular as their costs have decreased. Most auto pricing services provide detailed cost information on particular models, usually for less than $10 per model. Normally it takes two to four weeks to process your specific vehicle request. Also, auto pricing services may offer to buy the desired car for you and have it delivered to a local participating dealer. The USAA Auto Pricing/Buying Service provides both services, offering savings below the dealer MSRP on popular models. USAA also provides vehicle invoice prices at dealerships in your local area. Some other car buying services serve as car concierges who use a national directory of new or used cars to find the car the buyer desires (e.g., AutoNation Direct.com).

Buying from a private party

Although this option can lead to savings by a buyer and more money in the seller's pocket (the middleman is no longer taking a large cut), it can also lead to a deal that leaves one party very unhappy (usually the buyer). A prospective buyer who finds a vehicle for purchase through a private party must be careful to confirm the history of the car. It is possible to find great deals from individuals who rarely used a car, maintained and serviced it, and protected its exterior and interior; however, it is also possible that you may get stuck with a lemon (a car with mechanical or workmanship flaws). The issue is that the seller has more information about the car than the buyer (asymmetric information). Since the seller establishes the initial price point, he or she can signal (sometimes falsely) the quality of the car through its offering price. To counteract this advantage of sellers, you should take any car you are interested in purchasing to a reputable mechanic for a complete mechanical assessment of the vehicle's condition. Another option is to take the car to a used car evaluation/assessment/sales service such as CarMax.com or AutoNationDirect.com and have them provide an assessment of the car's value. Additionally, prospective buyers should review the selling prices for the make and model of car they selected on car buying guide sites such as Kelley Blue Book and Edmunds (both discussed earlier in the chapter). Taking these steps will increase the likelihood that a purchase from a private party will result in a favorable result for both the buyer and the seller.

7

Money for Education

This chapter is for servicemembers (veterans, reservists, or active duty) who are saving for their own, their spouses', or their children's education(s).

Money for higher education is one of the greatest financial concerns of American families today. The cost of higher education has increased greatly, and beyond the pace of inflation, for over a decade. This trend is likely to continue. Education is an investment in human capital; therefore, when considering education you should follow similar investment planning principles as you would when saving for a house or retirement. You should first determine your long-term goals, which requires asking how education fits into your priorities. Second, you should determine the expected cost of education (including tuition, fees, books, and living expenses). Families should decide for themselves, based on their individual means and life goals, who—the child or the parents—in the family should bear the cost of education expenses. Third, veterans, reservists, and active-duty servicemembers should determine the eligible benefits available that can reduce the overall costs of higher education. Some of these opportunities include:

- The Post-9/11 GI Bill or the Montgomery GI Bill
- Financial aid
- Tuition assistance
- Tuition reimbursement
- Scholarships

Finally, with this information, you can determine the best financial plan that, through savings and investments, will meet your family's education needs. The sooner you start to execute a college saving plan, the better. This chapter begins by estimating the total cost of a college education. Then, the chapter explores various opportunities that exist to help families reduce that expense. The chapter concludes with financial planning advice for covering the remaining expected costs after obtaining possible financial assistance.

THE COST OF A COLLEGE EDUCATION
College is expensive, and costs continue to rise at about twice the rate of inflation. The components of the total cost of higher education include tuition and

fees, books and supplies, room and board, transportation, and other personal expenses. The College Board, a nonprofit organization that connects students to college opportunities, conducts annual trend analyses of college pricing and tuition inflation rates and posts them on the Internet at http://trends.college board.org (see Table 7-1 for an extract of the 2010 data).

Using data collected over the last few years, the College Board identified an average annual increase in college tuition, fees, and room and board of 4.3%, 6.1%, and 5.6% for private nonprofit, public (for in-state students), and public (for out-of-state students) colleges, respectively. Of these overall average cost increases, tuition and fees rose 4.5%, 7.9%, and 6.0% for private, public in-state, and public out-of-state schools, respectively. Looking at only projected tuition and fee increases over the next seventeen years (the least amount of time required to save for a newborn to go to college), the average cost for a student to attend a private college, an in-state public school, or out-of-state public university for four years will be over $246,000, $124,000, and $230,000 respectively. Other college expenses (such as room and board) historically increase at lower rates than tuition and fees. While the rate of increase for college incidentals may change, they do generally follow an upward trend.

You can make specific calculations, based on the schools you are considering attending, by using a college cost calculator (for example, FinAid [http://www.finaid.org/calculators/costprojector.phtml]). For the calculator, use the current annual cost found on the website of the college that you or your family member is interested in attending. Harvard serves as a good demonstration of how expensive college can be for a family: In 2010, tuition and fees were $40,279 and room and board were $12,308 at Harvard, for a total annual expense of $52,587. Compounded at 4.3% (using the College Board's estimated rate of total college cost annual increase), that same education will cost $458,858 for four years starting in 2027 (seventeen years from 2010). Using the calculations presented in chapter 1, you can estimate the required lump-sum savings or monthly contributions necessary to meet a fam-

TABLE 7-1
AVERAGE ESTIMATED UNDERGRADUATE EXPENSES, 2010–11
(ANNUAL ON-CAMPUS LIVING)

Type of Institution	Tuition and Fees	Estimated Total Cost
Private (Nonprofit)	$27,293	$40,476
Public (In-state tuition and housing rates)	$7,605	$20,339
Public (Out-of-state tuition and housing rates)	$19,595	$32,329

ily's college savings plan goals. For instance, if parents who want to send their newborn to Harvard in seventeen years have not yet begun their college savings and expect to earn a 3% rate of return on their savings, they would need to set aside $301,559 today! Alternately, they would have to allot almost $1728 per month for seventeen years to save enough to pay for this education. Remember that is the cost for one child to attend a high-cost private university; imagine how much the family would have to save if multiple family members wanted to attend similarly priced schools. The goal of an education savings and investment plan is to maintain a level of return that outpaces the rate of increase of education costs. Due to the risks involved, you do not want to gamble with your future education needs, so you should seek financial planning advice.

FINANCIAL ASSISTANCE OPPORTUNITIES

Now, the *good* news: As a veteran, reservist, or active-duty servicemember, you have a plethora of military-sponsored services and opportunities available to promote and finance higher education for you and your dependents. Additionally, U.S. citizens may be eligible for numerous other government and private programs that help finance higher education. All families should explore these options.

The armed forces highly encourage the continuing education of servicemembers and their dependents through a number of programs. A few of these programs deserve specific attention.

U.S. Department of Veterans Affairs (DVA) programs

Post-9/11 GI Bill. The Post-9/11 GI Bill provides financial support for education and housing to individuals with at least ninety days of aggregate service on or after September 11, 2001, or individuals discharged with a service-connected disability after thirty days. One must have received an honorable discharge to be eligible for the Post-9/11 GI Bill. The Post-9/11 GI Bill became effective August 1, 2009. Congress changes or updates benefits every year, so individuals should check online for recent changes before they plan to use the benefits. Approved training under the Post-9/11 GI Bill includes graduate and undergraduate degrees, vocational and technical training, on-the-job training, flight training, correspondence training, licensing and national testing programs, entrepreneurship training, and tutorial assistance. All training programs must be approved for GI Bill benefits. The Post-9/11 GI Bill will pay tuition based upon the highest in-state tuition charged by a public educational institution in the state where the school is located. The amount of support that an individual may qualify for depends on where they live and what type of degree they are pursuing. This Post 9-11 GI Bill will pay eligible individuals:

- Tuition and fees directly to the school for all public school in-state tuition rates, and an amount not to exceed $17,500 for private and foreign schools (for exceptions, see the GI Bill website [http://gibill.

va.gov]). For more expensive tuition at participating private institutions, a program exists that may offset the additional expense, dollar for dollar, between the government and the academic institution. This program is called the "Yellow Ribbon Program."
- A monthly housing allowance based on the Basic Allowance for Housing (BAH) for an E-5 with dependents at the location of the school (only provided while school is in session).
- For those attending foreign schools (schools without a main campus in the U.S.) the BAH rate is fixed at $1,368.00 for 2012.
- An annual books and supplies stipend of $1,000 paid proportionately, based on enrollment.
- A one-time rural benefit payment for eligible individuals.

This benefit is payable only for training at an Institution of Higher Learning (IHL). If you are enrolled exclusively in online training you will receive a housing allowance at one half of the national average for an E5's BAH. If you are on active duty, you will not receive the housing allowance or the stipend for books and supplies. This benefit provides up to thirty-six months of education benefits. Generally, you remain eligible to claim benefits for up to fifteen years following your release from active duty. The Post-9/11 GI Bill also offers some servicemembers the opportunity to transfer their GI Bill to dependents.

Montgomery GI Bill (MGIB). The Montgomery GI Bill (MGIB) is available for those who enlist in the U.S. Armed Forces. MGIB encompasses both the Montgomery GI Bill—Active Duty (Chapter 30) and the Montgomery GI Bill—Selected Reserve (Chapter 1606). Under Chapter 30, active duty members enroll and pay $100 per month for twelve months and are then entitled to receive a monthly education benefit once they have completed a minimum service obligation (thirty-six months for full entitlement). Under Chapter 1606, a reservist must be actively drilling and have a six-year obligation in the Selected Reserve to be eligible.

The Montgomery GI Bill–Active Duty (MGIB-AD) program provides up to thirty-six months of education benefits. This benefit may be used for degree and certificate programs, flight training, apprenticeships or on-the-job training, and correspondence courses. Remedial, deficiency, and refresher courses may be approved under certain circumstances. Generally, benefits are payable for ten years following the servicemember's release from active duty.

The Montgomery GI Bill–Selected Reserve (MGIB-SR) program may be available to members of the Selected Reserve. The Selected Reserve includes the Army Reserve, Navy Reserve, Air Force Reserve, Marine Corps Reserve and Coast Guard Reserve, the Army National Guard, and the Air National Guard. Reservists may use this education assistance program for degree programs, certificate or correspondence courses, cooperative training, independent study programs, apprenticeships and on-the-job training, and vocational flight training programs. Remedial, refresher, and deficiency training are available under certain circumstances. Selected Reserve components determines eligibility for this program, and the VA makes the payments. Reservists may be entitled to receive up to thirty-six months of education benefits. Eligibility for the program normally ends on the day the servicemember leaves the Selected Reserve. One exception to this rule exists if the servicemember is mobilized (or recalled to active duty from reserve status). In this case, eligibility may be extended for the length of the mobilization *plus* four months. For example, if a reservist is mobilized for twelve months, the eligibility period is extended for sixteen months. So even if you leave the reserves after mobilization, you may have additional eligibility for the MGIB-SR.

Reserve Educational Assistance (REAP). REAP was established as a part of the Ronald W. Reagan National Defense Authorization Act for Fiscal Year 2005. It is a Department of Defense education benefit program designed to provide educational assistance to members of the Reserve components called or ordered to active duty in response to a war or national emergency (contingency operation), as declared by the president or Congress. This program makes certain reservists who were activated for at least ninety days after September 11, 2001, either eligible for education benefits or eligible for increased benefits.

Survivors & Dependents Educational Assistance Program (DEA). Dependents' Educational Assistance provides education and training opportunities to eligible dependents of certain veterans. The program offers up to forty-five months of education benefits. These benefits may be used for degree and certificate programs, apprenticeships, and on-the-job training. Eligible spouses may use the benefits for correspondence courses. Remedial, deficiency, and refresher courses may be approved under certain circumstances.

Veterans Educational Assistance Program (VEAP). VEAP is available for individuals who were in the armed forces between 1977 and 1985 and who elected to make contributions from their military pay to participate in this education benefit program. Their contributions were matched on a $2-for-$1 basis by the government. Servicemembers may use these benefits for degree, certificate, correspondence, vocational flight training, apprenticeship, or on-the-job training programs. In certain circumstances, remedial, deficiency, and refresher training may also be available. The benefit entitlement is for one to thirty-six months, depending on the number of monthly contributions. If you participated in this program, you have ten years from your release from active duty to use VEAP benefits. If the entitlement is not used after the ten-year period, your portion remaining in the fund will automatically be refunded.

National Call to Service Program. The National Call to Service Incentive program requires a participant to perform a period of national service to be eligible for benefits. It is a Department of Defense program that is administered by the VA.

Military Officer Undergraduate Commissioning Programs

U.S. Service Academies (Military, Naval, Coast Guard, Merchant Marine, and Air Force). The five U.S. Service Academies are accredited colleges and well-respected and prestigious institutions of higher learning. For this discussion, they serve as a cost-saving and financially advantageous option; all admitted students receive a full scholarship that includes a modest monthly stipend and covers all associated expenses (fees, room, board, uniforms, etc.). It is important to note that in exchange for the full scholarship, the student will incur a commission and service obligation into the respective service. Additionally, admission is highly competitive and, with the exception of the U.S. Coast Guard Academy, requires a presidential, vice presidential, or Congressional nomination in addition to standard college application procedures.

Reserve Officer Training Corps (ROTC). With the exception of the U.S. Coast Guard, each of the U.S. military services offers the opportunity for merit-based scholarships through the ROTC that cover up to full tuition at civilian institutions of higher learning. In exchange for active-duty service in the respective services upon completion of the civilian academic programs, students are required to participate in a college-based program that incorporates military science, leadership development, strategic planning, professional ethics, and tactical training as electives within the academic program of study.

DoD Active Duty Assistance Programs

Tuition Assistance (TA). TA is an excellent way for servicemembers to further their education with very little, if any, out-of-pocket expense. Each service branch has its own application procedures and restrictions for TA. Courses and degree programs may be academic or technical and can be taken from two- or four-year institutions—on base, off base, or by distance learning. Tuition is usually paid directly to the school by one's service branch. All four DoD service branches offer financial assistance for voluntary off-duty educational programs, in support of servicemembers' personal and professional goals. The program is open to officers, warrant officers, and enlisted active-duty service personnel. In addition, reservists in active-duty status—including the Army National Guard—are eligible for TA. (Some servicemembers in Reserve status may also be eligible for TA. Check with your branch Reserve component to see if this applies to you.) In order to be eligible for TA, an enlisted service member must have enough time remaining in service to complete the course for which he or she applied. After the completion of a course, an officer using TA must fulfill a two-year active-duty service obligation that runs parallel with—not in addition to—any existing obligation. For more information about each of the services' tuition assistance programs, see http://www.military.com/education/content/money-for-school/tuition-assistance-ta-program-overview.html.

Service-specific Education Support Programs. In addition to the Tuition Assistance offered by the individual service branches, each of the service branches also offers other education programs that can help you pay for education. A good summary of these programs can be found at http://www.military.com/education/content/money-for-school/active-duty-education%20benefits-users-guide.html.

Scholarships. Believe it or not, there are countless institutions that want to pay for part or all of your higher education. Hundreds of millions of dollars are awarded to servicemembers each year for tuition and associated costs. These scholarships range from less than a hundred dollars to tens of thousands of dollars. The most likely beneficiaries of these scholarships are those who take the time to search and apply for them. Visit your post, station, or base's education or community services office to start this search. Another resource to turn to is the scholarship finder available at http://www.military.com/scholarship/search-for-scholarships.do

Non-Military Options

In addition to military-sponsored programs, U.S. citizens may qualify for other federally-supported education programs. For a comprehensive summary of available benefits, visit Benefits.gov. At this site, a prospective student can search for education-specific benefits offered by various U.S. government agencies and offices.

Furthermore, there are also many need- and merit-based scholarships awarded by the public and private sectors. Competition for these scholarships occurs at various levels, from school, through state and regional, to the national level. Scholarship search services are available through the College Board website at https://www.collegeboard.com/pay. The Princeton Review also offers a free scholarship search service at http://www.princetonreview.com/college/finance. Be wary of services that search for scholarships for a fee. There are many scams out there: Check with the Better Business Bureau to verify the legitimacy of such agencies.

Financial Aid

Financial aid is available to most families. Financial aid includes any type of economic assistance that is based on need. It can be provided by the federal or state government, or by the college itself, and involves two main categories of financial aid: grants and loans. Grants carry no obligation to repay the grantor, while loans must be repaid. Detailed information on federal student aid is found in the annual *Student Guide,* published by the U.S. Department of Education and posted on the web at http://studentaid.ed.gov/students/publications/student_guide/index.html.

Many states offer grants and subsidized loans to complement federal programs, so be sure to fully explore this option. Information on state-funded financial aid is available through the National Association of State Student Grant & Aid Programs at http://www.nassgap.org/membershipdirectory.aspx.

Additional financial aid opportunities are provided by many colleges. Most schools offer financial aid to help alleviate the financial stress on their students and enhance the student college experience. Most will have a financial aid office accessible through their websites. Financial aid now covers a growing portion of tuition and other expenses at most universities.

Bottom line: The high cost of college is subsidized by financial aid for *most* students. At some private institutions, financial aid alleviates up to two-thirds of the typical student's college bill.

Determining Financial Aid Need

Based on a family's financial situation, income, and other variables, colleges will expect a family to contribute a certain amount to their child's education. Imagine that a child gets accepted to three different colleges and the income of the child's parents merits a parental contribution of $10,000.

A student's need determines the amount of financial aid he or she might receive. Federal and state financial aid agencies determine need based on expected parental and student contributions. The expected contributions are in part determined by income history and earning potential, and in this example are simple assumptions of $10,000 from the parents and $1,800 from the student. Notice in Table 7-2, that although the total annual cost and the total need for College B and C differ significantly, the sum of parental contribution, student contribution, and self-help are identical for Colleges B and C ($14,800). Under this hypothetical scenario, based on assumed calculations of need related to income, this student would pay the same initial out-of-pocket costs for a $40,000 college (College C) or a $25,000 college (College B). The total need calculation included above illustrates what a college's financial aid office

TABLE 7-2
FINANCIAL AID NEEDS ASSESSMENT

	College A	College B	College C
Total Annual Cost	$10,000	$25,000	$40,000
Parental Contribution	$10,000	$10,000	$10,000
Student Contribution	$1,800	$1,800	$1,800
*Self Help (loan/job)	$3,000	$3,000	$3,000
*Total Need (College's View)	$0	$10,200	$25,200

* Some colleges will expect students to take out loans and/or work during their years at college to cover some of the costs when considering total need.

would use to determine an applicant's overall need. Remember, though, that some aid may be in the form of loans, so the student or parents may still have to pay the difference after the student graduates. For a college applicant, a much more relevant figure for planning a college savings program is the Expected Family Contribution (EFC), which offers the best estimate of the amount the family needs to save for college costs.

The EFC is determined in one of two ways: the federal methodology, used by federal processors and school financial aid administrators, or the institutional methodology, used by many private colleges and universities. While the two methods use similar factors to determine eligibility, you should find out the exact rules (such as the expectation for students to work to pay for a portion of college expenses) used by the schools you are considering when you are one year away from entering college.

Families can calculate their Expected Family Contribution at a number of different wesites. A couple of good online calculators are https://big future.collegeboard.org/pay-for-college/paying-your-share/expected-family-contribution-calculator and http://www.finaid.org/calculators/finaidestimate. phtml. Even if your children are not near college age, the calculator will give you some idea of how much a family should expect to pay for college. Answer the calculator's questions as if your child was starting college next year, and describe what the family's financial situation will be when the child starts college. After completing the calculator, be sure to multiply the annual result by four years.

If you do not have the patience to work through an online EFC calculator, consider some of the key factors upon which these calculators are built and on which colleges base their aid decisions. Both methodologies consider the family's after-tax income and readily available savings. Approximately one third of parental income is included in the EFC, and up to 5.5% of parental assets per year. Parental assets, under the federal methodology, do not include such items as insurance policies, individual retirement accounts and 401Ks, or home equity; however, the institutional methodology may include home equity. EFC calculations also consider any after-tax income that the child generates, as well as readily available savings titled in the child's name, such as trust accounts. Families should plan on counting half of the child's taxable income and up to 35% of his or her assets per year in the EFC. Family size and number of children enrolled in college in a given year are considered, along with demographic information, such as the family structure (single- or dual-parent home), and special expenses such as a family's obligation to care for handicapped children. The bottom line: Current income has a greater influence over EFC than savings, and students are expected to apply a much larger amount of their income and savings toward the cost of college than their parents. Of course, each individual college can customize the formula for calculating EFC.

Even if parents do not pay for their children to go to college, the federal government and schools take the parents' financial assets and income into consideration when calculating the students' financial aid qualifications. Simply not claiming a child as a dependent on tax forms is no longer compelling enough to allow students to claim to be independent of their parents' support when applying for financial aid. The current qualifications to be considered independent are as follows:

- The student is 24 years or older by the end of the year financial aid is awarded; or
- The student is an orphan or ward of the court until age 18; or
- The student is a graduate student or U.S. military veteran; or
- The student is married or has legal dependents other than a spouse.

Financial Aid Mistakes

While financial aid is an important consideration in meeting funding challenges, parents should caution themselves against some common financial aid mistakes.

- *The expected family contribution (EFC) is not set in stone.* Don't assume that the EFC is the exact amount the school will ask the family to pay. Often the school will ask the family to pay more or less, depending on the school's financial condition or admissions policies.
- *Don't focus too much on the financial aid rules.* As with any system, the rules governing financial aid may change. Parents should guard against trying to arrange their finances to maximize financial aid at the cost of sound financial decisions. Financial aid eligibility is an important consideration, but not a central one. Furthermore, many colleges are more willing to accept full-paying students than students they will have to support with financial aid.
- *Don't focus on the zero-tuition option and fail to shop for value.* Parents and students should remember that college is a once-in-a-lifetime value decision. The lower-cost college whose tuition drops to zero after applying financial aid is not necessarily a better value than the higher-cost college whose tuition is reduced to an affordable (though perhaps still painful) level. Parents and students should shop around, compare choices, and select the school that offers the best value for the price, given the preferences and ability of the student.
- *Remember: "No" is not final.* Parents with college-age children likely have many friends who can tell tales of negotiating with schools for better aid packages than the initial estimates indicated. Parents and students should actively seek out opportunities to maximize their financial aid package.

Applying for Financial Aid

When your child applies to colleges, pay close attention to the financial aid information provided with the admissions packet, and be sure to submit the documents required by each school, even if you do not think the family qualifies. Families may be pleasantly surprised to discover that they meet the criteria for a variety of subsidized loan programs. Often, schools will require families to submit both the Free Application for Federal Student Aid (FAFSA) from the Department of Education, and the PROFILE Application from the College Scholarship Service. The FAFSA can be submitted between January 1 of the year the student enters college and June 30 of the year the student completes his or her first year of college. However, submitting earlier is better as a financial aid award may be available before the prospective student has to make a final decision on which school to attend. The PROFILE Application should be submitted between January 1 and February 1 of the year the student plans to enter college. Both forms should be available from high school guidance counselors, financial aid offices at the colleges to which the student is applying, and online. The FAFSA can be found at: http://www.fafsa.ed.gov. The PROFILE Application is available at: https://profileonline.collegeboard.com/prf/index.jsp. Much of the information needed for the FAFSA is found on a family's income tax forms, so you should have them available when you begin to fill out the form.

DEVELOPING A COLLEGE SAVINGS PLAN

The first portion of this chapter highlighted the cost of college attendance and how financial aid can reduce college expenses. The first step to developing a college savings plan is to estimate the cost of college for each student in the family. Then, the family should calculate its Expected Family Contribution toward that cost for each student. The family's college savings goal should be whichever is less: its Expected Family Contribution or its estimate of the cost of college. If the cost of college is greater than the Expected Family Contribution, one can reasonably expect to receive financial aid to cover the difference, whether in the form of direct grants or loans (subsidized or unsubsidized). Keep in mind, though, that the student or family will have to repay the loans after graduation.

Now that the family has a college savings goal in mind, it must decide how to invest those college savings dollars.

Does it Matter How Old Your Children Are?

Chapters 10 and 11 explain general investment strategies that apply to all types of short-, medium-, and long-term goals. Saving for college tuition is just another financial goal. A family's time horizon and associated risk tolerance will inform the family's investment decisions. If a family starts saving for college shortly after a child is born, the eighteen-year time horizon allows the family to accept greater risk and the potential for higher returns associated with a portfolio heavily focused in equities (stocks), which have historically provided a greater rate of return than bonds or cash equivalent investments. As time nears for the child to enter college, the family will want to adjust the asset allocation for the child's savings plan to more of a fixed-income (bonds) portfolio that provides greater financial security. Once the child is in college the family will want to move investments over to more liquid and risk-free assets such as money market accounts and cash in order to have the flexibility to quickly withdraw money for necessary education-related expenditures.

The Affect of College Savings Plans on Financial Aid

If you complete the Expected Family Contribution calculations discussed in the first part of this chapter, it will become apparent that anything you manage to save for college will increase your EFC *per year* by 5.5% of the parents' savings and 35% of the child's savings. In other words, every $100,000 saved in the family's name for college increases the family's EFC by almost $22,000 over four years. If the family saves that $100,000 in a child's name, the family's EFC will increase by $140,000 over four years. To compensate for this effect, you should rerun the EFC calculator after making a college savings plan and include your expected college savings. You may have to increase your college savings goal if the EFC increases. There are three additional points you should bear in mind when developing a college savings plan. First, parents should exercise care in the amount of assets they place in their child's name. Student-owned assets lower eligibility for financial aid more rapidly than assets placed in the parent's name.

Second, family savings in the form of Thrift Savings Plan (TSP) and Individual Retirement Accounts (IRAs), employer-sponsored retirement savings plans (such as 401(k) accounts), and home equity (using the federal methodology) are not part of the financial aid consideration and therefore do not increase one's EFC. These sources can themselves be important investment vehicles against which families may borrow to finance college tuition. Consequently, families should place the priority on funding these savings vehicles above all others, as their limited impact on the financial aid calculation makes these already attractive savings vehicles even better.

Third, if a child has significant expenses before college (such as summer camps, orthodontic work, or a cross country trip to visit colleges), parents should carefully consider how they fund those expenses. If the parents have a choice between taking money from their savings and taking it from the child's trust account (more on these types of accounts are covered later in this chapter), they should choose to spend the child's money to reduce the EFC for college. This expense shifting is well within the law, since the parent is the trustee of the account until the child is twenty-one, and the expenditure is clearly for the benefit of the child.

As one can see, how a family saves and grows its money can have an impact on the family's eligibility for financial aid, but it is still advantageous to plan and save! Having a savings plan and adhering to it will ensure the certainty of being financially prepared to pay for education expenses. While financial aid can be a useful and beneficial program, it does not guarantee full educational funding.

Taking Advantage of the Tax Laws to Accelerate College Savings

Uniform Gifts to Minors Account (UGMA) / Uniform Transfers to Minors Account (UTMA). The federal government has established two types of tax-favored trust accounts in which parents may accumulate funds designated for their children's college education. These accounts are commonly referred to as UGMA and UTMA. Both of these investment vehicles represent a low-cost, tax-advantaged means of saving for a dependent's college education.

UGMA/UTMA accounts offer the same tax treatment and differ only in the types of assets that can be in the account. UTMA accounts allow parents to deposit any assets for the benefit of minors, while UGMA may only hold cash or securities. Parents may establish these accounts through a bank or investment company, usually designating themselves as the trustee. States that have adopted UTMA have repealed UGMA, so your state of residence will determine which account type is available to you. The decision to establish a UGMA or UTMA should be based on your child tax liability. Basically, these trust accounts allow you to save the income taxes that would normally occur with the more common practice of sheltering your income-producing assets by transferring them directly to your children; however, UGMAs and UTMAs can result in a loss of eligibility for need-based financial aid.

Under child tax liability, the government taxes all child income (earned income as well as unearned income from interest and dividends) at a lower rate than parents' income. Generally, for dependent children during tax year 2010, the first $950 in annual income (earned and unearned) was not taxed due to the standard deduction. Additional income was taxed at either the child's rate or the parents' rate:

- If the child's earned income exceeds half of the parents' cost to support the child, the tax rate that applies to the income depends on whether the child reached the age of eighteen by the end of the tax year. If the child did not reach the age of eighteen, then the next $950 of income is taxed at the child's income tax rate. Beyond the $1,900 (the original $950 to which the standard children's deduction applies, plus the next $950), earned income is taxed at the parents' marginal income tax rate. If the child reaches the age of eighteen, then all subsequent income (after the $950 subject to the standard deduction) is taxed at the child's rate.

- If the child's earned income is less than half of the parents' cost to support the child, the tax rate that applies to the income depends on whether the child reached the age of nineteen (or twenty-four for full-time students) prior to December 31. If the child did not reach age nineteen (or twenty-four for full-time students) then the next $950 (after the $950 subject to the standard deduction) in income is taxed at the child's income tax rate. Beyond the $1,900 (the original $950 to which the child's standard deduction applies, plus the next $950), earned income is taxed at the parents' marginal income tax rate. If the child did reach age nineteen (again, twenty-four for full-time students), then all subsequent income (after the $950 subject to the standard deduction) is taxed at the child's rate.

The current federal tax brackets will remain in place until 2012 and—without Congressional action and presidential approval—will return to 2006 rates at that time. The discussion below uses the 2006 tax rates, which were higher than the rates current at the time of the printing of this book. The 2006 tax rates are more representative of the long-term average tax rate.

The UGMA/UTMA provisions represent rather sizable tax savings for parents in higher tax brackets. For instance, a parent in the 25% tax bracket would pay $350 in taxes on $1,400 of dividends and interest generated in an ordinary account. Assuming the child was under eighteen and in the 10% tax bracket, the same $1,400 in dividends in a UGMA would be assessed a tax of $45 ($1,400 minus the $950 standard deduction, yielding $450 of taxable income at the 10% rate)—a savings of $305. While this may not sound like a large amount, if the family saves the $305 each year for eighteen years and earns just a 3% rate of return (after taxes with interest compounded monthly), the result is about $7,285. That will come in handy at tuition time!

Obviously, the tax advantages of UGMA/UTMA accounts come early in the child's life, so parents wishing to receive the full benefits of the account should establish them as close to birth as possible. Parents in higher tax brackets receive proportionally greater tax savings than parents in lower tax brackets from UGMA/UTMA accounts, but most families can still benefit from this opportunity. These accounts are especially important tools for dual-career couples who might find themselves in higher tax brackets.

The major disadvantage of the UGMA/UTMA is that assets transferred to these accounts are an irrevocable gift. Parents having any doubts about their child's financial discipline should consider carefully the wisdom of establishing UGMA/UTMA accounts. Also, parents might find themselves irrevocably giving assets to children who might be able to secure financial aid or scholarships on their own. *It is critically important to note that these types of accounts can result in a loss of eligibility for need-based financial aid.* Additionally, parents could find that they have transferred assets to one of their children that they more urgently need for another child's college fund or for their own retirement portfolio. The Coverdell Education Savings Account (CESA), covered later in this chapter, allows for transfer of assets from one child's savings account to the other, so that account may be a better option than the UGMA/UTMA. CESAs and state-sponsored Qualified Tuition Plans (QTPs), covered below, also receive tax benefits and are considered assets of the parents, so they do not increase the EFC as severely.

U.S. Savings Bonds. Some parents use series EE Savings Bonds as a partial way to fund their children's college education. The good news is that interest earned from Series EE bonds bought after 1989 is tax exempt if higher education costs in the redemption year exceed the principal and interest received. U.S. Savings Bonds are a safe form of investment offering a predictable rate of return further enhanced by the tax-free provision. EE bonds are guaranteed to double in value from their issue price no later than twenty years after their issue dates. If the fixed rate on the bond does not double the bond's value after twenty years, the Treasury will make a one-time adjustment. This means that EE bonds guarantee at least a 3.5% average return over the twenty years. However, parents might find that the 3.5% average rate of return on these bonds is lower than what is needed to build a sufficient college fund. (Chapter 11 discusses bonds in more depth.)

Savings bonds are now available only in electronic form. You can purchase Electronic EE bonds directly from the Treasury Department by opening a TreasuryDirect online account at TreasuryDirect.gov. It is important to note the restrictions on the use of these bonds to ensure that the interest is tax-free. Refer to IRS Publication 550, IRS Form 8815, and IRS Form 8818 to find the most up-to-date information on tax exemption rules for college tuition and fees.

You need to decide whether the safe, conservative investment in savings bonds will yield enough return to provide the income you need to finance your child's college education. Military families may put some of their college fund into tax-advantaged savings bonds, but most families will have a sizable portion of their children's college fund in stocks or mutual funds that invest in stocks.

Coverdell Education Savings Account (CESA). The CESA allows families to save for tuition expenses in a non-tax-deductible account and then withdraw earnings tax-free for qualified education expenses (QEEs). Qualified expenses include tuition, fees, books, supplies, equipment required for enrollment or attendance, and certain room and board costs at an eligible education institution (see IRS Publication 590 for specific information on QEEs: http://www.irs.gov/pub/irs-pdf/p590.pdf). CESA can also be used to pay for public, private, and religious elementary and secondary school expenses. The limit on contributions to education CESAs is $2,000 per year per child, until the child is eighteen. The IRS reduces this limit for joint tax filers with over $190,000 in adjusted gross income and disallows all new contributions from filers with over $220,000 in combined income—not an issue for most service-members. Anyone can open a CESA for a child, but combined contributions to all accounts in a child's name cannot exceed the $2,000 cap per year per child. CESA policies are evolving, and families can now fund both a CESA and a 529 Plan (see below) in the same year. A child can also use the CESA distributions to pay for college expenses tax-free at the same time that the parent is claiming education tax credits (which we will address at the end of this chapter), as long as they are not used for the same expenses. Further, assets from one child's CESA can be rolled over into another child's CESA. This is beneficial for parents who would like to keep balances equal for their children and it gives parents the flexibility to move assets from one child's account to the account of another child who may have less access to financial aid (because of differences in education expenses or differences in parents' income or assets at the time each child is applying for financial aid). Finally, if a parent owns the CESA, it is considered a parental asset, so families are only expected to contribute 5.5% of this asset in the EFC.

Roth IRAs. Roth IRAs are retirement savings accounts that are initially non-tax-deductible, but from which you can later withdraw your earnings tax-free. Contributions are capped at $5,000 per year for 2008-2012 (with a catch-up amount of $6,000 authorized for contributors over fifty years old). These contributions may be withdrawn tax- and penalty-free to fund education expenses and are not considered in the EFC calculations. This method of funding college expenses only makes sense for parents who have substantially met their retirement savings goals in another type of tax-advantaged retirement account, such as the TSP or a 401(k) account. Remember, it is better for a child to have some student loans than to have to help parents financially in their retirement years. A child who has earned income can also start an IRA of his or her own. The child's IRA contributions can be made with gifts or inheritance (it does not need to be funded with the child's own earned income). Withdrawals from the child's IRA can also be used tax- and penalty-free to fund education expenses; however, a child's IRA will count as the child's asset (35%) for EFC calculations.

State-Sponsored Qualified Tuition Plans (529 Plans). There are two types of QTP 529 plans (so called after section 529 of the Internal Revenue Code): prepaid programs and savings programs. Every state offers at least one of the two types. Eligible educational institutions also offer QTPs. The benefit of QTPs is that distributions used to fund qualified education expenses (QEEs) at accredited colleges and universities nationwide (which are not limited to the state that sponsors the plan) are non-taxable. State program information can be found at http://www.collegesavings.org and at http://www.savingforcollege.com.

States and educational institutions offering QTPs will limit either a family's total contributions to their 529 plans or the balances held in those accounts. The general rule is that QTP contributions are limited to the amount necessary to provide for QEEs. Once a family establishes a QTP, securities firms hired by the state or educational institution manage the QTP through a set of investment options, limiting the control a beneficiary or contributor has over the investment of the funds within their QTP. Many state plans provide state income tax exemptions for residents, so it pays to investigate your own state's offering before shopping for plans in other states. Many plans automatically adjust a 529's asset mix as a child approaches college age, which may cost a bit more in fees but relieves the parents from worrying about reallocating assets to reduce the volatility of their child's college savings. 529 plans are not limited by the gift tax, which generally permits tax-free gifts of up to $13,000 per year (2010 limit). Instead, the unique feature of the 529 plan is that in 2010 you can contribute up to $65,000 ($13,000 per year for five years made up front, as a one-time contribution), or $130,000 per couple, per beneficiary in a single year without incurring a federal gift tax impact. That's five times the annual gift tax exclusion. This large contribution is possible because one is allowed to prorate the gift over five years to avoid triggering the gift tax.

There are several other unique attributes of a QTP that may make it more attractive as a college savings choice. QTPs have no adjusted gross income phase-out, so even high-income taxpayers can take advantage of QTP benefits. A single beneficiary can have both a QTP and CESA (though the tax benefits on distributions are still restricted to those that pay for qualifying educational expenses). QTPs, like CESAs, also allow for rollover of distributions from one beneficiary to another related family member. As discussed earlier, this allows parents to provide equity in their children's savings plans or to move assets from one child to another, based on their EFC. Finally, there are thousands of companies that support 529 college savings plans by returning a small percentage of your purchases from them to a designated 529 account. This is done through a nonprofit organization, Upromise (http://www.upromise.com/welcome). There are tens of thousands of stores, thousands of restaurants, and hundreds of online retailers participating in the Upromise program, with more joining all the time. It may be worthwhile to fill out the free application in order to accelerate your 529 savings.

ADDITIONAL OPTIONS TO FUND A GAP IN COLLEGE SAVINGS

The goal of a college savings program is to pay for the expected costs of sending your children or yourself to college. In the end, even the most carefully planned savings program and financial aid package provision may not yield enough funds to cover a family's college expenses. This final section will touch on some other options that families may use to help finance college costs.

Gifts

Grandparents and relatives are important sources of funding, especially in the early years of a child's life. Often, it is the grandparents who have the most to gain from the tax advantages of UGMA/UTMA provisions, as they may be in higher tax brackets during the early years of their grandchild's life. Recognize that gifts to the student will reduce the level of financial aid available much more than gifts to the parents.

Financing College with Current Income (Working)

In addition, parents should not overlook the option of financing a part of college tuition from the family's monthly income. Claiming various tax credits and deductions can alleviate some of the pain of paying college costs with current income. The Hope and Lifetime Learning tax credits and the tuition and fees deductions can almost be as beneficial as a grant, since they can provide a great savings on tax "costs."

Parents should also consider the option of having their children bear some of the expenses with student jobs while in college. Many universities expect students to work when they calculate the Expected Family Contribution. Some financial aid packages require the student to work for the university.

Financing College with Future Income (Borrowing)

Families may also finance full or partial tuition costs through loans against their family's net worth. Federally subsidized student loans (e.g. Perkins and Stafford loans) are one important source of funding, but parents may also find that banks will provide more favorable rates for taking out unsubsidized loans against the equity in their house. The interest on these home equity loans may be tax deductible. Many employers will also allow employees to borrow against the assets of their 401(k) or employer-sponsored savings plans.

However, families should be careful about sacrificing the benefits of tax-deferred accounts to fund college costs if other alternatives exist. Liquidation of traditional IRA and tax-deferred retirement accounts can trigger tax penalties of 10% over normal income taxes. There is a possibility that withdrawals may be exempt from the 10% additional penalties if the withdrawals are not greater than qualified educational expenses (QEEs). Due to the possible tax penalties, a better option for parents, particularly older ones, may be to finance college tuition through loans and defer the final loan repayment until age $59^{1}/_{2}$, when they can begin drawing from IRA accounts and avoid early distribution penalties. Parents may also find that their retirement accounts will hold significantly more assets in this case, having been afforded the opportunity for longer tax-deferred growth.

There are also potential tax savings from children taking out student loans. A person with a student loan may deduct up to $2,500 of the interest they pay per year—even if they use the standard deduction (instead of itemizing their deductions)—if modified adjusted gross income is less that $65,000 for a single person or $130,000 for married couples filing jointly. The deduction can be taken for the life of the loan. Those with student loans can also save on interest payments after they start paying off student loans. Many lenders will reward on-time payments with a 2% point reduction in interest rates after 48 consecutive on-time payments.

8

Meeting Medical Expenses

Every year, American families incur medical expenses. These expenses range in price and predictability from low-cost, health-maintenance office visits to high-cost, major medical procedures that require specialized equipment and highly skilled medical professionals. Somehow, of course, the bills for these medical services must be paid. If families only used routine, low-cost medical services, they could budget for these expenses as they do with grocery or telephone bills. Expensive, but rare, major medical procedures are difficult to budget for, however. Since most of these major medical procedures are life-threatening, families cannot postpone them to save for them as they might for a home or college expenses. It is the urgent nature of the high-cost, life-saving medical procedures that necessitates a chapter on the issue of medical expenses.

There is a possibility that a family will face a significant life-threatening medical procedure in any given year. Generally, only the wealthiest Americans can pay for these high-cost procedures out-of-pocket. It is difficult to budget for these unfortunate events because of their unexpected nature. Most families choose to purchase insurance to protect against the risk of large unexpected medical expenses. This chapter discusses the basics of health insurance and then examines the particulars of TRICARE—the health insurance program available to military families. After reviewing this information, you will be able to make an informed decision about the health insurance coverage that best supports your family's needs.

HEALTH INSURANCE COSTS
Almost all health insurance plans purchased by American families contain two parts. The first part is a health-maintenance contract. This is like a service contract you would buy for your car or any complicated piece of equipment; it covers the expenses associated with routine health maintenance office visits like checkups, immunizations, and treatments of common ailments. The second part is an insurance policy, comparable to the auto and fire insurance that most drivers and homeowners have to protect themselves financially in the event of an accident. Health insurance policies cover people against the financial risk associated with rare, life-saving, major medical procedures.

A typical health insurance plan costs the average American family between $10,000 and $18,000 a year in premiums, based on the extent of the policy's coverage. However, employers cover a large portion of that insurance cost for many families as part of overall employment compensation packages. As a general rule, employers only pay a portion of employer-provided health insurance. For example, the employer might pay $10,000 of the employee's health insurance plan premium; the employee then pays a monthly enrollment fee, perhaps $300 each month. In this example, the employer gives the employee the opportunity to buy a $13,600 health insurance plan for $3,600. Since the employer does not offer to give the employee the $10,000 benefit in cash or in addition to the employee's salary, most employees enroll in the employer-offered health plan.

As a general rule, health insurance plans do not pay all of an enrollee's medical bills. Certain medical treatments, called *exclusions,* are not included in the health insurance coverage; elective cosmetic surgery usually fits into this category. The enrollee must pay entirely for these treatments.

Besides exclusions, enrollees may also have to contribute payments towards some medical expenses. Most insurance policies do not start paying until the policyholder has paid some set amount; this amount is called the *deductible.* For example, if a policyholder has a deductible of $1,000, the insurance company will not pay for medical expenses until the policyholder has paid for the first $1,000 of covered medical expenses.

The second required payments is called *co-insurance.* After the policyholder meets the deductible, the health insurance company pays only part of the bill for a medical procedure; the remaining part of the bill must be covered by the policyholder and is called co-insurance. For example, the insurance company may only pay 80 percent of the bill, leaving the policyholder responsible for the remaining 20 percent.

The third type of required payment is called a *co-payment.* The co-payment is a flat fee that the insurance company requires a policyholder to pay for a provided medical service. For example, some insurance companies require a $10 co-payment from patients for every doctor's office visit.

Most health insurance plans place an annual limit, called the policyholder's *out-of-pocket maximum,* on the combined total cost of deductibles, co-insurance, and co-payments. For example, if a policyholder has reached a $10,000 annual out-of-pocket maximum in medical payments, the health insurance plan will then cover 100% of all other non-excluded medical treatments that year.

Health insurance plans may also limit their risk exposure through *maximum dollar limits,* which are limits on how much the insurance company will pay per covered person during a prescribed time period. For example, some health insurance plans will not pay more than $10,000,000 during a covered person's lifetime. Further, some insurance plans place maximum dollar limits on particular medical procedures. For example, an insurance plan might not pay more than $1,000 per year for chiropractic treatments.

TYPES OF HEALTH INSURANCE PLANS

There are three basic types of health insurance plans that differ in the flexibility and ease with which enrollees can determine their own health care treatment needs. The basic health insurance plans are described below, from the most to the least flexible:

Preferred Provider Organization Plans (PPOs)

A PPO is a group of health care providers—physicians, clinics, hospitals, labs, and so on—organized by a health insurance company. This group agrees to provide medical services to those insured by the company as outlined by the PPO's medical practice policy and for the PPO's fee schedule. This group of health care providers is called the network.

The PPO encourages enrollees to use the network of health care providers by charging smaller co-insurance costs for medical procedures performed by health care providers in the network than for medical procedures provided by out-of-network providers. An enrollee in a PPO can use out-of-network health care providers, but with higher out-of-pocket expenses.

Point-of-Service Plans (POSs)

A POS is similar to a PPO in that there is a network of health care providers that agree to provide medical services according to the POS's medical practice policy and fee schedule. In a POS plan one chooses a primary caregiver who acts as a gatekeeper for all of a policyholder's specialized medical needs; the policyholder first goes to the Primary Care Manager (PCM) who evaluates the need for specialized medical treatment before writing a referral (or permission slip) to a specialist. The primary caregiver usually selects a specialist from within the POS network.

The policyholder can request a referral to an out-of-network specialist, but as in a PPO, this usually requires higher co-insurance. Often, the policyholder must pay the out-of-network bill and then file a reimbursement claim with the insurance company.

Health Maintenance Organization Plans (HMOs)

An HMO is a health insurance company that hires physicians and health care providers and owns clinics, labs, and hospitals to provide medical services to enrollees. The enrollee selects a physician as a PCM within the HMO (as in a POS plan) who then refers the enrollee to specialists within the HMO as needed. HMO enrollees rarely receive medical treatment outside of the HMO system. An HMO can be inconvenient for frequent travelers or those living great distances from the HMO's facilities.

As a general rule, health insurance plans, whether PPOs, POSs, or HMOs, also provide prescription drug benefits. These plans work in two ways. First a prescription drug plan may prescribe *preferred drugs*. Health insurance companies receive a discount for purchasing these drugs in volume, passing the savings on to enrollees. Additionally, the plan may entitle a policyholder to a prescription *subsidy*. For example, the policyholder may pay 50 percent of the pharmacy charges, while the insurance provider pays the rest.

HEALTH SAVINGS ACCOUNTS

Remember that health insurance plans essentially provide two services. The first is a health maintenance contract that covers routine, predictable, and low-cost medical services. Health insurance premiums will directly reflect these average expenditures. For example, if the average insured family spends $6,000 a year on health-maintenance procedures, their health insurance premium will include this $6,000 to cover the expected health-maintenance contract costs.

The second part of the premium that the policyholder pays is for insurance against the risk of unexpected medical procedures. If one has a health insurance plan whose premium is $13,600 annually, and $6,000 of that premium is for the health maintenance contract portion of the plan, then only $7,600 is being spent to cover the risk of unexpected, costly medical procedures.

You can find more affordable health insurance plans by reducing or removing the health maintenance contract portion of the plan, keeping only the medical insurance portion. One way to lower costs on the medical maintenance contract portion of the plan is for the enrollee to pay a larger deductible or co-payment. You can budget for these increased out-of-pocket expenses due to the routine, predictable nature of these medical expenses.

Another way for individuals to reduce their health maintenance cost is through a Health Savings Account (HSA). Congress created HSAs as tax-free savings accounts dedicated to paying medical expenses in order to provide individuals with similar tax advantages to those of employer-provided health care plans that pay for routine medical expenses. The money deposited into an HSA is tax deductible and earned interest is tax-free. Individuals must pair an HSA with a high-deductible health insurance plan; the minimum deductible is $1,200 for single coverage and $2,400 for family coverage. Additionally, the policy's out-of-pocket expenses cannot exceed $5,950 for individuals and $11,900 for families. After the age of sixty-five, money from the HSA can be withdrawn for any reason.

If a family's routine health care expenses are lower than those of the average insured family, they can save money by reducing their contribution to the insurance plan's health maintenance portion, putting money into an HSA, and paying routine health care expenses out-of-pocket. These savings can accrue interest in the HSA until retirement at age sixty-five, at which time they can withdraw the money for any use.

Choosing an HSA does come with risk: In a year of unexpected medical needs, the family could be liable for up to $12,000 in out-of-pocket medical expenses. If the family has not yet established a large enough cash balance in the HSA to cover these costs, it will have to sacrifice other financial needs to meet these obligations, compromising their standard of living.

MILITARY HEALTHCARE BENEFITS: TRICARE

The TRICARE system is a Department of Defense (DoD)-wide healthcare program that combines the assets of military treatment facilities (MTFs) with supplemental services provided by civilian healthcare professionals from the surrounding communities. The DoD, in an attempt to reduce medical costs and improve the quality of and access to care, adopted the same philosophy as many large companies—provide health care to servicemembers and their dependents through an HMO.

TRICARE is a health care program for servicemembers and their families, including retirees, broken into four regionally-managed networks that supplement the care provided by military treatment facilities. These four networks operate independently of one another, and you can only enroll in the regional network where you are stationed. Every military hospital is aligned with one of these four geographic regions (see Figure 8-1). Each TRICARE region relies on a major medical center for major surgeries, as well as several regional hospitals to provide specialized medical care. As a result, servicemembers and their families may have to travel to receive certain medical treatments.

Figure 8-1
TRICARE Regions

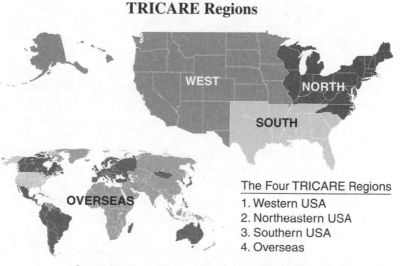

The Four TRICARE Regions
1. Western USA
2. Northeastern USA
3. Southern USA
4. Overseas

Source: http://www.tricare.mil/tricaresmart/default.aspx

The TRICARE program offers two basic options for all beneficiaries, except active-duty servicemembers. Active-duty servicemembers are automatically enrolled in TRICARE Prime during in-processing, while dependents of active-duty servicemembers are enrolled in TRICARE Standard and Extra and must voluntarily choose TRICARE Prime.

Option 1: TRICARE Prime (an HMO)

This is the managed-care network option. Family members who enroll in this option receive the majority of their care from MTFs. In return for this lower-cost option, beneficiaries give up the option to choose their doctors. This option is available to servicemembers and their families.

There are a few variations of TRICARE Prime:

- *TRICARE Prime Remote.* This is the managed-care network option for families who live more than 50 miles from a MTF. It works like TRICARE Prime through the TRICARE network of service providers. If a network service provider is not available, the family can choose a non-network provider as their PCM. Available to servicemembers and their families.
- *TRICARE Prime Overseas.* This is the overseas managed-care network option. Available to servicemembers and command-sponsored families.
- *TRICARE Prime Remote Overseas.* This is the overseas managed-care network option in areas designated as remote. Available to servicemembers and command-sponsored families.
- *US Family Health Plan (USFHP).* This is essentially TRICARE Prime but administered through six community health care networks instead of the TRICARE network or MTFs. Available to servicemembers and their families who live in one of the six plan districts.

Option 2: TRICARE Standard and Extra (a POS).

This is the traditional fee-for-service option. Enrollees can choose any health care providers they want. If the healthcare provider is within the TRICARE list of network providers, then the policyholder's out-of-pocket expense is 15 percent of the TRICARE-negotiated service price. If the healthcare provider is not within the TRICARE list of network providers, then the policyholder's out-of-pocket expense is 20 percent of the TRICARE allowable service price. If TRICARE Prime is not available where the policyholder is stationed, the policyholder's only option is to enroll in TRICARE Standard and Extra.

There are two variations of this program:

- *TRICARE Reserve Select.* This is a premium-based traditional fee-for-service option for qualified Selected Reserve members of the Ready Reserve and their families.

TABLE 8-1
TRICARE OPTION COMPARISONS

	TRICARE Prime	TRICARE Standard and Extra
Type of Program	TRICARE Prime is a health maintenance organization (HMO).	TRICARE Standard and Extra is a fee-for-service option—Point of Service (POS).
Main Features	• Servicemembers automatically enrolled • Family members need to be enrolled • Must choose your primary care manager (PCM) • Most care received from your (PCM) • Fewer out-of-pocket costs • No claims to file	• Not available for active-duty servicemembers • Family members automatically enrolled when enrolled in DEERS (Defense Enrollment Eligibility Reporting System) • Care from any TRICARE network or non-network provider • Referrals are not required • Some procedures require prior authorization • Non-network services may be paid out-of-pocket; SM files for reimbursement • TRICARE Standard is available worldwide • TRICARE Extra is not available overseas
Eligibility	• Active duty servicemembers (ADSM) • Active duty family members (ADFM) • Active duty servicemembers' surviving spouses and dependent children • Retired servicemembers and their families • Retired servicemembers' surviving spouses and eligible former spouse	• Active duty family members (ADFM) • Selected Reserve, Ready Reserve and National Guard in TRICARE Reserve Select • Retired Reserve and survivors in TRICARE Retired Reserve • Retired ADSM and family
Premiums	TRICARE Prime Active Duty • Servicemember $0 • Family $0 Other Beneficiaries • Individual $230 per year (proposed increase to $260 in 2012) • Family $460 per year (proposed increase to $520 in 2012)	TRICARE Standard and Extra • Servicemember N/A • Family $0 TRICARE Reserve Select • Member $53.16 per month • Member and family $197.72 per month TRICARE Reserve Retired • Member $408.01 per month • Member and family $1020.05 per month Continued Health Care Benefit Program • Individual $988 per quarter • Family $2,213 per quarter

table continued on next page

TABLE 8-1
TRICARE OPTION COMPARISONS

Deductibles	Network Providers • ADSM: $0 • ADFM: $0 POS Option • ADSM: N/A • ADFM: $300 • Active duty family total: $600	• Sponsor E-4 and below, individual: $50 • Sponsor E-4 and below, family: $100 • Sponsor E-5 and above, individual: $150 • Sponsor E-5 and above, family: $300 • All others, individual: $150 • All others, family: $300
Outpatient Service Fees	Military Treatment Facility • ADSM: $0 • ADFM: $0 • Other beneficiaries: $0 Network Provider • ADSM: $0 • ADFM: $0 • Other beneficiaries: $12 per visit Non-network Provider • With PCM referral: $0 • Without PCM referral: Point-of-service fees apply	Network Provider • ADFM: 15% of negotiated fee after annual deductible met • All others: 20% of negotiated fee after the annual deductible is met Non-network Provider • ADFM: 20% of allowable charges after the annual deductible is met • All others: 25% allowable charges after the annual deductible is met
Hospitalization Fees	Military Treatment Facility • ADSM and family: $0 Network Provider • ADSM and ADFM: $11 per day, ($25 minimum charge) • Others: $11 per day, ($25 minimum charge) Non-network Provider • ADFMs only: 50% of TRICARE allowable charge, after the annual deductible is met	Network Provider • ADFM: $16.85 per day ($25 minimum charge) • All others: $250 or 25%, whichever is less, for institutional services, plus 20% for separately billed professional charges Non-network Provider • ADFM: $16.85 per day ($25 minimum charge) • All others: $535 per day or 25% for institutional services, whichever is less; plus 25% for separately billed professional charges
Out-of Pocket Limit	• ADFM: $1,000 per family, per fiscal year • National Guard and Reserve families: $1,000 per family, per fiscal year • Retired families (and all others): $3,000 per family, per fiscal year	• ADFM: $1,000 per family, per fiscal year • National Guard and Reserve families: $1,000 per family, per fiscal year • Retired families (and all others): $3,000 per family, per fiscal year

Sources: www.tricare.mil/mybenefit/home/overview/compareplans
www.tricare.mil/mybenefit/Download/Forms/TRICARE_Prime_Handbook_Update_040811.pdf
www.tricare.mil/mybenefit/Download/Forms/TRICARE_Summary_of_Beneficiary_Costs_Br_021011_unlinked.pdf

- *TRICARE Retired Reserve.* This is a premium-based traditional fee-for-service option for qualified retired Reserve members and survivors. Enrollees can choose any health care providers they want. If the healthcare provider is within the TRICARE list of network providers then the policyholder's out-of-pocket expense is 20 percent of the TRICARE-negotiated service price. If the healthcare provider is not within the TRICARE list of network providers then the out-of-pocket expense is 25 percent of the TRICARE allowable service price.

TRICARE PHARMACY PROGRAM

TRICARE offers several convenient ways for beneficiaries to fill prescriptions based on a family's specific needs:

1. Beneficiaries may have prescriptions filled (up to a ninety-day supply for most medications) at a military treatment facility pharmacy free of charge. Be aware that not all medications are available at MTF pharmacies.
2. TRICARE Pharmacy Home Delivery is available for prescriptions taken on a regular basis. Beneficiaries can receive up to a ninety-day supply.
3. Prescription medications that a doctor requires a patient to start taking immediately can be obtained though a retail network pharmacy.
4. Non-network retail pharmacies are the most costly option for obtaining medications. Eligible beneficiaries usually receive reimbursement of 80% of the full retail price for medications, after they have met the TRICARE annual deductible amount ($150 per individual or $300 per family, or $50 per individual and $100 per family for lower-grade enlisted families). TRICARE Prime beneficiaries who use non-network pharmacy services pay the 50% point-of-service co-payment as well as a deductible of $300 per individual or $600 per family.

It is DoD's policy to substitute generic medications, when available, for brand-name medications. TRICARE will authorize dispensing of brand-name instead of generic drugs if the prescribing physician medically justifies the necessity. Table 8-2 summarizes the costs to beneficiaries for filling prescriptions from different sources.

The benefits described above are available to:

- Active-duty beneficiaries worldwide, including Reserve/National Guard personnel and their family members on Title 10 (federal) or Title 32 (state) active-duty orders for more than thirty days.
- TRICARE-eligible beneficiaries of all ages. (Note: Retired reservists, guardsmen, and former servicemembers and their families are not eligible for TRICARE until age sixty.) Servicemembers who enroll in the US Family Health Plan are not eligible for the TRICARE Pharmacy Program and must use USFHP pharmacy providers.
- Continued Health Care Benefit Program enrollees.

TABLE 8-2
TRICARE PHARMACY PROGRAM

Place of Service	Generic (Tier 1)	Brand Name (Tier 2)	Non-Formulary (Tier 3)
MTF (Up to 90 day supply)	$0	$0	Not Available
TRICARE Home Delivery (Up to 90 day supply)	$0	$9	$25
Network Retail (Up to 30 day supply)	$5	$12	$25
Non-network Retail (Up to 30 day supply)	TRICARE Prime • 50% cost share after POS deductible is met TRICARE Standard and Extra • $12 or 20% of total cost after annual deductable is met (whichever is greater)		TRICARE Prime • 50% cost share after POS deductible is met TRICARE Standard and Extra • $25 or 20% of total cost after annual deductable is met (whichever is greater)

Source: www.tricare.mil/mybenefit/Download/Forms/TRICARE_Pharmacy_Program_
Handbook_2011_LoRes.pdf

Beneficiaries who turned sixty-five before April 1, 2001, may participate in the program without being enrolled in Medicare Part B. Beneficiaries who turn sixty-five on or after April 1, 2001, must enroll in Medicare Part B and must ensure their DEERS profile is updated to participate.

WHO IS ELIGIBLE FOR ENROLLMENT IN TRICARE?

In order to receive care at military medical facilities, all beneficiaries must enroll in DEERS, including newborns after 120 days. The following groups are eligible for TRICARE medical coverage:

1. Active-duty servicemembers.
2. Spouses and unmarried children (under twenty-one years old) of active-duty servicemembers.
   - Handicapped children twenty-one years and older, if handicapped prior to twenty-first birthday.
   - Children under twenty-three enrolled full-time in school; however, they may not remain eligible for TRICARE Prime if they live in a different region from the servicemember.

- Children, including stepchildren adopted by the sponsor, remain covered if a divorced spouse remarries; however, they may not remain eligible for TRICARE Prime if they live in a different region from the sponsor.
3. Servicemembers and their eligible family members who separate from the military before retirement may receive TRICARE benefits for a period of 60 to 120 days after their separation date under the Continued Health Care Benefit Program.
4. Retirees under sixty-five years old and their spouses and unmarried children.
   - The same restrictions as above apply to children of retired servicemembers.
   - Medicare-eligible retirees are not covered as of the time of this writing. However, on October 1, 2001, retirees enrolled in Medicare Part B had their Part A eligibility restored if they lost it because of age.
5. Unremarried spouses and children of servicemembers who died. (Children have same restrictions as above.)
6. Spouses and children of reservists who are ordered to active duty for more than thirty consecutive days. (They are covered only during the reservists' activation period. Children have the same restrictions as above.)
7. Spouses and unmarried children of reservists who are injured or aggravate an injury, illness, or disease during active-duty training and die as a result of the injury, illness, or disease.
8. Former spouses of active or retired servicemembers who served for at least twenty creditable years. There are other restrictions for this category. Contact a TRICARE Service Center for complete eligibility rules.
9. Dependent parents and parents-in-law do not qualify for TRICARE benefits. However, they may use military medical facilities on a space-available basis.
10. Other categories of persons may be eligible for TRICARE benefits. Visit the TRICARE website or contact your TRICARE Service Center for the current information.

TRICARE FOR LIFE

The most common health insurance coverage for retired persons in the United States is Medicare. It is available to people over the age of sixty-five who have been legal residents of the United States for at least five years. Medicare Part A is inpatient hospital insurance, Medicare Part B is outpatient services insurance, and Medicare Part D is a prescription drug plan.

The Medicare insurance plans are premium-based. The government determines Medicare Part A premiums based on a retiree's or spouse's

Medicare tax payment contributions. The government waives the Part A premium if the retiree or his or her spouse has paid forty or more quarters of Medicare taxes. Those who have paid Medicare tax for thirty to thirty-nine quarters pay a $248 premium per month, while those who paid Medicare tax for less than thirty quarters pay a premium of $450 per month. The government scales Medicare Part B premiums to the retiree's income, ranging from a low of about $100 to a high of about $300 per month.

In addition to premiums, Medicare Parts A and B have deductibles, co-payments, co-insurance, and total payment maximums for specific procedures. These out-of-pocket expenses are considered gaps in Medicare health insurance coverage. Some people elect to buy supplemental health insurance to cover these out-of-pocket expense "gaps" in the Medicare insurance coverage; such policies are called medigap policies.

TRICARE for Life is a supplemental or medigap health insurance policy. The retiree must enroll in both Medicare Parts A and B to be eligible for TRICARE for Life. The only exception is for Medicare-eligible active-duty servicemembers and their spouses who only need Medicare Part A. Medicare is billed first when those enrolled in TRICARE for Life have a medical procedure covered by both Medicare and TRICARE for Life. Medicare pays its authorized limit and TRICARE for Life covers the remainder; the beneficiary will not have any out-of-pocket expenses. Retirees will pay out-of-pocket for medical procedures not authorized by either Medicare or TRICARE for Life.

TABLE 8-3
MEDICAL SERVICE CHARGE RESPONSIBILITY

Medical Service Characteristics	Medicare Pays	TRICARE for Life Pays	Patient Pays
Covered by TRICARE; covered by Medicare	Medicare-authorized amount	Remaining amount	Nothing
Not covered by TRICARE; covered by Medicare	Medicare-authorized amount	Nothing	Medicare deductible, co-pay and co-insurance
Covered by TRICARE; not covered by Medicare	Nothing	TRICARE-authorized amount	TRICARE deductible, co-pay and co-insurance
Not covered by TRICARE; not covered by Medicare	Nothing	Nothing	Total billed

Source: www.tricare.mil/mybenefit/Download/Forms/TRICARE_For_Life_Handbook_10_L.pdf

Most of the procedures that neither program would cover fall into the categories of elective or experimental procedures. It is unlikely that another medigap policy would cover such procedures, so it would probably not be worthwhile to acquire a second medigap policy, in addition to TRICARE for Life.

DEPARTMENT OF VETERANS AFFAIRS HEALTH BENEFITS

The Department of Veterans Affairs (VA) offers a comprehensive package of preventive outpatient and inpatient services. A national network of over 1,400 VA clinics, hospitals, and medical centers provides these services. Eligible veterans must enroll with the VA to receive these medical benefits. Once enrolled, veterans can receive care at their home facility or the nearest facility while traveling. For most veterans, eligibility for health care benefits is based solely on active military service, as long as they were not dishonorably discharged. Reservists and National Guard members called to active duty by a Federal Executive Order may also qualify for VA health care benefits.

The VA uses an electronic medical records program that allows VA medical practitioners access to a patient's medical records through the patient's bar-coded wristband. This technology helps prevent four of the most common medical malpractice errors: wrong medication, wrong dose, wrong dispensing time, and wrong patient. It also allows the attending medical practitioner instant access to diagnostic test results, radiographic images, and medical history. Many people are uncomfortable with the concept of electronic medical records for a variety of privacy and security concerns. If this is a concern for you, you must consider this factor when deciding whether to enroll for VA health benefits, which is a voluntary act.

9

Deployment

Deployments have become a routine occurrence in military life, especially since the beginning of Operation Enduring Freedom in 2001 and Operation Iraqi Freedom in 2003. For those getting ready to deploy for the first time, those who will deploy away from a spouse and children, or those redeploying, the challenges that deployments present are anything but routine. There are emotional and psychological needs to address that will undoubtedly impact the family's financial goals and plans.

When most people think of deploying, they think of risk: risk of injury, risk of separation, risk of infidelity or marital issues, risk to one's career, risk to one's financial situation, and risk to one's life. What is important to remember is that with added risk comes the potential for an increased reward. The trade-off between risk and reward is one of the fundamental principles of finance.

Firms, banks, and public entities pay higher rates of return to investors that are willing to finance riskier projects. In a similar fashion, employers provide extra compensation to workers who assume additional risk in the workplace. In the military, this compensation for risk, discomfort, and family separation comes at least partly in the form of tax-free military pay and special entitlements. Military deployments present a unique opportunity to take stock of a family's financial situation to develop a refined and oftentimes more aggressive financial plan. By using the principles of financial planning outlined in the previous chapters, a family can capitalize on the many financial rewards associated with deploying to fight and win our nation's wars or support full-spectrum operations.

The checklist that follows this section is a comprehensive, but not exhaustive, list of steps one should take before, during, and after deployment. Because deployments often come at short notice, you should not wait until you receive your orders to begin a review of your family's financial plan. If your family is already prepared with a financial plan, then these steps will be relatively simple to execute in addition to all of the other predeployment tasks that you must complete. Some of these tasks may require the assistance of a local finance office, a community services center, or the local Judge Advocate General (JAG). There are also countless lessons that may be gleaned from the experiences of other servicemembers or from information available on military websites. Several useful military websites are listed at the end of this chapter.

This chapter is formatted as a checklist to help servicemembers prepare for deployment under tight time restrictions, including special considerations for servicemembers whose deployment includes the care of a spouse or dependents. Interspersed are boxes where you will find key information regarding deployment benefits or available programs.

DEPLOYMENT CHECKLIST

Before Deployment

☐ Review your financial plan (see chapter 1).
- Update your budget based on the expected financial costs associated with your deployment. Most Forward Operating Bases (FOBs) are fully equipped with Exchange options that carry all necessities and some luxuries. Additionally, fast food chains and other snack items are available for sale. You should determine your budget for spending on these items in theater.
- Review and become familiar with the additional pays and benefits you will receive and account for those in your budget throughout the deployment. These include:
  - Combat Zone Tax Exclusion (CZTE)
  - Hostile Fire Pay/Imminent Danger Pay (HFP/IDP)
  - Family Separation Allowance (FSA)
- Reevaluate your financial goals. Determine if there are debts you can accelerate payment on or big-ticket items you may be able to pay cash for from deployment earnings.
- Assess the performance of your current investments.
- Reevaluate your life and personal property insurance needs (see chapters 13 and 15).
- Terminate a residential, business, or motor vehicle lease, if necessary.
- Terminate or suspend phone contracts, if necessary.

☐ Review your legal documents and preparations.
- Schedule an appointment with the post Judge Advocate General (JAG) office to handle legal concerns. Common ones include the creation of a will (provides legal transfer of property), a living will, or advanced health care directive (specifies health care treatment preferences in case the individual becomes incapacitated). You may also want to obtain a Power of Attorney (POA).
  - *Power of attorney.* A POA is someone an individual appoints to handle his or her affairs if he or she is unavailable or unable to do so. There are different types of POAs that can be assigned for specified time periods. Discuss which type may be appropriate in your particular situation. Often, a spouse or designee may

Combat Zone Tax Exclusion. IRS Publication 3 specifies that enlisted, warrant officer, or commissioned officer servicemembers serving in a combat zone may exclude the pay earned while in the combat zone from their taxable income. Commissioned officer personnel pay exclusion is limited to the highest rate of the senior enlisted servicemember (Sergeant Major of the Army) pay plus imminent danger/hostile fire pay received for each month served. The exclusion applies to the following payments:

- Active Duty pay.
- Imminent danger/hostile fire pay.
- Reenlistment bonuses when the reenlistment occurs in a month you served in a combat zone.
- Monetary awards for suggestions or inventions made while serving in a combat zone.
- Student loan repayments—enlisted members, warrant officers, and commissioned officers are allowed full- or partial-year exclusions. Officer exclusions are adjusted so as not to exceed the maximum allowed.
- Military pay earned while hospitalized as a result of wounds, disease, or injury incurred in the combat zone.

In addition, the IRS grants combat zone income tax filing extensions as well as extensions for contributing to Individual Retirement Accounts (IRAs).

need to handle important financial business in a servicemember's absence.

- *Will.* Discussing one's final wishes upon death can be difficult. However, it is best to have desires clearly outlined should an untimely death occur. Wills can be as general or specific as you wish. The more specific it is, however, the easier it will be for loved ones to honor your memory and preserve your legacy.
- Review your SGLI insurance policy to ensure the beneficiaries listed are consistent with your will.

☐ Familiarize yourself with benefits extended to servicemembers in combat.
- Savings Deposit Program (SDP).[1]
- Reduced interest rates on credit cards and loans (select banks).[2]
- Deferred or reduced minimum payments on credit cards and loans.

---

[1] SDP has a 10% guaranteed rate of return on savings up to $10,000 during a twelve-month deployment

[2] Ask your preferred lender about special discounted APRs on credit cards and consumer loans during the course of a deployment. The Servicemembers Civil Relief Act of 2004 (SCRA) caps interest payments on preservice debt at 6% APR.

Combat Zone Tax Entitlements. The following entitlements start upon arrival in a designated combat zone. Upon departure from the combat zone, the entitlements should stop automatically. If they do not, notify the local finance office or the government may deduct over-payments from your pay.

Entitlement	Amount	Remarks
Hardship Duty Pay	$50, $100, or $150/month (based on the location)	Prorated over 30 days. Does not start until in a combat zone for 30 days.
Hostile Fire Pay	$225/month	Prorated at $7.50 per day.
Family Separation Pay	$250/month (married servicemembers only)	Prorated over 30 days. Begins on first day of separation, but will not appear on LES until deployed for 30 con-secutive days.

- Tax filing extensions (For details, read Publication 3, *The Armed Forces Tax Guide,* or visit the IRS website at http://www.irs.gov).
- Maximum annual contributions to Roth IRA allowed, despite having no taxable income due to deployment, thanks to the 2006 Heroes Earned Retirement Opportunities (HERO) Act (see chapter 12).
- Combat zone tax exclusion.
- Combat zone leave. Servicemembers earn 2.5 days of leave per month (partial or full). Upon departure from the combat zone, any leave that is sold (that was earned in the designated combat zone) is free of federal and state tax when the leave is paid. Combat zone leave must be used prior to any other previous leave days accrued. The combat zone leave must be used within three years.
- Entitlements upon arrival in a combat zone.
- Increased contribution limits to Thrift Savings Plan (TSP).[3]

☐ Become familiar with opportunities to decrease personal expenses while in a combat zone.
- Suspend your cell phone usage plan.

---

[3] When deployed to a combat zone, servicemembers get additional benefits associated with TSP contributions. For instance, the elective deferral limit (the amount of your pay that can be contributed to your TSP account) is ordinarily $17,000. If you are in a combat zone receiving tax-exempt pay, there is no elective deferral limit, but there is an IRS provision that limits contributions to $50,000.

Thrift Savings Plan Tax Advantages. There are two tax benefits to making tax-deferred contributions to the TSP (see chapter 12 for detailed discussion):

- TSP contributions are taken out of your pay before taxes are withheld, so you pay less tax now.
- Taxes on contributions and earnings are deferred until you withdraw your money.

Additionally, when you serve in a combat zone or qualified hazardous duty area, most compensation you receive for active service is excluded from gross income on your IRS Form W-2, regardless of whether you contribute any of it to the TSP. Servicemembers receive no immediate tax benefit from contributing pay which has been excluded from gross income to the TSP; however, the earnings on those contributions are tax-deferred. When you make a withdrawal, money is taken from your total account balance proportionally from taxable funds and tax-exempt funds. The amount attributable to tax-exempt contributions will not be taxable. Services notify the TSP whenever contributions are from tax-exempt money. The TSP will then account for your tax-exempt contributions and, as indicated above, will ensure that these amounts are not reported to the IRS as taxable income. Consequently, those contributions will not be subject to taxation when you withdraw them. Your quarterly participant statement will show your tax-exempt balance separately. Visit http://www.tsp.gov for more information on the TSP.

- Consider storing your personal vehicle and suspending vehicular insurance (except for state-required coverage; see chapter 14). Ensure compliance with proper pre-storage maintenance to safely store a vehicle. Check online or with a local service center or dealer for the appropriate procedures.
- Consider putting household goods in storage (especially single soldiers or soldiers whose spouses decide to move closer to home).
- Consider subletting a room or entire apartment if your lease permits it, or consider breaking your lease altogether.[4]
- Maintain absolute minimal levels of heat/air conditioning and electricity. You may even cancel your utilities outright, but make sure not to run the risk of frozen pipes if your residence is in a cold climate or mildew if in a humid climate.

---

[4] SCRA also allows military personnel to break the terms of a lease or rental agreement upon receipt of PCS orders or deployment orders (greater than 90 days).

- Terminate or suspend subscriptions to magazines and newspapers (many companies will not forward correspondence to APO addresses).
☐ Wherever possible, establish online accounts for checking, savings, insurance, investments, and regular bills.
  - Make use of automatic bill payment functions for recurring bills (become familiar with these sites several months in advance to ensure that they are set up properly). Access to the Internet (unclassified) may be sporadic at best.
  - If a non-deployed spouse or designated POA holder will be in charge of your finances while you are deployed, make a list of usernames and passwords for each account and keep them in a secure place.
  - Notify companies that someone else will be managing your accounts. Ensure that the non-deployed spouse's name is on all joint accounts if full authority to make necessary transactions on accounts is preferred.
☐ Review TRICARE and DEERS status, benefits, and procedures with dependents to avoid costly medical expenses in your absence (see chapter 8).
☐ Review Veteran's Affairs and Survivor Benefits (see chapters 16 and 17).
  - Make these benefits known to your beneficiary.
  - Identify a point of contact to assist with these benefits in case of a tragedy.
☐ Review available continuing education opportunities.
  - If you are currently in school, notify teachers of the upcoming deployment and determine how the school handles deployed military professionals.
  - Research the online courses offered through the post or base education center. There may be opportunities to complete a significant portion of degree requirements during deployment.
  - Research and prepare for school admissions requirements by studying for and taking the SAT, GMAT, GRE, or other required standardized tests.
☐ Address family concerns. Deployments are especially challenging for the family. Take care to prepare your family members for the emotional as well as psychological challenges they will face.
  - Check out the services offered by the post or base community services office. There are special support programs for families of deployed servicemembers. This office provides a list of discount services offered by on-post centers as well as businesses in the surrounding area.
  - Connect with your unit's Family Readiness Group (FRG). The FRG is usually the first point of contact for timely information specific to your unit. It can also be an empathetic support network for families. The non-deployed spouse's or designee's contact information must be updated with the FRG administrator.

- Notify your family's child development center of your deployment. Childcare service discounts and evening and weekend specials are available at some centers.
- Determine the best way to keep in touch. Establish a Skype or other online phone/video account and do a few trial runs so the family gets familiar with the camera and computer software.
- Videotape yourself reading books to your children
- Discuss ways to capture and share family activities and special moments while you are deployed.
- Plan to spend quality time with your spouse and children before deploying. This could be an overnight stay at a local hotel or an extended vacation at a major theme park or national historic site.
- Transfer management of family maintenance activities to the non-deployed spouse. There are many household-upkeep items that he or she will need to be responsible for. Leave your spouse in the best position to easily continue maintenance of the household. Some items to consider include:
  - Bill payment
  - Vehicle tag renewals and registrations
  - Appliance repairs and purchases
  - Yard maintenance

During Deployment:
☐ Check your LES online at https://mypay.dfas.mil/mypay.aspx to ensure you are receiving your combat zone benefits.
- Confirm that hostile fire, family separation, and hardship duty entitlements have commenced. (Note: Family separation and hardship duty entitlements will not begin until the servicemember has been in theater for thirty days.)
- Confirm that federal income tax withholding has ceased.
- Confirm that combat zone leave days are accumulating.
☐ Confirm that new allotments have taken effect. These can be verified through the MyPay website as well.
- Increase TSP contributions.
- Increase contributions to other retirement portfolios (Roth or Traditional IRA, Savings Deposit Program SDP).
☐ Check your financial plan.
- Is the family (deployed and non-deployed members) staying on budget?
- Are the bills getting paid on time?
- Is the non-deployed spouse taking advantage of every possible deployment benefit?
- Are the family's goals realistic? Are they too high? Too low?

☐ Focus on your financial goals.
- Pay off debt with additional income.
- Eat at the dining facility as much as possible.
- Be conscious of special discounts offered to deployed servicemembers on certain big-ticket items (military car sales, watches, rugs, vacations, etc.), but only buy if the item is included in your budget.
- Maintain focus on long-term goals (house, child's education, and retirement).
- Maintain open communication between the deployed spouse and the non-deployed spouse regarding major financial decisions.

After Deployment:

☐ Check your LES online at https://mypay.dfas.mil/mypay.aspx to ensure combat zone benefits have stopped. This should occur automatically upon redeployment. Resubmit redeployment orders through the unit's personnel representative if benefits continue. If you continue to receive combat zone benefits for a period of time after redeployment, save the money you expect to repay to the government.

☐ Notify your creditors you have redeployed. Respond to any legal issues that may arise immediately. The Servicemembers' Civil Relief Act offers legal protection for servicemembers forced to deploy or relocate.
- Property owned may not be foreclosed on or seized without a court order.
- Anyone holding a lien on your property may not foreclose on or enforce any lien without a court order.

☐ Sign new property and car leases.

☐ Renew/start phone contracts.

☐ Reinitiate automobile insurance coverage if suspended during deployment.

☐ Reevaluate your predeployment financial plan in light of your current level of income and expenses.

☐ Review/adjust your budget based on current (non-combat zone) pay and allowances.

☐ Withdraw money invested in the Savings Deposit Program (SDP) and transfer to another investment or savings account.

☐ Resist the urge to splurge.

☐ Take a vacation.
- Discounted vacation packages may be offered to military veterans through local MWR offices or at travel websites such as the ones below:
  - http://www.armymwr.com
  - http://www.dodlodging.net
  - http://www.afvclub.com/ (Armed Forces Vacation Club)
  - http://www.shadesofgreen.org

- http://www.rockymountainblue.com
- http://www.halekoa.com
- http://www.dragonhilllodge.com
- http://www.edelweisslodgeandresort.com
- http://www.interliner.com
- http://www.vrbo.com

USEFUL WEBSITES WHEN PLANNING FOR DEPLOYMENT
General Military Information:
- http://www.militaryonesource.com
- http://www.military.com
- http://www.tsp.gov

Financial Planning:
- http://www.usaa.com
- http://www.usaaedfoundation.org
- http://www.aafmaa.com
- http://www.irs.gov ("Publication 3" addresses combat zone exclusions)

Relief Sites:
- http://www.redcross.org
- http://www.nmfa.org
- http://www.aerhq.org
- http://www.nmcrs.org

PART III

INVESTING FOR YOUR FUTURE

10

A Basic Investment Strategy— Mutual Funds and ETFs

Any investor, regardless of financial knowledge, must have an investment strategy in order to reach his or her financial goals. Investors must determine where they are, where they want to be, and how they will use their available resources to get from here to there. Here are six steps to develop a comprehensive investment strategy:

1. Determine how much you can afford to invest.
2. Set your investment horizon.
3. Assess your risk tolerance.
4. Identify investment instruments.
5. Evaluate investment performance.
6. Adjust/rebalance your investment portfolio periodically.

DETERMINE HOW MUCH YOU CAN AFFORD TO INVEST

> *"Pay yourself first . . . that simple step was easy to write,*
> *easy to say, and easy to ponder, but the true application*
> *of that simple step can be challenging for many."*[1]
>
> DARREN L. JOHNSON
> *AUTHOR, SPEAKER, AND PERSONAL DEVELOPMENT COACH*

Chapter 1 outlined the steps necessary to develop financial goals and a personal budget. There is no need to have an investment strategy if your monthly budget requires consumption of all your income for bare necessities. However, you should view investing a portion of your income as a priority and structure your budget accordingly. This may require trimming other parts of your budget that you might think of as "necessary" expenses, such as cell phone, cable, or entertainment. Establishing this "pay yourself first" mentality early in your investment career more easily enables you to establish and

---

[1] Darren L. Johnson, "Pay Yourself First," accessed on 24 July 2011 at: http://www.self growth.com/articles/pay_yourself_first.html.

achieve your investment goals. To start, it is helpful to establish a fixed portion of your income to invest (e.g. 6-10% of gross income). The percentage remains fixed, but the amount invested fluctuates as your income fluctuates. Most importantly, this investment amount comes out of the budget first— before any other expenses.

Once you have determined a manageable investment percentage, you should (especially if you are a beginning investor) set up automatic monthly allotments to transfer the money from your account following receipt of your paycheck. In addition to "paying yourself first," investing the same amount each month ensures you receive the benefits of "dollar cost averaging."

The dollar cost averaging investment strategy involves investing a constant dollar amount at specific intervals, usually each month, in a mutual fund or Exchange-Traded Fund (ETF). Over time, this method enables investors to pay less per share than the actual long-run average share price. The key to dollar cost averaging is that by purchasing the same dollar amount each period, investors buy more when the market is low (since shares cost less) and buy less when the market is high (since shares cost more). Consequently, investors will earn a positive return even if they sell their shares at a price per share equal to the long-run average price per share. Table 10-1 illustrates the mechanics of dollar cost averaging using $100 per month for three months in three different market scenarios.

Dollar cost averaging is the most common tool for investing in mutual funds. It is most frequently mentioned in financial news articles because it is the easiest investment method and requires little or no "active" participation by investors. If investors have not accumulated a sizable amount of money to

TABLE 10-1
DOLLAR COST AVERAGING

	Amount Invested	Rising Market		Declining Market		Fluctuating Market	
		Price Paid for Each Share	Number of Shares Bought	Price Paid for Each Share	Number of Shares Bought	Price Paid for Each Share	Number of Shares Bought
Jan	$100	$10.00	10.00	$10.00	10.00	$10.00	10.00
Feb	100	10.45	9.57	9.55	10.47	9.25	10.81
Mar	100	10.90	9.17	9.10	10.99	10.25	9.76
Total	$300		28.74		31.46		30.57
Average Share Cost to you[1]			$10.44		$9.54		$9.81
Average Share Price[2]			$10.45		$9.55		$9.83

[1] Average share cost = total dollars invested ÷ total shares purchased
[2] Average share price = sum of price paid per share column ÷ 3

invest, or feel uncomfortable taking an investment plunge with all their money at one time, slow integration into the market using dollar cost averaging is an attractive option.

Most mutual funds make it simple and convenient to dollar-cost-average by offering systematic investment plans. Under these plans, the fund will take a constant amount out of the investor's checking or savings account every month. Many funds will also reduce or waive the minimum initial investment if investors start a systematic investment plan. Therefore, investors who do not meet the minimum initial investment requirement may still be able to invest in the fund by initiating a systematic investment plan.

SET INVESTMENT HORIZON, ASSESS RISK TOLERANCE, AND IDENTIFY INVESTMENT INSTRUMENTS

Based upon your financial objectives, you must also consider how long you will invest in funds to meet a particular financial objective. Investments with greater risk (volatility) provide the greatest potential for higher returns but also the greatest potential for losses. Your tolerance for risk is driven by your investment horizon and your personality. If you need funds for a financial objective that is only a short time away (short investment horizon), then you should not be willing to accept as much risk. Additionally, if you cannot sleep at night due to the volatility of your portfolio, your risk aversion should drive you to select less risky investments. The length of the investment period, along with your risk tolerance, should dictate your investment selections.

Typically, you should select nearly risk-free investments such as money market funds as a vehicle to invest funds earmarked for financial objectives less than one year away; an example might be an emergency fund that could be needed at any time. For financial goals that are one to five years away, you might consider fixed-income mutual funds (corporate or government bond funds).

For financial objectives that are more than five years away, such as retirement, investors should consider a combination of fixed-income and equity mutual funds (those funds that buy and sell the stocks of publicly traded U.S. and foreign companies) with more emphasis on equity funds with longer investment horizons. For example, one guideline recommended to fairly conservative investors is that 100 minus one's age is the percentage of retirement investments that should be invested in equity-stock mutual funds. Investors can increase this percentage if they can tolerate the added risk, and should decrease this percentage if they have a risk-averse personality.

Once you have chosen your investment instruments, you should give consideration to initiating investment accounts online. Nearly all mutual funds have an online presence and a user-friendly interface to allow investors to easily open an account. You can make your initial contributions, as well as set up automatic investments in one sitting, all in the matter of minutes.

EVALUATE INVESTMENT PERFORMANCE AND ADJUST / REBALANCE YOUR INVESTMENT PORTFOLIO PERIODICALLY

Evaluating an investment's performance is an important step in attaining your investment goals. You should periodically evaluate your investments and objectives, and make changes as necessary. It is best to evaluate your investments against similar investments in order to judge their performance. This is more beneficial and informative than judging the performance of each investment or the collective investments in your portfolio against the market indices. For the average long-term investor, trying to time the market in order to "buy low and sell high" is often counterproductive and can result in missed opportunities. As discussed in previous sections, to maximize the expected value of returns, systematic investing over the long term is recommended for the majority of investors.

You should evaluate your investments' performance against funds in the same category as well as against benchmarks such as the S&P 500. Funds that consistently underperform against others in the same category or against their benchmarks may be reason for concern and warrant a change.

Coupled with evaluating individual investments, you should also evaluate your investment objectives. As your life situation changes over time, so should your investment objectives. For instance, as you near retirement or a child nears college age, preserving an investment's value becomes more important. This may require a reallocation of a portfolio toward more conservative investments (this chapter covers that process in greater detail in later sections).

Websites for Evaluating Investments

http://www.morningstar.com
http://finance.yahoo.com
http://www.marketwatch.com
http://money.msn.com
http://www.investopedia.com

WHAT IS A MUTUAL FUND?

Mutual funds provide an easy and effective means for investors of all experience levels to invest. With more than 7,500 different mutual funds, there is a vast spectrum of investment opportunities that vary in size (small, medium, or large companies), objective (growth or value), location (country, region, or global), and business model or industry sector (biotech, financials, manufacturing, etc.). There are also diversified mutual funds that capture large swaths of these characteristics in individual diversified funds (total market indexes).

Investment companies develop mutual funds by pooling money from different individual investors. Mutual fund companies sell shares in a particular fund to raise money to invest in additional securities. When investors buy shares, the fund uses the money, as well as the investments of other fund shareholders, to purchase stocks, bonds, and other financial instruments according to the fund's objectives. Some funds buy only one type of security—such as stocks of large blue-chip companies or stocks from companies in one specific industry. Others have greater diversification. A typical fund portfolio may include from thirty to several hundred different investment instruments.

Professional money managers direct the mutual fund by continually buying and selling securities. Investors (mutual fund shareholders) gain profits or losses in proportion to the number of mutual fund shares they own. Shareholders can track the status of a mutual fund by checking the fund's net asset value in the newspaper, by phone, via the Internet, and through monthly, quarterly, or annual statements.

By law, mutual fund companies must provide a prospectus for every fund they offer. The prospectus is a valuable tool for analyzing the fund's objectives, learning about the management team, viewing the performance of the fund's investments, and summarizing associated fees. Typically, the prospectus will also include quarterly and annual reports and discuss recent performance trends. The majority of mutual funds require an initial investment of $25 to $5,000, but some waive this minimum if investors enter into an automatic monthly investment plan of $25 or more monthly. Once investors have an account, they can usually make additional contributions whenever they like. The minimum additional investment is usually $25 to $200.

The Advantages of Mutual Funds

Diversification. The primary benefit of mutual funds for most investors is diversification of risk at a small cost. Mutual funds allow investors to achieve a diversified portfolio by investing only a few hundred dollars. Since most mutual funds invest in more than thirty different stocks or bonds, even a small investor can have a fully diversified portfolio—particularly if the manager invests in a number of different asset classes.

Convenience. Mutual funds permit small investors to have their money professionally managed. Professional managers have access to a wide range of information and can perform more extensive research than an individual investor when selecting securities for a portfolio. Mutual funds are convenient to buy and sell as all major funds have telephone and online exchange and redemption options. They also allow the investor to reinvest capital gains distributions and dividends in the fund or receive them directly, allowing investments to grow more quickly. Lastly, the ease with which an investor can open an account online and set up automatic investments makes mutual funds a very convenient option.

Flexibility. Liquidity, or the ability to quickly redeem shares for cash, is a great benefit of investing in mutual funds. This allows investors to quickly move money from one fund to another or redeem shares for cash as unforeseen personal expenses arise.

Families of Funds

Most mutual fund companies offer several different funds, typically called a family of funds. There are hundreds of mutual fund families that offer funds to everyday investors. Some of the largest mutual fund families are: Vanguard, American, and Fidelity. Other popular fund families include T. Rowe Price, Putnam, Janus, and American Century. These firms allow average investors to move money back and forth among the different funds in the family at no cost for retirement accounts (IRA transfers—direct transfers from one investment to another—can be performed with unlimited frequency; IRA rollovers—where the fund is completely liquidated and proceeds are provided to the investor to reinvest in a different fund within 60 days without penalty—can be performed one time per year) at little or no cost for taxable accounts (except for any short-term capital gains or losses due to changes in share price from purchase to redemption). The different funds within the family usually offer a broad mix of mutual fund types to appeal to a full spectrum of investor objectives. Consolidated account statements also make personal financial planning a less daunting task for the beginning investor. Fund families provide investors the ability to respond quickly to changes in market conditions, investment strategy, or risk tolerance, and to balance their portfolio by quickly transferring money from one fund to another.

Remember that profits and losses have tax implications. This is true even if you are redeeming shares to transfer from one fund to another within the same family of funds. Your mutual fund company will provide you with the information required for IRS reporting purposes. Before you decide to invest within a particular mutual fund family, you should consider whether the fund family offers the flexibility to transfer funds (at little or no cost) and the variety of funds available within the family.

Mutual Fund Categories

Mutual funds are usually classified by their investment strategy. Table 10-2 lists the common fund categories as determined by their objective and a general measure of their risk. Certain types of mutual funds may be better suited for some investors than others based on each investor's financial goals, retirement horizon, and willingness to accept risk.

The majority of mutual funds are open-end. The remaining funds are called closed-end funds—funds limited to a predetermined size (fixed number of shares). In contrast to closed-end funds, the more money investors put into open-end funds, the larger the fund grows (more shares created). Therefore, investors can buy or sell shares in open-end funds from the mutual fund itself, through a financial advisor, or through a broker. An open-end fund creates and

TABLE 10-2
MUTUAL FUND CATEGORIES

Category	Primary Objective	Risk	Potential Reward
Aggressive Growth	Capital Appreciation	Extremely High	High
Growth	Capital Appreciation	High	
Value	Capital Appreciation & Income	Moderate to High	
Income	Current Income	Moderate	
Balanced	Current Income	Low to Moderate	
Bond	Current Income	Low	Low
Specialized Funds			
Industry/Sector Fund	Capital Appreciation/Income	Low to high	Low to high
Location Fund	e.g., China, SW Asia, Global,	Low to high	Low to high
Index Fund	e.g., Sector, location, total market	Low to high	Low to high

sells as many shares as investors demand and must redeem investors' shares whenever investors want to sell them. The share price of an open-end fund depends on the underlying value of the securities in its portfolio. Small (dollar amount) investors generally favor purchasing open-end funds over closed-end funds and direct investment in individual stocks because of the relative ease of purchasing and redeeming shares and diversification of their portfolio. However, some closed-end funds, such as Exchange-Traded Funds (ETFs), are gaining popularity with some investors; the end of this chapter discusses ETFs in more detail.

Common Types of Mutual Funds

Index Funds. Since there are thousands of open-end mutual funds from which to select, the task of selecting representative investments for each asset class may seem daunting. A popular technique to avoid this process is investing in index or "passive" funds.

The intent of an index fund is to replicate the return of a particular index such as the S&P 500 (largest 500 U.S. companies) or the Russell 2000 (smallest 2000 U.S. companies). There are index funds for most asset classes, including U.S. equities, U.S. Treasury bonds, and international stocks. Index funds typically have low management and expense fees since they require less management. The fund manager uses computer models to replicate an already-determined portfolio of stocks or bonds based on defined characteristics. In a sense, the investor "owns the market" that the index represents. Also, since the index rarely changes, low portfolio turnover results in better tax efficiency for the fund shareholders. Finally, an index fund stays fully invested in the index it represents. Imagine if an individual investor tried to replicate the S&P 500 by buying 500 different stocks—the brokerage fees would be staggering. Mutual fund managers have the ability to do this with relative ease and low cost because of the volume of money available to them.

Index funds offer investors an inexpensive means to own a highly diversified portfolio. Investing in a broad-market index fund, such as an S&P 500 index fund, is a great starting point for a portfolio. As the investor begins to accumulate wealth, these funds serve as the core of a portfolio of mutual funds. The investor could subsequently diversify and build around this core by adding bond funds, industry funds, and international or regional funds (funds that invest in companies based outside the United States [international] or within a specific region [regional]). Within these international or regional classes of funds, investors can invest in companies ranging from small to large, or growth to value, allowing investors to select funds that match their desired risk/return profile. Returns from these funds move differently from U.S.-based equities and can help reduce volatility.

Active (Managed) Funds. Funds that are classified as active or managed usually carry higher fees or a type of load. Often, these funds are classified as Class A, Class B, or Class C funds. These funds have either a front-end load (a sales charge applied when you buy shares in a fund), a back-end load (usually referred to as a "contingent deferred sales charge"—a sales charge when you sell shares in a fund), 12b-1 fees (fees paid to third-party brokers who promote/sell their funds), or a combination of all three. Additionally, these funds might be solely invested in a specific industry such as life science, technology, or energy. The justification for this "fee" is usually that the fund will "beat" index funds on average because "more qualified" management is taking more of a hands-on approach to the stocks that make up the fund. In other words, the fee is simply the cost of being in a fund that requires more involvement by a fund manager(s) and that must buy and sell securities more often. Some stockbrokers buy and sell these funds exclusively because the commission on them can be significant over the long term. Many investors are led to believe that the return on load funds will more than compensate for the sales charge. On average, there is no evidence that this is typically the case.

Target-Date Funds. Target-Date funds, also known as life-cycle or age-based funds, allow individual investors to diversify their entire portfolio easily and with the least amount of time and effort by investing in just one fund. They blend together multiple mutual funds (usually within the same fund family), aiming at broad-based diversification. These funds allocate a percentage of the investment among different mutual funds based on the target date and selected risk profile (e.g., 60% U.S. stocks, 30% foreign stocks, 10% bonds). An investor simply picks one of these funds based on his or her target date, whether it is retirement or a child going to college, and the percentage of stock funds within the portfolio will decrease as the date nears. This way an investor can be appropriately diversified with the desired blend of mutual funds without ever having to switch funds over time.

Mutual Fund Expenses

Expenses related to mutual funds reduce an investor's return and should be taken seriously. Though mutual funds are one of the least expensive ways to invest, they still have expenses. Three common mutual fund expenses are: loads, management fees, and 12B-1 fees. Investors can find these fees disclosed in the mutual fund's prospectus.

Loads. Funds with front-end loads (called "Sales Charge (Load) on Purchases" in the prospectus) can, by regulation, charge as high as 8.5% of the initial investment amount. The typical range is 2 to 8.5%. Most importantly, front-end loads can significantly affect the amount of an investment actually used to purchase shares. An investor effectively starts with a negative return on day one of the investment.

Funds with back-end loads ("Deferred Sales Charge (Load)" in the prospectus) charge a commission (usually 2 to 6%) to sell fund shares. Funds commonly impose these fees to discourage short-term investing or market timing (switching in and out of a fund to make short-term profits). Back-end loads are not prominently advertised, so investors must carefully read the fund's prospectus to determine if the fund has any. Some funds have declining back-end loads that start out high and then decline to a low fee or no fee after investors hold shares for some time period.

No-load funds, when purchased directly from the mutual fund company, do not charge commissions. Most financial experts strongly encourage beginning and intermediate investors to choose only no-load funds.

Management and 12B-1 Fees. Management fees of most mutual funds range from 0.2 to 2.5%. The fund collects these fees out of the fund's assets. The greater the fees, the less an investor receives in returns. 12B-1 fees cover marketing and advertising costs. About 50% of all funds charge a 12B-1 fee which reduces an investment's total return, so it is wise to do the research on all associated fees. These two fees are included in the Total Annual Fund Operating Expenses disclosed in the fund's prospectus and should be weighed heavily when deciding on a mutual fund. You should view fees as money coming out of your pocket—because that's what they are. For example, a $10,000 investment that produced a 10% annual return before expenses and had an annual operating expense of 1.5% would be worth approximately $49,725 after 20 years. The same investment with a .5% annual operating expense would be worth $60,858. Such a seemingly minor difference in a fund's expenses can make a big difference in an investment's value over time. You can make similar comparisons analyzing the impact of fees using the actual fees of different mutual funds by using the Financial Industry Regulatory Authority (FINRA) Fund Analyzer tool (http://apps.finra.org/fund

analyzer/1/fa.aspx). The lower fees of typical passive funds are one of the main factors that make them an attractive investment option.

Contractual Mutual Funds: A Cautionary Note. The most expensive type of front-end load fund you can buy is a contractual mutual fund. Insurance agents, commissioned financial planners, and other mutual fund peddlers prefer to sell this kind of fund because the salesman's compensation is much more lucrative than with other loaded funds. As a result of a 2004 *New York Times* article, firms selling these products came under great scrutiny because they tended to target service members, used "high-pressure" tactics, and used former military officers and noncommissioned officers to sell their products.

Contractual mutual funds obligate investors to invest a set number of dollars every month over a ten- to twenty-year time frame. This "contract" is generally not considered a legal obligation, and can be cancelled at any time. A significant drawback of contractual plans is that they often take 50% of the first year's investment as a commission, with an additional sales charge being applied (between 2 and 8.5%) for all investments, including the first year's. This means that up to 50% of the first year's investments goes into the salesman's pocket (and another 2 to 8.5% into the fund company's account), not into the investor's account! Also, if investors cancel their "contract," they may lose up to 50 % of their initial investment because the up-front commissions are nonrefundable after the grace period (usually eighteen months) expires. Fortunately, many recent laws have been implemented that require the sellers of these funds to be much more explicit in their explanation of the contract.

Should Investors Ever Buy a Load Fund? Be wary of investing in a load mutual fund. On average, load funds do not consistently outperform no-load funds. Remember that the load fee does not pay for superior research or better management; it simply compensates the salesman for selling shares to investors. See Table 10-3 for a comparison of an investment with different fees

TABLE 10-3
$10,000 INVESTED WITH 10% ANNUAL RETURN BEFORE EXPENSES

Fund	Total Annual Operating Expense	Front-end Load	Back-end Load	Investment Value after 10 Years
A	.5%	None	None	$60,858
B	1.5%	None	None	$49,725
C	.5%	5%	None	$57,815
D	.5%	None	5%	$60,358*

* Assumes the back-end load is applied to the initial investment amount only.

Source for investment value after 10 years: The U.S. Securities and Exchange Commission mutual fund cost calculator (www.sec.gov/investor/tools/mfcc/get-started.htm)

and load structures. All else being equal, a no-load fund with lesser fees yields a higher final investment value.

Researching and Selecting a Mutual Fund

Before researching specific funds or fund categories, you should complete the first three steps in developing an investment strategy. In general, the fund category you choose will depend on your own risk preference and time horizon. The longer your investment horizon, the more attractive riskier funds become. Other considerations include your tax situation and need for steady income.

As a basic guideline, you should invest savings for short-term goals (less than one year) in money market or low-risk bond mutual funds. For medium-term goals (one to five years), you should consider short-term government or corporate bond funds. To satisfy long-term goals, you should have a diversified mix of stock, balanced, international, and perhaps sector funds.

When the time comes to research different mutual funds, there are many independent websites that can help you. The five mentioned earlier in this chapter are a great starting point. They have user-friendly tools that can help you navigate through the countless funds available and narrow the list down to those that fit your needs. As an example, Morningstar's site (http://www.morningstar.com/Cover/Tools.html) allows you to screen the funds available by selecting criteria such as the fund's category or objectives (e.g., aggressive growth, large company growth, value, and income), manager longevity (e.g., one, three, five, and ten years), past performance (e.g., one-, three-, five-, and ten-year returns), loads (load vs. no-load), fees (complete expense ratios), turnover, and price-to-earnings ratios, among others. You should select your desired settings for each of the criteria (start with *very* strict criteria) and then allow the program to search all available mutual funds. Then loosen the criteria as necessary to have some funds in the pool. After narrowing the potential purchase options to a few mutual funds, use the website's reviews and commentary on funds to help you make your final choice. Most investors find these websites extremely helpful in weeding out funds that do not meet their criteria. The choice between the handful of funds that meet all investor criteria is difficult (and less important). Because the stock market is a random walk (no one can predict movement), it is impossible to determine which of these remaining mutual funds will outperform the others in a given year. Since you have already eliminated about 99 percent of all mutual funds, which did not meet your criteria, you should waste little additional energy in selecting one that you are comfortable with.

Once you decide on a fund, it is important to read the fund's prospectus to gain a better understanding of the fund's objectives, main asset holdings, and fees and expenses. You can request a prospectus from any mutual fund company by telephone, in writing, or by submitting a request online at the company's website. Company websites frequently allow investors to download the prospectus immediately.

The purpose of reading the prospectus and researching mutual funds is to determine whether a particular fund is consistent with your investment objective, time horizon, and risk tolerance. In particular, you should review a fund's prospectus for, at a minimum, the following fund information:

- Investment strategy
- Expenses
- Past performance, and a comparison of this performance to more common benchmarks, such as the S&P 500
- Manager longevity and the manager's philosophy
- Instructions for opening a fund account and/or an application to start one
- How and when distributions are made and taxed
- Important administrative data about the fund, such as contact information, changes to the fund (if relevant), etc.

Buying Mutual Fund Shares

After you feel comfortable with your selected fund, it is time to make an investment. Buying mutual fund shares is relatively easy, even for a beginning investor. The most convenient way to do this is to go directly to the selected mutual fund's website and open an account. Most websites allow investors to make an initial investment at the time of opening an account by transferring money from their bank. It is also possible (and advisable) to set up automatic investments at this time as well. It is possible to walk away from your account application session with a new investment account set on "autopilot." The only thing left to do is the periodic evaluation discussed earlier in this chapter. If you are not comfortable establishing an account online, you may request paper application materials, either online or by telephone, to complete and mail to the mutual fund company.

Selling Mutual Fund Shares

There are several reasons to sell mutual fund shares. These reasons include a change in investment horizon, an unforeseen personal expense, and poor fund performance. Of these, one of the most common reasons investors sell their shares is performance. If the return is consistently below the returns of funds with similar objectives, then you may consider selling shares and investing elsewhere. However, you should avoid the temptation to sell a fund's shares just because the fund or the market has a bad quarter or year, as even the best funds have periods of subpar performance. Always focus on the long-term record. Many inexperienced and undisciplined investors sell out at market bottoms, missing the ride back up to the top, and then buy back at the market peak when it is too late. This behavior directly contradicts the old Wall Street adage of "buy low, sell high." Our economy is affected to a large extent by random, unpredictable events. Experts who spend their whole lives analyzing the economy have trouble accurately forecasting what will happen next or to what degree. Studies of experts that claim their ability to "time the market" show that few—no more than would be expected by random chance—are able to beat the return of those that buy and hold their mutual funds over the long-term. The major results of attempting to time the market are more taxes, higher transaction costs, and lower average returns. A good compromise if your fund is doing poorly is to simply hold on to the investment and withhold future investments until you have more confidence in the investment's expected future performance.

Another consideration into the "sell" decision is the potential tax impli-cation. That is, you could pay taxes on any capital gains received from the sale, reducing the amount available for your next investment.

When you make the decision to sell shares, it is relatively easy and can be done by phone or online with the fund company.

Mutual Fund Returns

Mutual fund returns come from three sources: dividends, capital gains distrib-utions, and changes in the share price of the fund. When a mutual fund earns dividends or interest on its securities, the fund passes those along to the investor in the form of dividends. If a mutual fund sells some of its securities for more than it paid for them, it must pass that profit along to the shareholders in the form of capital gains distributions. Finally, changes in the share price of the fund translate to profit or loss for the shareholders. If an investor sells fund shares for more than they paid for them, he or she will earn a profit, or capital gain, on those shares. Conversely, an investor could incur a loss on the shares by selling them for less than he or she paid. The total return on the mutual fund includes profits or losses from all three sources. Of course, any loads and oper-ating expenses will also reduce the total return. You should also be mindful of the impact taxes have on your overall return. Most fund companies send annual summaries; you should file these as part of their record keeping practices.

Record Keeping

One of the biggest problems for investors in mutual fund shares is that of good record keeping. Many investors pay too much in taxes when they later sell mutual fund shares because they did not keep all the records of purchases that their fund sent. You should keep records of purchases, reinvestments, div-idends, capital gains distributions, and sales proceeds received for as long as you own any shares in a fund—and then a few years after any sales to satisfy the IRS. At a minimum, keep the annual summary statements, as well as all tax documents. To help investors with tracking investments, many companies offer software that tracks investment transactions and performance.

EXCHANGE-TRADED FUNDS (ETF)

An Exchange-Traded Fund, or ETF, is an index fund that trades on the market similarly to how a stock trades. ETFs are very practical and allow investors to follow major stock indexes, such as the Dow Jones Industrial Average, the Standard & Poor's 500 Index, and the Nasdaq Composite. Almost every major index, from gold to real estate to international trusts, has an ETF. Investors should understand that this form of investing is simply another method of diversifying assets. Instead of picking stocks, investors are literally buying a particular market of similar stocks, much like buying shares in a mutual fund. ETFs share many similarities with mutual funds but also have many differences—many of which are beneficial to the investor.

ETFs blend the benefits of stock trading together with the benefits of traditional index fund investing. The annual expenses for ETFs are comparable to passively managed (index) funds and are much lower than expenses for actively managed funds. However, ETFs must be bought through brokerage firms just like stocks are purchased, so there is a transaction cost (brokerage fees range from about $5 per trade to hundreds of dollars per trade—see chapter 11, "Advanced Investment Strategy," for details about brokerage firms). For example, an investor who makes a systematic, monthly investment of $100 into an ETF and pays a $10 brokerage commission on each purchase is effectively paying a 10% load. Investors who make larger lump-sum purchases can minimize the effects of the brokerage fees (making a $1,000 investment with a $10 brokerage commission is paying a 1% load). ETFs can be traded intraday at a price set by the market, whereas mutual funds are priced at the end of the day after all trading has ceased. In other words, investors cannot quickly sell a mutual fund during a daily market rally or downturn, while they can sell or buy an ETF during the day just as they would a stock. This "flexibility" in purchasing and selling shares is seen as a benefit to some investors. Finally, ETFs tend to generate fewer capital gains than actively managed mutual funds (but a similar number to passively managed [index] funds) because of the low turnover of the securities that comprise them. On the other hand, investors may generate sizable capital gains or losses by conducting intraday trades just as they would with stocks.

Mutual funds and ETFs allow individual investors a convenient opportunity to invest in a broad mix of securities (stocks and bonds). They both achieve the same goal of diversification, although they operate and are classified differently. In response to the introduction of ETFs, many major mutual fund companies have lowered the management fees of their index funds. However, recent data shows money flowing out of mutual funds and into ETFs. ETFs provide yet another reliable method for investors to diversify assets at little cost.

ETFs Versus Mutual Funds

Since ETFs and mutual funds are similar in concept, investors may wonder which one they should invest in first. Perhaps the biggest consideration in deciding where to invest rests on your initial investment. If, at any given time, you are making large purchases of an amount over $1,000, it might make sense to invest in an ETF, because one-time brokerage fees and ETF maintenance fees will be lower than mutual fund maintenance fees. Alternatively, if you plan to make monthly systematic investments over time, then you should consider a mutual fund rather than an ETF to avoid brokerage fees for each share purchase. In summary, mutual funds are generally best (have lower expenses) for more frequent purchases of shares, while ETFs are often best for large-dollar, lower-frequency purchases.

Although there are no guarantees of profit, mutual funds and ETFs offer the investor a convenient and low-cost method of achieving diversification. Investors should consider both of these types of investments as part of their overall financial strategy.

ADDITIONAL INVESTING GUIDES

Bernstein, William J. *The Four Pillars of Investing: Lessons for Building a Winning Portfolio.* New York: McGraw-Hill Companies, 2002.
Edleson, Michael E. *Value Averaging: The Safe and Easy Strategy for Higher Investment Returns.* Chicago: International Publishing, 1991.
Morris, Kenneth M. *Wall Street Journal Guide to Understanding Money and Investing.* New York: Lightbulb Press, 2004.

11

Advanced Investment Strategy

As discussed in chapter 10, there are six steps that you must take in order to develop a comprehensive investment strategy: (1) determine how much you can afford to invest; (2) set your investment time horizon; (3) assess your risk tolerance; (4) identify investment instruments; (5) evaluate investment performance; and (6) adjust/rebalance your investment portfolio periodically.

This chapter uses these same six steps to introduce some advanced investment concepts and theories for those servicemembers wanting to take a more hands-on approach with their financial assets and have a full understanding of the topics introduced in the previous chapter. Some readers may not find this chapter "advanced" enough for their interests. Readers who are looking to understand technical financial analysis, sophisticated investing techniques, or trading derivatives, currencies, and other alternative assets, may want to seek advice from one of the many guides found in the personal finance section of a local bookstore. Those topics are beyond the scope of this book and the needs of most servicemembers. However, most readers should find this chapter extremely beneficial when putting together personal investment strategies.

SELECT AND OPEN A BROKERAGE ACCOUNT

In order to buy and sell financial assets on an exchange you must open a brokerage account. The two main types of brokerage accounts are full service and discount. Full-service accounts involve more interaction with a stockbroker who, for a fee, provides advice, executes trades, and/or makes investment decisions on a client's behalf. Conversely, discount brokerages typically allow clients to conduct online trades with little or no interaction with a live broker. As a result, discount brokerages charge significantly lower commissions and associated expenses. Since the advent of the internet, discount brokerages have proliferated.

When selecting a brokerage firm, you should consider the costs associated with the tools the trader expects to use. For most investors, trading cost is the primary consideration in selecting a broker. A share of stock purchased with a $50 commission is identical to the same share purchased with a $4.99 commission. You should also consider brokerage firms' margin rates, research capabilities, quality of service, other available services, and execution times when choosing a firm. It is also convenient to keep an IRA account at the same brokerage firm as your taxable brokerage account. Given the higher costs of full-service brokers and the ease of conducting transactions with a discount broker, a discount broker is a better fit for most investors' needs.

DETERMINE HOW MUCH YOU CAN AFFORD TO INVEST
Chapter 1 discussed the development of financial goals as well as a personal budget. There is no reason to have an investment strategy if your family monthly budget requires consumption of all disposable income for necessary goods and services. However, in most cases, your budget should support some level of investment. Advanced investors normally have performed this basic budget analysis and already have determined the amount available for investment.

SET YOUR INVESTMENT HORIZON
Based upon the financial objectives that you identified in chapter 1, you should know how long to invest your funds to meet a particular financial objective. Investments with greater risk (volatility) provide the greatest potential for higher returns but also the greatest potential for losses. How do you determine the best combination of investment assets? Part of the answer lies in understanding your time horizon and the most relevant risks. Table 11-1 illustrates the impact of an investor's time horizon and asset type on historical returns. Note that Table 11-1 includes only domestic investments; Table 11-2 (page 180) and Figure 11-1 (page 173) address additional investment asset classes.

Most investment managers equate the risk of a financial asset (e.g., stocks or bonds) to the volatility of its expected return. Historically, the financial markets have rewarded investors with higher returns for their investment in more volatile assets. That is to say, if investors accept the risk of having some bad years with negative returns, the long-term average gains of the good years will offset the losses in the bad years and yield higher average returns. Viewing Table 11-1 from left to right demonstrates the reduction in the risk one assumes by investing in each asset category. Table 11-1 displays the variation of volatility in these financial assets, demonstrating the wide range of annual returns for stocks (potentially greater rewards with greater risk) compared to the relatively low variation of returns for treasury bills (lower risk, yielding lower but more stable returns).

> *The risk of a financial asset equates to the*
> *volatility of its returns.*

Examine the one-year holding period returns at the top of Table 11-1. Note that either small- or large-company stocks had the highest return in fifty-five of the eighty-five one-year holding periods. However, they both had a

TABLE 11-1
DOMESTIC INVESTMENT COMPOUNDED ANNUAL RETURNS
FOR VARIOUS TIME PERIODS

	U.S. Small-company Stocks	U.S. Large-company Stocks	U.S. Corporate Bonds	Long-term U.S. Government Bonds	T-Bills	Effect of Inflation
	HIGH		RISK		LOW	
One-Year Holding Periods (85)						
Arithmetic annualized average	16.74%	11.88%	6.23%	5.88%	3.67%	3.07%
Highest annual return	142.87%	53.99%	42.56%	40.36%	14.71%	18.16%
Lowest annual return	-58.01%	-43.34%	-8.09%	-14.90%	-0.02%	-10.30%
Negative periods	26	24	17	22	1	N/A
Periods with best return	38	17	12	16	12	N/A
Five-Year Holding Periods (81)						
Arithmetic annualized average	13.24%	10.07%	5.96%	5.57%	3.73%	3.17%
Highest annual return	45.90%	28.56%	22.51%	21.62%	11.12%	10.06%
Lowest annual return	-27.54%	-12.47%	-2.22%	-2.14%	0.07%	-5.42%
Negative periods	9	9	3	6	0	N/A
Periods with best return	43	23	4	9	2	N/A
Ten-Year Holding Periods (76)						
Arithmetic annualized average	13.87%	10.64%	5.95%	5.56%	3.81%	3.43%
Highest annual return	30.38%	20.06%	16.32%	15.56%	9.17%	8.67%
Lowest annual return	-5.70%	-1.38%	0.98%	-0.07%	0.15%	-2.57%
Negative periods	2	2	0	1	0	N/A
Periods with best return	47	20	6	2	1	N/A
Twenty-Year Holding Periods (66)						
Arithmetic annualized average	14.46%	11.30%	5.75%	5.41%	4.05%	3.77%
Highest annual return	21.13%	17.88%	12.13%	12.09%	7.72%	6.36%
Lowest annual return	5.74%	3.11%	1.34%	0.69%	0.42%	0.07%
Negative periods	0	0	0	0	0	N/A
Periods with best return	58	8	0	0	0	N/A

Source: Computations from Ibbotsons, 2011.

negative return nearly a third of the time. Thus, if the time horizon for a particular goal were only a year away, stocks would not be a prudent selection for meeting the goal. Treasury bills make a better choice, since they only had one instance of a negative return over a one-year time horizon.

Lengthening the investment time horizon, look at the five-year holding periods. Notice that small and large company stocks provided negative returns in nine out of eighty-one five-consecutive-year periods. That means that someone who had invested in stocks in a randomly chosen five-year period would have lost money about 11% of the time. Comparatively, government bonds provided negative returns in only six periods—less than 8% of the time.

Now look at the twenty-year holding periods. Stocks not only had no periods with a negative return, but they also had the best rate of return, compared to the other investment instruments, in all of the sixty-six different twenty-year periods. Of those periods, small-company stocks and large-company stocks provided superior returns fifty-eight and eight times, respectively. The important implication for developing an investment strategy is this: The longer your investment time horizon, the more risk you should consider taking in a portfolio to gain a higher rate of return. Over time, the good years can offset the bad years. On the other hand, the shorter the time horizon, the more important it is to invest in less volatile financial assets to reduce the impact of negative returns.

Stock and bond market volatility is the greatest short-term risk to an investor's portfolio. Thus, you should place funds designated for short-term goals in an investment that provides lower volatility—and, correspondingly, a lower return. The greatest long-term risks to an investor's portfolio are inflation and taxes. Therefore, you should invest money with longer-term objectives in assets that provide the greatest possibility of providing returns that outpace inflation and taxes—thereby achieving your financial goal.

> *Funds designated to meet short-term goals should be placed in investments that earn positive returns with the lowest volatility.*

ASSESS YOUR RISK TOLERANCE

Potential investors must look at the risk associated with returns (especially high returns) to determine if the risk is worth the potential reward. As already shown, an investment with the highest expected return will make a portfolio grow most quickly. Based on the average historical returns in Figure 11-1, stocks realized the quickest growth. So, should everyone invest his or her entire portfolio in stocks? No. Your risk tolerance, investment time horizon, and personality traits should be the factors used to determine the best investment vehicle for you. If you have a short-term financial objective, you should

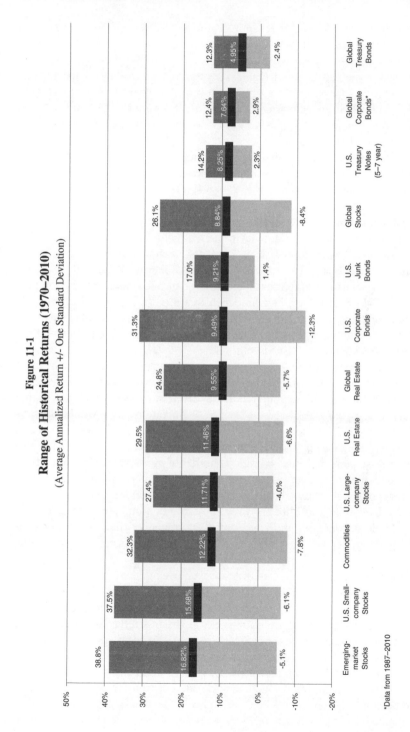

Figure 11-1
Range of Historical Returns (1970–2010)
(Average Annualized Return +/- One Standard Deviation)

*Data from 1987–2010

not accept as much risk. If potential volatility (seeing a stock rise and fall everyday in price) will keep you from sleeping at night, then you have not accurately assessed your risk tolerance.

Risk is the extent to which an asset's returns vary from the expected rate of return. Stocks provide the greatest return, but also the greatest risk, as reflected by their greater variation of returns. If not for the trade-off between risk and return, most investors would choose the investment that provides the highest rate of return.

Standard deviation, a mathematical measure of variability, serves as a convenient measure for risk, showing the level of confidence that a particular year's returns will fall inside a range. Figure 11-1 depicts the range of returns that are within one standard deviation of the average return for twelve major investments. One can see that there is more fluctuation in investments with greater historical rates of return, as measured by the standard deviation. Table 11-1 shows that the lower-risk investments, such as treasury notes, have a smaller distribution of (or variation in) historical returns. Returns also fall outside of these displayed returns, since a range of one standard deviation provides only a 68.2% level of confidence that a particular year's return falls inside the range. For example, if investors faced a situation such as investing in an emerging-market stock one hundred times, the rate of return would fall between 38.8% and -5.1% sixty-eight times.

There are two principal risks associated with financial assets, as measured by standard deviation: systematic (or market) risk and unsystematic (or idiosyncratic) risk. Systematic risk arises from macroeconomic factors that affect a large number of risky assets, or an economy as a whole, such as changes in GDP, inflation, and interest rates. Systematic risk factors affect all assets to one degree or another (the economy in general). Unsystematic risk comprises factors that affect a limited number of assets, industries, or particular companies or countries, such as labor strikes, parts shortages, or other asset specific risk factors. Investors can reduce or eliminate unsystematic risk with a diversified portfolio; however, they cannot eliminate systematic risk.

While standard deviation measures the cumulative effect of both systematic and unsystematic risks, the correlation coefficient is a metric of just the systematic risk, measuring how closely an asset's returns move relative to another asset's returns. If the assets' returns move at the exact rate (positive or negative), the correlation coefficient is +1.0. If the assets' returns have exactly the opposite rates (i.e., +5% and -5%), the correlation coefficient is -1.0. If the assets' returns have no correlation (i.e., one asset's return does *not* change along with a change in another asset's return), the correlation coefficient is zero. Correlation coefficients range from -1.0 to +1.0.

Figure 11-2 uses the returns of U.S. large-company stocks as a proxy value representing the entire U.S. market, showing the correlation coefficient (the value of the vertical axis) between a given asset class (labeled on the horizontal axis) and U.S. large-company stocks. The figure demonstrates that all

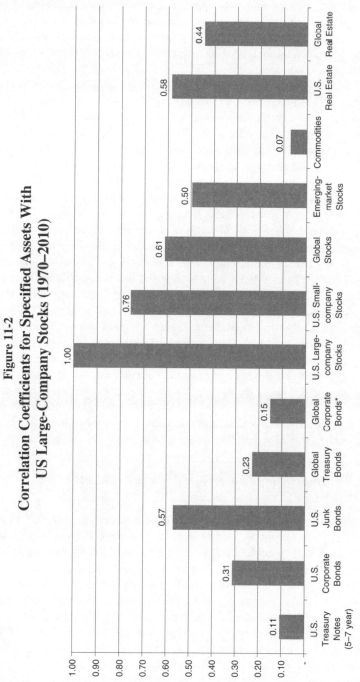

Figure 11-2
Correlation Coefficients for Specified Assets With
US Large-Company Stocks (1970–2010)

*Data from 1987–2010

investment vehicles carry some systematic risk (market) from the overall U.S. economy, with varying correlation levels between the investments. By developing a diversified (mixed) investment portfolio, with different correlation coefficients, you can minimize your exposure to systematic risk and eliminate the effects of nonsystematic risk.

IDENTIFY INVESTMENT INSTRUMENTS

As stated previously, your investment time horizon and risk tolerance should influence your investment selections. The previous section discussed how diversification could help mitigate investment risks. Figure 11-3 demonstrates why you have heard that you should not put all of your eggs in one basket. Figure 11-3 shows two available investment choices, depicted by curves A and B. Both investments have positive returns and fluctuate with the economy (i.e., the stock market, technological progress, and other systematic factors). Both investments have periods of positive and negative returns, but overall positive returns in the long-term, as the positive returns outweigh the negative ones. Since you cannot consistently predict when the swings will occur, and you may need the money from your investment just when it is in a trough instead of at a peak, buying just one of the investments leads to high levels of volatility and risk. To minimize that effect, you can buy equal amounts of both investment A and investment B so that the upswings of one can counter the downswings of the other. Line C in Figure 11-3 represents an investor portfolio with equal investments in instruments A and B. Portfolio C maintains the rates of return of A and B while reducing the volatility associated with investing only in A or B. Due to the differences in systematic and non-systematic risk, some investments react differently to the same general economic conditions, making it possible to reduce the volatility of your portfolio while maintaining a desired rate of return. This is the advantage of diversification.

> *Diversifying a portfolio will reduce its volatility.*

Chapter 10 explained that mutual funds and exchange-traded funds (ETFs) invest in multiple companies in order to diversify assets and reduce risk associated with specific companies (unsystematic risk). Following the same logic, it is also important to diversify your portfolio across sectors and asset classes to provide additional protection for your long-term investments from systematic and nonsystematic risks. Diversifying in this manner is called asset allocation. Any asset class can perform best in a given year because the business cycle impacts the performance of asset classes (see Figure 11-4). Therefore, it is important to invest in a combination of asset classes consistent with your risk tolerance and investment horizon.

It is important to understand how general economic conditions affect the general performance of different asset categories. Figure 11-4 illustrates a

Figure 11-3
Benefits of Diversification

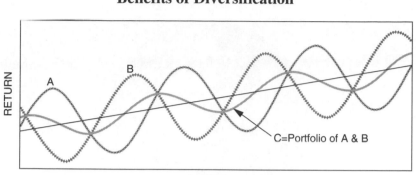

stylized, general relationship between asset class performance and the stage of the general business cycle. It highlights the four primary periods of the business cycle as characterized by capacity and economic growth. Capacity refers to the gap between actual and potential Gross Domestic Product (GDP), or national production. Spare capacity roughly corresponds to "slack" in productive ability, or underutilization of existing productive resources. In contrast, tight capacity refers to the full utilization of existing productive resources. Growth refers to a change in GDP—the increase or decrease in national production. A quick review of the chart illustrates that the different assets perform

Figure 11-4
Asset Class Returns: Tied to the Business Cycle

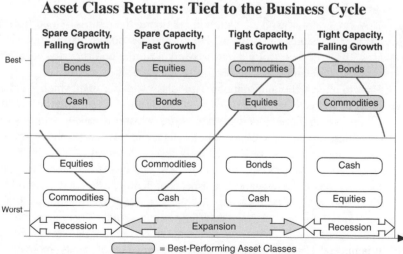

• The chart depicts the business cycle in terms of the GDP Output Gap (When Actual GDP exceeds Potential GDP)
• Note that the four business cycle periods above are not equal in duration.

Figure 11-5
Broad Asset Classes

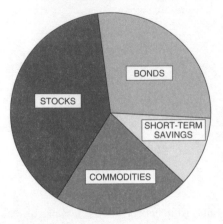

better than other assets at different points in the business cycle. As it is nearly impossible to accurately predict the business cycle, you should diversify your portfolio in order to capture each asset category's periods of outperformance relative to the other investment categories.

An asset allocation model is a plan for allotting funds to different asset classes within a portfolio. Figure 11-5 shows an asset allocation using four broad asset classes: stocks, bonds, commodities, and short-term savings (savings accounts, CDs, and money market accounts). This figure shows a potential allocation of these asset classes, but you should adjust these proportions to fit your own time horizon and risk preference.

How important is asset allocation in relation to the returns of a portfolio? According to a study by Brinson, Hood, and Beebower, asset allocation explains 91.5% of a portfolio's return. Market timing and security selection explain only 1.8% and 4.6%, respectively, of a portfolio's returns.

How to allocate holdings among asset classes, rather than which specific securities or funds to select or when to get in or out of the market, is one of the most important initial investment decisions. Most investment publications have countless articles on security, mutual fund, and ETF selection, as well as market timing strategies, yet few discuss asset allocation (although this is changing). As a result, many investors believe that investment selection and market timing are the most important aspects of their investment decisions. As described above, these decisions are not the primary drivers of returns. Even the *Wall Street Journal* discounts the importance, and ability, of portfolio managers to pick individual securities that outperform the market by pitting these managers' selections against a dartboard selection of stocks; more often than not, the dartboard wins!

You should keep some portion of your portfolio readily accessible for everyday life and current spending. Short-term savings, the first category in Figure 11-5, represents the portion of your portfolio made available to meet everyday needs and emergencies. The three other major categories of financial assets have different features that associate them with achieving other financial goals. The rest of this section provides an overview of the remaining three categories, while the end of this chapter discusses specific investment instruments in more detail.

The second major asset class, bonds, includes all types of debt instruments—situations where the investor loans money to some financial intermediary, such as a bank, the government, or a corporation, in return for a specified interest rate over a fixed period. At maturity (the end of the loan period), the borrower returns the principal (the amount loaned). Debt instruments are often called "fixed-income assets" because the fixed repayment schedule (interest payments that appear as income from the investor's perspective). Bond prices move in the opposite direction of interest rates because if one can get a higher interest payment for a new bond, one will pay less for a lower interest rate payment of an existing bond in order to gain the same overall yield.

The third major category in Figure 11-5, stocks, includes various equity instruments, investments in which the investor takes an ownership stake in a company. Equity investments do not earn a set interest rate. Rather, the rate of return depends on the company's performance over time.

The final major category, depicted in Figure 11-5, is commodities. Commodities are the marketization of specific categories of goods or services. Speculating in individual commodities is extremely risky and not advisable. However, investing in a broad-based commodities futures index, such as the S&P GSCI (formerly the Goldman Sachs Commodity Index), significantly reduces overall portfolio volatility. This index and others, like the Deutsche Bank Liquid Commodity Index, mimic the return of a rolling basket of commodities futures.

How do investors determine the appropriate allocation of funds to invest in these different asset classes? Largely, time horizon and risk tolerance determine asset distribution in an investment portfolio. Investors should select assets for their investment portfolios (to achieve their different financial goals) by comparing expected returns, risks, and time horizons across investment assets.

It is important to understand the different investment vehicles that exist within the four broad asset classes depicted in Figure 11-5. Table 11-2 provides a more detailed and comprehensive review of these investment vehicles.

You may not want to take much risk with money saved to achieve short-term goals. After working for several years to save enough for a house down payment, it would be a shame to see those savings lose 30% when you need them because of an unexpected downturn in the stock or bond market. Since few people can predict such downturns correctly (and none can do it consistently), the safe thing to do is to put money for short-term goals in an

TABLE 11-2
ASSET CLASSES

Cash	Debt Instruments (Bonds)	Equity Instruments (Stocks)	Other
Checking Account	Savings Bonds	Small-company Growth Stocks	Balanced Funds
Savings Account	Treasury Bills	Small-company Value Stocks	Real estate
Money Market	Treasury Notes	Medium-company Growth Stocks	Precious metals
Certificates of Deposit	Treasury Bonds	Medium-company Value Stocks	Commodities
	Treasury Inflation-Protected Securities	Large-company Growth Stocks	
	Municipal Bonds	Large-company Value Stocks	
	Mortgage-backed Bonds	International Stocks	
	Corporate Bonds	Emerging-market Stocks	
	High-yield Corporate Bonds		
	International Bonds		

investment that will provide a high degree of principal safety. In this case, the extra return that you might earn by leaving the money in the stock or bond market over the following year is not worth the risk that the market might take a dip at the very time you need the money. To achieve short-term goals (up to one-year) or to invest money for emergency needs, most investors place their money in the asset classes listed under "Cash" in Table 11-3.

You can accept more risk to achieve medium-term (one- to five-years) goals in order to overcome the impact of taxes and inflation on your investments. While you may accept some risk during this period, you do not want to accept too much risk, as market downturns may last several years, limiting your recovery time if you intend to use the money for a specific expenditure goal. It would be sad to think that a couple's well-deserved second honeymoon cruise might be delayed or cost 18% more (typical credit card interest rate) because of a gamble for a slightly higher return. In this case, short-term bonds, longer-term CDs, and treasury notes may make sense as investment alternatives (Table 11-3). Once a goal is only a year away, it then becomes a short-term goal, and you should move the funds into a cash equivalent investment, such as a CD, money market, or savings account.

For long-term goals (greater than five years), inflation and taxes pose the greatest risk to increasing your wealth and achieving your goals. Stocks offer

TABLE 11-3
INVESTMENT VEHICLES AND THEIR CHARACTERISTICS

Cash	Returns	Risk	Horizon	Remarks
Checking Account	Low	Low	Short	Daily use funds
Savings Account	Low	Low	Short	Stand-by funds
Money Market Account	Low	Low	Short–Medium	Less liquid than savings
Certificates of Deposit	Low–Moderate	Low	Short–Medium	Early withdrawal penalties
Debt Instruments (Bonds)	**Returns**	**Risk**	**Horizon**	**Remarks**
US Govt Savings Bonds—Series I	Low	Very Low	Medium–Long	Inflation protected, check penalties
US Govt Savings Bonds—Series EE	Low	Low	Medium–Long	Discount buy, doubles in 20 years
US Treasury Bills	Low	Low	Short	Zero-coupon bond; all less than 1 year
US Treasury Notes	Low	Low	Medium–Long	Coupon bond; Federal tax only; liquid
US Treasury Bonds	Low–Moderate	Low	Long	Coupon bond; Federal tax only; liquid
Treasury Inflation-protected Securities	Low	Very Low	Medium–Long	Coupon bond; adjust w/inflation; liquid
Municipal Bonds	Low–Moderate	Low–Moderate	All horizons	Usually tax-free at federal and state level
Mortgage-backed Securities	Moderate	Moderate	All horizons	Diversifies exposure to real estate
Corporate Bonds	Low–Moderate	Low–Moderate	All horizons	Coupon bond; company pays you
High-yield Corporate Bonds	High	High	All horizons	Coupon bond; riskier companies
International Bonds	Low–High	Low–High	All horizons	Research host country laws

table continued on next page

table continued from previous page

TABLE 11-3
INVESTMENT VEHICLES AND THEIR CHARACTERISTICS

Equity Instruments (Stocks)	Returns	Risk	Horizon	Remarks
Small-company Growth Stocks	High	Very High	Long	Most earnings growth potential
Small-company Value Stocks	High	Very High	Long	"Bargain" picks selling at discount
Medium-company Stocks	Moderate	Moderate	Medium–Long	Less risky, established stocks
Large-company Growth Stocks	Low–Moderate	Low–Moderate	All horizons	Blue chips with growth potential
Large-company Value Stocks	Low–Moderate	Low–Moderate	All horizons	Blue chips selling at discount
International Stocks	Low–High	Low–Very High	All horizons	Numerous unknowns; research
Emerging-market Stocks	Moderate–Very High	Moderate–Very High	All horizons	Diversify your exposure; research

Other	Returns	Risk	Horizon	Remarks
Balanced Funds	Moderate	Moderate	All horizons	Use to stabilize your portfolio
Real Estate	Low–High	Low–Very High	All horizons	Local conditions rule; tax friendly
Precious Metals	Low–High	Low–Very High	All horizons	Requires speculation; read forecasts
Commodities	Low–High	Low–Very High	All horizons	Avoid speculation; use total or excess return index

the best opportunity to outpace the impact of inflation and taxes. However, asset diversification remains important in order to mitigate risks.

> *Stocks offer the best chance to outperform inflation and the negative impact of taxes.*

A simple technique for allocating investments to achieve long-term goals is to put:

1. 20% of the money into an index fund or exchange-traded fund (ETF) (introduced in chapter 10) that holds large-company stocks,
2. 20% into small-company stocks,
3. 20% into international stocks,
4. 20% into an ETF or mutual fund that tracks a commodities futures index such as the S&P GSCI, and
5. divide the remaining 20% among bonds or the other asset classes shown in Table 11-2.

Investors can adjust the allocation of assets in this hypothetical portfolio to accept more or less risk depending on their risk tolerance and financial goals. An increase in the percentage of small-company and emerging-market stocks will increase risk and potential return, while investing more in bonds or large-company stocks will reduce risk. (Figure 11-1 shows risk measurements based on the standard deviation of returns for each asset class, while Figure 11-2 displays the systematic risk correlation between potential investments.)

Once you determine the appropriate asset class allocation to meet your goals, you must select specific investments. As the Brinson study mentioned earlier suggests, this decision is much less important than the asset allocation decision. You can choose specific investments, such as the stock of a particular company, or you can invest in mutual funds or exchange-traded funds that diversify investments within a specific asset class. Mutual funds make investing easier, because of their professional management, low costs, and further diversification of risk. For those investing larger amounts, exchange-traded funds offer lower commission charges and reduced capital gains taxes. Chapter 10 describes both mutual funds and exchange-traded funds in detail.

The three main factors that influence the purchasing power of accumulated savings are: rate of return, inflation, and taxes. Only the rate of return may contribute to wealth expansion; the other two factors diminish wealth.

> *Rate of return, inflation, and taxes influence the ability of your savings to achieve increased purchasing power.*

Rate of Return

Figure 11-6 plots the increase of $1 invested in 1970 over forty years across seven asset classes. The historical returns for emerging-market stocks and U.S. small-company stocks is significantly greater than those of U.S. large company stocks and commodities, which in turn are greater than those of real estate and fixed-income investments. While the return of emerging-market stocks and U.S. small-company stocks is high, so is the variation from year to year. This annual variation causes the peaks and valleys on the emerging-market stocks and U.S. small-company stocks plots compared to the relatively smooth graph of bonds. Additionally, observe how the assets tend to move together to varying degrees (Figure 11-6 depicts the correlation shown in Figure 11-2). Figure 11-6 is not adjusted for inflation or taxes.

Inflation

You should keep the impact of inflation in mind when investing. Table 11-4 shows why investors would not want to invest all their money in conservative investments like U.S. treasury bills and certificates of deposit (CDs). Column three shows that a 100% treasury bill portfolio would actually lose purchasing power, because the rate of return associated with treasury bills is not enough to offset the negative impacts of taxes and inflation over time. This can have a significant impact on an investor's ability to maintain or increase wealth. However, some investors do invest solely in these instruments because the negative growth is less than it would be to just keep piles of cash.

Taxes

Taxes reduce the investor's earnings on most investments. Table 11-4 shows the average annual rate of return for each asset class. The first column shows the annual return; the second column is what is important to most investors: the return after taxes (assuming a 27% marginal tax rate). Paying taxes on returns reduces the overall return of the portfolio. Investors must consider taxes in conjunction with the broad goal of increasing wealth. Although there are some investments that provide tax-favored treatment, such as retirement plans, IRAs, and variable annuities, most only permit tax deferment. Certainly, the prudent investor takes advantage of these opportunities, but the deferral does not completely negate the impact of taxes; it just delays tax payments until later. The exceptions to this include the Roth IRA and the Roth 401(k) (which eliminate taxes on all earnings and are strongly recommended as a first choice in retirement savings options [see chapter 10]).

You should take all of the factors shown in Table 11-4 into account when selecting investment vehicles. The returns associated with government bonds barely maintain purchasing power for the investor after accounting for taxes and inflation. In contrast, returns for stocks not only outpace inflation and taxes but also permit an increase in wealth. Keep in mind, however, that these returns are historical averages. Year-to-year results can vary significantly, as shown

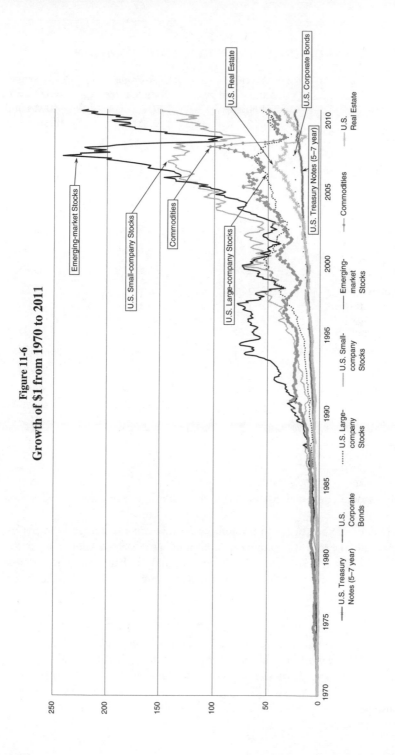

Figure 11-6
Growth of $1 from 1970 to 2011

TABLE 11-4
ANNUAL RETURN, TAXES, AND INFLATION

	Average Annualized Return (%)	Average Return after 27% Taxes (%)	Average Return after Taxes and Inflation (%)
Emerging-market Stocks	16.82	12.28	9.21
U.S. Small-company Stocks	15.68	11.45	8.38
Commodities	12.22	8.92	5.85
U.S. Large-company Stocks	11.71	8.55	5.48
U.S. Real Estate	11.46	8.36	5.29
Global Real Estate	9.55	6.97	3.90
U.S. Corporate Bonds	9.49	6.93	3.86
U.S. Junk Bonds	9.21	6.72	3.65
Global Stocks	8.84	6.45	3.38
U.S. Treasury Notes (5–7 year)	8.25	6.02	2.95
Global Corporate Bonds*	7.64	5.58	2.51
Global Treasury Bonds	4.95	3.61	0.54
U.S. Treasury Bills**	3.67	2.68	-0.39
Inflation**	3.07	N/A	N/A

*Data from 1987–2010
**From 1926–2010

by the standard deviation associated with each of the investments (see Figure 11-1).

One of the best ways to implement an investment strategy is to put as much of an investment program on "autopilot" as possible. Allotments, automatic checking account withdrawals, and mutual fund automatic investment plans are great ways to enforce the savings commitments you make when developing a budget.

> *Use allotments, automatic account withdrawals, and mutual fund automatic investment plans to enforce your commitment to savings.*

EVALUATE INVESTMENT PERFORMANCE PERIODICALLY

At least annually, you should compare the performance of selected funds to the benchmarks against which they compete. If a fund is not performing consistently well against the benchmark, you might consider moving to a different fund or investing in the benchmark index itself. Remember that the fund must beat the index on a regular basis, after considering all fees associated with an actively managed fund—an uncommon and particularly difficult task to accomplish—to be the best investment choice. Chapter 10 details the advantage of investing in the index itself rather than an actively managed fund.

PERIODICALLY ADJUST/REBALANCE YOUR INVESTMENT PORTFOLIO

There are two main reasons to adjust or rebalance a portfolio. The first has to do with changes to a time horizon; the second has to do with necessary changes to asset allocation to "protect" gains from volatile assets. First, you should continue to monitor your financial objectives as their deadlines approach. You should move funds to relatively more conservative short- or medium-term asset allocation portfolios as financial goals get closer.

Second, risks vary and some assets may not perform as expected, based on different economic conditions. You will have to rebalance the asset allocation of your portfolio after unusually strong or weak growth periods. Because different asset classes react differently to economic conditions, you should periodically check the values of each asset class to see if they are still in line with percentages originally selected. In all likelihood, some investments, typically the more volatile assets, will have done so well that their percentage of the long-term portfolio has grown. To achieve the desired asset allocation, you can either add new funds to other assets to bring them back up to the desired percentage or sell some of the investment that has done well to bring it back in line with the desired asset allocation. Selling a portion of the better-performing asset classes serves to protect some of these gains. Keep in mind that if you sell an investment that has performed well, you will incur tax on the capital gain; therefore, adding new funds is the more tax-efficient option. If you choose to sell or buy mutual funds, you should inquire about the funds' annual or quarterly distribution dates for capital gains and dividends. By buying at the "wrong" time, you can trigger an adverse tax event and end up buying a capital gains tax liability that you did not earn. If the funds are in an IRA or 401(k), you can move money between accounts without immediate tax implications, provided you follow the IRA transfer/rollover rules. Further, you should consider the brokerage fees and commissions associated with reallocating investments.

Once you have made the necessary switches, you can forget about the investment plan until the next year. The peace of mind of knowing you have a workable plan will give you confidence that you will achieve your financial goals.

Investors who do not have the time or inclination to directly manage their portfolios can consider "life cycle" or "target-date" funds. These mutual funds automatically adjust the proportional representation of asset classes during a set period of time. The portfolio typically adjusts from higher to lower risk as the mutual fund reaches its target or event date, such as retirement, or a child reaching college age. These funds represent a trade-off between convenience and the ability to fine-tune a portfolio in accordance with your goals and risk tolerance. For those who do not want to manage their own portfolios, life cycle and target funds are options worth considering.

A NOTE (AND CAUTION) ON INDIVIDUAL "STOCK PICKING"

You should invest, not speculate, in your financial future. Investors have consistent, long-term strategies, whereas speculators respond to and attempt to time the market. Chasing the market—trying to find the hot sector or asset class—rather than simply rebalancing periodically can lead to poor portfolio performance. Unless the speculator is very lucky, an investor's portfolio will consistently outperform a speculator's portfolio in the long term.

The majority of investment professionals *do not* consistently outperform the market. These professionals, the same ones who tend to underperform the market, typically have years of experience and education. Thus, a certain level of hubris is inherent in the common investor trying to pick individual stocks. In the long run, a well-balanced index portfolio will generally provide a greater rate of return. With that said, a very small proportion of retail investors do occasionally outperform the market, and there are those who enjoy stock picking as a hobby. For this minority we provide an overview of the two main stock picking methodologies.

There are two broad categories of securities analysis: technical analysis and fundamental analysis. Technical analysis attempts to identify market trends, while fundamental analysis attempts to determine the actual value of a security. Technical analysis involves evaluating securities by analyzing their price patterns using charting techniques, with the goal of predicting market trends. Fundamental analysis seeks to determine the intrinsic value of a company by discounting estimates of future performance. The interested investor should conduct further research into these methods.

EXPLANATION OF FINANCIAL INSTRUMENTS

The following information was compiled from a variety of sources. A useful source for additional information is Investopedia.com. Please visit the website for more information on these topics and a wealth of other financial explanations.

Cash

Checking Account

- Definition: A deposit account for funds intended for frequent use and quick turnover.
- Rate of Return: Checking accounts offer very low interest on unused cash balances. For a comparison of available rates of return on checking accounts, see Bankrate.com.

Savings Account

- Definition: A deposit account that is intended for money that you need for unexpected or planned short-term expenses.
- Rate of Return: A savings account generally offers lower returns than money market accounts, but higher than checking accounts; such an account is appropriate for emergency funds and short-term requirements. A limited number of monthly free withdrawals is generally permitted. For a comparison of available rates of return on savings accounts, see Bankrate.com.

Money Market Account (MMA)

- Definition: A savings account that offers a competitive rate of interest (real rate) in exchange for larger-than-normal deposits. Many money market accounts place restrictions on the number of transactions an investor can make in a month (e.g., six or less).
- Rate of Return: Investors usually have to maintain a certain balance in the account to receive higher rates of interest. Some banks require at least $500 dollars, while others require a much higher balance. As a general rule, the higher the minimum balance (the more money you provide for the bank to lend for profit), the higher the return. For a comparison of available rates of return on money market accounts, see Bankrate.com.

Certificate of Deposit (CD)

- Definition: A savings certificate that entitles the bearer to receive interest from money loaned to a financial institution. A CD bears a maturity date, has a specified fixed interest rate, and can be issued in any denomination. Commercial banks generally issue CDs, and the FDIC insures them. The term of a CD generally ranges from one month to seven years. A CD is a promissory note issued by a bank. It is a time deposit that restricts holders from withdrawing funds on demand. It is possible to withdraw the money before the maturity date, but this action often incurs a penalty.
- Rate of Return: A CD's rate of return will vary with the length of maturity and the current interest-rate environment. As a general rule, the

longer the maturity (the longer you give up your money), the higher the rate of return. For a comparison of available rates of return on CDs see Bankrate.com.

Debt Instruments (Bonds)

U.S. Government Savings Bond—I Bond

- Definition: U.S. government–issued debt security that offers an investor inflationary protection, as its yield is tied to the inflation rate. Available directly from the U.S. Treasury, this debt security is an exceptionally low-risk investment suitable for the most risk-averse investor; it has virtually zero default and inflationary risk.
- Rate of Return: An I Bond earns a guaranteed real rate of return (inflation adjusted) that compounds interest monthly and is paid out at maturity. It is important to note that if you use the I Bonds proceeds to finance education, you can deduct the interest earnings from federal income tax. Interest on an I Bond is exempt from state and local taxes. If you redeem an I Bond within the first five years, you forfeit the three most recent months' interest. For more information and current rates on the I Bond, see Treasury Direct (http://www.savingsbonds. gov).

U.S. Government Savings Bond—EE Bond

- Definition: An interest-bearing U.S. government electronic bond that sells for face value (i.e. $50 bond sells for $50). The paper savings bonds that were issued at a discount from par and sold at half face value (i.e., one paid $25 for a $50 bond) are now discontinued (they were last sold in January 2012). EE bonds are available in denominations of $50, $75, $100, $200, $500, $1,000, $5,000, and $10,000. A savings bond must be held a minimum of one year, and there is a three-months'-interest penalty applied to a bond held less than five years from issue date. At a minimum, the U.S. Treasury guarantees that a paper bond's value will double after twenty years (from its purchase date), and it will continue to earn the fixed rate set at the time of issue unless a new rate or rate structure is announced. If a paper bond does not double in value as the result of applying the fixed rate for twenty years, the Treasury will make a one-time adjustment at maturity to make up the difference. All bonds issued after May 2005 earn a fixed rate of return.
- Rate of Return: The Treasury adjusts rates for new issues each May 1 and November 1, with each new rate effective for all bonds issued through the following six months. Interest accrues monthly and is compounded semiannually. Interest on Series EE Bonds is exempt from state and local taxes. Investors can defer federal income tax until redemption, or until the bonds stop earning interest. Additionally, interest earned towards qualified education savings are tax exempt

when investors redeem bonds to pay for post-secondary tuition and fees. If investors redeem EE Bonds within the first five years, they forfeit the three most recent months' interest; after five years, there is no early redemption penalty. For more information on the EE Bonds, see Treasury Direct (http://www.savingsbonds.gov).

U.S. Treasury Bills

- Definition: A short-term debt obligation backed by the U.S. government with a maturity of less than one year. T-bills are sold in denominations from $1,000 to $5 million with maturities of one month (four weeks), three months (thirteen weeks), or six months (twenty-six weeks).
- Rate of Return: A T-bill is issued through a competitive bidding process at a discount from par, which means that rather than paying fixed interest payments like conventional bonds, the appreciation of the bond provides the return to the holder. For example, if you buy a $10,000 thirteen-week T-bill priced at $9,800, the U.S. government writes you an IOU for $10,000 that it agrees to repay in three months. Your return is the difference between the amount received at maturity and the discounted value originally paid ($10,000 - $9,800 = $200). In this case, the T-bill pays a 2.04 percent interest rate ($200 / $9,800 = 2.04 percent) over a three-month period. For more information and current T-bill rates, see Treasury Direct (http://www.savingsbonds.gov).

U.S. Treasury Notes

- Definition: A marketable, U.S. government debt security earning a fixed rate of interest every six months until maturity. T-notes are issued in terms of two, three, five, and ten years. T-notes can be bought either directly from the U.S. government or through a bank. When buying from the government, you can put in either a competitive or a non-competitive bid. With a competitive bid, you specify your desired yield; however, your bid may not be accepted. A non-competitive bid is where you accept the yield determined at auction. Due to a very large secondary market, T-notes are extremely popular investments.
- Rate of Return: Interest payments on the notes are made every six months until maturity. The income for interest payments is not taxable on a municipal or state level, but it is taxable federally. For more information and current rates on T-note, see Treasury Direct (http://www. savingsbonds.gov).

U.S. Treasury Bonds

- Definition: A marketable, fixed-interest U.S. government debt security with a maturity of more than ten years. The U.S. government initially issues U.S. treasury bonds in denominations between $1,000 and $5 million through auctions. A competitive bid states the rate that the bidder is willing to accept; it will be accepted or rejected based on how it compares to the set rate of the bond. A noncompetitive bid ensures that the bidder will get the bond, but he or she will have to accept the set rate. After the auction, the bonds trade in secondary markets.

- Rate of Return: The bonds make interest payments every six months, and the income that holders receive is taxed only at the federal level. For more information and current rates on T-bonds, see Treasury Direct (http://www.savingsbonds.gov).

<u>Treasury Inflation-Protected Security (TIPS)</u>
- Definition: A special type of treasury note or bond that offers protection from inflation. Like other treasuries, an inflation-indexed security pays interest every six months and pays the principal when the security matures. The principal received on a TIPS increases with inflation and decreases with deflation (as measured by the Consumer Price Index). When a TIPS reaches maturity, you are paid the adjusted principal or original principal, whichever is greater.
- Rate of Return: If U.S. treasuries are the world's safest investments, then one might say that TIPS are the safest of the safe. This is because the real rate of return, which represents the growth of purchasing power, is guaranteed. The downside is that, because of this safety, TIPS offer a lower return. For more information and current rates on TIPS, see Treasury Direct (http://www.savingsbonds.gov).

<u>Municipal Bonds</u>
- Definition: A debt security issued by a state, municipality, or county, in order to finance its capital expenditures, such as the construction of highways, bridges, or schools. A municipal bond may be exempt from federal taxes and most state and local taxes, particularly if you live in the state where the bond was issued.
- Rate of Return: "Munis" are bought for their favorable tax treatment and are popular with people in high-income tax brackets. For more information and current rates on municipal bonds from across the nations, see MunicipalBonds.com.

<u>Mortgage-Backed Securities (MBS)</u>
- Definition: A type of asset-backed security that is secured by a mortgage or collection of mortgages. This investment instrument represents ownership of an undivided interest in a group of mortgages. An MBS is a way for a smaller regional bank to offer a large number of mortgages to its customers and then effectively sell the mortgages to reduce their risk/exposure. The bank acts as intermediary between the homebuyer and the investment markets.

- Rate of Return: Investors receive principal and interest from the group of individual mortgages (MBS) (also known as "mortgage pass-through"). When you invest in a mortgage-backed security, you are lending money to a homebuyer or business. In the recent credit crisis, poor lending practices in the mortgage industry, in addition to other factors, led to a significant increase in the number of mortgages in default. This significantly reduced the return of most of these securities and in many cases, led to a loss of principal. For more information and current rates, see FannieMae.com.

Corporate Bonds
- Definition: A debt security issued by a corporation, as opposed to those issued by the government. A corporate bond typically has a par value of $1,000, is taxable, has a term maturity, and is traded on a major exchange.
- Rate of Return: Every bond issue is given a rating to indicate the risk associated with the bond issue. Bonds with lower risk have lower returns and are sometimes called "investment grade" while others with higher risk have high returns and are called "high-yield" bonds. For more information on the rating system used for bond issuance, see http://www.moodys.com or http://www.standardandpoors.com. For a comparison of corporate bond rates, see Zions Direct (https://www.zionsdirect.com).

High-Yield Corporate Bonds
- Definition: A bond rated "BB" or lower because of its higher default risk (see the Moody's or Standard and Poor's websites above for more information on the rating system). One may also hear these bonds referred to as a "junk bond" or "speculative bond." Investors generally purchase these bonds for speculative purposes, meaning the investor has some comfortable intuition about the future of the company issuing the bond or is willing to take a greater risk for a potentially greater reward.
- Rate of Return: Junk bonds typically offer interest rates three to four percentage points higher than safer corporate or government issues. For a compilation of high-yield corporate bond rates, see Zions Direct.com.

International Bonds
- Definition: A bond issued by a nondomestic (non-U.S.) entity. International bonds include foreign corporate bonds and foreign sovereign (government) bonds.
- Rate of Return: Just like other bonds, international bonds' returns are subject to risks—the magnitude of which determines the yields.

Default, liquidity, currency, interest rate, and event risk are factors in bond prices and yields. For more information about international bonds, see Finra.org.

Equity Instruments (Stocks)

Prior to defining equity assets, it is important to understand how markets measure a company's total value. Market capitalization (or "market cap"), the metric investors use to measure a company's value, is the total dollar value of all outstanding shares of the company. It is calculated by multiplying the number of shares outstanding by the current market price of one share. For example, if a business has fifty shares, each with a market value of $10, then the business's market capitalization is $500 (50 shares × $10/share). Companies generally fall into the following market capitalization-based classes:

- Mega Cap: $200 billion and greater
- Big/Large Cap: $10 billion to $200 billion
- Mid Cap: $2 billion to $10 billion
- Small Cap: $300 million to $2 billion
- Micro Cap: $50 million to $300 million
- Nano Cap: Under $50 million

Small-Company Growth Stock

- Definition: Refers to a stock with a relatively small market capitalization whose earnings are expected to grow at an above-average rate, usually as a function of accepting additional risk to expand current or develop new product lines. One of the biggest advantages of investing in small-cap stocks is the opportunity to beat institutional investors. Because mutual funds have restrictions that limit them from buying large portions of any one issuer's outstanding shares, some mutual funds would not be able to give the small cap a meaningful position in the fund. A growth stock usually does not pay a dividend, as the company prefers to reinvest earnings in capital projects.
- Rate of Return: You can expect that the relative prices of stocks in this asset class will be higher than those of their peers because the high growth rates will create greater demand that pushes up stock prices. Higher growth rates translate into higher rates of return, but also more volatility and the chance of greater losses. You should invest in this asset class for the longer term.

Small-Company Value Stock

- Definition: As a value stock, this asset tends to trade at a lower price relative to its fundamentals (i.e., dividends, earnings, sales, etc.) and is thus considered undervalued. Common characteristics of such stocks include a high-dividend yield, a low price-to-book ratio, and a low price-to-earnings ratio. A value investor believes that the market is not always efficient and that it is possible to find companies trading for less than they are worth.

- Rate of Return: People buying value stocks are searching for "bargains" within the small-cap asset class. The speculation is that the "bargain" will lead to appreciation in the stock's price. The higher risk associated with this speculation leads to greater volatility, meaning greater possible returns or losses. Again, you should only invest in this asset class over the long term.

Medium-Company Stock
- Definition: This asset is also referred to as "mid-cap" or "medium cap." As the name implies, mid-cap companies are not too big, but they have a respectable market capitalization.
- Rate of Return: This larger asset class is less risky than small caps and therefore, on average, provides lower returns.

Large-Company Growth Stock
- Definition: This category includes the largest companies in the world. Some of these stocks, including Wal-Mart, Microsoft, and General Electric, are called "mega caps."
- Rate of Return: The large-cap companies are generally well established with lower risk and therefore, lower returns; they are the least risky of the individual equity choices. Large-cap companies, also known as "blue chips," are generally very stable with lower risk.

Large-Company Value Stock
- Definition: Value stocks tend to trade at a lower price relative to their fundamentals (i.e., dividends, earnings, sales, etc.) and thus are considered undervalued by a value investor. Common characteristics of such stocks include a high dividend yield, a low price-to-book ratio, and a low price-to-earnings ratio. A value investor believes that the market is not always efficient and that it is possible to find companies trading for less than they are worth.
- Rate of Return: Value investors believe that the "bargain" will lead to appreciation in the stock's price. The lower risk associated with this kind of stock leads to generally less volatility, meaning slightly lower possible returns or losses compared to growth stocks. Again, as with other stock investments, you should generally only invest in this investment vehicle over the long term. Value investors search for "bargains" within the large-cap asset class.

In general, risk increases as the size of the company decreases (established companies vs. fledgling companies) and as the company's focus on growth increases (stable products [value] vs. new products [growth]). So within equities, small-cap growth is *very* risky, whereas large-cap value is at the other end of the spectrum.

International Stock Fund
- Definition: A mutual fund that can invest in companies located anywhere outside of its own country. Many people confuse an international fund with a global fund. The difference is that a global fund includes the entire world, and an international fund includes the entire world excluding its home country. There are many different options to choose when investing outside the United States. If you want exposure to the higher growth rates found in different regions or specific countries, then you must build some understanding of the social structures, political structures, and governments within your area of interest.
- Rate of Return: Rates of return vary according to the economic development level of the countries included in the fund. International stock funds can be comprised of well-established European countries, emerging-market countries, or any combinations in between. As always, returns are a function of the risk of the underlying assets.

Emerging-Market Stock Fund
- Definition: A mutual fund investing a majority of its assets in the financial markets of a developing country, typically a small market with a short operating history. It is in your best interest to diversify emerging-market investments across a few regions of higher growth. Hopefully, success in one region will mitigate a loss in another.
- Rate of Return: These funds offer higher potential returns in exchange for greater risk.

Other
Balanced Funds
- Definition: A mutual fund that invests its assets in money market accounts, bonds, preferred stock, and common stock with the intention to provide both growth and income. This asset class is also known as an "asset-allocation fund." A balanced fund is geared towards investors looking for a mixture of safety, income, and capital appreciation. The amount the mutual fund invests into each asset class usually must remain within a set minimum and maximum.
- Rate of Return: The security of a balanced fund may slow upside potential, but it will also slow any downside pressure as well.

Life Cycle or Target-Date Funds
- Definition: A special category of balanced or asset-allocation mutual funds or ETFs in which the proportional representation of an asset class

in a fund's portfolio automatically adjusts during the course of the fund's time horizon. The automatic portfolio adjustment moves from a position of higher risk to one of lower risk as the investor ages and nears retirement. These funds are also referred to as "age-based funds." Another variation of this theme is the "target risk fund." Investment companies offer these funds in low-, medium-, or high-risk varieties. Investors select an appropriate fund depending on their risk tolerance.
- Rate of Return: By design, this type of fund should offer a higher return, with greater volatility, in early years and a lower return, with lower volatility, in later years. As with any mutual fund or ETF, you should consider the transaction fees and other costs, as they can add up quickly.

Real Estate
- Definition: Land plus anything permanently fixed to it, including buildings, sheds, and other items attached to the structure. Unlike other investments, real estate prices are a function of the condition of the immediate area where the property is located.
- Rate of Return: Since real estate is affected by local conditions, it may be better to diversify holdings as in an index (discussed above in this chapter). An investor who would like to gain some real estate exposure while minimizing local area risks can invest in Real Estate Investment Trusts (REITs). REITs are like a mutual fund for real estate (oftentimes owning shopping malls, apartment complexes, and other similar assets) in which the company plans to sell the assets and reap benefits for investors (see chapter 5). Before buying a single property, an individual investor should research forecasts about future real estate appreciation (or depreciation) within the local area. The risk and reward of any real estate investment will be governed by the conditions within its local area. For more information, see Reit.com.

Precious Metals
- Definition: A precious metal, such as gold, iridium, palladium, platinum, or silver, generally increases in value during market uncertainty and inflationary periods. Investing in a precious metal can be done either by purchasing the physical asset, or by purchasing futures contracts for the particular metal. For example, if you think the price of gold is going to climb, you can buy an option to buy gold in the future at some set price. If the price of gold rises above the set price, then the option to buy (at the lower set price) can be sold to another person in a secondary market. This allows you to benefit from the appreciation without ever owning or paying the price of the actual gold.
- Rate of Return: Speculation in precious metals, especially through futures contracts, involves high risk, leading to potentially higher

returns, as well as potentially great losses. For more information, see Monex.com.

Commodities
- Definition: Commodities are most often used as inputs in the production of other goods or services. When traded on an exchange, commodities must meet specified minimum standards, known as a basis grade. The basic idea is that there is little differentiation between a commodity coming from one producer and the same commodity from another producer—a barrel of oil is basically the same product, regardless of the producer. In comparison, with electronics, the quality and features of a given product will be completely different depending on the producer. Some traditional examples of commodities include grains, gold, beef, oil, and natural gas. More recently, the definition has expanded to include financial products such as foreign currencies and market indices. Technological advances have also led to the development of new types of exchanged commodities, such as cell-phone minutes and bandwidth. The sale and purchase of commodities is usually carried out through futures contracts on exchanges that standardize the quantity and minimum quality of the commodity being traded.
- Rate of Return: Few individual investors participate directly in commodities exchanges. Most personal investors who want to invest in commodities purchase a commodity index. A commodity index tracks a basket of commodities and is often traded on an exchange. The value of these indexes fluctuates with the trading price of the underlying commodities. There is a wide range of market-traded commodity indices available to personal investors.

12

Investing for Retirement

What is retirement? For many people, retirement is simply the point in their lives when they stop working for money. But retirement can mean different things to different people. The traditional view of retirement resembles an extended vacation, with time to relax, travel, and visit with grandchildren. For others, retirement represents a "second life" that provides an opportunity for adventure or the pursuit of a lifelong passion. But the reality is that for some, retirement can be an unhappy and anxious period as their lives gradually wind down. Individuals must often accept a retirement far short of their vision as they draw down their savings to live rather than enjoying the life they envisioned. So when people think about retirement, they often think about how much money they need to build a sufficient "nest egg" so they can achieve their goals for retirement while living worry-free for the remainder of their lives. Additionally, most individuals want to ensure they will never become a financial burden on their children. How early individuals retire depends on their desired lifestyle in retirement and how much wealth they have accumulated during their working years.

While each individual has his or her own vision for retirement, it is important to remember that the resources necessary to achieve this vision are not guaranteed. The three major sources of income in retirement are company pension plans, Social Security, and personal savings and investments. Previous generations relied on Social Security and pension plans to fund retirement. However, the basic structure of company-sponsored pension plans has changed drastically in the last few decades and the future of Social Security is widely debated. For most retirees, pension plans and Social Security benefits alone are not sufficient to maintain their desired standard of living. Likewise, servicemembers who retire from the military often find that their retirement income is not enough to sustain the lifestyle they envision for retirement. Therefore, in order to achieve your retirement vision, enjoy financial independence, and prepare for any emergencies that may arise later in life, you must start saving for retirement now.

You must first determine how much you can afford to invest—the preliminary step in developing an investment strategy, as discussed in chapters 10 and 11. After putting together a budget using the procedures outlined in chapter 1,

197

you should identify how much disposable income you have available to contribute to retirement savings. If higher-priority expenses—such as repaying credit card debt, servicing family necessities, and funding emergency savings—consume all your income, you cannot afford to put savings toward retirement and realize the associated tax benefits. Once you determine how much to invest, your first priority should be to put that money in a retirement investment program.

The three major retirement investment programs for servicemembers and their families are:

1. Individual Retirement Arrangements (IRA),
2. Company sponsored pension plans (e.g., 401(k)), and
3. Government-sponsored Thrift Savings Plans (TSP).

Since the purpose of these programs is to help individuals save money for retirement, they each have rules that restrict when and how individuals can invest and withdraw from their accounts. While these retirement plans have some constraints, their most significant benefits are their distinct tax advantages. Taxes can drastically erode the value of a lifetime of savings. By deferring, or legally avoiding taxes, through these retirement programs, investors can increase their wealth faster and reach their financial goals sooner. This chapter discusses each of these options and provides individuals with information to maximize their wealth, minimize their taxes, and achieve their financial objectives. The following retirement savings priorities list identifies the order in which you should consider funding these retirement investments. The remainder of this chapter explores the major retirement investment programs in detail and provides basic investors with some considerations to help ensure they can achieve their goals for retirement.

Retirement Savings Priorities

1. Max out spouse's 401(k) (to the extent the company matches contributions)
2. Max out servicemember's Roth IRA
3. Max out spouse's Roth IRA
4. Max out spouse's 401(k) (even if company does not match contributions)
5. Contribute to servicemember's TSP
6. Taxable accounts for mutual funds, ETFs, and stocks
7. Taxable accounts for bonds, CDs, and money markets

INDIVIDUAL RETIREMENT ARRANGEMENT (IRA)

An Individual Retirement Arrangement (IRA), commonly called an Individual Retirement Account, is a personal retirement savings plan offered by the U.S. government. Basically, the Internal Revenue Service (IRS) provides a big tax break to individuals as an incentive to set aside money for retirement. Because the tax benefits are so generous, the IRS sets limits on maximum annual contributions and eligibility requirements, based on income and employment status. For investors under the age of fifty, the maximum contribution limit is $5,000 each year; individuals can withdraw IRA funds without penalty after the age of fifty-nine and a half.

Starting an IRA account is a simple process. Most financial institutions, from local banks to major mutual fund companies, offer the ability to open an IRA account. Enrolling can take less than twenty minutes, with the click of a mouse, at any one of hundreds of online banking or mutual fund websites. Some of these companies may charge an annual fee to maintain an IRA account, but many do not. As with any other economic decision, it pays to shop around to find the best deal. Most institutions also offer automatic transfers to fund an IRA account on a monthly basis (as recommended in chapters 10 and 11). Once individuals establish an IRA account, they have until the federal income tax deadline, usually April 15 of the following year, to make contributions for the current tax year. For example, individuals have until April 15, 2013 to make contributions to their 2012 IRA. Individuals may also contribute to their 2013 IRA starting January 1, 2013. So the IRA contribution window spans $16^{1}/_{2}$ months: from January 1 through April 15 of the next year.

A common misconception is that an IRA is an investment in and of itself; it is not. Rather, individuals may choose to put the money in their IRAs into any investments they like; the IRA simply provides a tax shelter for the money invested in the program, up to the annual contribution limits. Think of an IRA as a "basket" to hold investments. For example, a servicemember can invest in any number of mutual funds, ETFs, common stocks, bonds, certificates of deposits, or even standard savings accounts. If the servicemember places these investments in an IRA "basket" the financial institution tags the account(s) as an IRA and the IRS recognizes that no taxes are due on money inside the account.

Another advantage of the IRA is that investors can change instruments held inside their IRA "basket" at any time. For example, individuals can adjust their asset allocation within their IRA "basket" by moving funds from high-risk assets to low-risk assets as they approach retirement age. Once the money is inside your IRA account, you can buy and sell securities without tax consequences. While trading within an IRA account occurs tax-free, you must still consider the cost of trading. Trading costs and brokerage fees degrade the real returns from your investment. In many cases, you can simply adjust your asset mix (balance your portfolio) incrementally by buying more of an asset class to achieve your desired allocation, rather than trading. Keep in mind that IRAs are part of a long-term retirement strategy, and adjustments should be made primarily to manage risk as you near retirement. Apply the principles learned in chapters 10 and 11 for long-term goals to select the type of investments and asset mix to hold in your IRA account to best suit your financial goals.

You can also move your IRA funds between different financial institutions if you are unhappy with the performance of an existing IRA or want to consolidate accounts, or for other personal reasons. Two primary methods of moving retirement funds between IRA accounts are "rollover" and "transfer." In most cases, a transfer is much easier and the preferred method. A transfer moves investments directly from one institution to the other, sometimes called a "trustee-to-trustee" transfer. Transfers do not have to be reported to the IRS, are tax-free, and require very little involvement from the owner. Additionally, individuals may make unlimited transfers between IRA accounts. With a rollover, the investment funds are distributed from the old institution to the owner, usually in the form of a physical check; the owner generally has sixty days to make the rollover contribution to another qualifying retirement account. Rollovers must be reported to the IRS to ensure individuals abide by rollover rules and deposit their funds in a timely manner. Additionally, individuals can conduct only one rollover per year without incurring taxes or penalties, and the entire balance must be deposited into a new IRA account. In all instances, individuals must maintain good records for the life of their IRA to correctly determine their tax liability, or lack thereof, when they start taking distributions.

> *An IRA is not itself an investment instrument; it can be a combination of mutual funds, CDs, brokerage accounts, and/or standard savings accounts.*

There are two major types of IRAs: traditional and Roth. The traditional IRA originated from the first IRA plan established in 1974 with the Employee Retirement Income Security Act (ERISA). In 1997, Congress passed the Taxpayer Relief Act with a new offering called the Roth IRA, named after its chief legislator, Senator William V. Roth of Delaware. The primary difference between traditional and Roth IRAs is when the money is taxed. Basically, traditional IRAs are taxed on the back-end, or after the money grows; whereas, Roth IRAs are taxed on the front-end, or before the money grows. In other words, money invested in traditional IRAs use before-tax dollars and become tax-deferred (taxed upon withdrawal), while money invested in Roth IRAs use after-tax dollars and are tax-exempt (tax-free upon withdrawal). In both cases, money grows tax-free while in the IRA account or "basket." The following section highlights the advantages and disadvantages of each IRA. While it is feasible for servicemembers to own either or both types of IRAs based on their financial situation, in most cases it is in their best financial interest to choose a Roth IRA.

> *For most servicemembers, a Roth IRA is a better retirement investment than a traditional IRA.*

ROTH IRAS

Anyone—regardless of age or participation in another pension plan—can set up a Roth IRA provided he or she has taxable earned income during the year. Current law allows annual contributions of up to $5,000 in 2012 for a Roth IRA. Individuals aged fifty or older can take advantage of "catch-up" provisions and contribute an additional $1,000 each year until retirement. A spouse with less than $5,000 in earned income may contribute the maximum $5,000 to an IRA, as long as the married couple's combined income is greater than their combined contribution.

Additionally, if an individual's annual taxable income is less than the contribution limit, their contribution cannot exceed their taxable income. For example, if a part-time worker earned only $3,000 in taxable income this year, her maximum allowable contribution would be $3,000. Servicemembers who deploy to a combat zone and receive tax-free income (i.e., taxable income = $0) are covered by the Heroes Earned Retirement Opportunities (HERO) Act. Passed by Congress in 2006, this law allows servicemembers earning tax-exempt combat pay to make maximum contributions to their Roth IRAs.

Qualified distributions are withdrawals from the Roth IRA account that are tax- and penalty-free. For Roth IRAs, contributions and earnings are treated differently. Contributions, or the after-tax dollars originally invested (the principal), can be withdrawn at any time without penalty. However, earnings that accrue on the contributions must remain in the Roth "basket" for a five-year holding period and until age fifty-nine and a half, or the account-holder incurs a 10% penalty fee assessed by the IRS. So if an individual is at least age fifty-nine and a half and five years have passed since he or she first established the account, earnings can be withdrawn tax- and penalty-free. Non-qualified or early withdrawals of earnings are subject to a 10% fee, plus income tax. This penalty may be waived, however, for early qualified expenses such as the first-time purchase of a home, excessive medical costs, or higher education. For a complete listing of the withdrawal rules, limitations and qualifications of the Roth IRA, see Publication 590 on the IRS website (http://www.irs.gov/publications/p590/index.html).

Some people advise individuals to use their Roth IRAs as emergency funds, because you can withdraw contributions at any time for any reason with no tax or penalty; however, you should do this with caution. Building an emergency fund is a critical step in successful personal finance planning, just as building a retirement fund is another critical step. Using a Roth IRA for double-duty should only be a consideration for individuals who do not have sufficient funds to save for both emergency funds and retirement funds in a given year. In this specific case, it may be worth contributing to a Roth IRA in a low-risk, stable investment so that you do not forego the long-term tax-benefits of the Roth IRA. This way, you secure your money in the Roth IRA "basket" and it stays there until retirement, unless you need it for an emergency. However, you must keep in mind that this is a temporary strategy and you should establish a dedicated emergency savings account at the earliest opportunity. The importance of a separate emergency fund outside the Roth IRA is twofold. First, it allows you to maximize the tax-free growth potential of your Roth IRA "basket" by investing in higher-yield investments. Second, it helps to ensure that you commit your IRA investments for your future rather than for current unplanned expenses.

For many servicemembers, especially younger ones, committing investments to a retirement account until they are nearly sixty years old may deter them from selecting a Roth IRA. However, the advantages of a Roth IRA are well worth the wait. First, as mentioned, there are opportunities to make early, penalty-free withdrawals for specific life events should you need funds before you turn fifty-nine and a half. Also, you can withdraw contributions (not earnings) at any age for any reason. Undoubtedly, the greatest advantage is that withdrawals of distributions after the age of fifty-nine and a half (or earlier for qualified expenses) are tax-free. This means that every dollar invested in a Roth IRA and every additional dollar that those investments earn go straight into the investor's pocket and not Uncle Sam's.

To highlight how powerful this retirement option is, Figure 12-1 uses an example of a twenty year-old second lieutenant (O-1) in 2012. She contributes the maximum allowed under current law for her entire twenty-year military career to her Roth IRA and does not contribute any more after military retirement. The example assumes that the $5,000 annual contribution limit does not increase, so her contributions at the end of her military career total $100,000. If she invests this money in a mutual fund that grows tax-free in her IRA "basket," by the time she retires at age sixty, her IRA investments will have a value of $625,276 if she earns 6% on average, $1,151,792 at 8%, or $2,119,243 at 10%. Remember, these savings are tax-free. Table 12-1 provides the compounding growth values for the lieutenant's possible investments at different ages.

There are two disadvantages of Roth IRAs worth mentioning: Annual contributions are not deducted from annual income when filing taxes, and a family's taxable income could disqualify them from participation if it exceeds set amounts. While uncommon for most servicemembers, the maximum income limit has affected some military families with dual incomes, prevent-

Figure 12-1
Roth IRA Growth

$5,000 contributed annually for 20 years ($100,000 total investment)

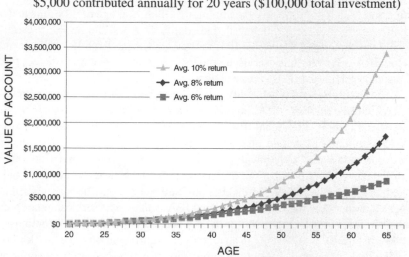

ing them from taking advantage of the tax benefits that a Roth IRA provides. The IRS determines the maximum income limitations each year. For 2012, individuals cannot contribute to a Roth IRA if they meet one of the following criteria:

- Combined taxable income is greater than $183,000 if married filing jointly or a qualified widow(er).
- Taxable income is greater than $123,000 if single, head of household, or married filing separately and lived apart for the entire year.
- Taxable income is greater than $10,000 if married filing separately and lived together at any time during the year.

TABLE 12-1
ROTH IRA COMPOUNDING VALUE OF RETURN
$5,000 contributed annually for 20 years ($100,000 total investment)

Age	Average Annual Return		
	6%	8%	10%
20	$5,000	$5,000	$5,000
40	$194,964	$247,115	$325,012
58	$556,493	$987,477	$1,751,441
59	$589,883	$1,066,475	$1,926,585
60	$625,276	$1,151,792	$2,119,243
65	$836,760	$1,692,361	$3,413,062

TRADITIONAL IRAS

An alternative retirement savings plan is the traditional IRA. The Roth and traditional IRA share many of the same rules. For example, annual contribution and "catch up" amounts, the minimum withdrawal age of fifty-nine and a half, penalties for early withdrawal, and qualified early withdrawals are essentially the same for a traditional IRA as they are for the Roth IRA. While the Roth IRA is best for most servicemembers, there are some circumstances that make the traditional IRA a better option.

There are several notable differences between Roth IRAs and traditional IRAs. Unlike the Roth IRA, individuals can never withdraw their contributions early from a traditional IRA. Once the money is placed inside the "basket," individuals cannot take it out until age fifty-nine and a half unless one of the qualified early withdrawal justifications is met. Traditional IRAs also include mandatory distributions in the year individuals turn seventy and a half and restrict individuals from making any additional contributions after that year. Another drawback of the traditional IRA is that some servicemembers or their spouses may be ineligible for the tax deductions on their contributions if they are already participating in an employer's retirement plan (i.e. 401k). For individuals or spouses covered by a retirement plan at work, the amount of contribution deductible from adjusted gross income—and therefore annual taxes—is eventually phased out, depending on the spouse's taxable income level. The IRS website explicitly defines these restrictions in Publication 590.

The primary difference between the Roth IRA and the traditional IRA is the timing of the tax benefits. As discussed earlier, Roth IRA contributions are not tax-deductible, but qualified distributions are tax-free. The IRS treats traditional IRAs in the exact opposite manner, giving them their most distinct advantage: Contributions to traditional IRAs are tax-deductible (meaning an individual's annual taxable income will be less, which translates into tax savings today). Saving on taxes today sounds like a financially prudent decision, especially when compared to a regular taxable account without a protective IRA "basket." However, when comparing the tax savings gained today with a traditional IRA to the tax savings gained at retirement with a Roth IRA, the Roth is the clear winner in most cases (especially for servicemembers).

> *Traditional IRAs are taxed when individuals withdraw their funds (at retirement), but they reduce taxable income in the year that individuals contribute to them (today).*

To demonstrate the Roth IRA's advantage, let's use the same second lieutenant from our example above (Figure 12-1). If she contributed to a traditional IRA instead of a Roth IRA and withdrew her entire savings at age sixty,

TABLE 12-2
TAX BENEFITS OF ROTH IRA VERSUS TRADITIONAL IRA

	Roth IRA	Traditional IRA
Value at age 60*	$625,276	$625,276
Investment returns on tax-deferred savings	$0	$60,549
Taxes due on withdrawal	None	Ordinary income tax
Tax liability	$0	$93,791
After-tax value	$625,276	$592,034

*Assuming $5,000 invested for 20 years starting at age 20; 6% average annual returns; 15% ordinary income tax rate

she would be forced to pay income taxes on all her distributions (assuming a 15% ordinary income tax rate). In other words, she would pay $93,791 (at 6% growth), $172,769 (at 8% growth), or $317,886 (at 10% growth) to the IRS. Although the Roth IRA does not provide any tax deductions in the years the $100,000 was invested, the second lieutenant would get to withdrawal all her savings tax-free. The tax deductions from a traditional IRA would have equaled $15,000 in total tax savings over the course of her twenty-year career (assuming an income tax rate of 15%). If the tax-deferred savings were invested in a taxable account over the same time period, the $15,000 would have grown to $60,549 by age sixty with 6% growth (ignoring the capital gains tax that would be owed on this investment). Table 12-2 presents the tax benefits of the Roth IRA compared to those of the traditional IRA. In this example, the investor would have saved $33,242 by choosing a Roth IRA over a traditional IRA, even with a constant tax rate. These savings would be much higher if her income tax rate increased over time—current marginal tax rates are at historically low levels.

So when is the traditional IRA a better option? This question really amounts to whether it is better to be taxed now (Roth IRA) or taxed later (traditional IRA); and the answer depends on your expected income tax rate in retirement compared to your current tax rate. Most people, including service-members, expect to be in a higher tax bracket in retirement, in which case a Roth IRA is better. But for those individuals who expect to be in a lower tax bracket in retirement, the traditional IRA may result in less overall tax liability. For example, consider an individual who is at the peak of his working years and currently falls in the 28% marginal income tax bracket. If this individual contributed $1,000 to a traditional IRA, he would essentially save $280 in income taxes now. If this same person expects to be in a 15% marginal income tax bracket in retirement, the tax-deferred savings from a traditional IRA may prove to be a better option for him than the Roth IRA. This is especially true if the individual does not have a defined benefit pension plan, such as the military retirement plan, in which the employer pays a specific amount each month. If retirement income is drawn primarily from retirement accounts (rather than pension plans), then the taxes on these withdrawals would be spread across the lower income tax brackets, greatly reducing the average tax rate in retirement. As individuals or couples increase their household income and move into higher tax brackets, the traditional IRA may start to become a more attractive choice. Additionally, current marginal tax rates are at historically low levels. If an investor believes tax rates may increase in the future, the Roth IRA becomes more attractive. You should continue to reevaluate your financial situation based on income and marginal tax rates to determine which IRA provides the greatest benefit.

The fundamental problem is that no one really knows what tax rates will be in the future, and you can only estimate what tax bracket you will be in when you start withdrawing funds. Since many investors plan to have other "tax-deferred" accounts (401(k), TSP), it may be prudent to also own "tax-free" accounts (Roth IRA). Diversifying retirement accounts provides you with more options in the future when you decide to make withdrawals. For example, if tax rates in retirement are very high, you can draw from your Roth account tax-free; if tax rates happen to be very low, then you can draw from your traditional IRA at low marginal tax rates.

A more obvious reason to choose a traditional IRA is if you exceed the maximum income limits for a Roth IRA, and are thus disqualified from making direct Roth IRA contributions. For those who do not qualify for the Roth IRA, the traditional IRA becomes the only choice. While all income earners can contribute to a traditional IRA, the tax-deductible benefits vary depending on participation in employer retirement plans and income levels. Individuals who are not covered by an employer retirement plan receive full tax-deduction benefits, regardless of their income level. Additionally, there are new provisions for high-income earners to contribute to a traditional IRA and then convert it to a Roth IRA, if desired.

IRA conversions allow traditional IRA owners to convert their investment into a Roth IRA. Because contributions held in a traditional IRA were pre-tax dollars (tax deferred), individuals must pay income taxes on the amount they convert. Prior to 2010, IRA conversions were reserved for those individuals who made $100,000 or less in taxable income and who were not filing using the status "married and filing separately." Currently anyone, regardless of income or filing status, can convert a traditional IRA to a Roth IRA. This new rule largely benefits high-income earners who now have access to the Roth IRA by way of a conversion.

The decision to convert to a Roth IRA can be complicated and depends on your expected future income tax bracket, age, and long-term goals. From a tax perspective, it may not make financial sense to convert, due to the immediate tax burden and the loss of future principal growth. For example, an individual in the 15% marginal income tax bracket with $10,000 in a traditional IRA would have to pay $1,500 in additional taxes to convert to a Roth IRA. Generally, you should only convert if you can pay the taxes with available cash from outside the IRA. Tapping into IRA money to pay taxes not only degrades future tax-protected growth, but the IRA money used to pay the taxes may also be subject to an additional 10% early withdrawal fee if you are under the age of fifty-nine and a half. You may also consider the benefits of a partial conversion. There are numerous calculators and guides available online to help make this conversion decision. Based on individual circumstances, the best option for many investors may be to simply stop contributing to the traditional IRA and open a second IRA account and establish it as a Roth. There is no restriction on the number of traditional and Roth IRAs an individual can maintain. There is just a restriction on the total contribution an individual can make per year ($5,000 for 2012 under age fifty). For example, if you designate five different accounts with five different financial institutions as Roth IRAs, you could spread your $5,000 contribution for 2012 across all five accounts.

SUMMARY IRA COMPARISON

Again, for most servicemembers the Roth IRA is a better investment option than the traditional IRA. While traditional IRAs allow tax deductions today, Roth IRAs allow individuals to take qualified distributions completely tax-free. Additionally, the Roth IRA has less stringent eligibility requirements, does not require forced distributions after a certain age, and provides more flexibility for withdrawing funds. Remember, Roth IRA contributions (not earnings) can be withdrawn without tax or penalty at any time, for any reason.

A Roth IRA is a powerful means of building wealth and helps augment an individual's retirement income. The tax-free compounding gains on annual contributions and reasonable restrictions set by the government make it a very attractive addition to any long-term financial plan. In almost every situation, the benefit of not paying income taxes when the funds are distributed with the Roth IRA outweighs the benefit of the tax deductions that could be taken when the funds are purchased with the traditional IRA. Table 12-3 summarizes the key differences between the traditional IRA and Roth IRA. Visit the IRS website (Publication 590) for more details regarding traditional and Roth IRAs: http://www.irs.gov/publications/p590/index.html.

COMPANY-SPONSORED QUALIFIED PLANS FOR SPOUSES

Employers establish qualified plans to provide retirement benefits for employees and their beneficiaries. These plans are either defined-benefit (like the military retirement system, in which retirees receive monthly predetermined payments after retirement) or defined-contribution (plans in which a certain amount or percentage of money is set aside each year for the benefit of the employee). This section will focus on defined-contribution plans because most working spouses who are not in the military will have the opportunity to participate in such arrangements. Additionally, National Guard and Reserve members may have civilian jobs that offer these plans as part of their compen-

TABLE 12-3
TRADITIONAL IRA AND ROTH IRA COMPARED

	Traditional	Roth
Contributions	*Before-tax* dollars	*After-tax* dollars
Tax Treatment	Contributions are tax-deductible, but distributions are taxed at ordinary income tax rate.	Contributions are not tax-deductible, but qualified distributions are tax-free.
Maximum Contribution	$5,000 per year; $6,000 per year if age 50 or older. Maximum contribution is for traditional and Roth IRAs *combined.*	
Age Limitations	Age 70.5 and older cannot contribute	No age limitation
Qualified Distributions (without penalty)	Qualified distributions can begin at age 59.5 (with exceptions).	Earnings can be withdrawn at age 59.5 *provided* at least 5 years have passed since account was first funded. (Contributions can be withdrawn at any time, for any reason, without tax or penalty.)
Early Distribution Penalty	10% penalty plus income taxes for distributions withdrawn before age 59.5 (with exceptions)	10% penalty plus income taxes on *earnings* withdrawn before age 59.5 or within 5 years after account was first funded (with exceptions)
Qualified Early Distributions (exceptions)	First-time home purchase (up to $10,000) Higher education expenses of owner, children, and grandchildren For a disability or medical insurance if unemployed Medical expenses (non-reimbursable if exceed 7.5% of taxable income) Beneficiary distributions if owner dies before the age of 59.5	
Forced Distribution	Must start withdrawing funds at age 70.5. Penalty for not withdrawing is a 50% tax on minimum required distribution.	None

sation. It is important to know the details of these plans because they offer employees a great means to accumulate retirement savings. The two most common forms of company-sponsored plans are the 401(k) and Roth 401(k).

Company-Sponsored 401(k) Plan

This is the most common form of plan offered by companies. 401(k) plans are retirement accounts established by employers to which eligible employees may make salary-deferral contributions (thus reducing their taxable income in the years they participate). However, just like a traditional IRA, distributions are taxed upon withdrawal after age fifty-nine and a half. As with both types of IRAs, employees designate the types of financial instruments they contribute to within their 401(k) plans. Also, the contributions to this type of plan are subject to limits set by the IRS. For 2012, the maximum employee annual contribution to a 401(k) plan is $17,000. Maximum contributions will increase with inflation for future years at $500 increments. A "catch-up" provision allows employees over the age of fifty to contribute an additional $5,500 per year.

Many employers make matching contributions to 401(k) plans on behalf of eligible employees and may also add a profit-sharing feature to the plan. (Since this is less common, we will not focus on this feature.) The amount that employers match varies by company; currently employers are limited to matching up to 6% of the employee's total pre-tax compensation. Therefore, if the employee earns a pretax salary of $100,000, the employer can contribute (match) up to $6,000. The benefits of employer matching contributions should be obvious—employers are adding up to $6,000, in this example, to the contributions of the employee (which have a maximum of $17,000) resulting in a maximum of $23,000 in the employee's retirement savings pool ($28,500 for those fifty or older). Individuals should maximize any matched contributions as their first retirement investment priority, as this represents guaranteed, zero-risk returns on investment. Never pass on the opportunity for free money!

> *Individuals should maximize contributions to a company-sponsored employer matching program as their first priority. Receiving a full match represents an immediate 100% return on investment with zero risk!*

Individuals must pay careful attention to the restrictions employers place on matching contributions. Frequently, employers will tie "vesting" criteria to matching funds. Vesting simply means that the employee gains the rights (takes ownership) of these matching contributions. The employer is authorized to stipulate the conditions upon which vesting occurs. Typical vesting criteria require the employee to remain with the company for a minimum number of years. Once that minimum time is met, the employee gains the rights (i.e., is vested) to the matching contributions the employer made during that time.

Company-Sponsored Roth 401(k) Plans

The Roth 401(k) plan offers the same advantages of a Roth IRA over the traditional IRA. While the standard 401(k) offers pretax contributions with tax-deferred growth, the Roth 401(k) requires post-tax contributions, but allows for tax-free growth and withdrawals. The Roth 401(k) has the same contribution limits as normal company 401(k) plans. Therefore, for 2012, an employee has the option to invest the maximum amount his or her employer allows (as a percentage of income), up to the maximum government contribution limits ($17,000, or $22,500 for those over fifty years old). Typically, qualified distributions can be made tax-free after the owner reaches age fifty-nine and a half, and the account has been established for at least five years. While matching contributions are allowable for Roth 401(k) plans, the employer's matching contributions are treated like traditional 401(k) contributions that invest pretax dollars and are taxed at ordinary income tax rates upon withdrawal.

In short, the Roth 401(k) combines the best aspects of both the Roth IRA and 401(k) plans. The Roth 401(k) provides tax-free growth and distributions, while offering larger contribution limits (three times more than IRAs) and is eligible for employer matching programs. However, the most beneficial 401(k) plan depends on each individual situation. For example, a young person in a low tax bracket is better off with a Roth 401(k) than with a regular 401(k) plan. This is because the benefit a young person receives over a long time horizon of not paying income taxes on withdrawals will far outweigh the tax-deductible benefits provided by a regular 401(k). However, if a person is currently in a higher tax bracket, or he or she expects to be in a lower or similar tax bracket in retirement, that person may want to consider the benefits associated with the tax-deferral of regular 401(k) contributions. The central question is whether the benefits of a tax reduction now with the regular 401(k) outweigh the benefits of tax-free income later with the Roth 401(k).

THRIFT SAVINGS PLAN

The Thrift Savings Plan (TSP) is a retirement savings and investment plan offered to federal employees and military servicemembers. The TSP is a defined contribution plan that offers participants the same type of savings and tax benefits that many private corporations offer their employees under regular 401(k) plans. The TSP allows participants to save a portion of their pay in a special retirement account administered by the Federal Retirement Thrift Investment Board. The money that participants invest in the TSP comes from pretax dollars and reduces their current taxable income. Contributions and earnings grow tax-free and are not taxed until they are withdrawn, which gives the TSP the same tax-deferred characteristics as a traditional IRA. In early 2012, the Federal Retirement Thrift Investment Board announced that a

Roth TSP Plan would be enacted in May 2012. No further details were available at the time this book went to press.

While the TSP and traditional IRAs have similar tax-benefits, the biggest difference is the availability of fund choices. Remember that with IRAs, individuals are nearly unlimited in the choice of investment instruments to place inside their "basket." The TSP, however, is limited to five individual TSP funds and a family of Lifecycle funds. The five individual TSP funds are:

- Government Securities Investment (G) Fund
- Fixed Income Index Investment (F) Fund
- Common Stock Index Investment (C) Fund
- Small Capitalization Stock Index Investment (S) Fund
- International Stock Index Investment (I) Fund

The G Fund is a unique, non-marketable government security fund exclusively issued to the TSP. It offers yields similar to those of intermediate-long

TABLE 12-4
THRIFT SAVINGS PLAN (TSP) INDIVIDUAL FUNDS

TSP Fund	Name	Description	Tracked Index
G Fund	Government Securities Investment (G) Fund	Short-term U.S. treasury securities; interest rates similar to those of long-term government securities with no risk of losing principal	No equivalent
F Fund	Fixed Income Index Investment (F) Fund	Broad U.S. bond index fund	Barclays Capital U.S. Aggregate Bond Index (www.barcap.com)
C Fund	Common Stock Index Investment (C) Fund	Equity stock index fund of 500 large-to-medium-size U.S. companies	Standard & Poor's 500 Stock Index (www.standardand poors.com)
S Fund	Small Capitalization Stock Index Investment (S) Fund	Equity stock index fund of small and medium-size U.S. companies not included in the S&P 500	Dow Jones U.S. Completion Total Stock Market (TSM) Index (www.djind exes.com)
I Fund	International Stock Index Investment (I) Fund	Broad international market index, primarily large companies in developed countries (no emerging markets)	Morgan Stanley Capital International EAFE Stock Index (www.msci.com)

term securities, but with no risk of losing principal. The G Fund is a secure investment that provides zero risk with potential rewards that outpace inflation; it is only available through the TSP. The other four TSP funds (F, C, S, I) are index funds that track indices in four major market segments: bonds, large-cap stocks, small-cap stocks, and international stocks. Table 12-4 provides a summary of each fund with its corresponding tracked index.

If index funds are part of your long-term retirement strategy, then the TSP can be an ideal investment choice. Investors value index funds for their low "expense ratios" or management fees, as discussed in chapter 10. Expense ratios represent the cost of administering and managing a mutual fund. Lower expense ratios means the investor keeps more of the returns. While seemingly small, these fees can have a significant impact on long-term investment performance. Most index funds have expense ratios that range from 0.20% to 0.50%, which is low compared to actively managed funds whose expense ratios range from 0.50% to 2.5%. In contrast, the TSP funds have average expense ratios of 0.025%—that is, ten times lower those of than many index funds, and forty to a hundred times lower than those of most actively managed funds. Nowhere else can individuals invest in the market for such a low cost!

> *The Thrift Savings Plan offers servicemembers access to extremely low-cost index funds, with tax-deferred growth and generous contribution limits.*

The TSP also offers five Lifecycle funds or "L Funds" that invest in a mix of these five individual funds. The TSP Lifecycle funds operate in the same manner as Target Date Retirement Funds, which reallocate funds over time based on an individual's time horizon or expected retirement date. The Lifecycle funds are designed for those servicemembers who do not have the time, experience, or interest to manage the correct mix of five individual funds. The main advantage of the L Funds is that they provide a low-cost, worry-free method of investing. Also, since L Funds are simply a mix of individual TSP funds, there are no additional fees beyond those paid for the individual funds.

Each L Fund is based on its own time horizon, allowing each asset allocation to adjust gradually over time, shifting automatically to a more conservative investment mix as its "target" date approaches. For example, the L Funds available as of 2012 are L 2050 (for those people who plan to retire or use their money in 2050), L 2040, L 2030, L 2020, and L Income (for those in retirement in need of a steady income with little fluctuation). Since most individuals investing in a TSP will also have retirement savings in a Roth IRA, investors must consider the asset allocation of all their investments when contributing to an L Fund. Table 12-5 shows the asset allocation of the TSP Lifecycle funds as of January 2012.

TABLE 12-5
ASSET ALLOCATION OF TSP LIFECYCLE FUNDS (AS OF JANUARY 2012)

Fund	L2050	L2040	L2030	L2020	L Income
G	4%	12%	23%	37%	74%
F	8%	9%	8%	7%	6%
C	43%	39%	35%	30%	12%
S	19%	17%	14%	10%	3%
I	26%	23%	20%	16%	5%

Once servicemembers enroll in the TSP, their contributions are automatically invested in the G Fund (the default), since there is no risk of losing principal. Individuals must submit a "contribution allocation" to invest in different funds. Contribution allocations can be changed at any time online, over the phone, or through a request by mail. Servicemembers may diversify their TSP contributions across any number of individual or Lifecycle funds, according to their investment horizons, risk profiles, and financial goals (topics discussed in chapter 11).

TSP contribution limits are very generous, and mirror those of 401(k) plans. Servicemembers can contribute any percentage (from 1% to 100%) of their basic pay each month. Individuals may also contribute up to 100% of any incentive pay (e.g., flight pay, hazardous duty pay), special pay (e.g., hardship duty pay), or bonus pay (e.g., enlistment and reenlistment bonuses) as long as they are contributing some amount from base pay. However, the total annual dollar amount cannot exceed the Internal Revenue Code's (IRC) elective deferral limit for that year ($17,000 for 2012). For those uniformed members who earn tax-exempt pay while deployed for any part or all of the year, they may contribute up to the lower of their tax-exempt pay or the IRC's limit ($50,000 for 2012).

The only way to contribute to the TSP is through monthly deductions. While servicemembers cannot make direct contributions, automatic payroll deductions provide a convenient and hassle-free method of saving for retirement. Additionally, TSP account information and contributions are detailed on the servicemembers' monthly Leave and Earnings Statements (LES). Once a servicemember establishes a TSP account, he or she can easily change contribution amounts through the DFAS myPay portal.

There are three primary methods of accessing money from the TSP account: (1) a loan, (2) in-service withdrawal (if still employed by the federal government), and (3) post-separation withdrawal (after separation). TSP loans provide servicemembers the ability to borrow from their own TSP accounts at low interest rates (interest rate of the G Fund at the time of loan processing).

Individuals can borrow $1,000 to $50,000, which will be repaid through pay-roll deductions over five years for general-purpose loans, or over fifteen years for residential loans. Loan repayments restore the amount of the loan plus the interest into the TSP account. However, loan repayments use after-tax money, and individuals miss out on any earnings they might have accrued on the bor-rowed money. In-service withdrawals can be made at any time, but individuals must pay ordinary income tax on the withdrawal—and may also be subject to a 10% early withdrawal fee. Post-separation withdrawals can be full or partial and also incur income tax liability. Federal employees who retire the year they turn fifty-five or older are exempt from the 10% early penalty tax. However, employees who retire before the age of fifty-five must wait until age fifty-nine and a half to avoid the 10% early withdrawal fee. In all cases, individuals should consider the cost of withdrawal from their TSP account and the impact on future earnings.

Servicemembers who separate from the uniformed services have the fol-lowing options regarding their TSP accounts:

- Receive a single "lump sum" payment, or transfer funds to an IRA, other eligible retirement plan (such as a 401(k)), or a civilian TSP account (if they continue to work for the government), without paying a penalty or taxes.
- Request a series of monthly payments based on a dollar amount (requesting a monthly fixed-dollar disbursement; the account is exhausted when value = $0) or life expectancy (TSP calculates and disburses monthly payments based on the IRS life expectancy tables; account is exhausted at end of life expectancy and the payment is recalculated yearly based upon changes to account value). All or a portion of certain monthly payments can be transferred to an IRA or other eligible retirement plan without incurring a penalty or taxes.
- Request a TSP annuity (a guaranteed specific monthly payment for life). An individual must have at least $3,500 in his or her account in order to purchase an annuity. It is important to find out more informa-tion before considering this option, as the rules are quite extensive and not covered in detail in this book.
- Keep money in the TSP account, where it will continue to accrue earn-ings. Once individuals leave the service, they cannot make additional contributions. If servicemembers retire on or after the age of fifty-five, they avoid the 10% early withdrawal penalty; otherwise they will have to wait until age fifty-nine. Servicemembers must begin withdrawing from their TSP account no later than April 1 of the year after they turn seventy and a half.

The advantages and disadvantages of the Thrift Savings Plan are summa-rized below. The TSP is an attractive retirement savings option for service-members that provides access to extremely low-cost index funds with tax-deferred growth and generous contribution limits. More information on the TSP can be found at https://www.tsp.gov or by calling ThriftLine toll-free (1-TSP-YOU-FRST).

Advantages of the TSP:

- Contributions use pretax dollars and reduce current year taxable income
- Investment earnings grow tax-deferred
- Extremely low expense ratios for funds
- Automatic payroll deductions facilitate hassle-free monthly contributions
- Generous contribution limits up to $17,000 per year for 2012, and up to $50,000 if deployed
- Account value does not count toward Expected Family Contribution (EFC) to determine child's eligibility for financial aid (see chapter 7)
- Portable retirement account that moves with the servicemember and offers a variety of withdrawal options

Disadvantages of the TSP:

- Withdrawals are subject to ordinary income tax
- Investment options limited to five individual TSP funds
- Servicemembers cannot make direct contributions to their accounts
- Monthly payroll deductions are the only method of contributing
- No matching contributions for uniformed military personnel

PRIORITIES FOR INVESTING

Based on the relative benefits of each retirement savings program, the authors of this guide recommend that investors consider the following priorities for retirement investing:

1. Max out spouse's 401(k) (to the extent the company matches contributions)
2. Max out servicemember's Roth IRA
3. Max out spouse's Roth IRA
4. Max out spouse's 401(k) (even if company does not match contributions)
5. Contribute to servicemember's TSP
6. Contribute to taxable accounts for mutual funds, ETFs, and stocks
7. Contribute to taxable accounts for bonds, CDs, and Money Markets

If a spouse's company provides matching contributions to his or her 401(k) plan, this should be the first priority. Matching contributions provide immediate and guaranteed returns on investment. For example, if an individual invests $1,000 to a dollar-for-dollar matched 401(k) program, the company contributes an additional $1,000 and now there is $2,000 total in retirement savings—that's an immediate 100% return on investment with zero risk! By comparison, investing $1,000 into an IRA account at 10% average annual returns would take roughly seven years to equal the same returns, and that's not guaranteed. While each matched 401(k) plan is different, individuals should, at a minimum, contribute up to the amount that their employers match—it's free money.

Beyond a spouse's company-sponsored plan with matching contributions, servicemembers should maximize their Roth IRAs for both themselves and their spouse. The Roth IRA is one of the single best investment options for retirement, as it provides tax-free growth and tax-free withdrawal upon retirement. One of the most important lessons of this chapter is that individuals should maximize their Roth IRA contributions each year.

After maxing out the Roth IRA, investing in a spouse's 401(k) plan or the servicemember's TSP is a near equal-value proposition that families should decide based on their individual circumstances. Investors should maximize investment in a spouse's Roth 401(k) for the same reasons as with a Roth IRA. Standard 401(k) plans can vary widely across companies and may provide more diverse investment opportunities. For all 401(k) plans, individuals should consider the investment fees and restrictions unique to each company. The TSP provides servicemembers access to low-cost index funds, a unique investment opportunity in the G Fund, as well as automatic payroll deductions. If index funds are part of a servicemember's investment strategy, the TSP offers an ideal investment option with expense ratios that are often ten times lower than similar funds available in the market. Individuals should assess the distinct benefits of each plan and determine which option best meets their financial goals.

Additionally, maximizing TSP contributions ($17,000 for 2012) may not be feasible or advisable for many people. Because TSP offerings are limited to five core investment funds, individuals may be better off diversifying their retirement portfolio into some other taxable investment instruments. For example, the TSP does not offer the opportunity to invest in individual common stocks, ETFs, CDs, money market accounts, emerging markets, or REITs. See chapter 11 for more on advanced investment strategy.

In conclusion, the most important thing individuals can do to secure their financial future is to start saving now. One of the oldest and most commonly used personal finance principles is to "pay yourself first." While individuals usually remember to pay their rent, cell phone bills, or buy groceries each month, they often forget to pay themselves. This practice, established early in one's career, can build tremendous wealth. By committing some portion of their earnings toward their future, individuals can ensure they achieve the life they envision for retirement.

PART IV

RISK MANAGEMENT

13

Life Insurance

Life insurance is one of the most important components of a family's financial plan. Unfortunately, life insurance is often misunderstood and misused. Mistakes made by the family's financial planner invariably cause great hardship for the survivors. The goal of this chapter is to provide you with a firm understanding of Servicemembers' Group Life Insurance (SGLI) so you can review the amount of money survivors will receive in the event of a family member's death, identify how much additional life insurance your family might need, and examine what type of policy might best fit your family's situation. The ultimate goal is to be a better prepared and savvier consumer of life insurance as a component of a family's financial plan.

Answering the following three questions will help you determine the life insurance protection your family wants and can afford prior to looking at options with an insurance agent.

1. Does the servicemember or spouse need life insurance at all?
2. If so, how much life insurance does the family desire for each family member?
3. What type of policy best fits the family's needs?

The primary function of life insurance is to provide protection for the family from the economic consequences of the death of a member of a household. Three factors complicate the buying process. First, most people hesitate to confront their own or a spouse's death. Second, some life insurance policies have both an insurance component and an investment component. These differences can make it difficult for some families to focus on the primary goal of life insurance protection, which is to replace family income in the event of a family member's death. Finally, there is the somewhat mysterious nature of the life insurance business. The use of statistics and proprietary actuarial (life projection) techniques to price insurance tends to discourage even the most careful shopper from doing good comparison shopping.

Adding to the confusion are the special terms developed by the life insurance industry to make the subject more appealing and the product more marketable. The typical insurance buyer must comprehend terms like "premium," "permanent insurance," "whole life insurance," and "term insurance" in order to understand the full range of options. The confusion created by this jargon causes many people to use and trust an agent's recommendations rather than selecting an insurance category or analyzing specific products themselves. This can be a very costly decision.

A life insurance company is a for-profit business. Insurance agents operate primarily on commission, so they have an incentive to sell policies that produce the highest commissions, rather than the policies that fit each family best. Reputable agents do attempt to match an insurance plan to a family's needs, but you should be aware of the substantial commissions involved and the possibility of high-pressure sales techniques. By doing your homework before talking to an agent, you increase the likelihood of making the best economic decision for your family.

THE PRINCIPLE BEHIND INSURANCE

Insurance is based on a very simple concept: Spreading the high cost of infrequent but catastrophic events among a large group of people reduces the cost to each member of the group. Individuals share the risk at a fraction of the cost of the catastrophic event. Life insurance is perhaps the best example of insurance that "pays off" for an event that happens most infrequently (death is a once-in-a-lifetime event), but with truly catastrophic effects. Life insurance is not designed to protect the insured; it safeguards the future well-being of the survivors or the beneficiaries of the policy. The policyholder benefits from the peace of mind that the insurance provides.

It is critical to understand what you are buying, and why, in order to purchase a life insurance plan that best meets your family's needs rather than those of an insurance company or agent.

Life insurance provides protection from the economic consequences of a family member's premature death. Insurance will not help with the emotional loss; however, it can remove the fear of economic hardship. Remember that the amount of insurance does not demonstrate your love for your family, nor does it delay your departure from this world. Life insurance is not an investment, although some policies have an investment component. Too much insurance can result in high premiums that reduce a family's monthly disposable income and, therefore, quality of life—the ability to enjoy other things important to the family.

SERVICEMEMBERS' GROUP LIFE INSURANCE

Servicemembers and their families should first understand the insurance and survivor benefits available to them through the military before assessing additional insurance needs.

The primary insurance for active duty military personnel is Servicemembers' Group Life Insurance (SGLI). SGLI is low-cost term life insurance available to active duty servicemembers, ready reservists, service academy cadets and midshipmen, and members of the Reserve Officer Training Corps. The coverage is available in increments of $50,000, up to a maximum of $400,000. It costs $.065 per $1,000 of coverage, regardless of age. This translates to monthly premiums ranging from $3.25 for $50,000 of coverage to $27 for the maximum $400,000 of coverage. This premium includes both SGLI ($26) and TSGLI ($1) coverage. TSGLI, Traumatic Injury Protection under Servicemembers' Group Life Insurance, is a rider to SGLI that pays servicemembers with severe injuries resulting from a traumatic event (on or off duty) who suffer from a qualifying loss covered under TSGLI. Servicemembers who have SGLI automatically have TSGLI, which cannot be declined. The most up-to-date premiums are available at http://www.insurance.va.gov/ sgliSite/SGLI/sgliPremiums.htm.

Another life insurance option for servicemembers is Family Servicemembers' Group Life Insurance (FSGLI). This program provides insurance for spouses and children of servicemembers. Spouses qualify for a maximum of $100,000 of life insurance, and each dependent child qualifies for $10,000 of life insurance. Premiums depend on family members' ages and can range from $.50 to $50.00 per month. Refer to the website for the latest premiums (http://www.insurance.va.gov/sgliSite/FSGLI/fsgliPremiums.htm). Remember that life insurance exists to protect a family from the economic consequences of a family member's death. Families analyzing the appropriateness of FSGLI (or some other supplemental insurance for family members) must consider what costs the insurance must cover (e.g. funeral, lost spouse's income, childcare, etc.), because some family members may require little to no insurance. Be sure to carefully compare insurance premiums before purchasing a policy, because individual circumstances may make FSGLI more or less attractive than other options.

When servicemembers leave the military, they have the option of converting their SGLI coverage to a Veterans' Group Life Insurance (VGLI) policy. VGLI is a post-separation renewable term life insurance policy, issuing coverage in multiples of $10,000 up to a maximum of $400,000. However, a servicemember's VGLI coverage amount cannot exceed the amount of SGLI coverage at the time of separation from service. Current premiums for VGLI are available at http://www.insurance.va.gov.

The "Servicemembers' and Veterans' Group Life Insurance Handbook" answers additional questions concerning SGLI and VGLI (see http://www. insurance.va.gov/sgliSite/handbook/handbook.htm). The VA's life insurance website at http://www.insurance.va.gov/sgliSite is also an outstanding source of information for military members researching their life insurance options.

SGLI will meet the life insurance needs of most military members. It is reasonably priced, nontaxable, and provides substantial coverage for servicemembers and their families. Thus, we recommend that military members purchase SGLI life insurance. However, servicemembers should carefully review VGLI and its competitors (e.g. USAA, etc.) as the family plans their transition to retirement. VGLI does not require a health assessment if the servicemember signs up within 120 days of retirement, but premiums tend to be quite a bit higher than premiums for many comparable privately available life insurance policies, especially in the older age categories. Families should conduct a careful assessment of their insurance needs and the servicemember's current health prior to deciding on life insurance for retirement years.

DEATH BENEFITS FOR MILITARY MEMBERS

Once you understand the life insurance benefits available through the military (SGLI), the next step is to learn about the death benefits available to survivors of military members in the event of an untimely death. In addition to SGLI lump-sum payments, survivors of military personnel also receive benefits through the Department of Defense (DoD), Social Security Administration (SSA), and the Department of Veterans Affairs (VA).

Department of Defense Benefits. The military provides a number of lump-sum death benefits to the survivors of its veterans. The first is the Fallen Hero Compensation (formerly known as the Death Gratuity). This benefit is an immediate cash payment of $12,420 to eligible beneficiaries of a servicemember who dies within 120 days of retirement or as a result of non-hostile action. In addition, The Emergency Supplemental Appropriations Act of 2005 increased this payment to $100,000 for "survivors of those whose death is as a result of hostile actions and occurred in a designated combat operation or combat zone or while training for combat or performing hazardous duty." The military also pays survivors the balance of any accrued leave at the time of the death. This leave payment consists of base pay and is taxable.

Social Security Benefits. Based upon a servicemember's lifetime credits earned through Social Security (i.e., how much he or she has paid to Social Security through FICA taxes), the Social Security Administration will pay survivor benefits to the servicemember's surviving spouse, if the spouse is eligible for retirement (age sixty for reduced benefits and "full retirement age" for 100% benefits), or for the children (if spouse is not eligible for retirement and is caring for dependent children under age eighteen). First, the family (either an eligible spouse or child under eighteen) receives a one-time family payment of $225. Second, surviving children under eighteen years of age receive a monthly percentage of the deceased's benefits. Finally, a surviving spouse that does not meet retirement eligibility and is caring for children under sixteen receives a monthly percentage of the deceased's benefits. The Social Security Administration has a calculator on its website (http://www.ssa.gov/planners/calculators.htm) that can help you determine available estimated benefits. This calculator also estimates a family's maximum possible benefits.

VA Benefits. The VA also has numerous nontaxable survivor benefits for military members, the first of which is Dependency and Indemnity Compensation (DIC). The following rates are effective as of Dec 1, 2011. A basic monthly payment of $1,195 to $2,738 (based on the servicemember's rank) goes to the surviving spouse. This amount increases by $296 per child under age eighteen, by $139 if the spouse is housebound, and by $254 if the veteran had been rated totally disabled for the previous eight years while married to the surviving spouse. The benefit increases by an additional $296 if the spouse is entitled to additional allowances (A&A), which is the case if any of the previous three conditions are met (children under 18, housebound, veteran rated totally disabled for previous eight years). These quoted benefits assume a veteran's death after 1993. Benefits for veterans' deaths prior to 1993 and summary DIC tables are listed at http://www.vba.va.gov/bln/21/rates/comp03.htm. Additionally, for veterans' deaths after 2001, the VA will pay up to $2,000 in burial expenses for service-related deaths or $300 for non-service-related deaths (plus an additional $300 interment plot allowance for non-service-related deaths).

The VA also pays a death pension to survivors of wartime veterans. This is a need-based monthly benefit primarily paid to nonworking spouses. If the spouse's yearly income is less than a specified income level, then the spouse receives a pension. Details on the income limits are at http://www.vba.va.gov.

The Survivors' and Dependents' Educational Assistance Program (DEA), another VA program, provides up to forty-five months of monthly allowances for a survivor's education, including degree and certificate programs, apprenticeships, and on-the-job training, as well as correspondence courses for spouses and children of deceased veterans. The type and length of schooling determine the monthly allowances. Details on this program are available at www.gibill.va.gov/pamphlets/CH35/CH35_Pamphlet.pdf.

The VA also extends home loan benefits to surviving spouses with no down payment required. However, there is a small fee involved. For details regarding these loans, see the VA website, http://www.homeloans.va.gov.

Veterans' surviving family members must apply for the VA and Social Security survivor benefits. Casualty assistance officers—military personnel trained about the survivor entitlements specified in AR 600-8-1—provide servicemembers' families with help in the application process.

Example: ARMY Captain (O3)

In the following example, we estimate the survivor benefits for the spouse of a married Army Captain (O3) who dies while deployed to a combat zone. This example assumes that the spouse works and that the captain is twenty-six years old with four years of active-duty service, military SGLI of $400,000, and thirty days of accrued leave at death. (All calculations are based on 2011 military pay.)

DOD BENEFITS (LUMP SUM)

Fallen Hero Compensation:	$100,000
Accrued Leave (30 days):	$4,952
SGLI:	$400,000
Total DoD Lump Sum Benefit:	$504,952

SOCIAL SECURITY BENEFITS

One-Time Lump Sum Benefit:	$225
Total Social Security Monthly Benefits*:	$1,887 per month

* All Social Security benefits were calculated using the benefit calculator at www.ssa.gov/planners/calculators.htm. This monthly benefit will be paid to the eligible spouse only when he or she reaches eligible retirement age.

VA BENEFITS (MONTHLY)

DIC-Spouse:	$1,154
Educational Assistance (Full-Time School)*:	$827
Total VA Monthly Benefits:	$1,981

* Survivors can receive educational assistance for a maximum of forty-five months (combined). Rates vary depending on the type of program selected. Spouses and children are eligible within certain criteria.

EXAMPLE: Army Sergeant (E-5)

In this example, we estimate survivor benefits for a spouse and two children of a married Army Sergeant (E-5) who dies in a non-combat-related accident. This example assumes the spouse does not work, the two children are under sixteen years old, and the sergeant is twenty-four years old with six years of active-duty service, military SGLI of $400,000, and thirty days of accrued leave at death. (All calculations are based on 2011 military pay)

DOD BENEFITS (LUMP SUM)

Fallen Hero Compensation:	$12,420
Accrued Leave (30 days):	$2,620
SGLI:	$400,000
Total DoD Lump Sum Benefit:	$415,040

SOCIAL SECURITY BENEFITS

One-Time Lump Sum Benefit:	$225
Spouse Caring for Children under 16 (75% of Estimated $1,049 Social Security Benefits):	$812
Surviving Children ($812 × 2)*:	$1,624
Total Social Security Monthly Benefits**:	$1,925.50 per month

* Be aware that surviving spouses will receive benefits for themselves only while they have a child under the age of sixteen who is eligible for Social Security benefits or after they (spouses) reach sixty years of age.

** All Social Security benefits were calculated using the benefit calculator at www.ssa.gov/planners/calculators.htm. This benefit calculator gave this maximum monthly amount of $1,925.50 instead of $2,436 because of what is known as a "family maximum." This limit is not set but "is generally between 150 and 180 percent of the deceased's benefit amount. If the sum of the benefits payable to a spouse and the children is greater than this limit, the family will receive a benefit amount that is proportionately reduced."

VA BENEFITS (MONTHLY)

DIC-Spouse:	$1,154
DIC-Transition benefit*:	$250
DIC-Children:	$572
Death Pension**:	$924
Educational Assistance (Full-Time School) ***:	$827
Total VA Monthly Benefits:	$3,727

* The family receives this allotment for up to two years.

** The Death Pension pays the difference between income and yearly income limits found on the VA website at www.vba.va.gov.

*** A survivor can receive educational assistance for a maximum of forty-five months.

Remember that the monthly benefits calculated in the two examples above are subject to change, based on the ages of one's children and spouse and the employment status of the spouse. The Social Security Administration and VA websites have the most up-to-date information about rules and monthly allowance amounts. Suggested websites are listed throughout this chapter and provide excellent starting points for further research based on one's personal situation.

NEEDS ANALYSIS

Once you have a better understanding of the survivor benefits available to servicemembers from the DoD, SSA, and VA, the next step is to analyze how much additional life insurance your family might want. The reason for determining insurance needs is to estimate your family's actual financial situation in the event of a family member's death. Life insurance is not a measure of devotion to loved ones or a monument to an individual's self-importance. It is insurance to protect dependents against undue financial hardship in the event of a family member's premature death.

Financial Obligations. Start your family's needs analysis by determining the family's financial obligations following the death of the servicemember or spouse. These financial obligations consist of burial costs, outstanding debts, and income that a family will require for future planned expenses. Burial costs include funeral expenses, burial fees, and headstone fees. Examples of typical outstanding debts are mortgages, credit card debt, and car loans. Future planned expenses may include children's college expenses, special medical care needs, and a reserve for emergencies. The DoD's lump-sum Fallen Hero Compensation and other VA funeral benefits should cover the majority of burial costs, while SGLI should adequately cover outstanding debts and future planned expenses.

Monthly Income Needs. After you determine your family's financial obligations at death, consider the monthly income that survivors will need to sustain a preferred lifestyle. If you do not know where to start in estimating these expenses, a good rule of thumb is two-thirds of your family's present monthly income while children remain at home, and one-half if the spouse is the only surviving household member. Typical monthly expenses to consider include childcare, health insurance, utilities, car and renters' insurance, rent or mortgage payments, car payments, food, and entertainment. As previously discussed, surviving families of servicemembers receive numerous allowances from Social Security and VA. As the E-5 example illustrated, these allowances are substantial ($4,825.50), even when not including spouse and child education allowances. You should also consider whether the surviving spouse would earn additional income, as this affects the family's monthly financial needs. Determining how much the spouse earns or will earn tells you how much to decrease the family's income needs by, reducing the amount of necessary life insurance coverage. The spouse's future income will also affect the amount of allowances provided by the VA.

Assets. Lastly, the family's needs analysis should consider the family's assets. Assets include money in savings accounts, mutual funds, stocks, CDs, or other investments. They also include other things such as whole life insurance and real estate.

Remember that life insurance is one way to provide an "instant estate" to meet the financial needs of survivors. You can easily estimate the expected income that accumulated financial assets will generate. Just multiplying the total value of income-generating assets by the interest rate (less the inflation rate) they earn. For example, if a family has saved $50,000 and will receive $400,000 from SGLI, the survivors will have $450,000 of assets. If the family invests this money and receives a 4% real rate of return (for example, if return = 6% and inflation =2%), they will receive $18,000 of income per year (without drawing down the principal). Detailed information and calculators can be found at http://www.insurance.va.gov.

Use this formula to calculate your additional life insurance needs:

$$\frac{\text{Financial}}{\text{Obligations}} + \frac{\text{Net Income Needed to}}{\text{Support Survivors}} - \text{Assets} = \frac{\text{Insurance}}{\text{Needs}}$$

> *Life insurance is not a measure of devotion to loved ones or a monument to an individual's importance. It is insurance to protect dependants against undue financial hardship in the event of a family member's premature death.*

Because of the more complicated calculations associated with the time value of money and inflation, we recommend families use an online life insurance calculator or consult a financial planner to conduct more accurate needs assessments. One financial planning service available to military members is the Army and Air Force Mutual Aid Association. The services this association offers include a needs analysis for servicemembers and their families. There are also useful online tools for estimating additional life insurance your family might need. A comprehensive life insurance calculator that incorporates the VA and social security survivor benefits discussed in this chapter is available at http://www.insurance.va.gov/sgliSite/calculator/intro Calc.htm.

As an individual lives longer, the financial needs of survivors often decrease. For example, if your children have finished college, you do not need to leave money for their education. Thus, families should reevaluate insurance needs periodically as survivors' situations change. In any case, the purpose of insurance is not to make your family wealthy upon the death of a family member; the purpose of life insurance is to provide the coverage necessary to take care of the survivors' identifiable needs.

LIFE INSURANCE TERMINOLOGY

If you determine that your family needs additional life insurance beyond SGLI, it is important to understand the types of insurance and terminology used by insurance companies and salespeople, so you can select the type of life insurance that best fits your family's needs. All life insurance policies contain a face amount, a policy period, a premium, and possibly a savings component. Individuals can adjust each of these to meet their needs.

Face Amount. The face amount of the policy is the amount paid to a beneficiary (designated survivor) in the event of the policyholder's death. The larger the face amount, the higher the benefit to the beneficiary and the higher the policy premium.

Policy Period. The length of life insurance policies can vary from a year to the policyholder's entire lifetime, which also impacts the premium (or cost of the policy). Policies set for a specific time period are renewable for additional periods unless explicitly stated otherwise. Renewable policies guarantee renewal without conditions (no physical exam required), and the premium will change only with age, not with the policyholder's health condition. Nonrenewable policies expire at the end of the term and a new policy must be purchased (generally requiring a physical exam). Reentry/requalification policies also require a new physical examination at the end of the coverage period; however, a favorable exam results in premiums lower than those of a new policy—hence the term reentry. The premiums for renewable policies are generally higher because insurance companies cannot raise premiums during the policy period, should the policyholder's health deteriorate, or end their obligation to insure the policyholder.

In general, nonrenewable policies, policies with shorter renewal periods, and policies that base future premiums on new physical exams have lower annual premiums today. Companies charge lower premiums for these policies because they have a chance to learn more at each renewal point about the factors (health, in particular) that affect the probability of death, and they can refuse insurance or raise premiums based on higher risk factors. If you are in excellent health, the cheapest possible coverage will be a one-year, nonrenewable term policy.

Premium. A premium is simply a payment (the cost of the policy), like a car payment or a mortgage payment on a house. The premium pays the insurance company for administering the policy and includes the agent's commission. With certain types of policies, part of the payment goes to a form of "savings." Premiums can stay the same, increase, or decrease over the length of the policy, depending on the policy type.

Savings. Permanent and variable insurance policies (discussed in the next section) include a cash value that you can use as a form of savings. There are some advantages to this type of policy. You can borrow from your account, although this incurs interest charges. After a specified number of years, the savings generated by your premiums may pay your insurance policy in full, so you will no longer need to make premium payments. Alternatively, you may elect to end the policy and cash out the "savings" portion to spend or invest elsewhere. Some disadvantages are that you typically earn a lower rate of interest on these savings than on alternative financial investments. Further, because these policies include both insurance and savings components, their premiums are much higher.

TYPES OF LIFE INSURANCE POLICIES

There are three main types of life insurance: (1) term, which lasts for just a specific period and has no savings component; (2) permanent (also known as whole), in which the policyholder pays premiums until the insured's death and the policy builds savings; and (3) variable, which has a flexible structure designed to allow greater return on the savings portion of the policy. Within these major categories, many variations exist to meet a policyholder's life insurance needs. As the policyholder gets older, premiums increase. To avoid this problem, the insured person may select level-term or permanent insurance.

Whatever the specific insurance option's finer points, the underlying principle of distributing the risk over a large group remains the goal of any type of insurance. After reading this information about each of the specialized types of life insurance, think about how the different options fit your family's personal needs.

Term Insurance. Term insurance protects the policyholder for a specified time period—one year, five years, twenty years, or more. It is pure insurance: the policy "pays off" only if the insured person dies within the specified period. In this sense, it provides protection to the survivors only from the economic effects of death. It has no savings feature and thus no "cash value," so you cannot borrow against the policy. You must renew term insurance at the end of the term. Usually, renewal requires a physical examination, although some companies may waive this requirement.

Generally, term policy premiums are lower than those of permanent policies since none of the premium goes toward savings. Thus, a young person with a low income who needs a large death benefit, perhaps in excess of $200,000, may be able to afford term, but not permanent, coverage.

Many insurance agents sell both permanent (insurance plus savings) and term (insurance alone) insurance policies. Due to higher commissions, many agents might try to steer clients towards permanent rather than term insurance (or temporary insurance, as the agents like to call it) policies. Even agents who sell term insurance often try regularly to get clients to convert the policy to permanent insurance. So beware of high-pressure tactics. Fortunately, some good companies specialize in term insurance, and a number, such as SGLI and USAA, cater especially to the military community.

Companies offer incentives to insurance agents to sell permanent policies because of the excess premiums they generate. With the excess "savings" held in permanent accounts, the insurance companies can invest those excess premiums in stocks, bonds, real estate, or other investment mechanisms to make more money. Since term policies have no savings component, insurance companies cannot make any additional money from excess premiums.

One disadvantage of term insurance is that premiums increase with age. At age twenty, one might pay $150 per year for a $100,000 term policy, but the same policy could cost the same person over $300 per year at age forty-five. The premium increases could make a term policy more expensive in the long-term than a permanent one (purchased now) for the same face amount. (Note: This chapter later discusses how the insurance portions of permanent policies effectively have the same characteristics.) But your insurance needs will likely peak and then lessen with age; for example, you need less insurance after your children have completed school. Some older people do not need any life insurance; however, for those who do, several types of term insurance can meet this need.

Level Term. The face value and the premium for level term insurance remains the same throughout the coverage period. This type of insurance extends the term of the policy in order to spread out the high cost of later-year term insurance across the entire length of the policy. Essentially, the policyholder overpays during the first half of the policy period and underpays during the second half. This agreement to pay premiums for an extended period helps keep level term policy premiums lower in the long term than permanent policy premiums.

Servicemembers' Group Life Insurance (SGLI) is level term insurance. Currently, a servicemember may elect to take the maximum $400,000 of coverage for $.065 per $1,000 of coverage, regardless of age. This is very inexpensive insurance for older officers and noncommissioned officers. In effect, the large numbers of young servicemembers make the low premiums for older servicemembers possible. For this reason, and because it is convertible after you leave the service, SGLI should be the basic building block of your family's insurance program.

Decreasing Term. Decreasing term insurance has a constant premium over the term of the coverage, but the face value of the policy declines to reflect the higher risk of death as age increases. For example, a twenty-five-year-old male may buy $100,000 of insurance protection for $10 a month, but that same male will only have $15,000 of coverage for the same premium at forty-five. A decreasing term policy makes sense for individuals whose insurance needs decrease as they age. For instance, an individual with decreasing obligations, such as a mortgage that the individual is paying off, will need less insurance to ensure that his survivors can pay the remaining mortgage obligation.

> *The underlying principle of distributing the risk over a large group remains the basis of any type of insurance.*

Renewable, Nonrenewable, and Reentry Term. These term policies have special features that allow individuals to renew their policy at the end of the policy period if they meet certain standards. Renewable term policies eliminate the physical examination requirement—a person injured in combat or who has contracted cancer would still be able to renew the term policy. In this regard, term insurance is not really "temporary" at all. However, most policies do not allow renewal past the age of seventy, when the cost of the policy outweighs the benefit. Most of the companies that cater to the military sell renewable term insurance.

The second type, nonrenewable, means that the policy ends at the conclusion of the term and the policyholder must buy a new policy to replace it. Most new policies require a new physical exam, which can impact the cost of the policy's premium. For a reentry term policy, the policyholder must pass a physical after the end of the term to "reenter" the low-cost policy. Reentry term policies are generally less expensive than renewable term policies. The danger is that if you fail the physical examination, you cannot reenter and must pay a higher premium or find a different policy. For example, suppose a thirty-five-year-old male bought a $250,000 five-year reentry term policy with an annual premium that started out at $400 and gradually rose to $550 over the five-year term. At the reentry point, the now forty-year-old man must take a new physical exam. If he passes, his premium drops to $500 and gradually rises from there, but if he fails, his premium rises to $750 and gradually rises from that new starting point. At forty-five years of age, when he has to take another new physical, the premium will increase to $600 (passing) or $1,100 (not passing).

In comparison, once an individual passes the initial physical examination for a renewable term policy, the policy premiums over time are the same for all policyholders in the same age category, regardless of the individual's health status. Reentry term is best for only a very select group: people who need a substantial amount of insurance at a lower cost for a short period of time. In the long term, due to the potentially marked increase in reentry premiums, the costs of these policies generally outweigh the benefits of the small savings they provide.

Convertible Term. Many term policies offer a feature that allows the policyholder to convert the term policy to some form of permanent insurance without having to provide evidence of insurability, such as through a medical examination. While policyholders will pay the higher premium associated with their age at conversion (some policies will allow a retroactive calculation to the original age of buying the policy), they are protected from the loss of insurability. This is a very desirable feature, as it protects policyholders and their survivors in the event the servicemember's insurability changes for the worse at the time that the term policy expires. See Table 13-1 for a summary of the advantages and disadvantages of term insurance.

Permanent Insurance. The words "permanent," "ordinary," and "whole" life insurance have the same meaning in the insurance industry. These policies combine pure (term) insurance with an automatic savings feature (called "cash value") that provides the companies with funds that they invest to produce most of their profits and to provide the assets to fulfill their obligations if a policy becomes due. The premiums on these policies include two components.

TABLE 13-1
TERM LIFE INSURANCE

Advantages
- Premiums are initially lower than those for permanent insurance, allowing individuals to buy higher levels of coverage at a younger age, when the need for protection often is greatest.
- Coverage protects against expenses that will disappear in time, such as mortgages, children's education, or car loans.

Disadvantages
- Premiums increase or coverage decreases as the insured grows older.
- Coverage may terminate at the end of the term or become too expensive to continue.

One portion goes to the insurance company, and the other goes into a savings account. Insurance salespeople are offered the largest commissions for selling permanent policies and therefore emphasize them in their sales presentations.

Perhaps "ordinary insurance" really refers to the fact that this is the type of insurance that a company would prefer to sell. With a permanent insurance policy, as the years go by, the interest earnings on the savings portion of the premiums will accumulate, slowly at first, but then faster in later years, until there is enough in the account to cover the face value of the policy. This, in effect, gradually replaces the insurance provided by the company with the policyholder's own savings. The company eventually accumulates enough of a cash value from the policyholder to simply hand it back to the survivors when the policyholder dies. Permanent insurance is really a combination of a decreasing term insurance policy bundled with an enforced savings feature. The company, in paying the face value totally out of cash value, essentially no longer provides any pure insurance. The accumulated savings represent a cash value that the policyholder may borrow against (with an interest charge) after some number of years.

An advantage of permanent insurance is that the policyholder is insured for life with a constant premium. No matter when the policyholder dies, if the policy is still in force, the company pays the face amount to the policyholder's beneficiary. Although the premium payments are much higher than term insurance early in life, they may be less costly in the long run because of the accumulated savings portion of the premium. The majority of permanent or whole life policies fall into two categories: straight life and limited-payment life.

Straight Life. Straight life (also called whole or ordinary life) is the most common form of life insurance sold. It provides both protection and savings for the policyholder, who pays premiums throughout his or her life and builds up a cash value in the policy. It has the same premium throughout the life of the policy (which is where the term "straight" comes from): The premium charged to the policyholder at age twenty is the same premium charged at age fifty. The premium amount is determined primarily by the policyholder's age when he or she buys the policy. The policyholder's physical condition may impact the cost of the premium, with a healthier or less risky person paying a lower premium.

Whole life policies build cash value each year that the policy is in force. But these savings accounts accumulate little cash value in the early years, so you will not have much saved if you close your account early. Insurance companies know that policy cancellations happen regularly, and establish rules with that in mind. For example, one company's most popular permanent policy returns an average interest rate of 0.2% on the accumulating savings if you cancel it at the ten-year point. A Senate subcommittee gathered data on sixty of the leading U.S. insurance companies and found that 25% of permanent policy buyers discontinue their policies within the first year, 46% within ten years, and nearly 60% before twenty years.

The return for a whole life policy does depend on the length of time one keeps the policy. Most policies forfeit all cash value if the policy is in effect for less than two years, with the average break-even point at eight years (this is where the accumulated savings have earned a zero percent return). Generally, a savings account at a local bank will earn as much interest as, and in some cases even more than, the savings portion of a whole life policy. However, the interest accumulated on a whole life policy is tax-deferred; no taxes are paid on the gains in the account until the funds are actually withdrawn.

Another often-stated feature of whole life insurance is the availability of loans against the cash value of the policy. This feature can come in quite handy as a ready source for short-term loans. Although these loans tend to cost less than most signature loans, you must realize that by borrowing from your own policy's savings, you reduce the interest you'll earn on the remaining savings. Some policyholders may not have to pay back these loans, but this reduces the death benefits payable to their survivors.

Limited-payment Life. A limited-payment insurance policy provides life insurance protection throughout the policyholder's life, similar to whole life insurance. But instead of the same payment throughout, the policyholder pays the same (higher) premium for a limited number of years (perhaps for ten, twenty, or thirty years). At that point, the policy is "paid up," meaning that the policyholder no longer has to pay any premiums. In comparison, a whole life policy does not get "paid up" until the policyholder reaches the age of one hundred. Insurance protection, in the sense that the beneficiaries get the face amount of the policy upon the policyholder's death, remains throughout the policyholder's life.

In order to pay off a policy earlier you must pay a greater premium. Therefore, limited-payment policies generally have the most expensive short-term premiums of all life insurance policy types. For example, a thirty-five-year-old

---

TABLE 13-2
PERMANENT LIFE INSURANCE

Advantages
- Protection is guaranteed for life as long as the premiums are paid.
- Premium costs can be fixed or flexible to meet personal financial needs.
- You can borrow against the cash value accumulated from the policy (you must repay the loan with interest or beneficiaries will receive a reduced death benefit).
- You can borrow against the policy's cash value to pay premiums or use the cash value to provide paid-up insurance.
- The policy's cash value can be surrendered, in total or in part, for cash or converted into an annuity (an annuity is an insurance product that provides an income for a person's lifetime or a specific period).

Disadvantages
- Premium level (required) may make it too expensive to buy enough protection.
- Cost—it may be more costly than term insurance if you do not keep it long enough.
- Returns—interest rates on the savings portion may be below market returns.

---

man who purchases a $10,000 twenty-year limited-payment policy might pay $340 per year, compared to $220 for a whole life policy. With these larger payments, you usually have to accept a lower face amount for the policy, causing some policyholders to remain underinsured compared to the obligations faced by their survivors. As a note, these are the most profitable policies for insurance companies due to the higher up-front premiums and lower corresponding face amounts.

Variable Insurance. In the 1970s, high interest rates available on alternative savings vehicles made the low rates of return on the savings component in whole life and limited-payment life financially unattractive. Sales of these products declined, and the insurance industry developed a new range of products with higher rates of return and increased flexibility. Some of these plans allow the policyholder to move between term and permanent insurance for a small fee, adjusting the savings and insurance components of the policies to meet the customer's needs over a period of years. Other new policies simply improve the return on the savings component of the policy. The most common types of these new policies are "adjustable life," "universal life," and "variable life" insurance. Most of these policies feature a single premium—one large up-front premium—and are unsuitable for most servicemembers due to this high initial cost.

Adjustable Life. Adjustable life insurance allows policyholders to adjust the terms of the policy as their needs change. Policies may start as whole life and later convert to term insurance, providing policyholders with the option to either reduce premiums or increase the policy's face value as their needs dictate. Another type of policy initially offers low-cost term coverage with little or no cash value buildup. Later, when the policyholder has more income, the policy can convert to permanent insurance with higher premiums that include an accumulation of cash value. The policyholder may use dividends to pay premiums or to increase the face value of the policy. The major advantage of this type of policy is flexibility. The disadvantage of adjustable life is that the policy owner has to compromise between the best term policy and the best permanent policy.

Universal Life. Universal life insurance is a combination of term insurance with a tax-deferred savings account that is tied to a market interest rate. In many respects, universal life acts like an adjustable life policy in that the policyholder can adjust the face value and premiums to meet changing needs. The major difference is that the interest rate paid on cash values in universal life is closer to market rates than in whole life policies, so the investment portion grows faster. Universal life usually invests the savings portion of the premium in short- or medium-term bond investments that in the past have offered superior rates of return to those of whole life savings components. The return, however, is not guaranteed; what a policyholder earns depends on the actual performance of the insurance company's investment portfolios.

It is probably true that the rate of return on a universal life policy's savings component will be higher than the return on a similar whole life policy, simply because the company attempts to tie the return to the performance of its investments. However, it is not clear that the actual return that is earned on a universal policy will be much higher when you consider all of the additional fees and restrictions. Beware of sales claims that advertise a rate of return paid on the cash value after all fees and costs have been deducted from your premium payment. You should calculate the relevant rate of return based on what you have to pay, minus the amount necessary to pay for the pure insurance—an amount that you may approximate by calculating the cost of a decreasing renewable term policy.

As with all insurance policies, it is important to shop for the best universal life policy, as different companies offer slightly different options. Some companies will only pay 3% interest on the first $1,000 in the savings portion of the account. Other companies allow you to vary the amount of insurance coverage without incurring additional fees. And some companies charge high first-year fees. The return on universal life insurance policies is usually guaranteed for one year, then fluctuates with market conditions over the long term. Many companies will guarantee a high rate for the first year and a nominal rate after that. Look for maximum flexibility, highest guaranteed minimum rates of return, and lowest fees.

Variable Life. Variable life policies are designed to allow the insured to earn possibly higher rates of return by putting the cash value component of the policy into higher-risk investments: common stocks, bonds, money market instruments, or government securities. There is no guaranteed cash surrender value (the amount paid by the insurance company) for a policyholder voluntarily terminating a policy, because the cash value depends on the return actually earned on the investments. Additionally, you will not know exactly what the face amount of your coverage is, although some minimum is normally guaranteed. If the investment portion of policy grows, the cash surrender value and face amount of the policy will rise. If the investment does poorly, the face amount of the policy will decline. It is important to recognize that the death benefit that survivors will receive from a variable life policy depends in part on the performance of the investment strategy from the insurance company you select.

For example, if you choose to have the company invest the savings component of the variable life premium in common stocks, the death benefit paid to survivors will increase or decrease with the price of the stock. It is true that in the past long-term bonds and common stocks have paid higher average returns than more conservative investments, but it is also true that the variability of those returns has been greater. Beware of counting on an assumed rate of return on an investment portfolio to deliver the insurance protection your family needs. Companies do not guarantee the rates of return you may see in variable life sales literature. You should base the amount of insurance you buy on your family's needs and choose a policy that guarantees that death benefit. The potential gains from higher investment returns in variable life policies should be viewed as a means to earn higher expected returns on the cash value by accepting greater investment risk.

PURCHASING A POLICY

Now, with a basic understanding of the various types of life insurance available, you have the difficult task of choosing the best policy for your family.

Almost all active-duty members elect to take Servicemembers' Group Life Insurance (SGLI) at some level of coverage. The maximum coverage is currently $400,000 in term insurance for $27 per month. Servicemembers should check their Leave and Earnings Statements to see if they are paying for SGLI and are therefore covered. You should only reduce this low-cost term insurance coverage after carefully reviewing the family's insurance needs. Upon separation or retirement from active duty, you can convert SGLI into Veterans' Group Life Insurance (VGLI). VGLI is a renewable five-year term policy with a premium based upon a servicemember's age at separation. Servicemembers can learn more about VGLI at http://www.insurance.va.gov, which also has links to VGLI premiums.

For term insurance other than SGLI and VGLI, servicemembers must inquire about rates and collect data from different insurance companies. Since the profit margins are low with term insurance, many companies that sell it do not have a sales force. Individuals must decide the amount of insurance they need and then find the best deal for the insurance.

Some financial planners say, "Buy term and invest the difference," when giving advice concerning life insurance. Before relying on this adage, you must evaluate your own discipline to stick to the plan. If you buy term and do not invest the difference between the term life insurance cost and the higher permanent life insurance cost, you will not accrue any savings. In this case, you will not do better than the permanent insurance policy's cash value buildup (any return is better than no return).

> *Insurance companies with the least expensive policies will probably not have a sales force, so do not expect the best deals to come knocking at your door.*

When shopping for permanent insurance, you should select an insurance agent. The agent will meet to discuss your needs and available products. Be aware that agents work on commission and usually are eager to show their products. You must avoid getting caught up in the salesperson's enthusiasm and buy the right type and amount of insurance to fit your family's needs, not the agent's. This is not an easy thing to do. Remember, over half of the people who take out permanent policies cancel them within ten years. The best offense is a good defense: Know something about your insurance needs and the available insurance options before the agent makes the sales pitch.

It is important that you select a financially secure company; insurance companies are subject to mismanagement, fraud, and poor economic conditions that can bankrupt the weaker ones. You can find insurance company ratings in most libraries in *Best's Insurance Reports,* and in magazines such as *Consumer Reports, Changing Times,* and *Money.* Each state also monitors the insurance companies licensed to sell policies within its jurisdiction. Insurance commissioners in your state can advise families about complaints or company performance, as can the Better Business Bureau.

In conclusion, it is important that you have a focused and organized plan to protect loved ones in the event of your untimely death. First, you must determine whether you need additional insurance. This entails understanding how much insurance you already have, and what additional survivor benefits are available to family members. Second, you must conduct a needs analysis to determine the approximate amount of life insurance necessary for the family. Finally, you must understand the types of life insurance available, which enables you to make an educated and informed decision concerning the type of life insurance you should buy to supplement your current coverage. Table 13-3 provides a summary of the three main insurance options. Armed with this knowledge and a focused plan, you should have no problem making an assessment of your life insurance needs and finding an appropriate life insurance plan to meet the needs of your loved ones.

TABLE 13-3
TYPES OF LIFE INSURANCE QUICK REFERENCE CHART

Type	Purpose	Costs	Risks	Payouts	Other
Term	Provides survivors protection from only the economic costs of insured's death	Low, depending on age and coverage duration	Costs increase as one gets older; no "borrowing" against the policy; renewal subject to health exam	Face amount	Variants: Level (e.g., SGLI); Decreasing; Renewable; Nonrenewable; Reentry; and Convertible
Permanent (Whole Life)	Protects from the economic costs of insured's death and provides a savings component that one can borrowed against	High	Costs exceed term; interest on savings may be below market returns	Face amount using the accumulated savings and interest from the savings portion of the monthly payment	Also called ordinary insurance, variants include straight and limited-payment life insurance
Variable	Provides the ability to move between Term and Permanent plans or take advantage of higher interest rates than those earned through permanent insurance	Varies depending on the type (usually the highest cost of all three options)	"Compromise" plan may result in getting neither the best term nor the best whole life plan, but a lesser mix of the two; very complex	Depends on the plan chosen and the returns earned (market) on selected investments throughout the life of the plan	Types: Adjustable; Universal; and Variable

14

Automobile Insurance

Owning and operating a motor vehicle can be a risky adventure. In addition to personal injuries or damages incurred while driving, the car can inflict injury on other individuals or damage property. The owner or operator of a motor vehicle assumes the risk and responsibility for compensating anyone injured and for replacing damaged property when he or she is responsible for an accident. Automobile insurance provides a necessary protection against these financial risks. All states require automobile owners to carry some basic minimum insurance coverage.

The goal of an insurance policy is to protect policyholders from the many financial risks associated with owning and operating a vehicle. An insurance policy attempts to cover each type of risk through a specific category of insurance. The cost for each type of coverage is called a premium. The sum of these risk premiums is the total cost of the policy. As a policyholder, by adjusting the level (amount) of risk coverage and the related deductibles (the amount you must pay prior to the insurance company paying for a loss), you can change your total policy cost. As a general rule, the lower the risk coverage, the lower the premium; however, premiums do not increase in proportion to the increase in coverage. For example, increasing liability coverage from $10,000 to $25,000, a 150% increase, may increase the premium by only 10%. The trade-off between premiums and coverage is important, since your primary concern should be to ensure that your assets are adequately protected against loss. Ensuring that you will have adequate protection is the most important concern when choosing car insurance; after this, you may consider other factors like firm reliability, ease of making claims, and cost.

SELECTING AN INSURANCE COMPANY

You should select your insurance company with the same diligence you used to select your car. Policy prices, coverage, and service differ significantly among companies, so comparison shopping is important in order to make an informed decision. Several Internet sites provide a comparison of the policies offered by several different insurance companies based on your specific information. Examples include http://www.carinsurancecomparison.org and htp://www.carinsurancequotescomparison.com. Additionally, letting an insurance agent know that you are actively looking at policies from different companies may give the agent some leverage in pricing the policy.

The company you select should have a reliable, established reputation in the insurance business. Longevity is typically an indicator of sound company management policies. Since military personnel move often, it is probably best to select an insurance company that will continue to provide coverage as you move from state to state and internationally. Though many Americans prefer dealing with the personal service of a local agent, military families may prefer the convenience of a toll-free number or Internet access that provides contact to an insurance professional from virtually anywhere, twenty-four hours a day.

Table 14-1 (Automobile Insurance Checklist) allows you to break down and track the costs of the various types of coverage (liability, collision, comprehensive, etc.) as well as special coverage options and discounts. Once you have narrowed down your search to a few companies, completing this table can help you make informed comparisons between companies and the various coverage options. In order to narrow the options down to a few for comparison, you might consider a few broad attributes like reputation, Internet access, bundling (e.g. also offering homeowner's insurance), and overseas coverage.

HOW INSURANCE COMPANIES EVALUATE A DRIVER'S POTENTIAL RISK

Insurance companies continually analyze each driver's financial risk, meaning the likelihood that the company will have to pay a claim to the driver. Since these companies cannot know everything about each and every policyholder, they make simplifying demographic assumptions and "pool" those policyholders with similar characteristics together. Insurance premiums are then based on the "pool" to which an insurance company assigns a driver; the riskier the pool, the higher the premium. By understanding how insurance companies assign drivers to these pools, you can influence the cost of your insurance premiums.

The common characteristics that determine a driver's pool membership are the type of car and the driver's record, as well as age, sex, marital status, frequency and length of commute, annual mileage, zip code, and academic performance. After assigning an initial pool, insurance companies reassess drivers' categorizations as their personal demographics change. For example, when a twenty-five-year-old male marries, he moves to a new category and his premiums decrease. Whatever you do, be honest with your insurance agent when discussing the demographics that affect your pool. You can get into serious trouble by providing false information just to save a few dollars.

An increase in a driver's insurance premium following a ticket or an accident can last three years, depending on the situation, and is one cost you should consider when making decisions related to safe driving. Based on historical statistics, drivers who speed excessively have a greater probability of being involved in an auto accident, and insurance companies take this information into account when they adjust a driver's rates. While a speeding ticket may

TABLE 14-1
AUTOMOBILE INSURANCE CHECKLIST

	Company A	Company B	Company C	Example*
Liability Coverage**				
Bodily injury protection	_____	_____	_____	$154.20
Property damage liability	_____	_____	_____	$203.40
Personal injury protection	_____	_____	_____	$181.30
Uninsured motorist	_____	_____	_____	$9.00
Underinsured motorist	_____	_____	_____	Incl. above
Medical payments	_____	_____	_____	$1.40
Collision**				
$100 deductible***	_____	_____	_____	$726.70
$250 deductible***	_____	_____	_____	$584.20
$500 deductible***	_____	_____	_____	$420.50
$1,000 deductible***	_____	_____	_____	$313.60
Comprehensive**				
$100 deductible***	_____	_____	_____	$69.20
$250 deductible***	_____	_____	_____	$58.50
$500 deductible***	_____	_____	_____	$54.90
$1,000 deductible***	_____	_____	_____	$42.90
Special Coverage Options				
Towing and labor	_____	_____	_____	$4.60
Rental reimbursement	_____	_____	_____	$34.90

*Six-month totals for a 22-year-old single male with no accidents, driving a 2010 Hyundai Elantra. Quote from sales2.geico.com; obtained on May 23, 2011.

**Special discounts may be given for certain technologies. It is often difficult to determine the exact amount of the discount, since the technology affects several coverage options (collision, comprehensive, liability, etc.). If your car has any of the following technologies, you should make sure your insurance company knows about them: dual airbags, side airbags, anti-lock brakes, daytime running lights, and anti-theft systems. Some companies also give discounts for certain habits, such as safe driver discounts, good student discounts, and discounts for completing driver's education.

***For collision and comprehensive deductibles, choose one deductible level for each category and pay the amount of insurance premium associated with that particular deductible.

result in an immediate $150 fine, the change in your driving record (your record of previous tickets and accidents) may result in insurance premium increases several times the cost of the ticket. Similarly, an accident claim can cause your insurance to increase by up to 30%, depending on the severity of the accident and the driver's history of previous claims. Therefore, you should take these "hidden" costs into consideration when weighing your personal tolerance for risk in your daily driving habits.

CAR TYPE INFLUENCES PREMIUM

Since your automobile insurance premium is major budget expenditure, you should consider this cost prior to purchasing a car. Different brands and car models have different claims histories. The claim history is the typical frequency that the model of car is involved in accidents and the costs of settling all claims from those accidents. Insurance companies use these claims histories along with drivers' personal information to calculate premiums. For example, a car with a poor claim history (typically involved in more accidents and repaired at a high cost) can have a significantly higher cost of coverage than a car with a better claim history. Also, "safe" cars, equipped with dual air bags, antilock brakes, and active theft-deterrent systems, are sure bets for lower premiums compared to cars without these options. These lower premiums can, over several years, offset the initial cost of purchasing these options on a new car. Likewise, when you are buying a used car, a better claim history can make the more expensive model actually cheaper than a car with a poor claim history. Insurance companies can calculate your expected premiums if you provide the relevant information (year, make, and model) on the cars that you are considering purchasing. Additionally, many insurance company websites will provide the same information.

The following websites will assist you in obtaining policy information and premium quotes: Allstate.com, Geico.com, Nationwide.com, Progressive.com, Safeco.com, Statefarm.com, and USAA.com. Some of the sites will provide quotes online; others will have a local insurance agent contact you to discuss coverage options and prices.

To review the claim history of a car, you can visit USAA.com or ConsumerReports.org and receive a copy of *The Car Guide*. Also, the Highway Loss Data Institute publishes insurance costs resulting from accidents for various makes and models of vehicles on its website (http://www.hldi.org). These historical costs affect insurance premiums in several ways. For example, large SUVs can cause greater damage to other vehicles (on average); thus, liability premiums for these vehicles tend to be higher. Also, some vehicle types, like sports cars, may serve as an indicator of the risk profile of the driver, so insurance companies use this information to set a driver's premium.

The far right column of Table 14-1 shows the six-month premium cost for a single, twenty-two-year-old male second lieutenant with no previous accidents, for a 2010 Hyundai Elantra. To get a sense of how vehicle type affects premium, if that same individual wishes to drive a 2010 Mustang GT and have a $500 deductible, then his collision coverage goes from $420.50 to $609.60, and his comprehensive insurance goes from $54.90 to $91.50. This $450 annual difference makes a very real impact on the total cost of ownership.

INSURANCE POLICY:
EXPLANATIONS AND RECOMMENDATIONS

The typical automobile insurance policy consists of five basic types of coverage: liability, medical payments, collision, comprehensive, and uninsured motorist. There are also other optional coverage choices. The following sections describe the types of coverage options as well as some guidelines to consider. You must balance these guidelines with your personal financial situation and attitude toward assuming risk.

Liability Coverage

Liability coverage pays for injuries and property damage that a driver (or someone using the driver's car) causes to another as a result of driving negligently. Liability coverage, mandatory in nearly all states, is the most expensive type of coverage and the most necessary. Individuals injured in an automobile accident in which someone else is at fault often seek compensation for personal injury through the courts. Drivers risk losing current and future assets if they fail to purchase adequate liability insurance. Therefore, liability coverage is the last place you want to skimp. There are two types of liability coverage: bodily injury and property damage.

Bodily Injury Coverage. Bodily injury (BI) coverage pays for medical expenses and associated litigation fees for losses resulting from injury or

---

Bodily Injury Insurance Guidelines

1. Carry no less than $100,000/$300,000 (split-limit) or $300,000 (single-limit) coverage.
2. Buy as much bodily injury liability coverage as you can afford. Increasing liability coverage does not raise your premium proportionately. Even if you increase coverage from $50,000 to $300,000 (a 500% increase), your premium might increase by only 25%.
3. Follow guidelines 1 and 2 even if you live in a no-fault state.
4. If you own a home and/or assets worth more than $300,000, consider an umbrella policy that will provide even more protection (see chapter 15).
5. Obtain insurance that covers any car you legally drive, even if it is a rented or borrowed vehicle.

death in an accident in which the policyholder was at fault. Losses can result from medical bills, lost wages, and pain and suffering. Court awards for pain and suffering can be enough to ruin a policyholder financially if he is underinsured. A policyholder can expect to be sued if he or she causes an accident that results in personal injury or death.

You should consider your personal situation when deciding on coverage amounts. Things to consider include your level of wealth (which you are protecting with insurance), your current income, the insurance requirements in your state, the way your state's laws deal with accidents (e.g. whether you live in a "no-fault" state), and any other insurance policies you already own.

There are two types of bodily injury (BI) coverage: single-limit and split-limit (or multiple-limit). Single-limit BI coverage pays a maximum single amount per accident, regardless of the number of individuals injured. For example, if you carry a policy with $300,000 single-limit bodily injury coverage, a single injured person could claim up to $300,000 from your insurance company, with the remainder coming out of your pocket. The second type of BI coverage, split-limit, is more common. It pays a maximum amount to each person injured in an accident, subject to a maximum limit per accident. For example, $100,000/$300,000 split-limit coverage means that the insurance company will pay up to $100,000 to each person injured, but no more than $300,000 per accident. If a single individual suffers damages of $150,000, the insurance policy would cover only $100,000 of the damages, and the policyholder would have to pay the remainder. If the policyholder injures six people in an accident, the company would be liable for a maximum of $300,000 worth of damages.

Most states mandate minimum limits for liability coverage. The typical amount is $25,000/$50,000, which is very low. A number of states have no-fault laws, meaning that an injured party receives compensation from his or her own insurance company after an accident, regardless of who is at fault. The theory behind no-fault laws is that the need for litigation after an accident decreases, so insurance premiums should decrease.

Property Damage Coverage. The second type of liability coverage is property damage (PD). PD pays for the necessary repairs when someone else's property (usually a vehicle) is damaged. PD also covers other types of

---

Property Damage Insurance Guidelines

1. Carry property damage coverage of at least $50,000. State minimums may be less, but consider the financial liability you could incur by damaging someone else's new Mercedes Benz.
2. Obtain insurance that covers any car you legally drive.

property. The average state minimums are around $10,000, which, generally, is not enough to cover the cost of a new car.

Medical Payments Coverage

Medical payments coverage pays the medical expenses of individuals injured in the policyholder's car. This coverage is normally optional in states without no-fault laws, and coverage amounts range from $1,000 to $100,000 per person.

Most people already have some type of medical and hospital insurance so some may choose to forgo this duplicate coverage. Military families have hospital benefits, but remember that all passengers may not be immediate family members. A small amount of additional coverage may make sense because medical payments coverage often includes a funeral benefit.

Medical Payments Insurance Guidelines

1. Consider $10,000 in medical payments coverage, even if you have a good health insurance policy for yourself and your family. This will help cover any medical expenses for non–family members.
2. If your state requires Personal Injury Protection (PIP), purchase $10,000 coverage (or the state minimum, if it exceeds $10,000).
3. If your state requires PIP coverage and the state's no-fault rules allow you to coordinate benefits with your health insurance policy, do so. This coordination may result in sizeable premium savings and means that you would seek reimbursement from your health insurance company before applying to your auto insurer. Military families should ask for coordination of benefits because of their access to the military healthcare system.
4. Obtain insurance that covers you if you are injured while using someone else's car.

States with no-fault laws may require drivers to carry PIP coverage. This is a more comprehensive form of medical payments coverage that covers medical bills, lost wages, and some funeral expenses for injuries to the driver or any passenger, regardless of who is at fault. Some states require a minimum amount of PIP, usually around $10,000, but amounts vary by state.

Collision Coverage

Collision coverage pays for physical damage to the policyholder's car regardless of who is at fault and accounts for approximately 30 to 40% of the total insurance premium on a new car. Collision coverage carries a deductible (an amount the policyholder must pay before the coverage becomes effective). By selecting the size of the deductible—ranging from $100 to $1,000—you can

---

Collision Insurance Guidelines

1. Carry collision on a car with a substantial Blue Book value, but choose the highest affordable deductible.
2. Drop collision coverage altogether on an older, lower-value car if its replacement cost is not prohibitive.
3. Financing institutions will require collision insurance if you have a car loan with a remaining balance.

---

affect your premium since the higher the deductible, the lower the premium. For example, increasing your deductible from $100 to $500 or $1,000 could save from 25 to 40% on premiums. But remember that if you cause an accident, you will have to pay the deductible out of pocket in order to repair your car.

Collision coverage is related to the "Blue Book" value of a car. The Blue Book value (provided by your insurance company, bank, or http://www.kbb.com) is the maximum amount your insurance company will pay if the car is totaled. For newer cars, collision coverage is essential and in fact required if the car owner borrowed money to purchase the car. For cars between four and six years old, the decision to carry collision coverage depends on the financial risk that the owner is willing to assume in the event that the car is totaled. Policyholders will generally need to wait until they have completely repaid any outstanding loan on the vehicle before dropping collision coverage. For cars with a low Blue Book value, collision coverage is usually a waste of money, since the cost of coverage will not cover replacement if the car is totaled.

Comprehensive Coverage

Comprehensive coverage reimburses the policyholder for damage caused by mishaps other than a crash, including vandalism, theft, falling objects, floods, glass breakage, and collisions with animals. It carries a deductible that normally ranges from $100 to $1,000. Further, for a relatively small additional

---

Comprehensive Insurance Guidelines

1. Choose the highest affordable deductible.
2. Adapt your comprehensive coverage to your post location. In cities with higher crime rates, it is a good idea to maintain comprehensive coverage.
3. Cancel coverage on a car with a low resale value, once you have clear title (no outstanding loan) to the car.
4. Financing institutions will require comprehensive insurance if a balance remains on your car loan.

---

premium, you can typically get full glass-damage coverage with no deductible. As discussed earlier, comprehensive coverage varies by car type; the insurance quote discussed earlier (Table 14-1) increased from $54.90 to $91.50 when the driver opted for a Mustang over the Elantra.

Uninsured Motorist Coverage

Uninsured motorist (UIM) coverage protects policyholders and their passengers from damages caused by uninsured motorists and hit-and-run drivers. It is especially important in states without no-fault laws. UIM coverage reimburses policyholders for bodily injury or death in accidents where the uninsured motorist is responsible. UIM covers payments for medical expenses and losses due to permanent disability or death, loss of income, and any other damages entitled by state law. It does not reimburse policyholders for property damages. Because some insurance companies will not allow policyholders to carry a larger UIM limit than the limit they carry on bodily injury liability, it can be difficult to determine the true cost of increasing your UIM. When the driver from Table 14-1 doubled his UIM coverage, described in Table 14-1, his UIM premium went from $9.00 to $13.50; however, in order to double the UIM, the second lieutenant had to increase his bodily injury liability, and that cost is not immediately obvious.

The minimum coverage offered by insurance companies normally coincides with a state's particular laws. Although UIM is a normal part of every insurance policy, you may generally elect to reject it. However, you must do so in writing. UIM premiums are on the rise because increasing numbers of drivers violate state laws and do not carry insurance. Therefore, the probability of having an accident with an uninsured motorist is also increasing.

Underinsured Motorist Coverage

There is a newer category of insurance called underinsured motorist (UNM) coverage. UNM coverage applies if you have an accident with another driver who is at fault but whose insurance coverage cannot provide sufficient compensation. UNM coverage pays when the other party's coverage stops. You can buy coverage limits similar to those available for liability. Different insurance companies treat UNM coverage differently. With some companies, UNM is an integral part of your policy. Other companies treat UNM as a separate coverage with a separate premium. State law determines what constitutes a UNM loss and under what conditions the policyholder receives payment.

Optional Coverages

Insurance policies can have as many options as the car itself; and just as you can save money by purchasing a car with fewer options, you can do the same with your insurance policy. There are many coverage options; however, we will discuss only a couple of the more prominent ones. If you have adequate personal property, health, and life insurance policies, you can reject any

---

UIM/UNM Insurance Guidelines

1. Carry UIM in an amount comparable with your bodily injury liability coverage.
2. Carry UIM coverage unless you live in a state with outstanding no-fault laws or have an excellent medical insurance policy for yourself and your family.
3. Check with your insurance company to determine if UIM coverage includes UNM coverage; if not, ask for it.
4. Check to see if UNM coverage pays only if your policy exceeds the liability coverage of the underinsured motorist, or if it pays for damages in excess (up to your limit) of the underinsured motorist's coverage.
5. Check with your insurance company each time you move, to determine the requirements of the new state.

---

options related to these risk categories. If you need more life insurance, buy more life insurance: Do not sign up for limited life insurance on your automobile insurance policy.

Rental Reimbursement Coverage. If the policyholder has an accident that requires car repairs, rental reimbursement will offset the cost of temporary transportation until repairs are complete. This coverage pays a certain amount per day, for a specified number of days. Reimbursement options typically include a maximum of $30 or $50 a day and last for two weeks. You will want to consider your rental needs and typical rental costs for your area before choosing rental reimbursement coverage. If you own more than one car or if alternate transportation means are available (such as a company car or local mass transit), rental reimbursement may not be necessary.

Towing and Labor Coverage. The insurance company pays the cost of towing the policyholder's car to a repair shop and pays for any immediate labor involved. If you are a member of an auto club that already provides this service, you should not carry this coverage. Also, read the fine print in order to understand the limits of the towing arrangement and exactly which labor costs are reimbursable. In our example (Table 14-1), towing and labor insurance would cost $4.60 for six months.

LEASED AUTOMOBILE COVERAGE
Leasing an automobile is becoming a popular alternative to buying. Insurance coverage for a leased vehicle is similar to insurance for a vehicle you own, but there are a few significant differences. The first is that leasing companies often require higher insurance requirements than the state minimums. Thus, if you lease a car, the leasing agent may require more insurance than you might

otherwise obtain. You need to consider these added costs when deciding whether to lease or buy a car.

Another difference is that most leasing companies consider a stolen or totaled vehicle as an early contract termination. In such a situation, the lessee will generally owe the lessor more than the lessee's insurance company will pay due to depreciation of the leased vehicle. The lessee must cover the difference between what he or she owes and what the insurance company will pay with what is called gap insurance or total-loss protection. Some leases include gap insurance in the cost of the payments. Others do not, and the lessee will need to buy separate coverage or potentially face a large financial loss if something happens to the leased automobile.

DEPLOYMENTS

During long deployments, you may be able to save money on car insurance by temporarily suspending certain types of insurance. For example, lending institutions require collision and comprehensive coverage, but you can petition the bank/credit union for a temporary exemption from these coverages (especially if the vehicle will be in storage). In addition, many states will let drivers suspend liability insurance if they agree to turn in the vehicle's license plates. This requires coordination with the department of motor vehicles, and qualifications and restrictions will vary by state. Your insurer should be able to answer any questions about this process.

MISCELLANEOUS ISSUES

Generally, if you drive someone else's vehicle and are in an accident, the insurance company will consider that vehicle's insurance as the primary policy (as long as the personal-use insurance is adequate), and your insurance will serve as the secondary coverage. But because this can vary by state, it is always best to consult your insurance policy before borrowing or loaning a vehicle. Similarly, you should consult with your insurance agent to determine the extent of coverage you have while renting a vehicle.

Finally, as military service can result in frequent relocations, it is important to update your residence information with your insurance company as soon as you complete your move.

AUTOMOBILE INSURANCE CHECKLIST

The checklist included in Table 14-1 (page 240) provides a list of most of the possible coverage categories, as well as other factors that are important to consider when shopping for insurance. It also provides an example to help benchmark some of the typical costs of coverage options. You should remember that the appropriate coverage depends a great deal on each driver's personal circumstances. Use the list in Table 14-1 to construct a spreadsheet for comparing insurance companies. Some companies (such as Progressive, http://www.progressive.com) may give potential customers the quotes of other reputable companies along with their own quotes; this is another useful insurance-shopping tool.

15

Protecting Wealth
with Insurance

As a person's wealth increases, insurance of all types becomes increasingly important. At its core, insurance is a tool by which individuals and families can protect themselves against catastrophic loss in the future for a relatively small payment today. Without insurance, you could see your hard-earned assets lost through accidental damage, theft, or liability in a civil lawsuit. This chapter provides you with the knowledge necessary to protect against such losses by exploring homeowners insurance, personal property insurance, and liability insurance, and gives advice for selecting an insurer.

HOMEOWNERS AND PERSONAL PROPERTY INSURANCE
Servicemembers who own homes need to insure both real property (the structure) and personal property (the contents) against loss. Home insurance policies cover both types of property.

Policy Selection
The term *homeowners insurance* is to some extent a misnomer. The standard homeowners policy can cover just about anything you own. It can provide protection against property loss, personal liability, and additional living expenses during times of loss; some policies cover medical expenses as well. Table 15-1 (page 250) describes six basic types of homeowners insurance. These types are usually identified by what are called "HO numbers," based on the forms that insurance companies use.

Amount of Coverage
Whether you rent or own a home, you have three options when deciding on your amount of coverage against loss: actual cash value, replacement cost, or guaranteed replacement cost. An actual cash value policy pays to replace an individual's home or possessions minus any depreciation in their value. For example, such a policy would only pay its owner a fraction of the purchase cost of a damaged older television, since the insurance company would take depreciation into account in its appraisal of value.

TABLE 15-1
HOMEOWNERS INSURANCE

HO 02	HO 03	HO 04	HO 05	HO 06	HO 08
Basic policy. Covers dwelling against limited number of perils.*	Most common form. Provides open peril** coverage on dwelling.	Renters' policy. No coverage on dwelling.	Provides open peril** coverage on both dwelling and contents.	Condominium insurance.	For older homes built with methods and/or materials not used today.

*Peril: A cause of loss such as fire, hail, or wind.
**Open peril coverage: More generous coverage. Covers all perils except those specifically excluded.
Source: www.iii.org/individuals/homei
All homeowners insurance offers two basic coverage or protection plans:
Property Protection (Section I) reimburses the policyholder for losses or damages to his or her house or personal property, regardless of location.
Liability Protection (Section II) covers any legal liabilities as a result of any unintentional bodily injury or property damage that occurs on an individual's property.
For the most updated information on homeowners' insurance policies, visit the Insurance Information Institute website at www.iii.org/individuals/homei/.

On the other hand, a replacement cost policy covers all costs associated with rebuilding a home or replacing a damaged piece of property, up to the limit of the policy. To protect against sudden increases in replacement costs that might exceed a homeowner's policy, insurance companies also offer guaranteed replacement cost policies. These policies, for an additional fee, guarantee to replace the home or piece of property regardless of policy coverage limits. These types of policies prove particularly valuable during times of natural disaster, when replacement costs soar due to increased demand for builders and building supplies. Guaranteed policies also protect policy owners against the normal inflation of construction costs over time. Such policies effectively shift the inflation risk—and the responsibility for ensuring that such increases in cost are captured in the policy—from the policy owner to the insurance company.

You can determine the replacement value of your home based on estimated construction costs in your area; simply multiply the total square footage of the home by the local building costs per square foot. Other ways to determine replacement value are to ask the insurance company to calculate the replacement cost, or hire an independent appraiser.

Individuals generally do not need to insure 100% of the replacement value of their homes, because the probability of a total loss is very low. For example, even a severe fire will not destroy a house's foundation. For this reason, mortgage lenders will usually require that borrowers obtain only 80% coverage to meet their requirements for maximum payouts for partial losses. (In essence, insurance companies consider 80% to be "full coverage" for partial payouts—anything less than 80% reduces partial payouts proportionally.)

If a home with a replacement value of $150,000 is covered for $120,000 (80%), the insurance company will reimburse the homeowner the full amount for partial losses to a maximum of $120,000. If you insure your house for less than 80% of the replacement value, the insurance company will reimburse only up to the percentage insured. You must understand the nature of your coverage and how your insurance company reimburses policyholders, because different companies vary in how they reimburse for losses.

Example: A fire in a servicemember's garage totally destroys the garage and adjacent kitchen. The cost of repair is $25,000. If the servicemember has 80% coverage (on a $150,000 house), the insurance company will reimburse him the full $25,000, since the homeowner had purchased the recommended 80% coverage and the cost was below the maximum payout of $120,000. If he has only 70% protection, the insurance company will divide his actual 70% coverage by the 80% "required" coverage (since the homeowner did not meet the company's guidelines) to determine the level of reimbursement in the event of such a partial loss (e.g., 70/80 = 87.5% of $25,000, or $21,875). Therefore, he would not receive enough to fully cover his loss.

Coverage for personal property is usually set at 50% of the home's replacement cost. It also usually covers 10% of the home's cost for damage to an external structure (such as a shed or boathouse). There are, however, limits to coverage on specific types of personal property—for example, in many policies, silverware is limited to $2,500, computers to $3,000, and jewelry to $1,000. Often, antique and rare items are not covered at replacement cost, regardless of policy choices, due to the difficult nature of replacing such items at any cost.

Additional Homeowners Insurance Policies

A standard homeowners policy does not cover some perils. Among them are floods, earthquakes, sinkholes, landslides, and sometimes windstorms—if individuals live in a high-risk coastal region. You can usually get coverage for these perils through *endorsements*—provisions added to an existing insurance policy to modify its coverage—or by purchasing separate policies.

Flood Insurance. Homeowners insurance does not cover flood damage; however, most mortgage companies require borrowers to carry some flood protection, depending on the location of the home. Mortgage companies will purchase flood insurance and charge you for the policy if you fail to secure insurance yourself. If you live in a community susceptible to flooding and that community participates in the National Flood Insurance Program (NFIP), you can obtain flood insurance through the Federal Emergency Management Agency (FEMA). You can find out whether your community participates in NFIP at http://www.fema.gov or at http://www.floodsmart.gov.

Earthquake Insurance. Basic homeowners policies do not insure against damage caused by earthquakes. Therefore, you should consider adding earthquake insurance to your homeowners policy if you live in an earthquake-prone area. In major disasters, the federal government has generally provided some level of assistance to the owners of damaged homes, usually in the form of subsidized loans. As a result, many experts debate the need for this insurance. You have to balance the cost of purchasing private insurance against your family's tolerance for risk, and the degree to which you expect the government to respond rapidly and generously in the event of an emergency; the government guarantees neither of these. You can get more information on earthquake coverage from the California Earthquake Authority (CEA) and the Insurance Information Institute at: http://www.earthquakeauthority.com or http://www.iii.org/articles/what-type-of-disasters-are-covered.html.

Title Insurance. A title is a legal document establishing evidence of ownership and possession of land. There are two types of title insurance: One protects the lender, while the other protects the buyer. At settlement, the buyer pays for a policy to protect the lender; however, the buyer must purchase a separate policy to protect him or herself against a defective title.

"What could be wrong with the title?" you might ask. A lawyer or lender will tell any number of horror stories. For example, a previous owner may have had thousands of dollars in unpaid traffic tickets, and the state may have put a lien—a legal claim against an asset—on his or her property. If the purchase agreement does not note the lien against the property before the transfer of the property, the new buyer becomes liable for the unpaid tickets. It is better for an insurance company to deal with these rare but costly surprises. The cost of this additional policy is much less than you might think, and you may find it is worth the peace of mind the policy provides. For more information see http://www.homebuying.about.com/od/homeshopping/qt/TitleInsurance.htm.

> *You should consider purchasing a title insurance policy when buying real estate.*

Mortgage Life Insurance (or Credit Life Insurance). This insurance repays the remaining balance on a mortgage in the event of the borrower's death or the death of the borrower's spouse. The premium is added to the mortgage payment. This is normally a very expensive form of life insurance and can be three to ten times more expensive than term life insurance coverage for the mortgage or loan amount. You should consider holding adequate life insurance and avoiding mortgage life insurance. For more information, see chapter 13 on life insurance.

Insuring Rental Property

A military family may purchase a home and then decide to rent it out after making a PCS move. Since they still own the home, they are responsible for insuring it. It is very important to check with the insurance company to determine what your homeowners policy coverage protects once you move, and for how long that protection is in force. Also, verify whether it matters if the home is vacant. The following general guidelines apply if you decide to rent your home to someone else:

- Replace your homeowners policy with a fire policy. This provides coverage for the dwelling itself and for damage to personal property in the event of the perils named in the policy. It does not cover theft of personal property and furnishings left in the dwelling.
- The aforementioned fire policy may be extended to provide personal liability protection—any legal liabilities as a result of any unintentional bodily injury or property damage that occurs on the property—on request. However, if you have a homeowners or a personal liability policy in effect, you do not need additional liability coverage added to the fire policy.
- You can obtain a separate policy that covers the contents of the rental property that belong to you in the event of a theft.
- Make sure that the tenants understand that they are responsible for arranging for their own renters insurance to cover their personal property.

Renters Insurance
Given the high number of moves servicemembers make during their careers, they often rent houses or apartments rather than purchasing them. It is important to know that, as a renter, you have no vested interest in the building itself, but you may wrongly assume that losses sustained from fire, flood, or theft are covered by the landlord's policy. In fact, renters are provided little or no protection from the landlord's policy. Renters insurance (see "HO04" in Table 15-1) provides coverage against such perils for a renter's possessions. Additionally, renters insurance can also provide liability coverage for you in the event that you are responsible for injury to others—at the rental home or elsewhere—by you, a family member, or a pet. The policy may also cover legal defense costs if you are taken to court over a liability claim. Policies may also cover additional living expenses—those above normal monthly rent—in the event that the rental unit becomes uninhabitable, forcing you to live in a hotel or other temporary lodging facility.

Insurance in Government Quarters
If you live in government quarters, you are covered by government insurance. However, such coverage is normally limited to damaged or stolen personal property from the quarters, and the coverage limits are sometimes surprisingly low. Also, government insurance only provides limited personal liability protection. You should purchase specific insurance policies for personal property and personal liability protection, or purchase a renters policy (see "HO04" in Table 15-1) that covers both categories of risk. Such a policy can provide protection wherever you reside.

LIABILITY INSURANCE

Most homeowners policies offer $100,000 liability coverage as a minimum, and an automobile insurance policy will usually include liability coverage. Given the ease of litigation in America, the amount of coverage in these policies is usually inadequate. The need to protect your home and physical possessions is readily apparent; however, the necessity of protecting your future income is not so obvious. Liability judgments can include payment of a portion or all of an individual's future income to the injured party; therefore, you could lose not only everything you own today, but also a substantial portion of your future earnings from a liability claim. Therefore, you should maintain adequate liability coverage. In so doing, it is also important to accurately assess the value of current assets and the potential size of future assets in order to optimize the level of your coverage while not incurring excessive costs.

Automobile and homeowners policies provide only limited personal liability insurance. An *umbrella policy* picks up where existing coverage leaves off and goes to whatever limit the individual selects, normally the $1 million to $5 million range. Coverage extends well beyond damages assessed for physical injury. An umbrella policy covers judgments for injuries on property, unintentional libel or slander, catastrophic automobile accidents that exceed policy limits, sickness or disease, shock, defamation of character, mental anguish, wrongful entry, malicious prosecution, wrongful eviction, and more. This coverage also includes compensation for defense costs and court costs. For additional information on umbrella policies visit http://personalinsure. about.com/cs/umbrella/a/aa110503a.htm.

SELECTING AN INSURER

All homeowners policies are not the same, nor do all standard policies cost the same. As with all insurance, the first rule is to shop around, but with so many options this is not as easy as it sounds. The following websites offer excellent advice about selecting an insurer: http://www.iii.org/individuals/homei/hbs/pickco and http://www.smartmoney.com/plan/insurance.

There are hundreds of companies that provide homeowners and related insurance. Always get more than one quotation. Insurance price quotation sites like http://www.insurancequotes.com provide multiple quotes for a given level of coverage in a given area. Two popular insurance companies among servicemembers are USAA and Armed Forces Insurance, but many other firms can meet a servicemember's needs. You may find that local agents of nationwide firms have lower rates because they have better knowledge of the local housing market. You can also get more detailed information from insurance commissioners in your state. These offices can be found through the Insurance Information Institute website at http://www.iii.org. Additionally, ConsumerReports.org periodically publishes rankings of insurance companies and can serve as a helpful resource in picking one.

You should also research potential insurance companies for their financial health. Major rating agencies have this information available at the following websites: A.M. Best Company Inc. (http://www.ambest.com), Fitch Ratings Ltd. (http://www.fitchratings.com), Moody's Investors Service (http://www.moodys.com), Standard & Poor's Financial Services LLC (http://www.standardandpoors.com), and Weiss Ratings (http://www.weissratings.com).

PART V

TRANSITIONING FROM THE MILITARY

16

Transition Assistance, VA Benefits, and Social Security

"The 9/11 generation includes more than a million spouses and two million children of servicemembers, many of whom have lived their entire lives in a nation at war. More military women have served in combat than ever before. Hundreds of thousands of troops have deployed multiple times. They have all borne a heavy burden on behalf of the nation. But despite the enormous strains of ten years of continuous operations, our military remains as strong as it has ever been. [The] 9/11 generation is defined, just as every previous generation of America's veterans has been defined, by the virtues of selfless service, sacrifice, and devotion to duty. These men and women who serve and have served are the flesh and blood of American exceptionalism—the living and breathing embodiment of our national values and our special place in the world."
— *VA SECRETARY ERIC SHINSEKI,*
IN A SPEECH TO THE DISABLED AMERICAN
VETERANS ANNUAL CONVENTION, AUGUST 2011

Every servicemember leaves the military, whether by choice or necessity. Most leave the military through voluntary retirement, separation at ETS, or voluntary resignation from active or reserve duty. Some leave the military involuntarily because they have reached mandatory retirement age, have become ineligible for reenlistment, or have been separated under administrative or legal proceedings. Others leave the military for medical or health reasons, including injuries suffered in the line of duty. Regardless of the reasons for separation, military service qualifies servicemembers, and in many cases, their dependents, for a wide range of benefits and services (see Figure 16-1). This chapter provides a short summary of the many benefit programs that are

Figure 16-1

Benefit Programs to Help You With Your Financial Future After the Military

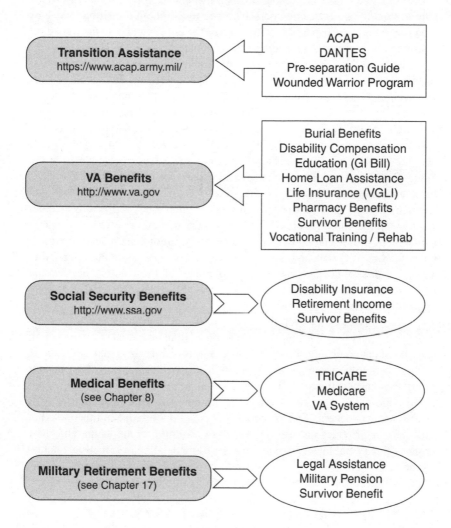

Transition Assistance
https://www.acap.army.mil/

ACAP
DANTES
Pre-separation Guide
Wounded Warrior Program

VA Benefits
http://www.va.gov

Burial Benefits
Disability Compensation
Education (GI Bill)
Home Loan Assistance
Life Insurance (VGLI)
Pharmacy Benefits
Survivor Benefits
Vocational Training / Rehab

Social Security Benefits
http://www.ssa.gov

Disability Insurance
Retirement Income
Survivor Benefits

Medical Benefits
(see Chapter 8)

TRICARE
Medicare
VA System

Military Retirement Benefits
(see Chapter 17)

Legal Assistance
Military Pension
Survivor Benefit

available to servicemembers and their dependents as they transition from the military to the private sector.

The first section provides an overview of the transition process. While each service is unique in its delivery of transition assistance, there are some key services common throughout the Department of Defense that are invaluable to separating servicemembers. The key to a smooth transition is to start the process as early as possible to maximize the aid provided by the transition assistance professionals and their partner agencies.

The second section provides informational coverage of the benefits and services available from the Department of Veterans Affairs (VA) while in service and after leaving the military. The VA provides comprehensive assistance for veterans of the armed forces. Servicemembers must ensure they receive thorough counseling on all of these benefits before they leave the military and take the time to become familiar with the VA's website at http://www.va.gov.

The final section of this chapter summarizes benefits available from the Social Security Administration (SSA) for those transitioning out of the work force due to death, disability, or old-age retirement. Social Security benefits can constitute a significant portion of a servicemember's retirement income. These benefits can also provide disabled servicemembers with a valuable supplement if they can no longer work. Finally, these benefits can provide a veteran's survivors with an important source of income should the veteran die. These benefits are not automatic. Servicemembers and veterans should become familiar with the SSA's website at http://www.ssa.gov, especially as they approach retirement.

Eligibility rules for each of the programs and services discussed in this chapter are rather complex and can vary substantially depending on the length and classification of service. The purpose of this chapter is to make you aware of these benefit programs, give you an indication of the value of these benefit programs, and encourage you to take these benefit programs into account when conducting personal financial planning. An exhaustive treatment of Social Security benefits and VA benefits is beyond the scope of this book, but this chapter provides an overview of their essential components and their impact on personal financial planning. For more detailed information, contact the nearest Social Security Administration (SSA) or Department of Veterans Affairs office, or browse the websites mentioned in this chapter.

TRANSITION: SEPARATING FROM MILITARY SERVICE

Transition is a normal part of life, but if it is not properly planned and prepared for, it can be stressful and even traumatizing for you and your family. Life, especially in the military, includes a series of transitions as people move continuously from one situation to another, sometimes undergoing multiple transitions simultaneously such as a promotion that occurs at the same time as a deployment. Whether you serve for three or thirty years, you experience a transition with every job change, PCS move, or deployment. Each time you make a transition, it is likely a unique experience, since personal, professional, and family considerations change over time. As a result, it is common to experience a fear of the unknown and a natural anxiety as a transition approaches. Transition is not a trivial experience for anyone. Some may handle it better than others, but it is certainly stressful for everyone and is not easy. In fact, a Department of the Army council identified a link between poor transition preparation and high-risk behaviors such as drug abuse and increasing rates of homelessness and suicide among veterans.

Most people could improve their quality of life by accepting some assistance when in a period of transition. A simple scan of the private market for transition services reveals a plethora of agencies ready to charge, and consumers willing to pay, thousands of dollars for transition assistance. Transition assistance includes services to prepare you for employment such as resume assistance, preparation for career workshops or job fairs, and information on how to apply for jobs in the civilian or federal sector. It also includes information to help you understand benefits you may be eligible for, such as unemployment compensation, educational assistance, or VA benefits. If the private market can charge for these services, the assistance provided must clearly be beneficial in improving the quality of life of those transitioning. Servicemembers should take advantage of free assistance in preparing for any transition. Each service, in partnership with the Department of Labor (DOL) and the Department of Veterans Affairs (VA), among other agencies, provides servicemembers transitioning from the military to the civilian sector the necessary assistance to be *confident in their preparedness* to achieve a successful transition back into the civilian world. Transition can be traumatic, but the key to success is preparing for the transition back to the civilian world throughout your military career, working with first-line supervisors, commanders, and career counselors along the way, not just in the last few days or even the last year prior to separation.

Congress recognized the importance of providing transition assistance for servicemembers transitioning to the civilian sector. By law, each service must conduct pre-separation counseling utilizing DD Form 2648 no later than ninety days prior to a servicemember's separation. However, Congress recognized that successful transition is unlikely if servicemembers begin transition assistance only ninety days prior to separation; therefore, servicemembers are eligible to access transition services one year prior to the end of their service for separating servicemembers; two years prior for retirees. Each service must also provide servicemembers with employment assistance and information on veteran's benefits. While some services make more transition services mandatory than others, it is in every servicemember's best interest to take full advantage of the transition assistance offered by his or her service.

The ninety-day mark is too late to sufficiently begin planning for your service separation. The average servicemember requires approximately seventy hours of transition assistance to ensure a well-prepared transition. These transition services are best spread out over a twelve-month period to enable the transition counselors to work with the transitioning servicemember on developing an Individual Transition Plan (ITP)—a comprehensive assessment to take the servicemember from where he or she is, to where he or she wants to go. A year may seem like a long time to prepare for transition into the civilian sector, but starting early will enable you to ensure that you are well prepared for this transition.

Each service operates a Transition Assistance Program (TAP). Transition Assistance Programs are managed and operated by the Army Career and Alumni Program (ACAP), the Family Support Center, the Fleet and Family Support Center, and the Personnel Services Center in the Army, Air Force, Navy, and Marine Corps, respectively. Transition Assistance Programs help servicemembers make the transition from a military career to a civilian career through the provision of special transition benefits, job assistance workshops, automated employment tools, guidance and referral tools, access to job networks, and many other types of information services. Each service also provides transition counselors, trained experts who help servicemembers develop a transition plan, create a résumé that effectively translates skills and experiences developed while in the military into language easily understood by civilian employers, gain access to civilian and federal job networks, and understand the financial and educational benefits available to those who have served honorably. In many cases, spouses and dependents of servicemembers are also eligible for transition counseling. If your service does not have a transition assistance office at the local installation, you may enroll in the transition program of your host installation.

It is important to remember that transition does not equate to separation from the service. Separation is simply the final stage of a comprehensive transition process that you will make while wearing the uniform. Starting the separation process early will help you identify whether you are ready to make the transition from military service to civilian life. You may realize that it is not the right time to separate, either because of a currently unavailable skill set, or a condition in the economy that will impact the likelihood of being offered a job in a desired profession or within a desired residence locale. Transition services can help you identify such gaps and connect you with services such as off-duty voluntary education programs through the Defense Activity for Non-Traditional Educational Support (DANTES). DANTES programs encourage servicemembers to pursue their education goals; they include testing, assessment, certification, tuition assistance, scholarships, higher education, and distance learning services. In most cases, servicemembers and eligible dependents can qualify for tuition reimbursement up to $250 per credit hour and $4,500 per fiscal year for education programs taken during off-duty hours. For more information, visit the DANTES website at http://www.dantes.doded.mil or stop by any installation's education center.

The services often operate special transition assistance programs for wounded servicemembers. These programs, known as Disabled Transition Assistance Programs (DTAP), provide specialized resources for servicemembers who are likely to receive a disability rating from their service, the VA, or both. One such program is the Army's Wounded Warrior Program, which supports soldiers who have become seriously injured while serving their country. The Army designed this program to meet the needs of both disabled soldiers who want to work and employers who actively recruit them. For more information, see http://wtc.army.mil/aw2/index.html.

A key component of a servicemember's transition is the Employment Workshop conducted by DOL. DOL conducts the workshop over two and a half days with experienced facilitators who employ the latest best practices to prepare servicemembers and their spouses for their transition. Prior to the workshop, participants conduct an online pre-assessment that inventories their current skills, so the facilitator knows how best to help during the workshop. Participants attend a workshop with a cohort of peers who are at the same level of job preparedness, so the facilitator tailors the briefing to the cohort's needs.

As part of their transition, servicemembers also receive a Veteran's Benefits Briefing from the VA. This half-day workshop is presented by experienced and knowledgeable VA benefits counselors and is held regularly on most military installations. VA counselors tell servicemembers about their benefits, outline eligibility criteria, answer questions, and give advice for completing and filing applications. Depending on your individual situation, this briefing can be overwhelming because of the sheer volume of information presented. Some servicemembers decide to attend the briefing twice to ensure they understand the benefits and know how to proceed. You will find it helpful to attend this briefing as early as possible in your transition process, since you may need medical appointments to ensure your benefits status is documented properly prior to your transition. Since the VA briefing discusses many benefits for families, the VA encourages spouses to attend as well.

Many servicemembers struggle with balancing their transition needs with their ongoing commitments in their military job. Fellow servicemembers may perceive those taking advantage of transition services as "quitting the team." Leaders within DoD recognize the danger of this attitude and are currently embarking on new programs to stress the vital importance of transition as a commander's and leader's imperative. Successful transitions contribute greatly to the wellness and readiness of the total force. DoD is reinforcing the importance of leader engagement, coaching, and support of transition assistance as part of professional military education courses. The particular challenges faced by many combat veterans from Iraq and Afghanistan, combined with an impending drawdown of forces in the coming years, reinforce the point that successful transition assistance is critical to the overall readiness and wellness of the armed forces.

The transition process can be overwhelming. However, a key to a successful transition is taking charge of your Individual Development Plan. The transition assistance provided by your service and by partner agencies empowers transitioning servicemembers with the tools to be confident in their preparedness to transition to the civilian sector.

VA BENEFITS

Most vererans are or will be eligible for one or more benefits provided through the Department of Veterans Affairs. VA benefit programs include burial benefits, disability compensation, education benefits, home loan assistance, life insurance, pharmacy benefits, survivor benefits, and vocational training and rehabilitation programs. The VA also provides medical care that promotes, preserves, and restores the health of eligible veterans. A complete description of benefits is in the VA's annual edition of a booklet titled "Federal Benefits for Veterans and Dependents," available at www1.va.gov/opa/vadocs/Fedben.pdf. These benefits are subject to regular change by Congress, so it is worthwhile to regularly check the VA website at www.va.gov. Members of the military still on active duty may qualify for home loans, use the GI Bill, and participate in VA vocational rehabilitation programs under some circumstances. In addition, active-duty servicemembers may begin the process of applying for benefits before discharge.

Eligibility for VA medical benefits is based on active service in the military and subsequent discharge under other than dishonorable conditions. Eligibility includes National Guard and Reserve members called to federal active duty. Veterans may determine their eligibility for VA health care benefits at www.va.gov/healtheligibility/eligibility/DetermineEligibility.asp. Nondisabled veterans whose income exceeds an income cap may not be eligible for some benefits due to means testing imposed by Congress. For more information about medical care, see chapter 8.

Education Benefits

There are various GI bills that provide servicemembers and veterans with education benefits. Two well-known VA programs are the Montgomery GI Bill (MGIB) and the Post-9/11 GI Bill. Under the MGIB, as of October 1, 2011, servicemembers can receive up to $1,473 per month (with annual increases to keep up with inflation) for a maximum of thirty-six months for eligible education programs after separating from the military. Veterans are eligible if they first enlisted on or after July 1, 1985, had a pay reduction of $1,200, and had continuous active duty service equal to or greater than their initial enlistment period. Persons discharged for the convenience of the government must have served twenty months of a two-year enlistment or thirty months of a three-year enlistment to be eligible. For those discharged early, the maximum number of months of eligibility is the same as the number of months served (20 months served equates to 20 months of education program benefits). The

TABLE 16-1
MONTHLY PAYMENT RATES FOR THE
ACTIVE-DUTY MONTGOMERY GI BILL (2011)

	Original Enlistment of Less than Three Years	Original Enlistment of Three Years or More
Full-time student	$1,196	$1,473
Three-quarter-time student	$897	$1,104
Half-time student	$598	$736.50
Less than half-time, more than quarter-time	$598	$736.50*
Quarter-time or less	$299	$368.25*

*Tuition and fees only. Payment cannot exceed the listed amounts.
Source: Department of Veterans Affairs, 2011.

length of your original enlistment determines your benefit rates based on the type of training or education program you undertake (i.e. whether you are a full-time, three-quarter time, half-time, or quarter-time student). Benefit rates are determined by Congress and usually change each year.

The Montgomery GI Bill buy-up program allows eligible active-duty members before discharge to make a one-time additional contribution of $600 to the fund, which will give the veteran up to $150 per month in addition to the amounts shown in Table 16-1. Also, some members enlisted for College Fund options, which were incentives to servicemembers who enlisted in specific job specialties. Veterans have ten years from the date of discharge to use their GI Bill benefits. Veterans can use the benefits in programs that lead to a college degree (Associate, Bachelor's, Master's, or Doctorate), vocational programs that lead to a degree or certificate, licensing and certification programs, flight training, and other types of training programs such as on-the-job or apprenticeship training.

An alternative to the Montgomery GI Bill is the Post-9/11 GI Bill. Veterans who served at least ninety days on or after September 11, 2001 or were discharged with a service-connected disability after thirty days are eligible for this program. The entitlements related to this program are different from those of the Montgomery GI Bill. Tuition rates vary by state, eligibility percentage varies based on level of service obligation completion, and recipients receive an allowance for housing as well as for books. Further, some schools offer additional funds, known as Yellow Ribbon funds, which the government matches (see Table 16-2 for a summary of the Post-9/11 GI Bill benefits). Additionally the veteran must have received an honorable discharge from the military in order to be eligible. In some cases, veterans can transfer their

TABLE 16-2
BENEFITS PAYABLE FOR THE POST-9/11 GI BILL (2011)

	Active Duty	Former Soldier (Honorably Discharged)	Dependent Spouse Transfer	Dependent Child Transfer
When Eligible (partial benefits)	90 days service after 9/11/01	90 days service after 9/11/01	No transfer for partial benefits	No transfer for partial benefits
When Eligible (full benefits)	36 months service after 9/11/01[1]	36 months service after 9/11/01[1]	Servicemember completed 6 years service; agrees to 4 more years[2]	Servicemember completed 10 years service[2]
State School	up to $17,500	up to $17,500	up to $17,500	up to $17,500
Private School Tuition[3]	up to $17,500	up to $17,500	up to $17,500	up to $17,500
Private School— Yellow Ribbon program[4]	Not Eligible	Varies	Not Eligible	Varies
Housing Allowance	Not Eligible	BAH for E5 with dependents[5,6]	Not Eligible	BAH for E5 with dependents[5,6]
Books and Supplies[7]	$1,000	$1,000	$1,000	$1,000
Rural Benefit	One-time payment of $500[8]	One-time payment of $500[8]	One-time payment of $500[8]	One-time payment of $500[8]

[1]Or disabled with less than 30 months of service.
[2]If disabled servicemember is separated for medical reasons the VA will allow for spouse/child transfer.
[3]On August 3, 2011, President Obama authorized the VA to pay more than $17,500 to certain students in Arizona, Michigan, New Hampshire, New York, Pennsylvania, South Carolina, and Texas to ensure their rates of reimbursement would not come down after they were enrolled, if they remained continuously enrolled in a program that charges more than $17,500.
[4]See chapter 7 for complete description of the yellow ribbon program.
[5]For online courses, students receive 1/2 E5 national average ($684.00 in 2012).
[6]For foreign schools, students receive E5 national average ($1,368).
[7]Paid proportionately based upon enrollment (course load).
[8]A one-time payment for recipients to pursue a program of education if they reside in a county with six or fewer persons per square mile (as determined by the most recent decennial census) and either physically relocate at least 500 miles to attend an educational institution or travel by air to attend an educational institution if no other land-based transportation exists.
Source: Dept. of Veterans Affairs, 2012 at http://gibill.va.gov/benefits/post_911_gibill/

Post-9/11 GI Bill benefits to dependants. For more information please see chapter 7 of this book or visit http://gibill.va.gov/benefits/post_911_gibill.

There are also two types of GI Bill programs for reservists. As of 2005, a new program called the Reserve Educational Assistance Program (REAP) was enacted to provide education assistance to members of the Reserves called to active duty in response to a war or national emergency. Furthermore, servicemembers who first entered active duty between January 1, 1977, and June 30, 1985, may have participated in the Veterans Educational Assistance Program (VEAP), the predecessor program of the GI Bill. For more information about these programs and the reserve duty version of the GI Bill, please visit http://www.gibill.va.gov.

Although generous, GI Bill payments may not cover the full costs associated with pursuing a degree or training certification. In most cases, the benefits will likely help the veteran cover a portion of tuition costs, book expenses, and administrative fees. A veteran who pursues full-time education or training will need to develop a plan for meeting the everyday living expenses related to housing, transportation, sustenance, and medical care. The Post-9/11 GI Bill will cover most of these costs at a public university in your home state. For those eligible for both the Montgomery GI Bill and the Post-9/11 GI Bill, it is generally better to opt for the Post-9/11 GI Bill over the Montgomery GI Bill. You cannot receive both benefits.

Finally, the VA provides education and training opportunities through the Survivors' and Dependents' Educational Assistance Program (DEA) to eligible dependents of those veterans who are permanently and totally disabled due to a service-related condition, or who died while on active duty or as a result of a service-related condition. The program offers up to forty-five months of education benefits that can be used for degree and certificate programs, apprenticeships, and on-the-job training. Benefit rates as of October 1, 2011, are $957 per month for full-time degree programs, $718 for three-quarter-time students, $476 for half-time, $476 for less than half-time and greater than one-quarter-time, and $239.25 for one-quarter time-students. For more information regarding the monetary benefits associated with these educational programs, please refer to chapter 7 of this book.

VOCATIONAL REHABILITATION

The VA's Vocational Rehabilitation and Employment (VR&E) service provides services to veterans with service-connected disabilities and military members with disabilities who have not yet exited the service (for example, some of those in Warrior Transition Units). The goal of this program is to enable injured veterans—soldiers, sailors, airmen, and marines—with disabilities to make a seamless transition from military service to a successful rehabilitation and on to suitable civilian employment. The desired outcome is to help eligible veterans prepare for, find, and keep jobs which suit their abilities and interests. For veterans with severe service-connected conditions that render them temporarily or permanently unable to work, VR&E may improve their ability to live as independently as possible. For more information and assistance with applying for VR&E services, visit http://www.vba.va.gov/bln/vre.

VA HOME LOAN PROGRAM

A VA-guaranteed home loan is a loan made by a private lender, such as a bank or a savings and loan association, to an eligible veteran for the purchase or refinancing of a primary residence home, condominium, or manufactured home. Based on the individual's personal financial situation, the maximum loan limit for which the VA will provide a guarantee is $417,000—with a few exceptions. The lender from whom the servicemember or veteran borrows money is protected against loss up to the amount of the guarantee, if the borrower fails to repay the loan. Since the VA provides this guarantee to the lender, the servicemember or veteran can qualify for a mortgage with an extremely competitive interest rate without making a down payment. Additionally, the VA home loan program has several provisions that safeguard veterans from unscrupulous lenders or homebuilders. For example, the builder of a new home is required to give the purchasing veteran a one-year warranty that the home has been constructed to VA-approved plans and specifications. Furthermore, the veteran who gets a VA loan can prepay the entire loan without penalty. As with most home mortgage loans, there are certain fees and closing costs that will apply, and the veteran must pay a portion of these fees at settlement.

In general, those purchasing a home should attempt to find the best value mortgage for which they are eligible (see chapter 5). In some cases, a servicemember or veteran may find better mortgage or refinancing options without using the VA home loan program. However, in light of the recent financial crisis, and given stricter private lending practices, the VA loan will often be a better option than conventional loans. The primary advantage of a VA loan is that it affords the veteran or servicemember the opportunity to purchase quality housing even if he or she has not had the opportunity to save enough money to make a normal minimum down payment or to cover settlement fees normally associated with conventional loans. If you can afford a relatively large down payment, then you may be able to find another mortgage option with a more cost-effective rate than you could find through the VA home loan program.

Veterans, active-duty servicemembers, Guard and Reserve members, and military spouses are potentially eligible for the VA home loan program. Eligibility for this program is based on an individual's (or a spouse's) service. Those currently on active duty are eligible after serving continuously for at least ninety days. Veterans (or unremarried spouses of veterans who died while in the service or due to service-connected disabilities, or were missing in action or a prisoner of war) with at least ninety days active wartime service, and who were discharged under other than dishonorable conditions, are also eligible.

Veterans with peacetime service of at least 181 continuous days of service and a discharge under other than dishonorable conditions are eligible. Eligibility rules for Guard and Reserve members vary but generally require at least six years of service. U.S. citizens who served in an allied armed force in World War II and various other groups (including cadets and midshipmen at the service academies) also qualify for the VA home loan program.

LIFE INSURANCE
The VA manages and operates several different insurance programs, including SGLI, VGLI, and special programs for disabled veterans. The Service-Disabled Veterans Insurance (S-DVI) program provides term or permanent life insurance with a maximum benefit amount of $10,000 for veterans with service-connected disabilities. (Those who become eligible for a waiver of premiums due to total disability can apply for supplemental S-DVI of up to $20,000.) You must apply for S-DVI within two years of rating a service-connected disability. (Application for the supplemental insurance must take place within one year of notification of eligibility for waiver of the basic policy premium.) Disabled veterans should investigate other life insurance options prior to purchasing S-DVI, as commercial policies, especially group plans through employers, may be better buys.

The Veterans' Mortgage Life Insurance (VMLI) is a program that provides mortgage life insurance to severely disabled veterans. To be eligible, a veteran must have received a Specially Adapted Housing Grant from the VA. (The purpose of the grant is to help the veteran build or modify a home to accommodate his or her disabilities.) VMLI is payable to the mortgage holder. If the veteran dies before being able to repay the mortgage, VMLI covers the balance of the mortgage still owed. VMLI allows severely disabled veterans to qualify for mortgage loans for which they would not otherwise qualify due to being high credit risks for lenders.

The most well-known insurance programs run by the VA are the Servicemembers' Group Life Insurance (SGLI) and the Veterans' Group Life Insurance (VGLI) programs. SGLI is a program of low-cost, group, term life insurance for servicemembers on active duty, ready reservists, cadets and midshipmen of the service academies, and members of ROTC. For more information on this program, see chapter 13. As of December 1, 2005, all servicemembers with SGLI were automatically enrolled in TSGLI for "traumatic injury" protection. TSGLI pays a benefit of between $25,000 and $100,000 to servicemembers covered by SGLI who sustain traumatic injuries that result in certain severe losses. The amount that will be paid under TSGLI is related to the type and severity of loss. For example, the total and permanent loss of sight in both eyes qualifies for a $100,000 payment.

The SGLI program also provides family coverage for the dependents of servicemembers. Family SGLI (FSGLI) provides up to $100,000 of insurance coverage for spouses (but not to exceed the amount of SGLI that the insured servicemember has in force), and $10,000 for each dependent child. There are no additional premiums for FSGLI coverage of dependent children. For more information about FSGLI, see chapter 13.

Veterans' Group Life Insurance (VGLI) is a post-service group life insurance program that allows servicemembers to convert their SGLI coverage to renewable term insurance. Servicemembers with full-time SGLI coverage are eligible for VGLI upon release from service. An eligible veteran must submit an application for conversion of SGLI coverage to VGLI coverage within one year and 120 days from the date of discharge. VGLI is available in increments of $10,000 to a maximum of $400,000. However, VGLI coverage cannot exceed the amount of SGLI that was in force at the time of separation from service. VGLI does not provide disability or other supplementary benefits; it has no cash value and does not pay dividends. VGLI premium rates are substantially higher than SGLI premiums because VGLI premiums are based on the separating servicemember's age. For example, as of 2012, a forty-year-old servicemember pays $27 per month for $400,000 of SGLI coverage but a forty-year-old veteran pays $68 per month for $400,000 worth of VGLI coverage. Still, VGLI is a relatively inexpensive option for life insurance, particularly for veterans with disabilities who may or may not qualify for preferred rates with other life insurance products. See chapter 13 for more information. A complete listing of current VGLI premium rates is available on the VA's Life Insurance Program webpage at http://www.insurance.va.gov.

The main advantage of VGLI is that service members need not complete a medical qualification exam if they apply for VGLI within 120 days of exiting the service. Furthermore, VGLI might be an attractive option for separating servicemembers, particularly if they have any health issue that might jeopardize their ability to obtain affordable insurance from civilian sources. Lastly, veterans can keep their VGLI coverage for life, as long as they continue to pay premiums.

With VGLI, as with any insurance policy, you must take care in evaluating your insurance needs. SGLI and Family SGLI provide valuable life insurance coverage at affordable rates. However, for veterans, other insurance options may be more affordable than VGLI. Refer to chapter 13 for more details. To file a claim for SGLI, FSGLI, TSGLI, VGLI, S-DVI, or VMLI, contact a VA office or a military personnel assistance center (refer to the phonebook or Internet for specific contact information).

DISABILITY COMPENSATION

Disability compensation is a benefit paid to veterans for injuries or diseases that occur while on active duty, or for preexisting conditions that were made worse by active military service. These benefits are tax-free. Veterans may be eligible for this program if they have a service-related disability rated at 10 percent or higher and were discharged under other-than-dishonorable conditions. The degree of disability represents the average loss in wages resulting from such diseases and injuries, as well as their complications in civilian occupations. As of 2012, the amount of the basic benefit ranges from $127 to $2,769 per month, based on the veteran's disability rating. Veterans may be paid additional amounts, in certain circumstances, such as if they have severe disabilities, limb amputations, dependents, or a seriously disabled spouse. Except in cases of the most severe injuries, VA benefits are only supplemental income, and most veterans will want to find other employment. Disabled veterans might also be entitled to priority medical care in the VA health system, clothing allowances, grants for specialty housing, federal employment preference, exchange and commissary privileges, vocational rehabilitation, service-disabled veterans' life insurance, and other forms of state and local veterans' benefits. Finally, under new legislation affecting only post-9/11 veterans, family members providing full-time care in a home environment may qualify for a monthly stipend, travel expenses, access to health insurance, mental health services, and comprehensive caregiver training. Caregivers wishing to check their eligibility for these services should first visit http://www.va.gov/healtheligibility/caregiver for an intial eligibility screening.

The Civilian Health and Medical Program of the Department of Veterans Affairs (CHAMPVA) is a comprehensive health insurance program for dependents of disabled veterans and, in certain cases, for surviving dependents of deceased veterans. This program is independent of CHAMPUS and TRICARE. For the veterans' dependents to be eligible for CHAMPVA, the veterans cannot be eligible for TRICARE/CHAMPUS and the dependents must be (1) the spouse or child of a veteran who has been rated permanently and totally disabled for a service-connected disability by a VA regional office, (2) the surviving spouse or child of a veteran who died from a VA-rated service connected disability, (3) the surviving spouse or child of a veteran who was at the time of death rated permanently and totally disabled from a service connected disability, or (4) the surviving spouse or child of a military member who died in the line of duty, not due to misconduct. For more information, visit http://www.va.gov/hac/forbeneficiaries/champva.

BENEFITS FOR SURVIVORS

There are additional benefits available that will have a significant impact on the emotional and financial stability of survivors. These benefits include one-time payouts, burial benefits, and monthly annuity payments. Survivors should seek assistance from veterans organizations for help in receiving available benefits.

Dependency and Indemnity Compensation

Dependency and Indemnity Compensation (DIC) is a monthly benefit paid to eligible survivors of a servicemember who died on active duty, a veteran who died as a result of a service-related injury or disease, or a veteran whose death resulted from a nonservice-connected disability. In general, to be eligible for

DIC benefits, the surviving spouse must have been married to the veteran, must have lived with the veteran until the veteran's death, and cannot be currently remarried. Specific eligibility rules can be quite complex, and those who might be eligible should consult www.vba.va.gov/survivors/VAbenefits .htm or contact their local VA office. Surviving children are eligible if they are not included in the surviving spouse's DIC, they are unmarried, and they are under age eighteen (or between the ages of eighteen and twenty-three but attending school). As of 2012, the basic monthly rate of DIC is $1,159 for an eligible surviving spouse. Other rates apply for various other family situations: Veterans or survivors should contact the VA for their authorization amount, which can be substantially more than the basic rate (and see chapter 13 for additional details). Survivors might also be eligible for health care through the VA, the VA home loan program, federal employment preference, and educational assistance. Several other federal agencies have programs for spouses and children of servicemembers who died in the line of duty. See www.vba.va.gov/survivors/agencies.htm for more information.

> *Survivors may be entitled to a monthly compensation benefit when a servicemember dies on active duty or when a veteran dies from a service-related injury or disease.*

Other Death Benefits for Survivors

Veterans discharged under other-than-dishonorable conditions and servicemembers who die while on active duty may be eligible for the following burial benefits: (1) burial in a national, state, or military installation cemetery, (2) a government-furnished headstone or marker, (3) a presidential memorial certificate, (4) a burial flag, and (5) reimbursement of a portion of burial expenses. Spouses and dependent children of eligible servicemembers and veterans may also be buried in a national cemetery. The funeral director or the next of kin makes interment arrangements for the eligible veteran or dependent at the time of need by contacting the national cemetery in which burial is desired. The VA provides headstones and grave markers for the graves of veterans anywhere in the world and for eligible dependents who are buried in military installation, state veteran, or national cemeteries. Niche markers are also available for identifying cremated remains in columbaria, and memorial markers are provided if the remains are not available for burial.

A certificate bearing the President's signature is issued to recognize the service of deceased veterans who were discharged under honorable conditions. Eligible recipients include next of kin or other loved ones. A certificate can be issued to more than one eligible recipient. VA regional offices can help in applying for certificates. A U.S. flag is provided, at no cost, to drape the casket or accompany the urn of a deceased veteran who served honorably in the U.S. Armed Forces. The flag is furnished to honor the memory of a veteran's military service to his or her country and is generally given to the next of kin, as a keepsake, after its use during the funeral service. When there is no next of kin, the VA will furnish the flag to a friend who makes a request for it.

> *Death benefits for veterans and servicemembers include burial in a national cemetery, a headstone or grave marker, a presidential memorial certificate, a burial flag, military funeral honors, and reimbursement of burial expenses.*

The VA will pay a burial allowance up to $2,000 if the veteran's death is service-connected. The VA might also pay the cost of transporting the remains of a service-disabled veteran to the nearest national cemetery with available gravesites. The VA will pay a $300 burial and funeral expense allowance for veterans who, at the time of death, were entitled to receive a pension or compensation, or would have been entitled to compensation but for receipt of military retirement pay. Note that the VA will pay burial costs only if the veteran was receiving benefits from the VA at the time of his or her death or if the veteran dies in a VA hospital. The VA's burial benefits are important items to include in personal financial planning because these benefits may reduce the amount of life insurance needed, which can help save money through lower premium payments. These benefits also allow servicemembers and veterans to leave more of their estates to their survivors.

DoD will, upon request, provide military funeral honors for the burial of military members and eligible veterans. A basic funeral ceremony with military honors consists of the folding and presentation of the U.S. flag by two or more uniformed members of the armed services and the playing of Taps. DoD maintains a toll-free number (877-MIL-HONR) for use by funeral directors to request an honors ceremony. Family members should inform their funeral directors if they desire military funeral honors for a veteran. Finally, the VA provides bereavement counseling for survivors.

When a servicemember dies on active duty, active-duty training, or inactive-duty training, the service pays a lump-sum death gratuity of $100,000 to the survivors. This death gratuity is 100 percent tax-free. Survivors can also stay in military housing or receive Basic Allowance for Housing (BAH) for 180 days following the servicemember's death. Unlimited exchange and commissary store privileges in the United States are available to surviving spouses of members or retired members of the armed forces, recipients of the Medal of Honor, and dependents and orphans of military retirees. For nonretirees, death must be service-connected. Dependents of Reservists also may be eligible. The VA provides a certification letter for use in obtaining commissary and

TABLE 16-3
ESTIMATED MONTHLY DEATH BENEFIT FOR SERVICEMEMBERS
WHO DIE ON ACTIVE DUTY

	E-4 2 Dependents	E-6 2 Dependents	O-2 2 Dependents
Dependency and Indemnity Compensation (DIC) (Taxable Equivalent)	$2,860	$2,860	$2,860
High-3 SBP Benefit	$1,007	$1,546	$1,826
$400,000 SGLI Annuity*	$1,333	$1,333	$1,333
Total (DIC + SBP + SGLI)	$5,200	$5,739	$6019
Estimated 2011 Monthly Regular Military Compensation (RMC)**	$3,073	$4,264	$4634.62
Fraction of RMC Replaced by Death Benefits (DIC + SBP + SGLI)	169%	134%	129%

*The SGLI annuity assumes that the surviving spouse invests the entire SGLI payout of $400,000 in an asset that yields a 4% after-tax annual return. The survivor could earn $1,333 per month without consuming any of the principal. An SGLI payment strategy which includes some consumption of the principal would yield a higher monthly payment to the survivors.
**RMC includes base pay, basic allowance for housing, basic allowance for subsistence, and the federal tax advantages associated with the allowances.
Source: Office of Economic and Manpower Analysis, U.S. Military Academy, 2011

exchange privileges from the armed forces. Eligible family members may receive inpatient and outpatient care, including pharmacy services at uniformed services medical treatment facilities where adequate services and facilities are available. Eligible family members of active-duty members who died while on active duty and who were on active duty for at least thirty days before death will continue to be treated as active-duty family members for three years after their active-duty sponsor dies. If a widowed beneficiary remarries someone outside the uniformed services, he or she is no longer covered.

Finally, the National Defense Authorization Act for FY2004 made a provision to provide a Survivor Benefit Plan (SBP) annuity for the surviving unremarried spouse or dependent children under eighteen (or twenty-two if the child is a full-time student) of a servicemember who dies while on active duty but is not yet eligible for retirement. Thus, for active-duty deaths occurring on or after November 24, 2003, eligibility for the SBP includes the servicemember's spouse, former spouse (if court ordered), or child (when there is no surviving spouse). Previously, active-duty members qualified for SBP only if they were eligible for retirement with twenty or more years of service or were medically retired prior to death. The current law treats members who die on active duty as 100 percent disabled in order to calculate their retired pay entitlement. Under the High-3 retirement plan, the retired pay entitlement would be 50 percent of the average of the basic monthly pay during the servicemember's three highest years of military earnings (normally the last three years of service). The monthly SBP payments would then be 55 percent of the retired-pay entitlement. See Table 16-3 for a comparison of current death benefits across grades for servicemembers who die while on active duty.

(Note: These calculations do not include all of the in-kind and cash assistance programs for which the survivors might be eligible from the VA, the SSA, or DoD. For example, these calculations do not include any death gratuities, burial benefits, continuation of basic allowance for housing, or SSA survivor benefits; nor do they include continuation of exchange, commissary, and medical facility privileges.)

In general, as a servicemember's rank and pay increase, death benefits from DIC, SBP, and SGLI replace a smaller portion of the servicemember's monthly regular military compensation.

Casualty Assistance Officers

There are many benefits and entitlements to assist the survivors of those killed or missing in action. As discussed previously in this chapter, some of these benefits include a death gratuity, housing assistance, dependency and indemnity compensation, commissary and exchange privileges, burial services, financial counseling services, and unpaid pay and allowances. Surviving spouses and dependents may have difficulty navigating their way through the bereavement process and the compensation process simultaneously. Thus, the military typically assigns a Casualty Assistance Officer (CAO) to assist the family members of those killed or missing in action. The CAO, among other responsibilities, helps the family members learn about and apply for all of the benefits DoD provides to survivors. When a soldier, sailor, airman, or marine is assigned duty as a CAO, the casualty assistance mission takes precedence over all other obligations. The CAO's mission is to provide assistance to the primary next of kin (PNOK) or the person authorized direct disposition (PADD) during the period following a military servicemember being declared missing or deceased. In the event that a family member is a PNOK or PADD for a servicemember who is declared missing or deceased and the family member is not assigned a CAO, the family member should contact the servicemember's unit commander, rear detachment commander, or the closest military personnel service center to ensure that he or she receives adequate support in accessing benefits.

A casualty assistance officer will guide beneficiaries through the process of applying for and receiving survivors' entitlements.

Remember, to receive these benefits, the beneficiary must apply for them. Servicemembers and dependents should receive counseling on all of these benefits before leaving the military, and take the time to become familiar with the VA's website at http://www.va.gov.

BENEFIT PROGRAMS FOR TRANSITIONING OUT OF THE WORKFORCE (SOCIAL SECURITY)

Social Security is a set of programs designed to provide income security for workers and their families. Several major programs come under the general heading of Social Security, including Medicare, Black Lung Benefits, and Supplemental Security Income. Also, the fifty states operate two other categories of "social security" programs: unemployment compensation and public assistance programs. However, the term "Social Security" is commonly used today to refer to only one set of these programs: Old Age, Survivors, and Disability Insurance (OASDI). This section explains the OASDI benefit.

Social Security insures workers and their families against the financial hardships associated with living an extremely long life, becoming disabled, or passing away prematurely. Social Security is not a personal retirement program. It provides income for workers and their dependents during their retirement years, but it is meant to supplement other sources of retirement income, not to comprise total retirement income. The average retired worker can expect to receive Social Security benefits replacing approximately 25 to 40% of pre-retirement income. To qualify for Social Security benefits, individuals must earn a specified amount of work credits. Military service counts towards these work credits. Benefits vary substantially based on a rather complicated set of rules. The purpose of this section is to inform servicemembers and their families of the benefits that they earn as they work so that they can account for them in their personal financial planning.

> *Servicemembers and their families should establish a long-term savings plan to supplement Social Security in their retirement.*

Today's Workers Pay for Today's Beneficiaries

Many Americans do not understand how the Social Security system works. Social Security is not a savings plan; it is a "pay-as-you-go" plan. Individuals do not pay their Social Security taxes into an account with their name on it from which they draw payments after retirement. Instead, they pay taxes into a general trust fund. The taxes individuals pay today are used primarily to pay the benefits of today's retirees and disabled persons. Social Security is a social contract. Individuals pay taxes today for the benefit of today's elderly, with the understanding that the government will provide benefits for them in their retirement or disability by taxing tomorrow's workers. Thus, individuals should pay close attention to the political decisions made today concerning the future of Social Security. The amount of benefits individuals can expect has implications for long-term savings plans (see chapter 1) and investment strategy (see chapters 10, 11, and 12).

> *Social Security is a "pay-as-you-go" social contract; taxes collected from current workers pay for the benefits of current beneficiaries while taxes collected from future workers will support future beneficiaries.*

Active-duty members of the uniformed services have been covered by Social Security on the same basis as civilian workers since 1957. Participation in the Social Security program is mandatory—individuals must pay the Social Security tax, which is annotated as FICA (Federal Insurance Contributions Act) on pay statements. For servicemembers, only basic pay is taxable for Social Security purposes, and each service withholds taxes by law in the full amount from each active duty monthly paycheck. If individuals have additional income from self-employment, they must pay a self-employment tax to the IRS. They must also file Schedule SE, "Computation of Social Security Self-Employment Tax," with their tax returns if their net annual earnings from self-employment are greater than $400.

As of 2012, the Social Security tax rate is 15.3% of earnings. Individuals pay a Social Security tax of 7.65% of their earnings (1.45% is applied to Medicare and 6.20% is applied to non-Medicare Social Security). Employers make a matching contribution of 7.65% of employee earnings. Self-employed workers must pay the entire Social Security tax rate of 15.3%. The Medicare portion of the tax (2.9%) applies to all earnings, while the non-Medicare rate (12.4%) is applied on up to $110,100 of earnings. The $110,100 limit increases automatically with inflation each year.

In 2011, the government temporarily reduced the employee's share of the non-Medicare Social Security tax to 4.2%. All other taxes and figures remained the same. Unless extended, this temporary payroll tax holiday will expire at the end of 2012, thereby returning employee contribution levels to 2010 levels.

Eligibility for Social Security Benefits
Eligibility for each type of benefit (Old Age, Survivors, and Disability Insurance programs) depends on insurance status, which, in turn, depends on employment history. Because servicemembers pay Social Security taxes, they become insured workers. Working spouses (who must also pay Social Security

taxes) become insured workers in their own right. Nonworking spouses are eligible for Social Security benefits based on the benefits of their working spouses. The rules on how individuals get insured and how much money they are entitled to receive are a bit complex. In general, what matters is how much and for how long individuals have paid into the Social Security system. Thus, the accuracy of potential beneficiaries' records at the Social Security Administration (SSA) is crucial.

Historically, the SSA sent an annual statement to each working American over the age of twenty-five. Individuals received this statement approximately three months prior to their birthday. However, as of April 2011, due to budget cuts, the SSA stopped mailing these statements. Effective 2012, only individuals over the age of sixty will receive them in the mail, while others will be able to access them online.

> *To be eligible for Social Security benefits,*
> *individuals must earn work credits and pay FICA*
> *taxes. Military service counts as part of this work*
> *history.*

Individuals are therefore encouraged to use the SSA online tools to ensure the accuracy of their records. When the SSA makes annual online statements available in 2012, individuals should compare the SSA's numbers to their records (W-2 statements or LES) and write to the SSA to correct any errors immediately. For more information, visit the official website of the U.S. Social Security Administration at http://www.ssa.gov, or visit the local Social Security Administration office (http://www.ssa.gov/locator).

> * *Visit the SSA website annually to receive*
>   *electronic access to the Social Security statement*
>   *(available in 2012).*
> * *Verify your earnings history and correct any*
>   *errors immediately.*
> * *Account for estimated benefits as part of*
>   *personal financial planning.*

Basic Benefits

This section explains the three types of Social Security benefits. The amount of each benefit is based on the primary insurance amount (PIA). This section shows briefly how to calculate the PIA. For further information, individuals

TABLE 16-4
SOCIAL SECURITY BENEFITS

Nominal Monthly Earnings Over the Course of 35 Years	Approximate Monthly Benefits at Age 67
$1,667	$981
$2,500	$1,255
$3,300	$1,529
$4,167	$1,803
$5,000	$1,972
$5,833	$2,100
$6,667	$2,229

Source: The authors tabulated these figures in September 2011 using the SSA online tool available at http://www.ssa.gov/retire2/AnypiaApplet.html, assuming a birth date of January 1, 1970, and nominal monthly earnings indicated above for the 35 highest-earning years. All figures are in today's dollars.

can get estimate their own projected benefits from the SSA. Since the purpose of Social Security is to help maintain a reasonable portion of the standard of living that a beneficiary achieved during his or her working lifetime, the benefits you receive from Social Security will depend on the wages you earned (and the taxes you paid). A secondary purpose of Social Security is to provide a minimum standard of living for all elderly persons. Therefore, workers who earned a lower level of wages will retain a larger percentage of those low wages in their benefits. For example, an individual who earned $20,000 before retirement will get a Social Security benefit of approximately 69% of this income, whereas a beneficiary who earned $90,000 before retirement will receive a benefit of about 36% of this income (according to Aon Consulting and Georgia State University, *Replacement Ratio Study: A Measurement Tool for Retirement Planning* at http://www.aon.com/about-aon/intellectual-capital/attachments/human-capital-consulting/RRStudy070308.pdf, page 6.) The assumption is that the lower-wage earner could not save enough to provide other income during retirement, while the better-paid worker could.

Calculating PIA. The primary insurance amount is based on a worker's average indexed monthly earnings (AIME), which is a function of an individual's thirty-five highest-earning years. The AIME adjusts actual earnings for inflation. You can determine your projected benefits by using the SSA's online calculator, available at http://www.ssa.gov/retire2/AnypiaApplet.html. Table 16-4 utilizes this calculator to outline approximate monthly benefits for seven different earning scenarios. For example, as of September 2011, if a worker earns an average of $3,300 monthly for thirty-five years, he or she should get

$1,529 of social security benefits per month at the age of sixty-seven. How-
ever, given the complexity of the formula for calculating AIME and social
security benefits, the best way to get estimates of your future benefits is to
access your annual statements online, as noted above.

> *SSA benefits for low-income workers replace*
> *about 60% of their working wages.*
> *For higher-income workers, the replacement*
> *ratio can fall to 25% or lower.*

Retirement Benefits. There are three options for retirement under Social
Security: (1) retire at the full retirement age and receive full benefits, (2) retire
earlier than full retirement age and receive reduced benefits, or (3) retire later
than full retirement age but prior to age seventy and receive increased benefits.
Full retirement age is determined by the SSA based on the year of your birth.

TABLE 16-5
FULL RETIREMENT AGE AND REDUCTION IN BENEFITS
FOR EARLY RETIREMENT

Year of Birth	Full Retirement Age	Benefit as a Percent of Full Retirement PIA if Servicemember Retires at Age 62 Rather than at Full Retirement Age
1937 or Earlier	65	80%
1938	65 and 2 Months	79.2%
1939	65 and 4 Months	78.3%
1940	65 and 6 Months	77.5%
1941	65 and 8 Months	76.7%
1942	65 and 10 Months	75.8%
1943-1954	66	75%
1955	66 and 2 Months	74.2%
1956	66 and 4 Months	73.3%
1957	66 and 6 Months	72.5%
1958	66 and 8 Months	71.7%
1959	66 and 10 Months	70.8%
1960 and Later	67	70%

Source: SSA, 2011.

TABLE 16-6
CHART OF DELAYED RETIREMENT CREDIT RATES

Date Attained Full Retirement Age	Annual Percentage
2000-2001	5.5%
2002-2003	6.0%
2004-2005	6.5%
2006-2007	7.0%
2008-2009	7.5%
2010 or later	8.0%

Source: SSA, 2011.

Workers who were born during or before 1937 (and who will retire before 2002) can normally retire at age sixty-five, whereas those born after 1937 cannot retire with full benefits until a slightly older age. Most current servicemembers (if born after 1959) cannot retire with full benefits until they are sixty-seven years old. Early retirement at age sixty-two is still possible under the rules outlined in Table 16-5, but retiring exactly on your sixty-second birthday will mean that your monthly check will be an even smaller percentage of the PIA. For example, workers born after 1959 who retire at age sixty-two will receive only 70% of the PIA.

Just as retiring before reaching full retirement age can reduce your Social Security benefits, you can increase your Social Security benefits by delaying your retirement past the full retirement age. When individuals retire after their full retirement age, they receive a delayed retirement credit. Each month in which they are at least at full retirement age, but not yet age seventy, is an increment month. For example, an individual who reached full retirement age after 2010 would receive 100% of his or her PIA plus 8% for each year that he or she continued to work past full retirement age (see Table 16-6). Once individuals reach age seventy, they no longer accumulate delayed retirement credits.

For 2011, the maximum Social Security benefit for a worker who retires at full retirement age is approximately $2,366 per month. The estimated average monthly Social Security benefit payable in 2011 for all retired workers is approximately $1,174 per month. For a retired couple, the average is about $1,907 per month. Benefits are adjusted each year to keep up with inflation.

Survivor Benefits. Another important goal of Social Security is providing for families when an insured worker dies if the family members are too young, old, or disabled to work. Benefits paid to the dependent family members of a deceased worker are called survivor benefits. There are many categories of survivor benefits corresponding to the many circumstances that qualify someone to be a dependent family member of an insured worker.

TABLE 16-7
SOCIAL SECURITY SURVIVOR BENEFITS

Benefit Insurance Status	Amount of Payment
Payment to Each Child under 18	75% of PIA
Payment to a Widow(er), any Age, Caring for any Children Under 16	75% of PIA
Payment to a Widow(er) Age 60 to Full Retirement	71.5 to 99% of PIA
Payment to a Widow(er) at or over Full Retirement Age	100% of PIA

Source: SSA, 2011.

Table 16-7 presents information about four of the most frequently used categories of survivor benefits.

From the table, you can see that each child under age eighteen receives a monthly check for 75% of the insured worker's PIA. However, in the event that the family has many children, the total amount paid to the family is subject to a cap. Notice also that nonworking spouses over age sixty who are not insured themselves are entitled to the benefits of the deceased spouse if that spouse was fully insured before dying. The benefit will range from 71.5 to 100% of the PIA of the deceased worker, depending on the age of the surviving spouse. Divorced surviving spouses receive the benefits of a deceased worker if the marriage lasted at least ten years. Generally, a surviving spouse over age sixty does not forfeit this entitlement by remarrying. There are several rules associated with remarrying, so you should contact the SSA directly with questions about your specific situation.

One final survivor benefit is the lump-sum death payment of $255. Surviving spouses living with an insured worker at the time of death or surving spouses if living apart and receiving benefits on the deceased person's record are eligible for this payment; divorced spouses are not.

> *Dependents of eligible workers are entitled to survivor benefits if the worker dies and the dependents are too young, too old, or too disabled to work.*

Disability Benefits. For the purposes of Social Security, disability means the inability to work by reason of any medically determinable impairment which can be expected to result in death or which has lasted for at least one year. If a worker has a qualifying disability, he or she will receive the full PIA. Benefits for a disabled servicemember involve not only the SSA but perhaps also the VA and the military disability compensation system. In this complex area, consult a legal assistance officer, the VA, and the SSA for details about all of the entitlements.

Other Factors Affecting Benefits

If individuals are receiving Social Security benefits and have a large amount of earnings, then they may receive reduced benefits. Workers who retire from the full-time workforce before reaching their full retirement age will have their benefits reduced $1 for every $2 of income over $14,160 per year. Workers who continue to work in the year they reach full retirement age will have their benefits reduced $1 for every $3 of income over $37,680 for those months before they reached the full retirement age. Once workers reach full retirement age, their Social Security benefits are no longer subject to the earnings test and are not reduced based on their income.

In addition to being offset in the manner described above, Social Security benefits also may be taxed as ordinary income for some retirees. This will apply only if individuals have other substantial income in addition to their benefits (for example, wages, self-employment, interest, dividends, capital gains, military pension, and other taxable income that must be reported on a tax return). The percent of social security benefits subject to taxation depends on an individual's combined income, which is the sum of adjusted gross income, nontaxable interest, and one-half of Social Security benefits, after any offset. Table 16-8 indicates the percent of social security benefits that may be taxable based on an individual's combined income. For more information about income taxes, see chapter 4.

Each year, Congress determines the Cost of Living Adjustment (COLA) that applies to Social Security benefits. The COLA is probably the most valuable provision in Social Security. Once the SSA determines an individual's

TABLE 16-8
TAXES ON SOCIAL SECURITY BENEFITS

Type of Return	Combined Income	Percent of Benefits Subject to Tax
Individual	$25,000–$34,000	50%
	Over $34,000	85%
Joint	$32,000–$44,000	50%
	Over $44,000	85%

Source: SSA, 2011.

benefit amount, the benefit adjusts every year to protect its purchasing power from inflation. The SSA calculates the COLA based on the Bureau of Labor Statistics' percentage increase in the Consumer Price Index for Urban Wage Earners and Clerical Workers (CPI-W). As was the case in 2011, if there is no increase in the CPI-W, there is no COLA.

As is the case with veterans' benefits, servicemembers and their eligible dependents will receive Social Security benefits only if they apply for them. The SSA does not award these benefits automatically. Become familiar with the SSA's website, http://www.ssa.gov, especially when approaching retirement age.

> *The SSA adjusts Social Security benefits annually for inflation.*

OTHER RESOURCES FOR TRANSITION

There are many good Internet sources that can provide information and advice to help you with your transition from the military to civilian life and with exploring the benefits available to you. Here are a few that we recommend.

Military.com is a free information service designed to provide resources to connect and inform servicemembers, veterans, family members, defense workers, military enthusiasts, and those considering military careers. This website is the online presence of Military Advantage, whose mission is to connect the military community to all the advantages earned in service. The website strives to help servicemembers make the most of military experience, enhance access to benefits, find transition support, and enjoy military discounts. See http://www.military.com.

MilitaryHOMEFRONT is the official Department of Defense website for reliable, up-to-date quality-of-life information, focusing on Department of Defense benefits and services. See http://www.militaryhomefront.dod.mil.

Military OneSource Online is an official Department of Defense website designed to serve American troops and their families by providing information related to a host of personal, financial, and legal issues, especially those pertaining to Department of Defense benefits and services. See http://www.militaryonesource.com.

An official Department of Veterans Affairs web portal, eBenefits, serves wounded warriors, veterans, servicemembers, and their families. It provides information about military and veterans benefits and allows individuals to apply for these benefits using online tools. See http://www.ebenefits.va.gov.

One further source of information for Social Security and VA programs is the local office of each administration; check your local telephone directory under "U.S. Government." The SSA and the VA have pamphlets explaining each of their programs, which they will send to you at no charge.

PREPARING FOR YOUR FINANCIAL FUTURE AFTER THE MILITARY

- Visit a Transition Assistance Center and make an appointment with a transition counselor one year prior to your separation.

   Army Career and Alumni Program
   (https://www.acap.army.mil)
   Air Force Family Support Centers
   (http://www.afpc.af.mil)
   Navy Fleet and Family Support Centers
   (http://www.cnic.navy.mil/CNIC_HQ_site/WhatWeDo/Fleet
   AndFamilyReadiness/FamilyReadiness/FleetAndFamilySupport
   Program/index.htm)
   Marine Corps Personal Services Center
   (http://www.usmc-mccs.org/tamp)
- Become familiar with the wide range of veterans' benefits.
- Regularly check your Social Security statement to ensure the SSA has an accurate record of your employment history.
- Discuss VA and SSA benefits with your spouse and dependents so they know about their entitlements should you die.
- Account for potential disability benefits from the VA and SSA if you are considering the purchase of private disability insurance.
- When making life insurance decisions, factor in your veterans burial benefits and Social Security survivors benefits.

17

Military Retirement Benefits

One of the largest financial benefits from military service is the inflation-adjusted pension that begins paying an annuity immediately following retirement. This chapter explains the structure of the Department of Defense's different retirement systems and an important decision that servicemembers must make at their fifteenth year of service. Additionally, it addresses the Survivor Benefit Program (SBP), TRICARE healthcare benefits, and other insurance alternatives available to servicemembers upon retirement. The chapter concludes with some tax considerations for retirees.

In the United States, military pensions for disabled veterans predate the Declaration of Independence. Under the Lincoln administration, the U.S. military adopted its first pension program that extended benefits to non-disabled veterans in order to retain its most experienced and knowledgeable members. This program subsequently transformed over the following 150 years into the military's current "length-of-service" retired pay. This retirement program is designed primarily to retain mid- to senior-grade officers and NCOs through twenty years of service. Presently, the military offers one of the few remaining pensions that allow retirees to draw retirement pay immediately upon retirement, regardless of age. The authority for non-disability retired pay, commonly known as "length-of-service" retired pay, is contained in Title 10, U.S. Code.

There are two primary methods for retirement from the armed forces. The first is length-of-service: You may retire after twenty years of active service (or "qualifying" years if in the reserve component), and in most cases, you must retire after thirty years of service. The other means of retirement is as a result of disability. The intent of this form of retirement is to ensure that servicemembers have a guarantee that the federal government will provide income for them and their families in the event of serious physical or mental disability.

RETIREMENT PAY

Currently, three unique methods of determining retirement annuities exist for active-component "length-of-service" retirees: the "Final Pay" system, the "High-3" system, and the "CSB/REDUX" system (see Table 17-1). Reserve-component retirees have "Final Pay" and "High-3" options available to them.

TABLE 17-1
DOD RETIREMENT SYSTEMS

Retirement System	Basis	Multiplier	Bonus
1: Final Pay	Final basic pay	2.5% per year up to 100%*	None
2a: High-3	Average of highest 36 months of basic pay	2.5% per year up to 100%*	None
2b: CSB/REDUX	Average of highest 36 months of basic pay	2% per year for the first 20 years; 3.5% for each year beyond 20, up to 100%**	$30,000 at fifteenth year of service with commitment to complete 20-year career

*The multiplier can exceed 100% for service beyond 40 years.
**COLA capped at 1% less than CPI with one-time catch-up at age 62.

The retirement system a retiree falls under or selects impacts only how much he or she receives in pension benefits or monthly annuities, not any other earned retirement benefits. The retirement pay a retiree receives depends upon the number of years served and the highest pay achieved prior to retirement. Active-component retirees begin receiving retirement pay immediately upon retirement, whereas Reserve-component retirees begin receiving retirement pay at age sixty (Congress recently passed a law moving the start date forward by three months for every ninety days deployed for war or national emergency since January 28, 2008). Although Congress has changed the retirement system twice in the past thirty years to reduce its future financial obligations, it has always "grandfathered" current servicemembers into the older, more generous system based on that person's date of initial entry into military service (DIEMS). Servicemembers can find their DIEMS in the remarks section of their Leave and Earnings Statement (LES). Updated information on military retirement pay is available online at http://militarypay.defense.gov/retirement/ad/18_summary.html.

In all three systems, retirement pay is subject to income tax but not payroll taxes (aka FICA or Social Security). Regulations also specify that the federal government must pay retirement annuities via direct deposit (electronic transfer) on a monthly basis. Eligibility for each retirement system is listed below.

1. If the servicemember entered service before September 8, 1980, retirement pay is based on his or her final base pay (System 1).
2a. If the servicemember entered service between September 8, 1980, and July 31, 1986, retirement pay is calculated using the average of his or her highest thirty-six months, or three years, of base pay, hence the name, High-3 (System 2a).

TABLE 17-2
RETIREMENT BENEFITS COMPARISON

LTC (O-5) with pay and retirement based on twenty years of active service, retiring in 2011

Retirement Program	Payment Year	Monthly Gross Pay
High-3 annuity	2011	$3,780
CSB/REDUX annuity	2011	$3,024
High-3 annuity	2031*	$6,827
CSB/REDUX annuity	2031*	$4,535**

MSG (E-8) with pay and retirement based on twenty years of active service, retiring in 2011

Retirement Program	Payment Year	Monthly Gross Pay
High-3 annuity	2011	$2,160
CSB/REDUX annuity	2011	$1,756
High-3 annuity	2031*	$3,901
CSB/REDUX annuity	2031*	$2,665**

*Assuming a 3% annual inflation rate
**Assuming that the retiree is not yet sixty-two years old

2b. The Career Status Bonus (CSB)/REDUX retirement system (System
2b) applies to those who entered service on or after August 1, 1986,
and who elected to receive a $30,000 Career Status Bonus at their fif-
teenth year of service. The National Defense Authorization Act
(NDAA) of 2000 allows those in this group to choose between the
High-3 retirement system and the REDUX retirement system.

The REDUX retirement system and Career Status Bonus is a "package
deal." In exchange for the bonus at the fifteenth year, the individual agrees to
a reduced monthly paycheck upon retirement. However, if he or she stays on
active duty through thirty years of service, the bonus does not affect his or her
retirement base pay percentage.

A servicemember who selects CSB/REDUX and retires at twenty years
receives 40% of the average of the highest thirty-six months of base pay, while
a retiree who selects the High-3 plan will receive 50%. In addition to the
reduced annual multiplier (2.0% for CSB/REDUX and 2.5% per year for
High-3), individuals who opt for CSB/REDUX also receive a 1% lower annual
Cost of Living Adjustment (COLA) following retirement than the High-3
plan. The CSB/REDUX plan does offer a one-time "COLA catch-up" for the
retiree at the age of sixty-two; however, following this adjustment, COLA
returns to an annual multiplier 1% lower than that of the High-3 system. Note

that the $30,000 Career Status Bonus paid out at the fifteenth year of service is the same regardless of rank, while the amount of the retirement annuity is highly dependent on rank.

For retirees of all ranks, choosing the CSB/REDUX option almost always results in greatly diminished retirement payments over the individual's lifetime. Even if a servicemember serves thirty years, the point where the CSB/REDUX base pay percentage equals the High-3 pay percentage, the reduced annual COLA will in most cases (unless the retiree invests the $30,000 and earns a substantial return) result in a greatly reduced retirement payout over time. Generally, only those individuals who anticipate not living very long after retirement will receive more money under this retirement option. See Table 17-2 for a comparison of retirement benefits under different programs.

A retirement calculator is available online at http://www.dod.mil/military pay/retirement/calc/index.html. Additionally, the Defense Finance and Accounting Service (DFAS) publishes a detailed overview of the preparation required for military retirement. It can be found online at http://www.dfas. mil/retiredmilitary/plan/estimate.html.

Cost-of-Living Adjustments (COLA)
Annual increases in retirement pay are indexed to the consumer price index (CPI) to ensure that inflation does not erode the retiree's purchasing power. The Department of Labor determines CPI based on the price of a "basket" of consumer goods selected to represent spending in an average urban family of four household. As mentioned in the previous section, COLA for a CSB/REDUX retiree trails that of a High-3 retiree by 1% annually. The Department of Defense does allow for a one time "catch up" in COLA once the CSB/REDUX retiree reaches the age of sixty-two. Under this provision, the government increases the CSB/REDUX pay level to that of a High-3 retiree pay level. Following the one-time catch up provision, the CSB/REDUX retirees again receive a COLA increase that is 1% less annually than the increase High-3 retirees receive. For the latest information on Retirement COLA, see http://militarypay.defense.gov/retirement/cola.html.

In addition to the government's effort to adjust retirement pay to keep up with inflation, every servicemember should have a personal savings plan to supplement his or her retirement pay. This financial plan and investment strategy, as discussed in part III of this book, will help provide retirees with the peace of mind that they will be able to maintain their standard of living in retirement.

Retirement Due to Disability
If a medical evaluation board finds a servicemember physically or mentally unfit for further military service and that servicemember meets certain standards specified by law, he or she is entitled to disability retirement. Disability

retirement may be temporary or permanent. If it is temporary, the government should resolve the status within a five-year period. The criteria for rating the severity of various disabilities are available online at http://www.access.gpo.gov/nara/cfr/waisidx_04/38cfr4_04.html.

The government determines the amount of disability retirement pay by one of two methods:

1. The first method is to multiply the servicemember's final base pay or, depending on the retirement system, the average of the highest thirty-six months of active duty pay, by the percentage of assigned disability. The minimum percentage for temporary-disability retirees is 50% and the maximum is 75%. This computation is sometimes referred to as "Method A."
2. The second method is to multiply the servicemember's years of active service at the time of retirement by 2.5% by his or her base pay, (depending on the retiree's retirement system). This computation is sometimes referred to as "Method B."

DFAS establishes a disability retirement account using the method that results in the greatest amount of retirement pay. For more updated information on disability retirement pay and tax implications, go to http://www.dfas.mil/dfas/retiredmilitary/disability/disability.html or http://militarypay.defense.gov/retirement/disability.html.

Severance Pay

Concurrent with each disability retirement, the government performs a line-of-duty investigation. If the disability is not due to intentional misconduct or willful neglect, and if it was not incurred while AWOL, then the disabled retiree may be eligible for severance pay. If a servicemember has less than twenty years of active service and a permanent disability rating of at least 30%, then he or she receives disability severance pay in the amount of two months' basic pay per year of service up to a maximum of twelve years. For example, a captain (O3) with five years of service would receive ten (2 months × 5 years of service) months of basic pay, and a master sergeant (E8) with eighteen years of service would receive the maximum allowable twenty-four months of basic pay because he has more than twelve years of service.

Severance pay is covered by Department of Defense (DoD) Pay Regulation, Volume 7A, Active Duty & Reserve Pay, chapter 35—Separation Payments. This regulation can be downloaded at http://www.dod.mil/comptroller/fmr/07a/.

Concurrent Retirement and Disability Pay

Concurrent Retirement and Disability Pay (CRDP) refers to receiving both military retirement benefits and VA disability compensation simultaneously. Receiving both forms of retirement was forbidden by law prior to 2004. Congress amended this law because it adversely affected the retention decisions of disabled individuals still wanting to remain on active status. Prior to 2004, in order to receive VA disability compensation, disabled military retirees had to waive all or part of their military pay. However, the amended law allows disabled military retirees with disability ratings of 50 percent or greater to get paid both their full military retirement pay and their VA disability compensation. For the latest updates on this change, visit http://www.dfas.mil/dfas/retiredmilitary/disability/crdp.html.

SURVIVOR BENEFIT PLAN (SBP)

One of the single largest benefits of a military retirement is the monthly retirement paycheck that the retiree receives for the remainder of his or her life. An individual who retires after twenty years of active service at the age of forty and lives to an average life expectancy will receive pay for nearly twice as long in retirement as while on active duty. However, retirement pay stops with the death of the military retiree. Without some form of insurance, this sizeable benefit would not be available for the retiree's family in the event of a premature death. The unexpected death of the retiree could potentially leave a spouse or dependent children financially vulnerable.

The purpose of SBP is to provide the retiree's spouse (or children, in certain circumstances) with an inflation-adjusted monthly income after the

---

TABLE 17-3
SURVIVOR BENEFITS PROGRAM

Advantages
- Government-subsidized plan
- Premiums paid with before-tax dollars; this lowers taxable income
- Benefits adjusted annually for inflation
- Spouse cannot outlive benefit payments
- Age, health, gender, and lifestyle not considered. All retired servicemembers may participate.
- Benefits can only be changed by Congress
- Peace of mind from risk transfer

Disadvantages
- Tax collected on annuity to survivor
- Premiums not returned if spouse dies first (SBP is not an investment, it is a risk-transfer device)
- Retirement pay reduced due to payment of SBP premiums
- Premiums are adjusted with inflation
- Plan accrues no cash value—you cannot cancel program and collect money paid
- Plan has no inheritance provision

retiree's passing. SBP continues to pay a portion of the servicemember's earned retirement pay to the surviving spouse after death. SBP guarantees that 55% of a *base amount,* chosen by the servicemember upon retirement, will be paid to the surviving spouse following the death of the retiree. The maximum base amount is the servicemember's gross monthly retirement pay. Thus, SBP protects up to 55% of retirement pay against the risk of an individual prede- ceasing his or her spouse. See Table 17-3 for a listing of the advantages and disadvantages to SBP.

If a servicemember is on active duty and retirement-eligible with depen- dents, he or she is automatically protected under SBP at no cost. For an up- to-date and detailed overview of the SBP, visit http://www.dfas.mil/dfas/ retiredmilitary/provide/sbp.html.

Cost of Participation in SBP

SBP is one additional benefit of military retirement; however, the program is not free for retirees. The SBP premiums for spouse coverage can amount to as much as 6.5% of a retiree's gross retirement pay. This percentage is the only method of calculating SBP costs for those who joined the military after March 1, 1990. For those who entered military service prior to this date, and who opt for less than the maximum SBP protection amount, the rate is 2.5% of the first $735.00 of the retiree's elected base amount (or the threshold amount) plus 10% of the remaining amount. The threshold amount is $735.00 as of January 1, 2011. The threshold amount increases at the same time and by the same percentage as future active-duty basic pay.

In addition to the most common "Spouse Only" form of SBP, "Spouse and Children Coverage" and "Children Only Coverage" are also available. The additional cost for children is based on the ages of the youngest child, the ser- vicemember, and the spouse; therefore, the cost varies considerably. Your local personnel officer can provide you with the details for your specific situation.

Participation in the SBP is voluntary. The government designed the pro- gram during an era when most military spouses did not work outside the home. Today, families are very different. For some families, the benefit may not be worth the cost. However, before making an informed decision regard- ing SBP enrollment, the retiree should understand that this program offers a form of annuity life insurance at a cost far below market value. The federal government subsidizes the cost of this form of life insurance as an added retirement benefit. Additionally, before declining SBP, the retiree must get signature approval from his or her spouse.

Note that SBP payments are no longer reduced once the spouse begins drawing Social Security, thus eliminating the need for a Supplemental Sur- vivors Benefits Plan.

Changes in Coverage

Except as permitted under the SBP open enrollment period, participation in SBP cannot be changed or modified once an application becomes effective—with one exception. As an SBP participant, a retiree has a one-year window to terminate SBP coverage, between the second and third anniversary of the date that he or she began to receive retirement pay. If the retiree cancels participation in SBP, the government will not refund premiums paid, and no annuity payments will be made upon the retiree's death. Additionally, the covered spouse or former spouse must consent to the withdrawal from the program. Termination is permanent, and participation may not be resumed under any circumstance.

SBP vs. Term Life Insurance

Some retirees believe that they can replicate SBP with term life insurance. The decision is between participating in SBP (and accepting the lower retirement pay that goes with it) or turning down SBP in favor of taking full retirement pay, then using part of that to buy term life insurance. Term life insurance is often cheaper in the short term. However, in the long term, the increasing year-to-year cost of insurance protection for cost-of-living increases, plus the rising cost of term life insurance with age and current health status, make the cost of term insurance greater than the cost of SBP.

In addition to the long-term cost advantages of SBP over private term life insurance, SBP also offers an important tax advantage. SBP payments are

---

TABLE 17-4
SBP VERSUS TERM INSURANCE

SBP
- Premiums are a constant percentage of retirement pay and therefore increase with COLA
- Premiums paid with "before-tax" dollars
- No health tests for insurability
- Benefits adjust with inflation
- Spouse cannot outlive benefit payments

Term Life Insurance
- Premiums rise or benefits decrease as you get older
- Premiums paid with "after-tax" dollars
- Must be insurable
- No inflation protection
- Spouse can outlive benefit payments

---

deducted from a retiree's pretax income. This essentially reduces the costs of SBP by the highest marginal tax bracket of the retiree for a given year. This same advantage does not apply to term life insurance. Table 17-4 summarizes the differences between these two options.

Veterans Administration (VA) Benefits
The annuity paid by SBP is reduced by any Dependency and Indemnity Compensation (DIC) payments paid by the Department of Veterans Affairs if death occurs on active duty, or if the servicemember meets other requirements (see chapter 16). To determine a spouse's actual SBP monthly payment, determine the SBP planned payment (either 55% or 35% of the base amount, depending on the spouse's age) and then subtract the DIC payment from that amount.

The DIC payment is tax-free, but the spouse's total payments are capped at either 55% or 35% of the base amount elected. If an individual dies on active duty, his or her spouse will never receive less than the DIC payment; however, the survivor benefits can be much greater than the DIC payment if retirement pay and, consequently, the SBP benefit is sufficiently large.

Should You Select SBP?
So, "Is SBP a good deal?" The answer is: "Yes, but . . ."

A similar system cannot be bought at a lower cost "on the economy." For a male servicemember and spouse of equal age with no other source of retirement income, the benefits will normally outweigh the costs as long as the servicemember dies before reaching age eighty-three.

There are circumstances, however, in which the benefits are not worth the costs. Clearly, if a retiree pays a premium for a number of years and the spouse dies first, there would be no SBP benefit; all SBP payments made until the spouse's death would be lost. Or if the spouse dies soon after the military retiree (before predicted life expectancy), he or she is not able to receive the SBP payments long enough to recoup the deductions from retirement pay.

Our recommendations:
- First, decide if the spouse needs the retirement pay to sustain his or her retirement needs.
- Buy SBP at retirement if the choice is between SBP and term life insurance. You can then reassess your financial situation between the second and third year of retirement.
- Evaluate SBP as insurance, not an investment; coming out ahead with SBP still means the retiree has died.
- If the retiree is male, you probably cannot beat SBP with commercial insurance.
- If the retiree is female, analyze the spouse's age against that of the retiree and consider the odds that the spouse might outlive the retiree. (Statistics show that women typically outlive men.)

- If retirees are both retired military, SBP is unnecessary. Explore the "Children Only" option.

SBP alone is not a complete estate plan. Other insurance and investments are important in meeting needs outside the scope of SBP. For example, SBP does not have a lump-sum benefit that some survivors may need to meet immediate expenses upon the servicemember's death.

On the other hand, insurance and investments without SBP may be less than adequate. Even if they could duplicate SBP, investments are more risky and require a degree of financial expertise many do not have.

It is important to look at SBP as an integral part of total estate planning. Base participation on family discussions with the advice of qualified personnel officers, insurance agents, bank trust officers, or organizations qualified in estate planning.

VETERANS' GROUP LIFE INSURANCE (VGLI)

Veterans' Group Life Insurance (VGLI) is a program of post-separation insurance which provides for the conversion of SGLI to renewable term coverage. While SGLI is highly subsidized by the government, VGLI is not, and therefore is more expensive for retirees. It is a form of level-term insurance with premiums fixed over time.

At the end of each term period, the insured has the right to renew coverage for another term period. A servicemember may convert this group insurance to an individual policy with any one of the participating companies at any time.

- VGLI is issued in $10,000 increments to a maximum of $400,000, but not for more than the amount of SGLI that the member had in force at the time of separation.
- If a retiree submits the VGLI application within 120 days following separation from service, he or she *does not* need to provide proof of good health to qualify.
- If a retiree submits the VGLI application *between 120 days and one year and 120 days* after separation from service, he or she needs to provide proof of good health.

Additional information on VGLI can be found in chapter 16 of this book and on the web at http://www.insurance.va.gov/sglisite/vgli/vgli.htm.

Individuals may be able to find less expensive policies by shopping around. For instance, in 2012, $400,000 of VGLI coverage costs $816 per year for someone in the forty to forty-four year age group and about $480 per year for a forty-two-year-old with a comparable policy from USAA (http://www.usaa.com). However, the commercial insurance market generally requires proof of good health. If you need life insurance and have preexisting health issues, converting to VGLI is likely to be the best available option. Review chapter 13 for more information on life insurance.

TRICARE

A retiree can remain enrolled in the TRICARE program for a fee. The same two TRICARE options as on active duty are available to retirees: TRICARE Prime and TRICARE Standard and Extra. The plan you should choose is dependent on your retirement situation. If you have additional health insurance that serves as your primary coverage (for example, if you continue working and your new employer provides medical benefits), Prime will only pay after the primary insurance has made payment. Visit the TRICARE website at http://www.tricare.mil to determine the best coverage for you. Also, see chapter 8 for more detailed information about TRICARE.

TRICARE-for-Life is a program that continues support for Medicare-eligible military retirees, their spouses, and other qualifying dependents. It functions as a supplement to Medicare. There are no enrollment fees and enrollment is automatic. In order to be eligible, retirees must ensure that their DEERS status and Military Identification card are current and they must be enrolled in Medicare Part B.

Pharmacy Benefits

Retirees also retain TRICARE pharmacy benefits upon retirement. There are four ways to have prescriptions filled:
1. Military Treatment Facility: Free of charge. Certain medications may have limited availability.
2. TRICARE Mail Order Pharmacy: Medications are mailed directly to the beneficiary; available on a prepaid, cost-share basis.
3. TRICARE Retail Network Pharmacy: Pharmacy in TRICARE network; paid on a cost-share basis.
4. Non-network Pharmacies: Pay full amount and then file a claim with TRICARE.

For additional and updated information see chapter 8 or visit the TRICARE Pharmacy website at http://www.tricare.mil/mybenefit/home/Costs/PharmacyCosts.

TRICARE Retiree Dental Plan

TRICARE has a dental plan for retirees. Both retirees and their dependents are eligible for this program. This plan is operated by Delta Dental and is not government subsidized. There is no standard monthly premium, and costs will vary based on location. The most current information on this program can be found at http://www.trdp.org.

If you get a job elsewhere after retiring from the military, you should compare the dental plan offered by your new employer to TRICARE's plan and determine which plan is more appropriate for your needs.

TAX CONSIDERATIONS

When deciding where to retire, you should consider state and local tax burdens in addition to the numerous family considerations affecting your decision. Some families may choose a retirement destination based on the lack of a state income tax. Several states also have tax benefits for military retirement pay. Information concerning military pay tax benefits can be found at http://usmilitary.about.com/od/taxes/Military_Income_Taxes.htm or http://retirementliving.com/RLstate1.html.

You should also take into account the costs of sales and property taxes when deciding on a retirement location. These can more than offset the lack of a state income tax and any tax breaks on retirement pay. The following website supplies information to retirees on state tax burdens: http://www.retirementliving.com.

Glossary of Financial Terms

The following financial terms, along with many others not listed below, can be further researched and defined at http://www.investopedia.com.

accumulation plan. An arrangement that enables an investor to purchase mutual fund shares regularly, usually with provisions for the reinvestment of income dividends and the acceptance of capital gains distributions in additional shares. Plans are of two types: voluntary and contractual.

actuary. One versed in the mathematics, bookkeeping, law, and finance of life insurance. Actuaries assign probabilities to adverse events and determine the appropriate premiums that insurance companies should charge for associated insurance.

add-on method. A computational method where (1) the finance charge for an installment credit contract as a whole equals the add-on rate times the principal amount of credit at the start of the contract times the number of years in the credit contract; (2) the finance charge is added to the principal; and (3) the credit user receives the principal and pays back the principal plus the finance charge in monthly (or other periodic) installments.

adjustable rate mortgage. (ARM) A mortgage loan for which interest rates are not fixed but vary with market interest rates.

adjusted gross income. (AGI) See taxable income.

adjusted-balance method of computing interest. Interest is charged on the balance outstanding after it has been adjusted for payments and credits.

amenities. The features of a property that are not a part of the space occupied and that create special attraction, such as recreation rooms, saunas, and pools, or natural amenities like a view or ocean frontage.

amortization. The process of retiring debt or writing off an asset. As regards a direct reduction of self-amortizing mortgage, amortization represents the principal repayment portion of an installment payment.

annual percentage rate. (APR) The effective interest rate applicable to a loan. It includes interest charges and fees on an annual basis to allow comparisons between loan options.

annual report. The formal financial statement issued yearly by a corporation to its shareowners. The annual report shows assets, liabilities, earnings, how the company stood at the close of the business year, and how it fared in profit during the year.

annuity. A stated sum of money, payable periodically at the end of fixed intervals.

annuity, certain. An annuity payable throughout a fixed (certain) period of time, irrespective of the happening of any contingency, such as the death of annuitant.

annuity, contingent. An annuity contingent upon the happening of an event that may or may not take place.

annuity, deferred. An annuity modified by the condition that the first payment will not be due for a fixed number of years. Thus, an annuity deferred for twenty years is one on which the first payment is made at the end of twenty-one years, provided the annuitant is still alive.

annuity, life. A fixed sum payable periodically as long as a given person's life continues.

annuity, survivorship. An annuity payable throughout the lifetime of one person after the death of another person or persons.

annuity, variable. A form of whole life insurance where the face value and cash value vary according to the investment success of the insurance company.

appraisal. The estimation of market value of property.

assessed value. The value assessed by the taxing authority for purpose of establishing real estate taxes. This value may not be directly related to market value.

assessment. A charge against real estate made by a unit of government to cover a proportionate cost of an improvement, such as a street or sewer.

asset allocation. The distribution of funds among asset classes in a portfolio, for example: 10 percent cash equivalents, 20 percent bonds, 70 percent stocks.

asset class. A group of investments with similar characteristics or features, for example: cash equivalents, which include savings accounts, checking accounts, money market funds, and Treasury bills.

asset. A resource with economic value owned by a country, firm, or individual with the expectation that it will provide future benefit.

assumption clause. A mortgage loan clause that allows the owner of a house to transfer the mortgage to a later buyer.

assumption of mortgage. The taking of title to property by a grantee, wherein the grantee assumes liability for payment of an existing note or bond secured by a mortgage against a property and becomes personally liable for the payment of such mortgage debt.

automatic paid-up insurance. An amount of insurance, which, without further action by the insured and upon failure to pay a premium when due, is continued as paid-up insurance. (The result will be a lesser value than the original protection guaranteed by the policy.)

average-daily-balance method of computing interest. Interest is charged on the average daily balance outstanding. The average balance is calculated by adding the balances outstanding each day and dividing by the number of days in the billing month. Payments made during the billing month reduce the average balance outstanding.

balanced mutual fund. A mutual fund that invests its assets in a wide range of securities with the intention of providing both growth and income.

balance sheet. A listing of what a person or business owns and owes at a certain point in a certain time period. It has three categories: assets, liabilities, and net worth.

bankruptcy. A legal procedure that allows a person or an organization to give up certain assets in return for release from certain financial obligations.

bear. A person who believes stock prices will go down; a "bear market" is a market of declining prices.

beneficiary. The individual or organization that receives the proceeds of a life insurance policy when the insured dies. The primary beneficiary has the first right to proceeds, and contingent beneficiaries receive the proceeds if the primary beneficiary is no longer living.

bid and asked. The bid is the highest price anyone has declared willing to pay for a security at a given time; the asked is the lowest price at which anyone will sell at the same time. In mutual fund shares, bid price means the net asset value per share, less a nominal redemption charge in a few instances. The asked price means the net asset value per share plus any sales charge. It is often called the "offering price."

blue chip stocks. Stocks of highly stable and financially strong firms.

bond mutual fund. A mutual fund whose objective is to provide stable income with minimal risk.

bonds. A bond is essentially an IOU. The person who invests money in a bond is lending a company or government a sum of money for a specified time, with the understanding that the borrower will repay and also pay interest for using it.

book value. The book value of a firm is equal to its total assets minus total liabilities.

broker. An individual or firm that charges a fee for buying and selling securities on behalf of an investor.

budgeting. A system of record keeping involving detailed planning to account for all incomes and expenses.

bull. A person who believes stock prices will rise; a "bull market" is one with rising prices.

business risk. Risk associated with changes in the firm's sales.

buying on margin. The investor borrows a portion of funds from the brokerage house to buy securities.

call loan. A loan that may be terminated, or "called," at any time by the lender or borrower.

cancellation clause. A unilateral clause in a lease or purchase and sale that terminates an agreement.

capital gain. An increase in the value of an investment that gives it a higher value than the purchase price. This gain is not realized until the asset is sold.

capital improvement. Any structure erected as a permanent improvement to real estate, usually extending the useful life and increasing the value of property. (The replacement of a roof would be considered a capital improvement.)

capital loss. The loss incurred when an investment decreases in value. The loss is not realized until the asset is sold.

cash surrender value. The amount available in cash upon voluntary termination of a policy before it becomes payable by death or maturity.

closed-end investment company. A mutual fund that invests in the shares of other companies. There are a fixed number of shares, and shares are available in the market only if original investors are willing to sell them.

closing. The culmination of a real estate purchase and sale when the title passes and certain financial transactions occur.

closing costs. Costs paid at closing, such as operating cost adjustments, legal and financial expenses, brokerage commissions, and transfer taxes.

closing date. The designated date of a purchase and sale transaction (see closing).

co-insurance. The portion of the total medical insurance bill for which the patient is responsible after the deductible is paid.

co-payment. The flat fee the insurance company requires the patient to pay for a medical service provided.

collateral. Property, or evidence of it, deposited with a creditor to guarantee the payment of a loan.

commission. With respect to insurance policies, a percentage of the premium paid to an agent as remuneration for services; for stocks or real estate, a sum due a broker for services in that capacity.

community property. Property owned in common or held jointly by husband and wife within the statutes of certain states.

compounding. The act of generating earnings from previous earnings.

conditional sales contract. A sales contract in which title to the goods remains with the lender, while the buyer has physical possession of them. The title goes to the buyer when the loan is repaid. This type of contract is often used with items such as appliances and furniture.

condominium ownership. A form of ownership wherein a multi-unit building is divided so that each owner has individual ownership of his unit and joint ownership in the common areas of the buildings and grounds. Condominiums are frequently used for residential housing and sometimes for office space. In addition to the initial purchase price, each owner in a condominium is liable on an annual basis for a predetermined portion of the expenses of maintaining the common areas.

contingency fund. A fund that provides cash to be used if an emergency arises.

contributions. Payments (investments) made into an individual's IRA.

conventional mortgage. A mortgage that is not insured by the FHA or guaranteed by the VA.

conversion. A right to change from a term insurance policy to a whole life policy without a medical examination. This feature is also called a convertability option.

convertible. A bond, debenture, or preferred share that may be exchanged for other stock in a company.

cooperative ownership. A method of indirectly owning a unit in a multi-unit property through a cooperation. A specially created legal corporation owns the building completely. Each shareholder of that corporation owns a predetermined number of shares that entitle him to a long-term lease on a specific apartment. After paying for the purchase of his or her shares, each shareholder is liable for an annual maintenance charge to support the basic services and debt financing in the multi-unit building.

corporate bonds. Debt securities issued by corporations.

cost index. An index developed by the insurance industry allowing the comparison of different policy costs. A surrender cost index is used to determine the value of a policy if the policyholder decides to terminate coverage. A net payment cost index determines the value of the policy assuming it is not surrendered and the cash value remains in the policy.

coupon interest. Refers to the rate of interest on bonds implied by the annual dollar amount of interest paid and the bond's face value.

credit life insurance. Term insurance designed to repay the remaining balance on a loan in case of the borrower's death.

creditor. A person, group, or company that extends credit; one to whom a borrower owes money.

credit union. An institution whose depositors are also its owners. It lends money only to its owners.

cumulative preferred stocks. Preferred stock that requires that any missed dividends that have accrued be paid first—before dividends can be paid on common stock.

current yield. For a bond, its annual interest divided by its current market price.

custodianship account for minors. An account set up for a child in the form of gifts and managed by an adult other than the grantor.

debenture. A bond not secured by liens against specific assets of the firm.

debit card. Like a credit card, except purchases are deducted from your checking account.

debt consolidation loan. A loan that is used to repay outstanding debts. One consolidated loan payment is substituted for many debt payments.

declarations section of an insurance policy. The section that contains the basic identifying details of the policy. It consists of the name of the policy owner, what is insured, the amount of insurance, the cost of the policy, and the time period covered by the insurance.

declination. The rejection of an application for life insurance, usually for reasons of the health or occupation of the applicant.

decreasing term life insurance. Insurance in which the amount of benefits declines over the life of the policy.

deductible. The amount that must be paid out-of-pocket by a policyholder before the insurance company will pay the remaining costs.

deductible clause. A clause in an insurance policy that allows the insured to retain the loss equal to the deductible amount.

deed. A legal document transferring title from owner to buyer, typically recorded with the clerk of the county in which the property is located.

deed restrictions. Limitations placed on the use of the real property through deed covenants such as land coverage, setback requirements, architectural approval, or construction timing.

DEERS. The Defense Enrollment Eligibility Reporting System, a computerized roster of people eligible to receive health benefits under the Uniformed Services Health Benefit Program.

demand deposit. An account in a bank or other financial institution subject to withdrawal by check.

depreciation. The decline in value of property due to normal wear and tear.

disability waver premium. A guarantee that premiums will be paid on your policy should you become disabled.

discount broker. A firm that processes securities transactions for relatively low commissions.

distributions. Gains made by the investments in an IRA.

diversification. A risk management technique that mixes a wide variety of investments within a portfolio. It is designed to minimize the impact of any one security on overall portfolio performance.

dividend. In insurance, the part of the premium returned to a policyholder after the company pays its expenses; dividends are paid only on participating term or whole life policies. For stocks, a dividend is usually paid quarterly, distributing some portion of earnings to shareholders.

dividend payout ratio. Dividends per share of stock divided by earnings per share.

dividend yield. Dividends per share of stock times 100% divided by the market value of a share.

dollar cost averaging. (DCA) Buying a fixed dollar amount of securities at regular intervals. Under this system the investor buys by the dollars' worth rather than by the number of shares. DCA can be an effective way to limit risk while building assets in stock and mutual funds.

double indemnity. An optional life insurance clause that provides payment of twice the face amount of the policy in death benefits if the insured is killed in an accident.

Dow Jones Industrial Average. Daily index of stock prices of thirty large industrial corporations; a popular measure of the stock market's performance.

down payment. The amount of money that the buyer puts up toward the purchase of a house, car, or other asset; does not include closing costs.

earnings. The net income, or profit, of a company or investment after taxes and dividends.

earnings per share. Net income divided by shares of the stock outstanding.

effective rate, annual or monthly. The finance charge as a percentage of the average unpaid balance of the credit contract during its scheduled life. Also called actual rate or annual effective rate.

emerging market. A financial market of a developing country with a short history but potential for growth.

endorsement. A statement attached to an insurance policy, changing the terms of the policy.

endowment life insurance. A life insurance policy that is fully paid (endowed) after either a specified time period or when the insured attains a certain age.

equity. The interest in or value of a property or estate that belongs to an owner, over and above the liens against it; asset value minus liabilities.

escalator clause. A contract or lease clause providing for adjustment of payments in the event of certain specified contingencies such as an increase in real estate taxes or certain operating expenses.

escrow account. Most mortgage lenders require that borrowers make monthly payments equal to one-twelfth of anticipated real estate taxes and insurance into this account. This assures the lender that there are funds from which the taxes and insurance can be paid.

estate. All of a person's assets, including the appropriate portion of any jointly owned property.

estate planning. The systematic accumulation, management, and transfer of a person's estate to achieve family goals.

estate taxes. Taxes levied on the transfer of estates that are larger than a certain specified sum.

evidence of insurability. Evidence of your health that helps the insurer decide if you are an acceptable risk.

exclusions. Certain medical treatments that are not covered by a patient's health insurance.

exclusive agency. An agreement of employment of a broker to the exclusion of all other brokers; if sale is made by any other broker during term of employment, the broker holding exclusive agency is entitled to commissions in addition to the commissions payable to the broker who effected the transaction.

executor. A person or a corporate entity or any other type of organization named or designed in a will to carry out its provisions as to the disposition of the estate of a deceased person.

face value. The dollar value of a security stated by the issuer. Usually associated with a bond, it is the value due to the lender at the maturity date.

Federal Deposit Insurance Corporation (FDIC). A government agency that provides insurance for accounts held at banks; most banks carry FDIC insurance.

Federal Housing Authority (FHA). A government agency that provides mortgage loan insurance to financial institutions.

fiduciary. A person who on behalf of or for the benefit of another individual transacts business or manages financial assets; such relationship implies great confidence and trust.

finance charge. The dollar charge or charges for consumer credit.

finder's fee. In real estate, a payment made for aid in obtaining a mortgage loan or for locating a property or tenant.

foreclosure. The procedure through which property pledged as security for a debt is "repossessed" and sold to secure payment of the debt in event of default in payment or terms. The rights of debtors and creditors in foreclosure vary from state to state.

grace period. Additional time allowed to perform an act or make a payment before a default occurs. In insurance, a period of time where if the premium is not paid, it is still in effect with or without penalty conditions. Generally an insurance grace period is thirty-one days after the premium due date. Some credit cards have a twenty-five-day grace period to avoid finance charges.

gross. Before any deductions.

growth stock. Stock that is characterized by the prospect of its increase in earnings and in market value rather than by the cash dividends it earns for the stockholder.

guaranteed insurability clause. A provision allowing policyholders to purchase additional insurance without having to pass a physical examination.

High-3. Military retirement system for individuals who entered service between September 8, 1980, and July 21, 1986. This plan pays the average of your highest thirty-six months of basic pay.

home loan. A real estate loan for which the security is a residential property.

homeowners warranty (HOW) program. Builders in this program guarantee that their workmanship, materials, and construction meet established standards.

house poor. Buying more house than one can afford to buy.

income. Money received in the form of a salary or investments. It is typically subject to income tax.

income bond. A corporate bond that pays interest only if corporate earnings reach a specified level.

income shifting. The process of transferring income from a high-income taxpayer to a lower-income taxpayer, or from a high-tax year to a low-tax year.

incontestability. In insurance, a provision that the company may not dispute the payment of the claim for any cause whatsoever except for nonpayment of premium. A life insurance policy in force for at least two years cannot be contested.

inflation. The rate at which the general level of prices for good and services is rising, and subsequently, purchasing power is falling.

insurance. A contract that provides protection from financial losses, provided by a company that pools the risks of its clients in order to make the policies affordable.

insurance, paid-up. Insurance on which there remain no further premiums to be paid.

interest. In practice, a payment for the use of money.

interest rate. The percentage of a sum of money charged for its use.

intestacy. The condition resulting from a person's dying without leaving a valid will.

joint account. A checking or savings account in the name of two or more persons. There are two types of joint accounts. One type allows any owner to withdraw funds. The other type requires the permission of all owners before funds can be withdrawn.

joint and survivorship annuity. An annuity that continues payment to a secondary beneficiary if the primary one dies. This annuity guarantees income for life to the surviving beneficiary.

joint ownership. Two or more persons jointly own the property in question. There are three forms of joint ownership: (1) joint tenancy; (2) tenancy in common; (3) tenancy by the entirety.

joint tenancy. A type of ownership wherein two or more persons hold property together, with the distinct character of survivorship. In other words, during the life of both, they have equal rights to use the property and share in any benefits from it. Upon the death of either, the property automatically passes to the survivor(s).

junk bonds. Bonds that investment advisors consider to be risky investments.

landlord. One who rents property to another.

lapse. The voidance of a policy, in whole or in part, by the nonpayment of a premium or installment on a premium date.

lease. An agreement in which one party gains long-term use of another party's property, and the other party receives a form of secured long-term debt.

lease-option. A lease written in conjunction with an option agreement, wherein the payments may be credited toward the purchase price if the option is exercised.

lessee. The party contracting to use the property under a lease.

lessor. The owner who contracts to allow property to be used under a lease.

lien. The right of an individual to retain possession of the goods of another until the debt has been paid.

limited-payment whole life insurance. Life insurance requiring premiums to be paid only for a specific time period but remaining in force after the payment period is over (e.g., twenty-pay life).

limited warranty. A guarantee that is much more restrictive than a full warranty.

liquid assets. Cash and other investments that can be converted into cash quickly, such as money in checking and savings accounts.

liquidity. The cash position measured by the cash on hand and assets quickly convertible into cash.

listed stock. The stock of a company traded on a securities exchange for which a listing application and a registration statement (giving detailed information about the company and its operations) have been filed with the Securities and Exchange Commission (unless otherwise exempted) and the exchange itself.

listing agreement. A written employment contract between a property owner and a real estate broker, whereby the agent is authorized to sell or lease certain property within specified terms and conditions.

load. The portion of the offering price of shares of open-end investment (mutual fund) companies that covers sales commissions and all other costs of distribution. The load normally is incurred only on purchase. Some funds also charge a "back-end" load or "redemption charge" when the shares are sold, or an annual "12b-1" charge.

loading. That addition to the net insurance premium that is necessary (1) to cover the policy's proportionate share in the expense of operating the company and (2) to provide a fund deemed sufficient to cover contingencies.

loan value. The amount of money that one can borrow from an insurance company by using the policy's cash value as collateral.

management fees. A fixed fee that a mutual fund manager charges investors for his services and work with the fund.

marginal tax rate. The amount of tax paid on an additional dollar of income. Relates directly to an individual's tax bracket.

market capitalization. The market value of a company's outstanding shares found by taking the stock price and multiplying it by the number of shares outstanding.

market value. The highest price that a buyer (willing but not compelled to buy) would pay, and the lowest price that a seller (willing but not compelled to sell) would accept.

maturity. The time at which a bond or insurance policy is due and payable. In insurance, the date at which the face value of an endowment policy is paid to the insured if still living.

mortality. The statistical measure of the probability of death at each age group. The same age groups can have different rates based on the amount of group risk. For example, a lower rate is charged for a twenty-five-year-old nonsmoking male than for a twenty-five-year-old male who uses tobacco.

mortality rate (death rate). The ratio of those who die at a stated age to the total number who are exposed to the risk of death at that age per year.

mortgage. A legal document pledging a described property for the performance of promise to repay a loan under certain terms and conditions. The law provides procedures for foreclosure. The notations of "first," "second," and so forth refer to the priority of the liens, with the lower number representing greater security for the mortgage holder. A direct-reduction mortgage involves a constant periodic payment that will eventually repay the entire loan, providing a specified return to the mortgagee.

mortgagee. The party who lends money and takes a mortgage to secure the payment thereof.

mortgagor. The person who borrows money and gives a mortgage on the person's property as security for the payment of the debt.

multiple listing. An arrangement among Real Estate Board of Exchange members, whereby each broker presents the broker's listings to the attention of the other members; if a sale results, the commission is divided between the broker bringing the listing and the broker making the sale.

mutual wills. Separate wills made by two or more persons (usually but not necessarily husband and wife) containing similar provisions in favor of each other or of the same beneficiary.

negative cash flow. Situation when cash inflows are less than cash outflows.

net. Remaining after all deductions.

net asset value of a mutual fund. The value of one share of a mutual fund. It is equal to the fund's total market value, less its liabilities, divided by the number of its shares outstanding.

net cost. In insurance, the total gross premiums paid, less total dividends credited for a given period.

net surrendered cost. The total gross premiums paid, less the total dividends credited for the given period and the surrender or cash value of the policy, plus the surrender charge (if any) for an insurance policy.

net worth. What a person or business would own after paying all liabilities. Assets minus liabilities equals net worth. Net worth is the same as "equity."

no-fault insurance. A form of automobile insurance where the insured collects from his own company regardless of who was at fault.

no-load mutual fund. A mutual fund that does not charge a sales commission on the sale of its stock.

nominal interest rate. The stated or advertised interest rate.

noncontributory pension plan. A pension plan in which the employee does not make any contributions. Military retirement is an example.

nonforfeiture provisions. Provisions whereby, after the payment of a given number of premiums, the contract may not be completely forfeited because of nonpayment of a subsequent premium but is held good for some value in cash, paid-up insurance, or extended term insurance. These values are usually stipulated in a table that is printed in the policy. One of the last two options is usually effective automatically; any other option is generally available only upon surrender of the policy.

notary public. A public officer who is authorized to take acknowledgments to certain classes of documents, such as deeds, contracts, or mortgages, and before whom affidavits may be sworn.

note. A legal document in which the borrower promises to repay the loan under agreed-upon terms.

NOW (Negotiable Order of Withdrawal) account. Equivalent to checking accounts paying interest on the funds on deposit.

odd lot. An amount of stock less than the established 100-share unit of trading: from one to ninety-nine shares for the great majority of issues.

offer. An initial, brief written contract submitted by a potential buyer of real estate for approval by the seller, giving the price and limited other details.

open-end investment company. A company, popularly known as a mutual fund, issuing redeemable shares, that is, shares that normally must be liquidated by the fund on demand of the shareholders. Such companies continuously offer new shares to investors.

open-end mortgage. A mortgage under which the mortgaged property stands as security not only for the original loan but for the future advances the lender may be willing to make. It is similar to a home-equity line of credit.

open listing. A listing given to any number of brokers without liability to compensate any except the one who first secures a buyer ready, willing, and able to meet the terms of the listing, or secures the acceptance by the seller of a satisfactory offer. The sale of the property automatically terminates the listing.

option. A legal agreement that permits the holder—for a consideration—to buy, sell, or otherwise obtain or dispose of a property interest within a specified time and on specified terms described in the agreement.

out-of-pocket maximum. The maximum amount that a health insurance company will require a patient to pay for medical services in one year. It is the sum of the insurance plan's deductible, co-insurance, and co-payment expenses.

over-the-counter. A market for securities made up of securities dealers who may not be members of a securities exchange. Thousands of companies have insufficient shares outstanding, stockholders, or earnings to warrant listing on a stock exchange. Securities of these companies are traded in the over-the-counter market between dealers and customers. The over-the-counter market is the chief market for U.S. government bonds, municipal bonds, and bank and insurance stock. NASDAQ is an organized, computerized OTC market handling a large number of stocks.

par value. See face value.

participating preferred stock. A preferred stock that shares with common stock in exceptionally large corporate earnings, thus getting a rate higher than the stated maximum rate.

personal property. Property that is not attached to land, such as furniture, appliances, clothing, and other personal belongings.

points. A loan fee charged by lenders. Each point equals 1% of the amount of the loan. Points are payable up front and add to the effective cost of a loan.

policy. The life insurance contract between the life insurance company and the owner of the policy. The policy outlines the terms and conditions for both the company and the policyholder.

policy, installment. A contract under which the sum insured is payable in a given number of equal annual installments.

policy, joint life. A policy under which the company agrees to pay the amount of insurance at the death of the first of two or more designated persons.

policy, limited payment. A policy that stipulates that only a limited number of premiums are to be paid.

policy loan. A loan made to the policyholder by the insurance company based upon the cash value in a whole life or other permanent insurance policy.

policy, nonparticipating. A policy that is not entitled to receive dividends. Such a policy is usually written at a lower rate of premium than a corresponding participating policy.

policy, participating. A policy that participates (receives dividends) in the surplus as determined and apportioned by the company.

policy year. The year beginning with the due date of an annual premium.

portfolio. The aggregate investment holdings of an individual or institution. A portfolio may contain individual securities (stocks and bonds), mutual funds, collectibles, or other forms of investment wealth.

power of attorney. A written instrument duly signed and executed by an owner of property that authorizes an agent to act on behalf of the owner to the extent indicated in the instrument.

premium. A stated sum charged by a company in return for insurance. It may be payable in a single sum or in a limited number of payments, or periodically throughout the duration of the policy.

prepayment clause. A clause in a consumer loan contract that provides for a refund to a debtor who chooses to repay an installment account early. Or a clause in a mortgage that gives a mortgagor the privilege of paying the mortgage indebtedness before it becomes due.

property. Real property consists of land and, generally, whatever is erected or growing upon or affixed to it, including rights issuing out of, annexed to, and exercisable within or about the same. (See personal property.)

prospectus. The official circular that describes the shares of a company and offers them for sale. It contains definitive details concerning the company issuing the shares, the determination of the price at which the shares are offered to the public, and other financial data as required by the Securities and Exchange Commission's rules.

purchase and sales agreement. A legal contract between buyer and seller of real estate that details the terms of the transaction.

rating. The basis for an additional charge to the standard premium because the person to be insured is a greater than normal risk. A rating can be the result of a dangerous occupation, poor health, or other factors.

real rate. An interest rate expressed in inflation-adjusted terms used to define the growth or decline in purchasing power; usually expressed as a percentage. It is computed by taking the difference between the nominal interest rate and the inflation rate.

real estate investment trust (REIT). Similar to a closed-end investment company. A REIT, however, specializes in buying real estate properties.

real estate syndicate. A partnership formed for participation in a real estate venture. Partners may be limited or unlimited in their liability.

real property. Land, buildings, and other kinds of property that legally are classified as real, as opposed to personal property.

realtor. A coined word that may be used only by an active member of a local real estate board affiliated with the National Association of Real Estate Boards.

reduced paid-up insurance. A form of insurance available as a nonforfeiture option. It provides for continuation of the original insurance plan, but for a reduced amount, and no further premiums.

return. The gain or loss of a security in a particular period. It consists of the income and capital gains of an investment, and is usually expressed as a percentage.

reinstatement. The restoration of a lapsed policy after the policyholder pays all unpaid premiums and charges.

renewable term insurance. Term insurance that can be renewed at the end of the term, at the option of the policyholder and without evidence of insurability, for a limited number of successive terms. The rates increase at each renewal as the age of the insured increases.

rent. The payment for use of someone else's property; the compensation paid for the use of real estate.

reserve (policy reserves). The amount that an insurance company allocates specifically for the fulfillment of its policy obligations. Reserves are so calculated that, together with future premiums and interest earnings, they will enable the company to pay all future claims.

retained earnings. On an income statement, changes in retained earnings come from net income minus dividends paid for the year. On the balance sheet, this is cumulative from year to year.

retirement. To give up one's work or business, especially because of age.

revenue bonds. Municipal bonds backed by special sources of income.

reverse annuity mortgage. Contract under which a homeowner can receive monthly income by borrowing against the equity in a home.

revocable trust. A trust that is controlled by the grantor and can be revoked by him or her.

revolving credit. A continuing credit arrangement between seller and buyer in which the buyer (1) agrees to make monthly payments equal to a stipulated percentage of the amount owed at the start of the month plus interest and (2) is permitted to make additional credit purchases as long as the total debt owed does not exceed an agreed-upon limit.

rider. Any additional agreement to an insurance policy, usually adding a benefit at an additional cost. A rider becomes part of the insurance policy.

rights or warrants. When a company wants to raise more funds by issuing additional stock, it may give its stockholders the opportunity, ahead of others, to buy the new stock. The piece of paper evidencing this privilege is called a right or warrant. Because the additional stock is usually offered to stockholders below the market price, rights ordinarily have a market value of their own and are actively traded. Failure to exercise or sell rights may result in actual loss to the holder.

risk. The chance that an investment's actual return will be different than expected.

sale-leaseback. A transaction in which the vendor simultaneously executes a lease and retains occupancy of the property concurrently sold.

sales charge. The amount charged in connection with the distribution to the public of mutual fund shares. It is added to the net asset value per share in the determination of the offering price and is paid to the dealer and underwriter. Also called a "load."

sales contract. A contract by which the buyer and seller agree to terms of sale.

savings. Amount of income not spent.

savings account. An interest-bearing liability of a bank, redeemable in money on demand or after due notice, not transferable by check.

savings and loan associations. Financial institutions that have historically specialized in offering savings accounts and in providing mortgage funds.

savings banks. Located in New England and eastern states, these banks provide services very similar to services provided by commercial banks.

secondary financing. A loan secured by a mortgage or trust deed that is secured by a lien subordinate to that of another instrument.

secondary markets. Buying and selling of securities that takes place between investors.

second mortgage. A mortgage next in priority to a first mortgage.

secured installment loans. Loans that are backed by collateral. Examples are loans for cars, home improvements, boats, furniture, appliances, and other durable goods.

securities. Things given, deposited, or pledged to assure the fulfillment of an obligation. In this narrow sense a mortgage is a security, but the term is now generally used in a broader sense to include stock as well as bonds, notes, and other evidences of indebtedness.

Securities and Exchange Commission (SEC). A federal agency that oversees securities trading.

Securities Investor Protection Corporation (SIPC). A federal agency that insures investors' accounts at brokerage houses.

securities markets. Places or networks where stocks, bonds, and other financial instruments are traded.

selling short. Selling borrowed securities with the expectation of buying them back later at a lower price.

Series EE bond. A nonnegotiable U.S. savings bond. Interest on these bonds is received only upon redemption.

Series HH bond. A nonnegotiable U.S. savings bond that pays periodic interest, can be redeemed after six months, and has a maturity period of ten years. Series HH bonds have been discontinued and can no longer be purchased, although bond holders can retain them until the last maturity date in 2014.

service contract. An agreement purchased by an appliance owner to keep the appliance in working order.

share. See stock.

simple-interest method. A computation method where the finance charge for a given month of an installment contract equals the monthly rate times the loan balance at the end of each month.

single-premium deferred annuity. An insurance product with a large up-front payment to provide for retirement income and tax savings for high-bracket taxpayers.

speculator. One willing to assume a relatively large risk in the hope of gain. His principal concern is to increase his capital rather than his dividend income. Safety of principal is a secondary factor. (See investor)

Standard & Poor's 500 (S&P 500). An index of five hundred large stocks, a broad measure of the stock market's performance.

standard deviation. As an investment term, standard deviation is used as a proxy for risk. It represents the possible divergence from the expected rate of return and can be used to establish a range of expected returns for an investment or portfolio.

stock. A type of security that signifies ownership in a corporation and represents a claim on part of the corporation's assets and earnings. Stock is also known as shares or equity.

stock dividend. A dividend payable in stock rather than cash.

stock mutual fund. A mutual fund whose objective is to provide the highest possible returns by investing in a number of different companies' stocks. These funds can be characterized by industry, company size, company objectives, or investment objectives.

subletting. A leasing by a tenant to another, who holds under the tenant.

suicide clause. A provision in a life insurance contract that cancels the proceeds from a policy should the insured commit suicide within two years of taking out a life insurance policy. A suicide clause is illegal in some states.

surrender (cash) value. The amount the insurer will pay the policyholder if the life insurance policy is canceled. Term insurance policies have no surrender value.

survey. The process by which a parcel of land is measured and its area ascertained; also the blueprint showing the measurements, boundaries, and area.

tax bracket. The rate at which an individual is taxed based on income level.

tax-deductible. Exempt from inclusion in one's taxable income.

tax deferred. Refers to the investment earnings such as interest, dividends or capital gains that accumulate free from taxation until the investor withdraws and takes possession of them.

tax-exempt. Not subject to taxation.

taxable income. The amount of net income used in calculating income tax. It is gross income minus all adjustments, exemptions, and deductions.

tenancy in common. The means of holding property by two or more persons, each of whom has an undivided interest. In event of the owner's death, the undivided interest passes to the owner's estate and heirs rather than to the surviving tenants in common.

tenancy by the entirety. A tenancy created by husband and wife, who together hold the title to the whole, with right of survivorship upon the death of either spouse. It is essentially joint tenancy, but it is used only for husbands and wives and only in some jurisdictions.

tenant. One who is given possession of real estate for a fixed period or at will.

term policy. An insurance policy that provides that the amount of the policy shall be payable only in event of death within a specified term.

testamentary trust. A trust that is created by placing an appropriately worded clause in the testator's will. The clause places the trust principal under the trustee's control on the testator's death.

testator. A person who has made and left a valid will at death.

thrift savings plan. A tax-deferred 401(k)-like investment vehicle that is available to military personnel.

time deposit account. A savings account in which the account owner receives interest but cannot withdraw funds prior to maturity without a penalty.

time-share homes. The buyer buys the use of the house for a short time period. The time varies from one week to six months.

title. The right to ownership of a property.

title abstract. A history of the ownership of the property.

title insurance. A policy of insurance that indemnifies the holder for loss sustained by reason of defects in the title.

title search. An examination of the public records to determine the ownership and encumbrances affecting real property.

traveler's checks. Checks that are readily accepted as payment because the person must buy them in order to use them. They are safer to carry than cash as they can be replaced if stolen.

TRICARE. A regionally managed health-care program for active duty servicemembers, retired members, and their families. The military has created fourteen civilian health-care networks based upon geographical regions to supplement the care provided by military treatment facilities.

TRICARE Extra. An option similar to TRICARE Standard except that if an insured uses providers who are TRICARE Extra approved, then the insured will receive a discount to the costs he or she would otherwise have to pay under TRICARE Standard. This option should be used by those who do not live in a TRICARE Prime network but wish to reduce their medical expenses.

TRICARE Prime. The managed-care network option. Treatment is received in either the Military Treatment Facility Network or the Civilian Health-Care Network. In return for giving up a personal choice of doctor, the cost of receiving medical treatment is reduced. Because of the high costs of setting up the networks, this option is currently available only in regions that have large military populations.

TRICARE Standard. This is the traditional fee-for-service option. The insured can choose any health-care provider, but his or her costs will be greater than if TRICARE had been used. If TRICARE Prime is not available where an insured is stationed, then he or she must enroll in this option.

trust. A fiduciary relationship in which one person (the trustee) is the holder of the legal title to property (the trust property) subject to an obligation to keep or use the property for the benefit of another person.

trustee. A person who manages a trust.

trustor. A person who establishes a trust.

underwrite. The insurance company's decision on whether an individual qualifies for life insurance based on reviews of his or her occupation, health, age, and so on. Underwrite also means the sale of original securities in the primary market.

variable annuity. An annuity in which the dollar amount of benefits depends on the investment performance of the insurance company's fund managers.

variable rate mortgage. A mortgage loan for which interest rates are not fixed. The rate applicable to the mortgage goes up or down as interest rates in general go up or down.

vesting. The gaining of rights by a worker to the pension contributions made by an employer on the worker's behalf.

volatility. A statistical measure of the tendency of a market or security to rise or fall within a period of time.

waiver-of-premium clause. A provision committing the life insurance company to make premium payments for a policyholder who suffers an injury or illness causing a disability.

warranty. The consumer's assurance that the product will work as it is supposed to. They are guarantees issued by manufacturers or suppliers of goods and services that explain their obligation and, generally, the user's or buyer's responsibilities also.

warranty deed. The safest deed for the buyer, since it guarantees that title is free of any legal claims. There are two kinds of warranty deeds: general warranty deeds and special warranty deeds. A general warranty deed contains a promise by the grantor to "defend the property against every person or persons whomsoever." In other words, it is a promise of protection against the whole world. A special warranty deed contains the more limited promise "to defend the property against every person or persons whomsoever lawfully claiming the same or any part thereof by, from, through, or under him." In other words, it is a promise to protect against the grantor, his heirs, or his assignees.

whole life insurance. Life insurance that remains in force as long as the insured continues to pay the insurance premiums. The premiums remain level and fixed as long as the policy remains in force, and the excess premiums collected in the early years of the policy's life accumulate interest as "cash value."

will. A legally enforceable declaration of a person's wishes in writing regarding matters to be attended to after his or her death, but inoperative until his death. A will usually relates to the testator's property, is revocable or amendable up to the time of his death, and is applicable to the situation that exists at the time of his death.

"window sticker" price. Lists the manufacturer's suggested list price for a car and the itemized prices of the options.

yield. The dividends or interest paid expressed as a percentage of the current price or, if you own the security, of the price you originally paid.

About the Contributors

The writers of this book are officers and civilian faculty members who either are or have been assigned to the Department of Social Sciences at the United States Military Academy (USMA). With graduate degrees from many of the nation's leading universities, we provide instruction in economics and finance at West Point. As important as a graduate school education is, our most relevant financial advice for the readers of this book stems from our previous roles as company-level commanders.

Major Hartleigh Caine is an aviation officer who previously commanded an attack helicopter company in Taji, Iraq, and currently teaches principles of economics at West Point. She earned a BS from USMA and an MBA from Columbia Business School.

Professor Dean Dudley is an associate professor of economics at West Point. His research includes economic manpower analysis for the armed services-applying economic labor models to military manpower data-and game theoric analysis of the art of war. He earned a BA from Eastern Washington University and a PhD from Indiana University Bloomington where he specialized in Game Theory, Public Economics, and Institutional Economics. He studied under Nobel Laureate for Economics Dr. Elinor Ostrom.

Major Matthew P. Fix is an aviation officer who commanded an attack helicopter company in the 101st Airborne Division at Fort Campbell, Kentucky, and deployed in support of Operation Enduring Freedom in 2009. He currently teaches economics at West Point and earned a BS from USMA and an MBA from the Naval Postgraduate School.

Major Daniel Gade is an instructor of American Politics, Policy, and Strategy at the United States Military Academy. He holds a BS from the United States Military Academy and an MPA and PhD in Public Administration and Policy from the University of Georgia, and previously worked at the White House as an Associate Director of the Domestic Policy Council. He remains on active duty despite severe wounds received in action during his service in Iraq, including the loss of his entire right leg.

Colonel S. Jamie Gayton teaches economics at West Point. He deployed to Desert Shield/Storm and Iraqi Freedom III. Colonel Gayton served as a battalion commander in Eastern Baghdad where he used principles of economics to help negotiate and manage over $300 million in reconstruction operations.

Colonel Gayton graduated from USMA in 1987, earned an MBA from MIT Sloan in 1996, and earned a PhD from RAND in 2009.

Ms. Nicole Gilmore teaches economics at West Point. She earned a BS from Tuskegee University and an MBA from the Kellogg Graduate School of Management at Northwestern University. She has worked in financial services as an advisor and has experience in small business development.

Major Jessica D. Grassetti is a military police officer who previously commanded the 65th Military Police Company (Airborne) at Fort Bragg, North Carolina, that deployed in support of Operation Iraqi Freedom from 2008 to 2009. She is an instructor of economics at West Point. She earned a BS from the United States Military Academy and an MPP from the Harris School of Public Policy at the University of Chicago.

Major Scott P. Handler teaches international relations at West Point. He earned a BS from USMA, a Master of Urban and Regional Planning (MURP) from the University of Hawaii at Manoa, and a PhD in political science from Stanford University.

Captain Liesl Himmelberger is a military intelligence officer and strategist who previously commanded a human intelligence company in INSCOM at Waegwan, Republic of Korea, and deployed in support of Operation Iraqi Freedom in 2004. She currently teaches economics at West Point and has a BS from USMA and an MA from the Johns Hopkins School of Advanced International Studies.

Major Jacob M. Johnston is an aviation officer who previously commanded an air cavalry troop in the 1st Infantry Division at Fort Carson, Colorado, and deployed in support of Operation Iraqi Freedom. He earned a BS from USMA and an MBA from Harvard Business School, and currently teaches economics at West Point.

Major Hugh W. A. Jones is an infantry officer who previously commanded an airborne infantry company and an airborne reconnaissance troop in the 82nd Airborne Division at Fort Bragg, North Carolina, and has deployed to Kosovo for Operation Joint Guardian, twice in support of Operation Iraqi Freedom, and for Hurricane Katrina relief. He currently teaches finance and economics at West Point and earned a BS from USMA and an MBA in finance from the Fuqua School of Business at Duke University.

Lieutenant Colonel Paul Kucik is the Director of the Operations Research Center at West Point. He has taught economics, systems engineering, and engineering management courses, and has served in a number positions in army aviation units and analytic agencies, deploying in support of Operation Iraqi Freedom in 2008. He earned a PhD from Stanford University, an MBA from the Massachusetts Institute of Technology, and a BS from USMA.

Major Conway Lin is a signal corps officer who previously commanded a satellite control company in Army Space and Missile Defense Command at

Camp Roberts, California, and currently teaches economics, money and banking, and comparative economics at West Point. He earned a BS from USMA and an MA in Public Policy from Harvard University's Kennedy School of Government.

Major Brian Miller is an army aviation officer who previously commanded an air cavalry troop of 3rd Squadron, 17th Cavalry Regiment in Baghdad, Iraq. He currently teaches economics at West Point, and has a BS from USMA and an MPA from the University of Texas at Austin.

Major Fran Murphy is an armor officer who previously commanded a re-missioned tank company in 1st Brigade, 1st Infantry Division at Ft. Riley, Kansas, and has twice deployed in support of Operation Iraqi Freedom. He currently teaches economics at West Point. He has a BS from USMA and an MBA from the Tuck School of Business at Dartmouth College.

Major Jeffrey S. Palazzini is an engineer officer who previously commanded a combat engineer company in the 4th Infantry Division at Fort Carson, Colorado, that deployed in support of Operation Iraqi Freedom. He currently teaches macroeconomics at West Point. He earned a BS from USMA and an MBA from the University of Pennsylvania's Wharton School of Business.

Major Riley Post is a Special Forces officer who previously commanded a Special Forces Operational Detachment-Alpha in the 5th Special Forces Group (Airborne) at Fort Campbell, Kentucky, deploying in support of Operation Iraqi Freedom in 2007 and 2009 and Operation New Dawn in 2010. He currently teaches economics at West Point and has a BS from USMA and an MSc from the University of Oxford.

Major Sukhdev S. Purewal is a foreign area officer who previously commanded a military intelligence company with V Corps in Darmstadt, Germany, and deployed with the Southern European Task Force in support of Operation Enduring Freedom. He currently teaches political science at West Point. He earned a BS from USMA and a MALD from the Fletcher School of Law and Diplomacy at Tufts University.

Major Lee Robinson is an aviation officer who previously commanded an attack aviation company in the 1st Air Cavalry Brigade at Fort Hood, Texas, and currently teaches American Politics at West Point. He earned a BS from USMA and an MPA from the Cornell Institute for Public Affairs.

Major Todd Schultz is an aviation officer who previously commanded two companies in the 160th Special Operations Aviation Regiment (Airborne) and currently teaches economics at West Point. He is a graduate of USMA and holds an MBA from the Tepper School of Business at Carnegie Mellon University.

PREVIOUS EDITIONS AND THEIR EDITORS

1st Edition
    Lieutenant Colonel Hobart B. Pillsbury, Jr.
    Lieutenant Colonel Robert H. Baldwin, Jr.
2nd Edition
    Professor Michael E. Edleson
    Colonel Hobart B. Pillsbury, Jr.
3rd Edition
    Dr. J. Kevin Berner
    Lieutenant Colonel Thomas Daula
4th Edition
    Lieutenant Colonel Michael J. Meese
    Lieutenant Colonel Bart Keiser
5th Edition
    Major David Trybula
    Lieutenant Colonel Richard Hewitt
6th Edition
    Colonel Margaret H. Belknap
    Major F. Michael Marty

Index